T0327719

Harvard Economic Studies / Volume 135

The studies in this series are published by the Department of Economics of Harvard University. The Department does not assume responsibility for the views expressed.

Capital Transfers and Economic Policy: Canada, 1951–1962

Richard E. Caves and Grant L. Reuber

with Robert W. Baguley, John M. Curtis, Raymond Lubitz

Harvard University Press / Cambridge, Massachusetts

1971

Canadian Economic Policy and the Impact of International Capital Flows,
by Richard E. Caves and Grant L. Reuber, published by University
of Toronto Press in 1969, was adapted from this study.

Preface

This study traces its origin to a day, several years ago, when Professor H. Edward English, then Director of Research for the Private Planning Association of Canada, invited Professor Richard Caves to prepare a pamphlet dealing analytically with the aggregative effects of international capital flows on the Canadian economy. Reflection on the intellectual merits of this exercise quickly showed that it might hold considerable interest. Reflection on scholarly research then in print dealing with international capital flows revealed, with equal speed, that most of the empirical work for such a study and some of the theory would have to be concocted ab ovo. The pamphlet was put up on blocks, as it were, to await the motivating power of a more extended piece of research.

As the larger project began to take shape, it became apparent that it would require a number of separate and separable statistical investigations to fill the indicated number of empty boxes. The output of each investigation was easy enough to define, but the best method of fabricating it would, in general, demand close study and experimentation; directions could not simply be written out in advance. The potential advantages of a division of labor became clearly apparent, and Professor Grant Reuber was asked to be coauthor. Furthermore, the ease of dividing several main investigations underlying the project into dissertation-size chunks called for taking into the fold the three junior authors, then in quest of thesis topics at Harvard.

Work on the project suffered more than a reasonable amount of disruption and delay due to administrative responsibilities of the two senior authors, not to mention their distraction along the way by other research. The authors gave concentrated attention to the project at different times and were to some extent geographically dispersed. Definite responsibility can and will be indicated for each segment of the research. Nonetheless, collaborative work in designing and executing the project has been extensive enough that we feel it to be a true joint product and not a collection of essays.

With these caveats, we can indicate the primary responsibilities of the individual authors. Richard Caves set the general research design of the volume and undertook the preparation of Chapters 1 and 7. He also supervised the three doctoral dissertations annexed to the project and oversaw the extraction from them of chapters for the book. Grant Reuber was responsible for Chapters 6 and 8. He also undertook the extensive exploratory study for Chapter 6 and helped to supervise the dissertation projects. Robert Baguley began working as a research assistant on material that was later to underlie Chapters 2, 3, and portions of 7; the problem of unscrambling the inter-relation of capital inflows and Canadian interest soon came to possess unexpected complexity (at the least); Chapters 2 and 3 and Appendix A are drawn from his thesis, "International Capital Flows and Canadian Monetary and Fiscal Policies, 1951–1962" (Harvard University, 1969). Raymond Lubitz developed Chapter 4 as a summary of his dissertation, "United States Direct Investment in Canada and Canadian Capital Formation, 1950–1962" (Harvard University, 1966), which also contains some exploratory research that provided useful background for a portion of Chapter 2. Chapter 5 was extracted from John Curtis' dissertation, "Direct Linkages Between Canadian and United States Prices and Wages: A Disaggregated Study, 1957–1966" (Harvard University, 1969). Appendix C was prepared by Peter K. Clark, of Harvard University.

Research support for this project came from a number of sources. Thanks are due the Private Planning Association of Canada; the Center for International Affairs, Harvard University; the Social Science Research Council, for an Auxiliary Research Award to Professor Caves; the Canada Council for a research grant to Professor Reuber; the Ford Foundation for Dissertation Fellowships to Dr. Baguley and Dr. Lubitz; and the Woodrow Wilson Foundation for a Dissertation Fellowship to Dr. Baguley. These agencies are disclaimed from responsibility in the usual way.

R. E. C.
G. L. R.

March 1969

Contents

Tables

Abbreviations

Listed below are the symbols for all statistical series used in the quantitative work for this study. All income and financial flows are for the Canadian economy, measured at quarterly rates in millions of Canadian dollars, in current prices unless otherwise indicated. Variables are not seasonally adjusted unless otherwise indicated. Interest rates are expressed as percent per quarter so that regression cofficients relating income or financial flows to interest rates can be employed for annual data without further adjustment. All series of international capital flows are defined so that a net inflow to Canada is positive. When a symbol is defined in terms of other symbols, entries for the latter can be consulted for further information.

A Change in constant-dollar Gross National Product; A is change from t-8 to t-2; A_1 is change from t-5 to t-1; A_2 is change from t-9 to t-5.

ATM Average term to maturity of Government of Canada long-term marketable securities at beginning of quarter, in months.

BM Balance of merchandise trade with all countries.

$BMTUS$ Canada's imports from the United States minus her exports to the United States, in constant dollars.

BTB Balance of international transactions in Canadian Treasury Bills and United States Treasury bills and certificates.

CA Balance of payments on current account with all countries.

CB Current-account balance less balance of interest and dividend payments ($CB = CA - ID$).

CFC Cost of forward cover in international transactions, expressed as percentage forward discount on the Canadian dollar ($CFC = 100(RS - RF) / RS$).

CL Interest rate on long-term Government of Canada bond bearing coupon rate 2.75 percent, maturing June 15, 1968 (callable after June 15, 1967), in percent per quarter.

CRS Quarterly change in spot exchange rate ($CRS = RS - RS_{-1}$).

ABBREVIATIONS

CS   Tender (auction) rate on three-month Government of Canada Treasury bills, in percent per quarter.

CTS   Term structure of Canadian interest rates, measured by differential between long-term and short-term rates ($CTS = CL - CS$).

D   Direct foreign investment flows to Canada from the United States, deflated by the Canadian capital-goods price index. D^* is a moving average of D.

DIC   Gross inflow of direct investment to Canada from all countries.

DL   Differential between Canadian and United States long-term interest rates ($DL = CL - USL$).

DR   Direct foreign investment flows to Canada from the United States plus retained earnings of United States-controlled firms in Canada, deflated by Canadian capital-goods price index. Quarterly distribution of retained earnings within a year is assumed same as direct investment. DR^* is a moving average of DR.

DRK   Differential between yield on Canadian common and preferred stocks held abroad and yield on foreign common and preferred stocks held in Canada.

DRSP   Deviation of spot exchange rate from parity ($DRSP = RS - \$1.00$).

DRST   Deviation of spot exchange rate from its trend over the period 1952-I through 1961-II.

DS   Differential between Canadian and United States short-term interest rates ($DS = CS - USS$).

FP   Forward premium (discount) on the Canadian dollar ($FP = RF - RS$).

FR   Gross investment in new machinery, equipment, and nonresidential construction less corporate profits, capital consumption allowances, and miscellaneous valuation adjustments.

GNP   Gross national expenditure, excluding military pay and allowances.

IB   Gross business fixed capital formation; nonresidential construction and new machinery and equipment expenditures, including both private and government enterprises, deflated by corresponding seasonally adjusted, currently weighted implicit price deflator from *National Accounts*.

ID Net balance of interest and dividend payments with all countries.

K Net balance of long-term capital inflows (direct, portfolio, outstanding securities, and miscellaneous).

MWL Average yield on 40 bonds (municipal, provincial, public utility and industrial) published by McLeod, Young, Weir and Co., Toronto, expressed in percent per quarter.

NFR Net financial requirements; gross financial requirements less foreign direct investment in Canada ($NFR = FR - DIC$).

NNS Net new issues of all long-term marketable securities.

NNSC Net new issues of all long-term marketable securities retained in Canadian portfolios ($NNSC = NNS - PC$).

NTOS Net inflow of portfolio capital via trade in outstanding Canadian and foreign securities.

OR Change in official reserves due to exchange-market operations.

P′ Change in index of production for industrial sector indicated in text, current year minus previous year.

PC Net inflow of portfolio capital via new issues and retirements of Canadian and foreign securities.

PCMS Percentage change in the money supply; quarterly change divided by money supply at beginning of quarter.

PIB Private gross fixed business investment; *IB* less estimated quarterly value of fixed capital formation by public corporations.

Q Quarterly dummy variables taking the values Q_1, Q_2, Q_3; the influence of the fourth quarter is picked up in the constant terms of regression equations.

R Residuals from equation specified in text.

RF Ninety-day forward exchange rate, number of United States dollars per Canadian dollar.

RS Spot exchange rate, number of United States dollars per Canadian dollar.

SK Total net inflow of short-term capital to Canada less trade in outstanding securities ($SK = STK - NTOS$).

STK Total net inflow of short-term capital to Canada, constructed as sum of all other balances (current, long-term capital, official reserves); for components, see p. 71.

T Time trend, 1952-I, . . . , 1961-II = 1, . . . , 38.

U Undistributed corporation profits after taxes plus depreciation, deflated by the capital-goods price index. U^* is a moving average of U.

UKS Interest rate on United Kingdom three-month Treasury bills, in percent per quarter.

UM Quarterly unemployment as percentage of total civilian labor force.

UR Undistributed corporation profits after taxes plus depreciation minus retained earnings of United States-controlled firms in Canada, deflated by capital goods price index. Quarterly distribution of retained earnings within a year is assumed to be the same as direct investment.

USL Interest rate on long-term United States Government bond bearing coupon rate 2.50 percent, maturing December 15, 1972 (callable after December 15, 1967), in percent per quarter.

USS Interest rate on three-month United States Treasury bills, in percent per quarter.

Capital Transfers and Economic Policy:
Canada, 1951–1962

1 Policy Problems and Theoretical Hypotheses

International capital transfers occur when citizens of different countries exchange financial assets for real goods and services. This exchange poses two critical questions for economic policy and analysis. The first is to determine by what process the flow of financial assets comes to be matched by the flow of goods and services. The second is to determine how these flows of financial assets affect the operation of nations' fiscal and monetary policies.

The interest of economists in these issues has waxed and waned along with the practical importance of international capital flows. The high tide of international transfers prior to World War I gave rise to a series of now classical studies. In the 1920's international capital flows occurred fitfully, in the shadow of the problems of German war reparations and the diminishing role of Britain as an international banker and lender. During the 1930's exchange control, uncertainty about exchange rates, and a plague of domestic ills combined to bring capital flows almost to a halt, except for reparations and speculative transfers.

The revival of all forms of private transfers on a major scale was heralded by the heavy flows of foreign capital into

Canada after 1950. From 1951 to 1962, $9,836 million of long-term capital flowed into Canada, of which 76 percent came from the United States. This flow represented the first international experience since before World War I with large transfers motivated primarily by market incentives. As nations recovered from World War II and as controls on trade and payments were progressively dismantled in Europe and elsewhere, countries other than Canada also received substantial flows of international capital, primarily from the United States, that were influenced mainly by national differences in the yield on capital and not primarily by speculative considerations. Table 1.1, based on International Monetary Fund data, shows Canada's predominance as a destination for long-term international private capital flows in the period 1957–1960 and its declining importance in 1961–1964.

Most economists have endorsed such flows as an improvement of the international allocation of capital among industrial countries. At the same time, they have increasingly recognized that such flows alter the operation of domestic economic policies in major ways. It has been apparent that the increase in capital exports from the United States after 1957 coincided with the appearance of a substantial deficit in its international payments. This deficit occurred at a time when employment would have been affected adversely if interest rates were increased to deter the capital outflow. In Canada, against a background of heavy unemployment in the late 1950's, the fear arose that capital inflows were proving deflationary: they were driving up the price of the freely fluctuating Canadian dollar, increasing imports, and reducing exports — thereby increasing domestic unemployment. Other concerns were also voiced over the impact of capital flows on the management of the economy. Because of the threat of massive short-term capital inflows, Canada would be unable to raise her domestic interest rate in order to restrain inflation. Moreover, fears were expressed that foreign borrowing would reflect a propensity of Canadians to live beyond their means, buying abroad more goods and services than they sold and incurring foreign debts that might someday prove troublesome.

TABLE 1.1. Canada's share of average annual long-term international private capital movements, 1957–1960 and 1961–1964 (millions of U.S. dollars)

Inflows	Annual average 1957–1960	Annual average 1961–1964
Gross inflows of direct investment		
Canada	$ 550	$ 360
Total, industrial countries	1,590	2,230
Canada, % of total	34.6%	16.1%
Total, all countries	3,010	3,360
Canada, % of total	18.3%	10.7%
Net inflows of other long-term private capital		
Canada	610	360
Total, industrial countries	1,220	1,480
Canada, % of total	50.0%	24.3%
Total, all countries	1,570	2,420
Canada, % of total	38.8%	14.9%

Source: Calculated from Marcus Diamond, "Trends in the Flow of International Private Capital, 1957–65," *IMF Staff Papers*, XIV (March, 1967), table 2.

With the decline of the inflow of long-term capital in the early 1960's, the pegging of the Canadian dollar in 1962, and the attainment of a more acceptable level of employment by 1964, discussion of these issues subsided in circles where Canadian economic policy is made. Nonetheless, a number of Canadian economists have since challenged the logical con-

3

sistency of the arguments underlying these concerns.[1] The analytical issues remain in part unsettled at the theoretical level, and certainly the quantitative empirical work done so far has been inadequate. To define these issues and to analyze the relevant quantitative evidence are the objectives of this study. The results of such an inquiry are important for several reasons. Canada's adjustment to international capital flows was sharply questioned as a result of some major alleged failures of Canadian domestic policy in the late 1950's, as reflected in the persistence of high unemployment along with high interest rates, slightly rising prices, and an appreciating foreign exchange rate. Were the difficulties due to simple inadequacies in the formation and execution of policy, or were they due to constraints (whether associated with capital flows or with other forces) that rendered the successful management of macroeconomic policy impossible? The answer to this question suggests how much we can expect from economic policy in a world where international capital flows are again important. No nation is immune from recurrent problems of maintaining full employment or stable prices, and these problems may be exacerbated by highly responsive international flows of capital. Within the context of Canadian policy, the issues of the late 1950's may well arise again in the same or closely related forms. Nothing has changed fundamentally in the environment that drew such strikingly large capital flows to this one country. Nor can the question of returning the Canadian dollar to a freely fluctuating exchange rate be regarded as forever dead.

The case for an intensive examination of Canada's experi-

---

1. For example, R. A. Mundell, "Capital Mobility and Stabilization Policy under Fixed and Flexible Exchange Rates," *Canadian Journal of Economics and Political Science*, XXIX (November, 1963), 475–485; Harry G. Johnson, *The Canadian Quandary* (Toronto: Macmillan, 1963); David W. Slater, *Canada's Balance of International Payments—When Is a Deficit a Problem?* (Montreal: Canadian Trade Committee, 1964).

ence with capital transfers is strengthened by the more recent outcropping of these questions among the nations of Western Europe. In order to deal with the balance-of-payments problem of the United States, efforts have been made to coordinate national monetary policies between America and the European countries in order to reduce differences in their short-term interest rates and thereby the size of United States short-term capital outflows. The issue of the impact of capital flows on money income levels and financial policies has also arisen in the complaints of countries with payments surpluses and overfull employment, suspecting that inflation was increased by the favorable balance on current account and its impact on income and domestic liquidity. The debate between deficit and surplus countries has then turned to whether or not monetary policy in the surplus countries could absorb the domestic liquidity created by the payments surplus[2] or, alternatively, whether or not deficit countries should be chastized for increasing inflation in their surplus partners. Occasionally, however, observers have noted that international payments components other than the current account may affect the level of aggregate demand significantly, so that such issues cannot be settled by examining trade balances alone. Häuser, writing about the German surplus, has suggested that German long-term capital exports and unilateral transfer payments have been noninflationary, implying that they reduced domestic demand by as much as they increased the current-account surplus.[3] It seems clear that the influence on domestic policy

2. Ira O. Scott, Jr., and Wilson E. Schmidt, "Imported Inflation and Monetary Policy," *Banca Nazionale del Lavoro Quarterly Review,* no. 71, (December, 1964), 390–398; Robert Triffin and Herbert Grubel, "The Adjustment Mechanism to Differential Rates of Monetary Expansion among the Countries of the European Economic Community," *Review of Economics and Statistics,* XLIV (November, 1962), 486–491.

3. Karl Häuser, "Das Inflationselement in den deutschen Exportüberschussen," *Weltwirtschaftliches Archiv,* LXXXIII (1959), 166–187; see also Patrick M. Boarman, *Germany's Economic Dilemma: Inflation and the*

of interest-elastic capital flows and their impact on domestic aggregate demand and price levels will be felt increasingly by the European countries unless something happens to reduce the volume of capital flows and their sensitivity to international yield differentials. Whatever can be learned about the effects of capital flows on the Canadian economy will very likely prove important knowledge for the other high-income countries as well: Canada's problems with international capital movements may easily become theirs.

In the remainder of this chapter we shall first set forth the theoretical background to an empirical analysis of international capital flows, then provide a brief narrative account of the behavior of capital inflows to Canada during the period under examination.

THEORETICAL FRAMEWORK

Theoretical work on international capital movements falls into two rather distinct categories: one has an ancient lineage in economic analysis, the other is largely a recent outgrowth of the theory of economic policy. The first is the theory of the "transfer problem," concerned primarily with the mechanism of adjustment of the current accounts of borrowing and lending countries to an *exogenous* change in the volume of capital transfers. Although models of the transfer problem concentrating on real variables normally stress the effects of a change in capital flows on the terms of trade, we will emphasize the income and monetary adjustments involved. The second body of theory, growing out of the Meade-Tinbergen analysis of policy instruments and targets, treats capital flows as *endogenous:* influenced by variations in interest rates, incomes, and

Balance of Payments (New Haven: Yale University Press, 1964), pp. 47–56.

the exchange rate. Here the emphasis is entirely on monetary variables and short time periods. The famous studies of capital transfers undertaken between the wars were based on the first type of models concerning exogenous movements. Our investigation, however, will draw in larger part upon the second, which has not yet inspired much research designed to confront theory with factual evidence. Both theories can be put quite briefly if the assumptions are picked strategically and attention concentrated on the equilibrium or final result. The following description will be somewhat loose and eclectic because the assumptions most suitable empirically are not immediately obvious, and because what theory says about processes of adjustment matters at least as much for our purposes as what it says about the positions of equilibrium that are approached.

The Theory of Exogenous Transfers

The theory of the transfer problem owes much of its modern development to the work of P. A. Samuelson and H. G. Johnson,[4] although histories of research on the subject trace it back many years.[5] As Johnson points out,[6] the transfer problem can be separated into two questions: (1) Will the process by which the transfer is financed in the lending country and expended in the borrowing country change the trade balance by enough, at unchanged prices, to effect or requite the financial transfer in real terms? (2) So far as the expenditure changes alone

4. Paul A. Samuelson, "The Transfer Problem and Transport Costs," *Economic Journal,* LXII (June, 1952), 278–304, and LXIV (June, 1954), 264–289; Harry G. Johnson, *International Trade and Economic Growth* (Cambridge, Mass.: Harvard University Press, 1958), chap. vii.
5. Carl Iversen, *Some Aspects of the Theory of International Capital Movements* (Copenhagen: Levin & Munksgaard, 1936); Jacob Viner, *Studies in the Theory of International Trade* (New York: Harper, 1937).
6. Johnson, *International Trade,* p. 170.

undereffect or overeffect the transfer, will adjustments involving price changes alter the trade balance in the right direction and enough to restore equilibrium? The second question merely raises the issue of the stability of the market for foreign exchange in response to disturbance from a particular source. Market stability is not usually thought to depend on the specific source of disturbance, and so it does not appear to require special consideration in the context of the transfer problem. Most discussions of the transfer problem have hence dealt with the first question: whether expenditure changes by themselves will undereffect or overeffect the transfer. In a neoclassical two-country model, with exchange stability assumed, this is equivalent to asking whether the borrowing country's terms of trade must improve or worsen in the price-adjustment process.

As shown by the Keynes-Ohlin debate of the 1920's and the archeological efforts of Iversen and Viner, an economist's views on the expected behavior of the terms of trade can depend in part on his recognition of changes in real income or purchasing power associated with the transfer. Leaving aside the question of the degree to which earlier writers simply erred in assuming that total income as well as total output was unaffected by the transfer, it seems clear that many of them suspected that incomes might not change to the full extent of the transfer. This is so, particularly because discussions of the transfer problem have often centered upon actual or hypothetical cases of reparations or other unilateral transfers, which common sense properly suggests may be less than fully spent in the receiving country.

Be that as it may, a neoclassical approach to the transfer problem, which assumes continuous full employment and thereby guarantees that the incomes of the borrowing and lending countries will change by the full amount of the transfer, yields a relatively simple criterion for whether the transfer will be accomplished by income changes alone. In such a two-country model, with no purely domestic goods (only import-ables and exportables) and no transport costs or tariffs, the transfer will be undereffected (overeffected) as the sum of the two countries' marginal propensities to spend on imports is less than (greater than) one or, equivalently, as the sum of the two marginal propensities to consume exportables is greater than (less than) one. Where tariffs exist or transport costs in-tervene, the critical value of the marginal propensities to import becomes higher; where nontraded goods also exist, the simplicity of the criterion disappears, since demand and sup-ply substitutability between traded and nontraded goods must be taken into account.[7] When the existence of more than two countries is allowed for, the changes due to income variations in the borrower's and lender's balance of payments no longer need be equal in size and opposite in sign, and different criteria can be stated for the lender and the borrower. In the case of the borrower's balance of payments, spending pro-pensities become the borrower's marginal propensity to import from all sources and the lender's marginal propensity to spend on the borrower's exportables.[8]

At this stage, neoclassical transfer theory supplies no defi-nite predictions about the adequacy of income adjustments in accomplishing a transfer. Those seeking to establish such a presumption on a priori grounds have noted the effect of such "realistic" factors as tariffs and transport costs on the relative prices of borrower-goods and lender-goods in the two coun-tries. Tariffs necessarily make home goods relatively cheaper within the country imposing them and, given consumers' pref-erence patterns, thus cause the expected values of the marginal

7. I. MacDougall, "Non-traded Goods and the Transfer Problem," *Review of Economic Studies*, XXXII (January, 1965), 67–84.

8. For a convenient summary of these cases, see Johnson, *International Trade*, pp. 171–176.

propensities to import to be lower than in the absence of such impediments; the likelihood that transfers will be underaccomplished becomes greater. Alternatively, the effect of such impediments can be viewed as causing the real outlay for a given bundle of goods in the importing country to exceed the receipts for them in the exporting country. If the transport costs incurred by a country in purchasing imports include some of that country's exportable goods, then the critical sum of marginal propensities to import what is needed for the transfer just to be effected will exceed one, and the chances that it will be undereffected again increase. The trouble with reasoning along either line, however, is that the conclusions pertain, not to any empirical distribution of the likelihood of outcomes, but rather to a comparison of alternative theoretical situations. The simplest case of no transport costs or tariffs is found to establish no presumption about the transfer, then a presumption is imputed in other cases because their most likely outcomes lie on one side or the other of the original case. But this is a presumption only against the simplest and most abstract theoretical model; its empirical or predictive content is near zero. Theory tells little more than what quantities to measure in analyzing a particular case.

These conclusions are changed only slightly if we shift from neoclassical to Keynesian assumptions: elastic supplies of total output in each country at the going domestic price level. The central difference between the two cases is, of course, that in the Keynesian theory income changes in the lending and borrowing countries may amount to less than the transfer and differ from each other. For the transfer just to be effected at constant prices, the sum of the marginal propensities to import associated with the financing and expenditure of the transfer[9]

9. In Keynesian analysis there is no compelling reason to assume that the marginal propensities to import associated with the institutional financing and expenditure of the transfer will be the same as those associated with other types of expenditure change. Specifically, designating the marginal

must be equal to a magnitude greater than one.[10] Thus the critical value of the sum of import propensities relating to the transfer is greater in the Keynesian case, and the chances of the transfer being undereffected is relatively greater. This is a perfectly plausible result because the difference between the two cases is that, in the Keynesian version, the change in total expenditure (including expenditure on imports) may be less than the transfer, whereas in the neoclassical version it equals it. Granting this difference, however, neither the Keynesian nor the neoclassical model supplies any a priori prediction about the result of the transfer. Each provides only guidance concerning the appropriate empirical relations to measure.

The Keynesian analysis yields an expression for the total effect of the transfer on income in the borrowing and lending countries, as well as on their balance of payments. The effect is more deflationary in the borrowing country, the greater the degree to which the transfer is overeffected and the larger the proportion of the transfer proceeds saved in the borrowing country. The impact on income may be inflationary in the borrowing country if the transfer is undereffected. Again, no clear a priori predictions can be developed.

The principal conclusions of the neoclassical transfer model can be stated without specifying whether exchange rates are fixed or flexible: the analysis of whether the financing and disbursement of a transfer will overeffect or undereffect it can be used to indicate either the direction of change of a flexible rate (assuming the stability conditions for the market are satisfied) or the sign of the disequilibrium remaining under a

---

propensities to spend and import by s and m respectively, using primes to indicate propensities describing the direct alteration of spending and saving associated with the transfer, and designating the lending and borrowing countries by subscripts a and b respectively, the transfer is just effected if

$$m'_a + m'_b = (m_a/s_a)s'_a + (m_b/s_b)s'_b + 1.$$

10. See Johnson, *International Trade*, pp. 177–181.

fixed rate. This correspondence fails to hold for the Keynesian analysis, however, because a fixed exchange rate must prevail if the size of the payments imbalance resulting at constant prices is to determine the equilibrating changes in income in the borrowing and lending countries. R. G. Penner[11] has suggested an approach to the effects of exogenous capital flows in Keynesian circumstances with a flexible exchange rate. A capital inflow drives up the price of the borrower's currency until the current account swings adversely by an amount sufficient to effect the transfer. Thus, if the stability conditions are satisfied, there is no question of the adequacy of the induced trade-balance change when the rate is flexible, as there is in the fixed-rate case. The current-account swing per se reduces real income in the borrowing country (and raises it in the lending country). As in the fixed-rate case, however, a conclusion about the total effect of the transfer on income requires knowledge of how the proceeds of the transfer are spent in the borrowing country, and raised in the lending country. If proceeds go to purchase imports (imported machines, for example), then the deflationary effect of the financial inflow on the current account is offset — indeed, there *is* no independent financial inflow. If they are exchanged for existing national assets (a takeover investment, for example, with the seller putting the proceeds into idle balances), then the full deflationary impact is felt. If they purchase currently produced goods and services of the borrowing country, then the deflationary impact may be offset or more than offset.[12] Thus, as in the fixed-rate case, the impact of capital flows on income

11. Rudolph G. Penner, "The Inflow of Long-term Capital and the Canadian Business Cycle, 1950–1960," *Canadian Journal of Economics and Political Science,* XXVIII (November, 1962), 527–533.

12. It is exactly offset if (1) the size of the associated purchase of goods is equal to the size of the transfer and (2) all other expenditures financed in the borrowing country are unchanged. See *ibid.,* p. 529.

depends critically on how the transfer is financed and spent.[13]

Penner's three examples of spending patterns associated with the transfer of capital provide useful reference points, but, as James Melvin has demonstrated,[14] they neglect both income disturbances in the lending country and the repercussions on spending of changes in the exchange rate induced by the capital inflow. (In this Keynesian model, domestic money prices are fixed and a change in the exchange rate alters the prices of foreign relative to home goods in the same proportion.) Penner suggests that a transfer spent wholly on currently produced domestic goods and services in the borrowing country will leave its income and employment unchanged; this requires certain assumptions about saving propensities and the demand elasticity for imports in the borrowing country, so that the price-induced fall in home expenditure equals both the initial transfer and the price-induced increase in spending on imports. Likewise, Penner's finding that a transfer spent directly on imports will leave both employment in the borrowing country and the exchange rate unchanged requires that expenditure in the lending country remain constant.

The details of these cases should not obscure the fact that the criterion for the sum of marginal propensities, taken from the neoclassical case with fixed exchange rates, provides a useful first approximation for analyzing the effects of a transfer in Keynesian conditions with a flexible rate. Complications

13. Egon Sohmen, *Flexible Exchange Rates: Theory and Controversy* (Chicago: University of Chicago Press, 1961), pp. 25–26, exaggerates the contrast between flexible and fixed cases by arguing that the monetary effects of the inflow under fixed rates must increase domestic spending; at the same time, he neglects the expenditure of the proceeds as a possible offset to the deflationary effect of the inflow under flexible rates through the current account.

14. James R. Melvin, "Capital Flows and Employment under Flexible Exchange Rates," *Canadian Journal of Economics,* I (May, 1968), 318–333.

stem from the dual forces operating on the borrower's employment level: the direct effect of the transfer on expenditure on domestic goods and services and its indirect effect via the current-account balance and changes in the exchange rate. We shall try to take these influences (and their respective time paths) into separate account in estimating the impact of capital-flow disturbances on the level of income and employment.

Extant empirical work on the transfer process, done mainly in the 1920's and 1930's, was based on classical transfer theory minus a clear recognition of the role of income changes in the adjustment process. Although they represented high-quality empirical work for their time, these studies suffer today from inadequate theoretical framework and scanty quantitative information. J. H. Williams, studying fluctuating exchange rates in Argentina between 1880 and 1900, found his evidence cluttered with the effects of disturbances other than capital inflows — principally domestic inflation and variations in the demand for Argentine exports. He noted the response of the trade balance to variations in capital inflows and, in explaining the behavior of domestic money prices and wages largely in terms of monetary developments, left the implication (for others to draw) that the visible part of adjustment to capital flows was due to income effects.[15] Viner's study of capital inflows to Canada found confirmation for a strictly classical transfer mechanism in the form of events consistent with the predicted monetary consequences of a transfer under fixed exchange rates, starting with an increase in the demand for bills on Canada, and leading to an increase in Canadian prices relative to those abroad and in the prices of Canadian non-

15. John H. Williams, *Argentine International Trade under Inconvertible Paper Money, 1880–1900* (Cambridge, Mass.: Harvard University Press, 1920), esp. chap. xii; A. G. Ford, "Flexible Exchange Rates and Argentina, 1885–1900," *Oxford Economic Papers,* X (October, 1958), 316–338.

16. Jacob Viner, *Canada's Balance of International Indebtedness, 1900–1913* (Cambridge, Mass.: Harvard University Press, 1924).

traded relative to traded goods.[16] Economists reviewing Viner's evidence have cast doubt upon his cautiously stated conclusions about the price adjustment mechanism.[17] More important, they have suggested that Viner's model was deficient in treating capital transfers as an exogenous disturbance, rather than as an endogenous component of a larger model in which income growth and factor inflows depend on actual and prospective export growth and changes in relative and money prices are explained by the impact of this general growth process.[18]

The lesson that deceptive conclusions can be drawn when endogenous capital flows are treated as exogenous, could be learned as readily from most other classic studies of the transfer process.[19] It directs our attention to the other class of theoretical models mentioned above, in which capital inflows are viewed as an endogenous component of a model of income determination. In them the international flow of capital takes place not for unexplained reasons but, rather, because of differentials between domestic and foreign asset yields. Theoretical reasoning establishes the impact of this responsiveness of capital supply on the balance of payments and other variables that are significant for the operation of domestic macroeconomic policy. Models of this type, now rapidly proliferating, cover both Keynesian conditions of elastic aggregate supply and downward-rigid domestic prices and neoclassical circum-

17. For example, John A. Stovel, *Canada in the World Economy* (Cambridge, Mass.: Harvard University Press, 1959), esp. pp. 181–189.

18. G. M. Meier, "Economic Development and the Transfer Mechanism: Canada, 1895–1913," *Canadian Journal of Economics and Political Science,* XIX (February, 1953), 1–10; Stovel, *Canada,* chap. xiii.

19. Professor George H. Borts has pointed out that, when capital movements are endogenous, numerous disturbances occurring elsewhere in the system can set in motion the same adjustments predicted in a neoclassical model to result from a change in exogenous capital flows; see his "A Theory of Long-Run International Capital Movements," *Journal of Political Economy,* LXXII (August, 1964), 341–359.

stances of flexible prices and full employment, and both fixed and flexible exchange rates.

The Theory of Endogenous Transfers and Internal and External Balance

The most familiar conclusion of this analysis, drawn for the case of fixed exchange rates, concerns the relative leverage of fiscal and monetary policy on domestic employment and the balance of payments when capital flows are interest-elastic. Consider changes in fiscal and monetary policy that would effect the same arbitrary increase in employment: either move would, in general, deteriorate the current account of the balance of payments by the same amount. But change in monetary policy would cause additional deterioration of the balance of payments through the capital account, because by lowering interest rates it would reduce the net capital inflow. The implications of this argument can be stated in various ways. In a static context, it suggests "assigning" the maintenance of payments equilibrium to the monetary authorities and the maintenance of full employment to fiscal policy; this recipe minimizes the incidental disturbances in one sector (employment or international payments) resulting from attempts to adjust the other. Alternatively, and in a dynamic context, correct assignment would avert instabilities resulting from the use of policy instruments.[20] Assignment is not relevant, however, if policy-makers enjoy full information on the size of disequilibria and the effects of their policy instruments; that case simply calls for simultaneous solution for the correct combination of policies.

With a flexible exchange rate, one policy objective is re-

---

20. Robert A. Mundell, "The Appropriate Use of Monetary and Fiscal Policy for Internal and External Balance," *IMF Staff Papers,* IX (March, 1962), 70–77, and a number of related papers.

moved, and the assignment problem becomes one of selecting the best instrument for maintaining internal balance. Still assuming Keynesian conditions, monetary policy becomes relatively effective for managing aggregate demand; it works through two complementary channels, whereas for fiscal policy one channel may frustrate the other's effects. Used to raise employment, monetary policy works directly on domestic expenditure to the extent that it reduces interest rates and eases credit availability. Any tendency for interest rates to fall also reduces the net inflow of capital, thereby depreciating the country's currency, improving the current-account balance, and raising aggregate demand in turn. More effect through one channel means less through the other, with the amount flowing through the external channel dependent primarily on the interest-elasticity of international capital movements. If capital flows are perfectly elastic, then the whole of the impact of monetary policy is felt through the external channel.[21]

Whether fiscal policy is effective for raising employment with the exchange rate flexible depends on how it is coordinated with monetary policy. If monetary authorities maintain domestic interest rates constant, fiscal policy becomes relatively effective. The multiplier operates without foreign leakage and thus attains a higher value than it would if exchange rates were fixed, since any income-induced increases in imports are offset by depreciation of the exchange rate and export expansion.[22] On the other hand, if the monetary authorities keep the money supply constant, fiscal policy is frustrated by the existence of interest-elastic capital flows. The government's borrowing

21. Mundell, "Capital Mobility," pp. 477–78.

22. Anne O. Krueger, "The Impact of Alternative Government Policies under Varying Exchange Systems," *Quarterly Journal of Economics,* LXXIX (May, 1965), 195–209. Treating the interest rate, rather than the monetary supply, as a basic policy instrument is subject to important theoretical difficulties within the framework of these models; see Ronald W. Jones, "Monetary and Fiscal Policy for an Economy with Fixed Exchange Rates," *Journal of Political Economy,* LXXVI, pt. 2 (July-August, 1968), 921–943.

17

operations to finance the increase in its deficit (or reduction of its surplus), the counterpart of the assumed net fiscal injection into the income stream, necessarily increase the net domestic supply of securities and tend to raise the interest rate. If capital flows are perfectly elastic, the interest rate remains constant, but capital flows in and the exchange rate rises. The exchange-rate appreciation must cause the current account to deteriorate until the net increase of the import surplus just offsets the net increase of the government deficit, and fiscal policy is entirely frustrated.[23] If capital flows are less than perfectly interest-elastic, fiscal policy still tends to drive up the exchange rate in this way; but it may generate its unfavorable monetary impact in part through a different channel — the direct discouragement of domestic spending by rising interest rates. A striking conclusion of Rudolf R. Rhomberg's econometric study of the Canadian exchange rate is that, with the money supply held constant, the monetary impact of easier fiscal policy — tending to appreciate the Canadian dollar — would swamp the direct tendency of increased spending on imports to depreciate the currency.[24]

These conclusions, drawn from recent work on the theory of economic policy with endogenous capital flows, suggest the need to explore several models before embarking on the empirical study we propose. Many different features of the economy, described by the diverse assumptions upon which models can be built, may affect the results fundamentally. Although economists have been busily creating such models, we have found it necessary to explore some theoretical problems not satisfactorily covered before; the results are detailed in Appendix A. We have investigated mainly two issues. First, when exchange rates are fixed, changes in foreign-exchange

23. Mundell, "Capital Mobility," p. 478.
24. Rudolf R. Rhomberg, "A Model of the Canadian Economy under Fixed and Fluctuating Exchange Rates," *Journal of Political Economy,* LXXII (February, 1964), 15.

reserves may be either allowed to or precluded from affecting the domestic money supply. If the second policy — sterilization — is in force, then actual changes in the money supply coincide with those intended by the monetary authorities; but without sterilization, the desired changes may be distorted when induced capital flows force the use of exchange reserves.[25] The effects of sterilization on leverages of policy instruments are considered in the Appendix.

Second, international capital flows may be responsive to changes, not only in the interest rate, but also in income or in the (flexible) exchange rate. The last type of sensitivity particularly has gone unexplored and is developed in Appendix A. The effect of the exchange rate on capital flows can be disposed of theoretically by assuming that the elasticity of expectations concerning future exchange rates is equal to one; this means that expected future rates change in the same proportion as the current exchange rate. A foreign lender or borrower normally faces a risk that the exchange rate may alter before a loan matures, causing the value of the repayment, and perhaps of some of the periodic interest payments, to differ from what was anticipated at the time the original contract was struck.[26] The interest differential between a borrowing and a lending country represents the market's evaluation of this risk (and perhaps other risks and frictions). In the case of unit elasticity of expectations, a current change in the exchange rate fails to affect the market's relative valuation of future and present payments and receipts and thus leaves

25. Differing assumptions about sterilization account for some variance in conclusions in the published literature. Mundell ("Capital Mobility") discusses the case of perfectly interest-elastic capital flows in which sterilization is impossible; sterilization is assumed, however, in Harry G. Johnson, "Some Aspects of the Theory of Economic Policy in a World of Capital Mobility," *Essays in Honor of Marco Fanno,* ed. Tullio Bagiotti (Padua: Cedam, 1966), II, 345–359.

26. In any particular transaction, the risk may be borne either by the borrower or the lender or it may be shared somehow between them.

capital movements unaffected. If expectations are elastic, the depreciation of a borrower's currency depresses the relative value of future proceeds expected by foreign lenders (or increases the cost of debt servicing expected by domestic borrowers) and tends to reduce the capital inflow and further depreciate the currency; if expectations are inelastic, the opposite effects are predicted and the exchange market stabilized. Consider the implications of inelastic expectations for the conclusions summarized above, concerning the relative effectiveness of fiscal and monetary policy. It is argued that an easing of monetary policy to raise aggregate demand and employment may be effective through discouraging capital inflows, depreciating the exchange rate and thereby improving the current-account balance. With expectations inelastic, the depreciation initiated by downward pressure of lower interest rates on capital flows itself tends to stay the reduction of the flows and stabilize the exchange rate, thus blocking the "indirect route" through which monetary policy might be effective.

Against this background we can summarize the results of Appendix A, which develops evidence on changes of the ratio of the leverage on employment of monetary policy to the leverage on employment of fiscal policy under various environmental conditions.[27] We assume Keynesian circumstances and explore the effects of fiscal policy either when the money supply is fixed or when it is changed only because of changes in foreign reserves; we explore the effects of monetary policy in the context of constant government expenditures and tax rates. With fixed exchange rates, using monetary policy to raise employment worsens the foreign balance unless capital inflows are highly sensitive to income changes; increased government expenditures are somewhat more likely to improve

27. Because leverages on the balance of payments are also considered, the findings could instead be phrased in terms of the "assignment problem." Given our primary interest in the case of flexible exchange rates, however, the device mentioned in the text is more relevant.

the foreign balance because they may induce income-elastic capital flows, and also because the increasing demand for money for transaction purposes raises interest rates and generates an inflow of interest-sensitive capital. If changes in foreign-exchange reserves are allowed to affect the money supply (in other words, reserves flows are not sterilized), the effectiveness of fiscal policy for raising employment is increased relative to monetary policy; this is because sterilization precludes an offset to the central bank's monetary injection through monetary contraction associated with the ensuing loss of reserves. The absolute effectiveness of fiscal policy probably rises when sterilization is eschewed; the absolute effectiveness of monetary policy almost certainly falls.

Considering flexible exchange rates, when capital inflows are totally exogenous (or absent), both monetary and fiscal employment multipliers are higher than in the case of fixed exchange rates; but they remain in the same proportion as when rates are fixed and changes in foreign reserves are sterilized. If capital flows are sensitive to interest rates, however, the relative effectiveness of fiscal policy falls[28] because the higher interest rates caused by increasing transaction needs for money attract foreign capital, precluding depreciation of the exchange rate and permitting a current-account leakage from the income circuit. As the interest-elasticity of capital flows increases, the effectiveness of fiscal policy approaches zero, whereas the effectiveness of monetary policy increases and approaches the value of the marginal velocity of circulation of money. If capital inflows increase when income rises, the effectiveness of both fiscal and monetary policy is reduced, as are the chances that either policy will prove more effective under flexible than fixed exchange rates; in the limiting case, as the income-sensitivity of capital inflows becomes infinite,

28. An exception occurs where the sensitivity of capital flows to interest-rate (and income) changes is high enough so that, under fixed rates, fiscal measures to raise employment also improve the balance of payments.

both instruments become completely ineffective for raising employment. Finally, inelastic exchange-rate expectations, like income-mobile capital flows, unambiguously reduce the effectiveness of monetary policy and probably reduce the effectiveness of fiscal policy as well.[29] As the sensitivity of capital flows to the exchange rate becomes infinite, the effects on employment of both fiscal and monetary policy approach their values under fixed exchange rates (private speculators are now performing exactly the same job as the exchange stabilization authorities); and exchange rate-sensitive capital flows reduce the effectiveness of monetary relative to fiscal policy.

The empirical questions raised by the these propositions do not call for direct testing; rather, they suggest an effort to select the empirically appropriate set of assumptions and to measure empirical magnitudes that the theory shows are critical, such as the elasticity of exchange-rate expectations and the time lags involved in the responses of international to domestic variables.

Capital Flows, Growth, and Inflation

Judging from discussion of economic policy in Canada during the floating exchange rate period, the most important effect of endogenous capital flows is on employment and the nation's ability to regulate it. Economic theory shows, however, that these endogenous flows can affect the attainment of other policy objectives besides full employment. We shall not closely attend to these objectives; nevertheless the relevant theory provides useful context and perspective.

One such case is the effect of capital inflows on the rate of economic growth — rather trivial, if capital inflows are viewed as exogenous. Unless the transfer proceeds are hoarded, spent only for consumption, or discourage an equivalent

29. Exception same as n. 28.

amount of domestically financed investment, capital inflows are associated with some net increase in the borrower's capital stock; they should thus increase the rate of aggregate growth over the period in which they occur. It is not very interesting to investigate the effect on a growth rate of one-shot events. What happens if capital inflows are themselves influenced by the growth of domestic income? And what about the increasing stream of interest and dividend payments associated with the borrower's increasing stock of foreign-owned capital? These questions, certainly close to concerns voiced in Canada, are readily answerable in a model of the Harrod-Domar type.[30] The change in foreign borrowings is assumed to bear some constant proportional relation to the change in income. The effect of debt-service obligations can be allowed for by computing the equilibrium growth rate for gross national income (which excludes net payments to foreign factors), rather than gross domestic product (which includes them). If this is done and a continuous balance of payments equilibrium assumed, it can be shown that the growth rate of gross national income will exceed the familiar value of Harrod-Domar growth in a closed economy: the product of the marginal output-capital ratio and the marginal propensity to save.[31] Since the encouragement of economic growth is now widely regarded as a policy objective, this theory suggests quantitative measure-

30. B. F. Massell, "Exports, Capital Imports, and Economic Growth," *Kyklos,* XVII, fasc. 4 (1964), 627–634

31. Let σ be the marginal output-capital ratio, s the marginal propensity to save, λ the ratio of extra dollars of foreign borrowing per extra dollar of income, and r the rate of interest. The closed-economy Harrod-Domar growth rate is σs. Under the present assumptions it becomes

$$\frac{\sigma s}{1 - \lambda(\sigma - r)},$$

which exceeds σs if $\lambda > 0$ and $\sigma > r$. As Massell points out, in the Keynesian Harrod-Domar model σ functions as the marginal productivity of capital, so the result can be given the very sensible interpretation that capital inflows speed the rate of growth if the marginal productivity of capital exceeds the rate of interest.

ments to evaluate the potential gain in leverage of domestic growth-inducing policies due to the availability of foreign capital supplies. The responsiveness of capital flows to income growth (policy-induced or otherwise) becomes important to evaluate, and there is an obvious need to know the extent to which capital flows are sensitive to income growth per se and the degree to which they respond to high interest rates that may result from rapid growth.[32]

Another impact of endogenous capital flows may be on the rate of inflation, its possible determinants in an open economy, and the ability of the authorities to control it by the usual methods. Here we make the theoretical analysis particular to the Canadian case, since these issues tend to be complicated by the multiplicity of theories of causes and mechanisms of inflation. The role of capital flows is easily identified if one accepts a theory of the causes of inflation in terms of excess real aggregate demand at the initial price level, and a theory of the inflationary process which explains the rate of inflation by a relation of the "Phillips curve" variety between the rate of price increase and the level of unemployment or excess capacity. Then the relation between capital flows and

32. Recent contributions to neoclassical growth theory have investigated the properties of an open economy or a two-country world in which capital is freely transferred internationally at the going world interest rate. In a two-country world, with the return to capital equated to its marginal product in both countries, balanced growth is possible only if both countries' labor forces grow at the same rate, so that one nation is a scale replica of the other; if labor-force growth rates differ, the faster-growing country imports capital and eventually dominates the determination of the world interest rate (Philip A. Neher, "Natural Rates of Economic Growth and International Interest Rates," *Kyklos,* XXI, no. 2 [1968], 326–335). Golden Rules of saving have been derived for economies too small to influence world interest rates and which will generally not have access to an equilibrium growth path unless their labor-force growth rates happen to equal the world interest rate (J. A. Hanson and P. A. Neher, "The Neoclassical Theorem Once Again: Closed and Open Economies," *American Economic Review,* LVII [September, 1967], 869–878). We found little useful guidance for empirical work in this literature, although it holds interest on other grounds.

inflation becomes very similar to the relation between capital flows and employment, discussed above in connection with the transfer process. The questions raised by Keynesian transfer theory about the direct impact of exogenous capital flows upon domestic spending, saving and imports can be phrased similarly, whether the effects of the associated variations in aggregate demand are expected to be felt on the price level, the rate of unemployment, or some combination of the two. Likewise, the impact of endogenous capital movements on the efficacy of fiscal and monetary policy should be fundamentally the same whether these policies are manipulated to control mainly the amount of unemployment or the behavior of prices.

Some examples may clarify these suggestions. Suppose that exogenous variations in capital inflows to a borrowing country (with a flexible exchange rate) alter domestic expenditure by more than the change in the transfer, and that transfers increase with the rate of price inflation in the borrowing country (perhaps because of the influence of inflation on profit expectations and direct investment). In that case, capital inflows would tend to increase the variability of the rate of inflation over time, augmenting it more when it is high than when it is low. The converse would hold if the tendency were for capital inflows to be associated with changes in expenditure of less than the amount of the transfer: they would reduce the variability of the inflation rate by exerting more deflationary pressure when it is high than when it is low.

A similar analysis would hold for the impact of endogenous capital flows on the effectiveness of policy to control inflation. The greater the interest-elasticity of capital flows, the greater the degree to which monetary policy operates on the price level indirectly through its impact on capital flows, the exchange rate, and the current-account balance. As before, inelastic expectations constrict this indirect channel by reducing the effective variability of the exchange rate; and if inflationary pressure results from a tendency for the current account to turn favorable in response to faster inflation abroad than at home, then inelastic expectations would reduce the effectiveness of the flexible exchange rate itself as a mechanism for protecting the price level from external disturbances.

The empirical guidance of these suggestions about the relation of capital flows to inflation is similar to that provided by other theories. Our attention is drawn to several measurements of the rate and magnitude of response of some variables to changes in others; these measures, appropriately combined, may suggest the net impact of international capital movements on inflation and policies to control it.

An important problem underlying the analysis of inflation along aggregative lines is the influence of "push" elements, especially those originating outside the country. Commentators on inflation in Canada sometimes invoke the proposition that Canadian wholesale prices are "simply world prices multiplied by the exchange rate" to support the conclusion that Canadian authorities cannot control their domestic price level when foreign money prices are rising. This is, of course, a nonsense application of the law of one price under a flexible exchange rate, or even under a fixed rate protected by suitable adjustment mechanisms or policy instruments. But it points to a valid source of concern about price behavior in an economy as open as that of Canada. The ownership links between firms in numerous Canadian industries and their United States counterparts, and the affiliation between Canadian and United States trade unions in certain economic sectors, raise the possibility that Canadian prices (and wages) may be marked up in the wake of adjustments made in the United States, regardless of market conditions in Canada. Alternatively, if prices are flexible upward but not downward, inflation might be transmitted to Canada via something resembling the "demand shift" inflationary process suggested by Charles Schultze[33] on the basis of United States experience. The prices of selected Canadian importables and exportables may rise as a result of shifts in demand (or cost) abroad, but the prices of Canadian domestic goods may not fall even if these or other sectors possess excess capacity. Either of these mechanisms, or others that might be considered, could produce increases in the Canadian price level that are not correlated with the states of aggregate demand, unemployment, or excess capacity in Canada.

How may international capital flows affect cost-push inflation? Direct investment in Canada by United States firms tends to increase the possible extent of direct price linkages, of course, by increasing, ceteris paribus, the proportion of decisions concerning Canadian prices that lie within control of the same administrative centers that make pricing decisions in the United States. Aside from this basically microeconomic effect, capital inflows would seem to bear little relation to the transmission of inflation through cost-push mechanisms, except by the constraints and opportunities they create for the use of macroeconomic policy. The empirical issue raised by these mechanisms is really the extent to which they explain observed movements of the Canadian price level. This is because their importance or unimportance may determine the significance of any restraints on macroeconomic policy that are due to interest-elastic international capital flows.

RESEARCH STRATEGY

The section above briefly identifies the models relevant to investigating the significance of international capital move-

33. Charles L. Schultze, "Recent Inflation in the United States," *Materials Prepared in Connection with the Study of Employment, Growth and Price Levels,* U.S. Congress, Joint Economic Committee, Study Paper no. 1 (Washington: Government Printing Office, 1959).

ments in Canada during 1951–1962. Two major impressions emerge concerning the research necessary to apply these theoretical materials. First: the task indicated is not to test hypotheses of the conventional sort (that monopolies earn higher profits than competitive industries, for example), but to measure the empirical magnitudes, the elasticities and propensities, that macroeconomic theory reveals are important for analysis and policy. Interpretation of the results requires an assembly of theoretical models and empirical estimates based on common sense as well as on statistical tests of significance. Second, not only are quantitative techniques required throughout the investigation; also, problems of general interdependence, autocorrelation, and the other bugbears of modern quantitative economics will unavoidably be present, and choices must be made among research procedures that involve numerous compromises and approximations.

Taking up the second judgment, it may seem that many of the analytical questions raised above are best answered by use of a large-scale econometric model or models theoretically capable of dealing with problems of simultaneous relations. We have chosen not to follow this course: our main interest has been to explore certain relations that have been left untouched, or largely untouched, in previous econometric work. The time claimed by these labors has not permitted the additional work of developing a full model of the North American economy. Such a task seemed particularly undesirable because two ambitious quarterly econometric models of Canada are already available,[34] and some of the multipliers and simulations needed to shed light on the questions raised above have already been developed. We make use of the results at appropriate places to check and supplement our own work; the techniques range from simple least-squares through simulta-

34. Rhomberg, "Model of the Canadian Economy"; Lawence H. Officer, *An Econometric Model of Canada under the Fluctuating Exchange Rate* (Cambridge, Mass.: Harvard University Press, 1968).

neous models smaller in scope than those of Officer and Rhomberg. In addition to the substantive advantages of these simple, flexible, and pragmatic methods, they offer the tactical advantage that a number of people can work on the project at the same time, somewhat independently of one another.

The following chapters reflect the division of labor in the underlying research work. Chapters 2 through 6 report some of the major quantitative investigations. Chapters 7 and 8 draw together their separate results (and describe minor quantitative work not covered in other chapters) in presenting our findings about the adjustment of the Canadian economy and the Canadian balance of payments to changes in capital inflows and their impact on Canada's policy instruments.

Chapter 2 investigates the sensitivity of capital flows into Canada to various magnitudes in the Canadian economy. Substantially, this is a question of the sensitivity of different classes of capital movements to the differential between Canadian and foreign (especially United States) interest rates. In contrast to capital movements elsewhere in the world, the interest sensitivity of long-term flows to Canada has been established for some time.[35] Nonetheless, it is important to secure measures that are as exact as possible of this sensitivity and to determine which Canadian interest rates can influence capital flows most. This must be done, furthermore, after allowing for other crucial influences to the greatest possible degree — in particular, the influence of spot and forward exchange rates. As the preceding theoretical discussion suggests, not only might these interact with interest rates in important ways, but the effect of exchange-rate changes on capital flows also comprises important factual information.

Chapter 3 goes beyond Chapter 2 to a problem of interdependent relations. If an increase in Canadian interest rates

35. R. A. Radford, "Canada's Capital Inflow, 1946–53," *IMF Staff Papers*, IV (February, 1955), 217–257.

(relative to those in the United States) increases capital flows to Canada, it is also likely that the response of the flows tends to curtail the increase in Canadian rates. The elasticity of demand for Canadian securities is elevated above what it would be in the domestic economy alone, and the discrepancies between Canadian interest rates and those abroad are reduced. This reverse influence of capital flows on interest rates is important for a number of reasons. If investment in Canada is viewed as dependent upon the interest rate and movements in the interest rate as damped by variations in the rate of capital inflow, then this connection comprises an important market link between real and financial investment. Its measurement should shed light on the influence of financial capital movements on both volume and variability of real capital formation. Furthermore, the effect of capital flows on interest rates influences the extent to which monetary authorities must intervene in the market to effect any desired change in interest rates.

Chapter 4 takes up a linkage between capital inflows to Canada and real capital formation not operating through the interest rates: the connection between gross business capital formation in Canada and foreign direct investment. Because of the entrepreneurial nature of direct investment, it depends not on interest rates, but on profit expectations. These, of course, can only be measured by proxy if at all. But the information needed is not the influence of anticipated returns, but rather the extent to which the response of Canadian capital formation to its various domestic determinants is altered by changes in the inflow of direct investment. Chapter 4 attempts this measurement by investigating the extent to which capital formation can be explained by foreign direct investment when principal domestic influences on capital formation are taken into account.[36]

36. It seems likely a priori that several categories of aggregate demand

Chapter 5, which detours the main line of argument some-what, is designed to assist in evaluating the effect of capital inflows on the ability of Canadian fiscal and monetary authori-ties to control inflation or otherwise attain macroeconomic balance at home. It is argued above that the effects of capital inflows on the control of the price level and employment level are similar unless the openness of Canada's economy afflicts it with "cost-push" inflationary pressures from abroad. Chapter 5 seeks to test this hypothesis, by discovering which industries of Canada and the United States show especially similar price and wage behavior and by investigating their common charac-teristics.

To evaluate the problems of adjustment created by capital flows to Canada and the constraints and opportunities that result for Canadian economic policy, we must know something about, first, the reaction times required for these disturbances to work themselves out and, second, the significance of ex-ogenous capital flows as a source of disturbance to the Canadian economy. Chapter 6 undertakes an investigation of lag struc-tures in the Canadian balance of payments and between pay-ments and national income magnitudes that is designed to shed light on both questions.

Chapters 7 and 8 draw together the results of the preceding chapters and the research previously published by other econ-omists to answer the two central questions of this study: What are the characteristics of the process of adjustment of the Canadian economy and balance of payments to exogenous variations in the rate of capital inflow? What are the con-straints and opportunities created by endogenous capital in-flows for Canadian economic policy?

----

in Canada, including inventory changes, residential construction, and pur-chases of consumers' durable goods, might be influenced in the same fashion by certain types of capital inflow. These hypotheses have been in-vestigated, but the results are used as needed in Chapter 7 and are not reported separately.

2 Influences on Canadian Net Capital Inflows

The primary objective of this chapter is to present empirical estimates of the response of inflows to Canada of portfolio and short-term capital to changes in the rate interest, the level of income, and the price of the Canadian dollar. The theory of economic policy summarized above identifies the important influence of these relations on the leverages of instruments of domestic economic policy when international capital flows are variable. Later they will be fitted into quantitative estimates of changes in the leverages of Canadian monetary and fiscal policies wrought by these sensitivities.

Most of the calculations described below amount to single-equation estimates of the determinants of various net inflows of external funds. Although the time series used to measure these flows generally record inflows from all countries, the predominance of United States capital allows us to concentrate on variables relating to U.S.-Canadian flows. Single equation estimation in this setting runs well-known risks. Emphasis here is on variables influencing the supply of funds; the problems of identifying supply and demand relations are considered in the next chapter. Our hypotheses about supply determinants are drawn from portfolio theory, yet stock-flow relations do not enter explicitly in most relations. The provisional justification for this lies in the similar growth rates and patterns of the United States and Canadian economies and of their stocks of financial assets over the period studied. Given the level of the United States interest rate, variations in the total intake of Canadian securities to U.S. portfolios should be highly correlated with variations in the *ratio* in which Canadian and U.S. securities are added, so that estimated flow relations give some idea of underlying portfolio preferences. We shall return to the problem of stock versus flow relations at the end of the chapter.

NET INFLOWS OF PORTFOLIO CAPITAL

The dependent variable explained in this section is the net inflow of portfolio capital in the form of new issues and retirements of Canadian and foreign securities,[1] henceforth referred to as *PC*. Some investigators exclude retirements on the ground that they arise through the mere passage of time since issuance of the securities; but Lawrence Officer has pointed out that retirements should logically be included in the portfolio capital series because retirements may be made to take place sooner than anticipated as a result of interest-rate and perhaps exchange-rate movements.[2]

1. Most of the statistical series used in this study were collected from official sources, analyzed, and reviewed with great care by Lawrence H. Officer in his dissertation "An Econometric Model of the Canadian Economy under the Fluctuating Exchange Rate" (Harvard University, 1964), where they are reproduced in full. We have either retained his notation or modified it slightly. Sources for Officer's data are given in his study and are not repeated here. Sources for series not included by Officer will be given in the text as they are introduced.

2. See Gerald K. Helleiner, "Connections Between United States' and Canadian Capital Markets, 1952–1960," *Yale Economic Essays,* II, no. 2 (1962), 377. *PC* in our notation is the same as *PNIR* in Officer's notation and is given on p. 277 of the unpub. diss. version of his study.

The Model: Explanatory Variables and Data

The net inflow of portfolio capital is determined by Canadian and United States interest rates, the Canadian term structure of interest rates, and a variable representing the demand for funds, each of which will be discussed in turn.

Interest rates. Ignoring considerations of portfolio balance, foreign investors will buy Canadian securities when they anticipate a higher return on Canadian relative to other securities. Canadian borrowers will sell securities abroad when they anticipate that the cost of funds obtained in this manner is less than the cost of funds obtained from Canadian residents. The return on the investment, or the cost of borrowing, reflects (a) interest on the security, (b) the change in capital value resulting from any expected change in market interest rates, and (c) the change in capital value resulting from any expected change in the exchange rate. The net inflow of long-term capital should increase, ceteris paribus, when the market as a whole ascribes a higher return to Canadian than to foreign securities.

Potential domestic returns are represented in this study by *CL* and *USL* — the yields on two comparable Canadian and United States government securities. The similarity of their characteristics is shown below.

Characteristic	Security Underlying	
	CL	*USL*
Type	Bond	Bond
Issuer	Federal government	Federal government
Coupon rate	2.75 percent	2.50 percent
Earliest call date	June 15, 1967	Dec. 15, 1967
Maturity	June 15, 1968	Dec. 15, 1972

The only significant divergence occurs with respect to the maturity date, but that date is far less important than the earliest time at which the security can be redeemed at the issuer's will.[3] The foreign interest rate is represented by the U.S. rate because the United States was the most important transactor between 1951 and 1961, accounting for 87 percent of new issues and retirements of securities.[4] It is important to emphasize that the difference between *CL* and *USL* is not the actual differential return payable in a certain period on investments made in that period, but rather proxies one component of the expected yield advantage of Canadian securities. Thus, as the yield differential increases, the probability that *CL* will fall also increases and this produces an expected capital gain on Canadian investments. By the same token, the probability of a rise in *USL* with a corresponding capital loss on United States investments increases with a rise in the Canadian-U.S. interest differential.

In addition to the fact that the differential between Canadian and United States interest rates is only a proxy for the actual return, estimation of the interest-sensitivity of portfolio capital inflows encounters other difficulties. Our portfolio investment equations may be weakened by the nonuniform lag between the time a contract is entered into and the time the proceeds are forthcoming. The relevant interest rate is the rate at the time of contract, but the flow figure in the balance of payments is the figure for deliveries. Gerald Helleiner was able to obtain unpublished material compiled by A. E. Ames and Company from which quarterly contract date statistics for the most important category of inter-capital market transactions — new issues by Canadians payable in U.S. dollars — were constructed. His regressions show significant interest-rate responses whether delivery or contract data are used. In comparable re-

3. See Officer, unpub. diss., p. 308. Officer denotes Canadian and U.S. long-run interest rates as *CIL* and *USIL,* respectively. The data are available pp. 310–311.
4. Officer, *An Econometric Model of Canada,* p. 76.

gressions (borrower and term to maturity are the same) where both delivery and contract date statistics were available, the delivery date statistics yielded more significant, but not substantially different, interest-rate responses in two out of three cases.[5] Although Helleiner does not use his material to develop any specific information on the length of the lag between sales and deliveries, we present some concrete evidence on the lag in Chapter 6. Our method involves the correlation of current values of offerings with successive lead values of deliveries. If, for example, the correlation coefficient is higher for deliveries, led one quarter, than for current deliveries, this would imply that deliveries *lag* about one quarter behind sales. The highest correlation coefficient is obtained between current values of sales and deliveries, and this suggests no lag or a lag of less than one quarter. When lagged values of offerings are correlated with current values of deliveries, the correlation coefficient for a one-quarter lag (offerings *lead* deliveries by one quarter) is only insignificantly higher than the coefficient for current values. Finally, it should be noted that, if deliveries lag sales by at least one and one-half months, the most significant measure of interest-rate sensitivity will be obtained by regressing current *PC* (reflecting deliveries of last quarter's sales) upon last quarter's interest-rate differential. But our experiments with lagged interest rates produced smaller and less significant regression coefficients than did regressions using the unlagged interest-rate differential. The evidence presented above therefore suggests the lag between contract and delivery dates will not greatly impede analysis based on delivery data alone.

A more subtle difficulty arises from the fact that the interest rate variables used should be the rates prevailing after the transactions being compared have actually taken place. Strictly speaking, the correct interest rates are those which would

5. Helleiner, pp. 386–387.

prevail in both countries if the contemplated transactions had actually taken place. The reason for this is that the Canadian borrower, in deciding whether to borrow in Toronto or New York, should look not only at existing bond rates, but also at what the rates would be if he borrowed in Toronto instead of New York and vice versa. This is most important on the Canadian side of the border, where thin markets and credit-rationing may inflate the potential cost of a large bond issue by an amount not necessarily proportional to the going interest-rate differential.[6] Helleiner suggests that the observed yields on submarkets of the Canadian capital market do not accurately reflect the information about these markets that would be relevant to the decisions of borrowers.[7] To circumvent this problem, the yields finally selected for this study are the federal government yields used by Officer — probably the best proxies for the general state of the capital markets. Experiments were conducted using a variety of interest-rate series constructed from data published by McLeod, Young, Weir and Company, but the results were always inferior to those that used Officer's federal yields. This suggests that Canadian borrowers (predominantly nonfederal) did indeed look at the general state of United States and Canadian capital markets, for which the federal government yield is probably the best proxy, rather than at the state of particular submarkets, when reaching their decisions as to which capital markets to use.

The final question involves the precise way in which Canadian and United States yields should enter the portfolio in-

---

6. This interpretation of borrowers' behavior in the market seems consistent with the suggestion often made in Dominion Bureau of Statistics (D.B.S.) documents that lenders' comparisons of financial investment alternatives may be complex and asymmetrical between countries (e.g., Canadian federal government bonds competing most closely with U.S. state and local issues) because of risk factors. See D.B.S., *The Canadian Balance of International Payments, 1960* (Ottawa: Queen's Printer, 1962), p. 39.
7. Helleiner, p. 388.

vestment equation. Both yields must enter the equations, of course, because the borrower is interested in relative costs and the investor is interested in relative returns. The interest-rate differential alone is inferior to the joint inclusion of both yields on a priori grounds — exchange risk increases and capital inflow decreases with a rise in absolute levels of Canadian and U.S. rates even if the differential remains unchanged. In other words, because of exchange risk, a given interest differential should attract different amounts of capital depending upon the absolute levels of Canadian and U.S. rates. During the period of the floating exchange rate, exchange risk was borne mainly by the Canadian issuer of securities because sales of Canadian new issues payable in United States dollars to U.S. investors (henceforth, U.S. pay bonds) was the most important class of intercapital market transactions in terms of size and volatility.[8] The Canadian who sells U.S. pay bonds faces the risk of a fall in price of the Canadian dollar that will increase the Canadian dollar cost of annual interest payments plus payment of principal at maturity.[9] To be specific, a Canadian who borrows X United States dollars at the interest rate USL will receive X/RS_0 Canadian dollars, given the initial U.S. dollar price of the Canadian dollar, RS_0. The total Canadian dollar outlay for the term of the loan is $(X \cdot USL)/RS_t$ dollars

8. Because this class of transactions accounted for about 80 percent of the 1952–1962 inflow, it might be concluded that the major part of the capital inflow was borrower-motivated in the sense that it was the Canadian issuer who had to enter the foreign exchange market in order to service his debt obligations. Presumably, most Canadian borrowers would prefer to avoid the exchange risk, except for subsidiaries of U.S. firms and other enterprises with substantial foreign-exchange receipts (thus able to hedge their overall position by foreign borrowing). The yield differential in the U.S. market between Canadian and U.S. pay bonds is of course market-determined, and the predominance of U.S. pay issues testifies mainly to differential preferences of borrowers and lenders as between yield and exchange risk.

9. The U.S. investor who buys Canadian dollar securities similarly faces the risk of Canadian dollar depreciation that will reduce the U.S. dollar value of Canadian dollar interest earnings and principal repayment.

annually plus X/RS_n dollars when the loan matures at the end of n years. When interest rates and exchange rates are both taken into account, the *effective* interest rate paid by the borrower is the rate of discount, i, which makes the present value of the repayments equal to the present value of the loan. If the effective interest rate computed from the equation

$$\frac{X}{RS_0} = \frac{X \cdot USL}{RS_1(1 + i)} + \frac{X \cdot USL}{RS_2(1 + i)^2} + \cdots + \frac{X(USL + 1)}{RS_n(1 + i)^n}$$

is less than the long-term Canadian interest rate CL, then it is profitable to borrow abroad. Suppose we solve for the percentage depreciation in RS that is required to completely eliminate the gain from borrowing abroad. In order to keep the arithmetic simple, we can assume the extreme case, where RS depreciates to the critical level immediately after the loan is contracted and remains there until maturity. If this information is substituted into the equation above, we obtain

$$\frac{RS}{RS_0} = USL \left[\frac{1}{1 + CL} + \cdots + \frac{1}{(1 + CL)^n} \right] + \frac{1}{(1 + CL)^n}$$

$$= USL \left[\frac{1 - (1 + CL)^{-n}}{CL} \right] + \frac{1}{(1 + CL)^n}$$

for the critical value of RS. To illustrate, assume that $CL = 3$ percent, $USL = 1$ percent, and $n = 5$ years. Then

$$\frac{RS}{RS_0} = .01(4.5797) + 0.8626 = 0.9084$$

and the percentage depreciation in RS is 9.16 percent.[10] The

10. Frederick C. Kent and Maude E. Kent, *Compound Interest and Annuity Tables* (New York: McGraw-Hill, 1963), tables 2 (pp. 46–73) and 4 (102–129).

2-percent cost advantage in borrowing abroad would be just offset by an immediate currency depreciation of 9.16 percent. Table 2.1, constructed similarly, shows that the percentage

TABLE 2.1. Depreciation required to eliminate the advantage of foreign borrowing in relation to interest-rate level and term to maturity (percentages)

Interest rates			Term to maturity (years)			
CL-USL	CL	USL	2	5	10	20
2.0	3.0	1.0	3.83	9.16	17.06	29.75
2.0	4.0	2.0	3.77	8.91	16.22	27.18
2.0	5.0	3.0	3.72	8.66	15.44	24.92
2.0	6.0	4.0	3.67	8.42	14.72	22.94
2.0	7.0	5.0	3.62	8.20	14.06	21.19

depreciation required to eliminate the advantage of foreign borrowing increases with the term to maturity of the loan and the level of interest rates. If exchange depreciation proceeds more slowly than is assumed in the examples above, the ultimate required depreciation can be considerably larger before the cost advantage of foreign borrowing is completely eliminated. The economic reason why the exchange risk faced by the Canadian borrower increases pari passu with the level of rates (even if the differential remains unchanged) is that the exchange losses on the series of annual interest payments are proportional to the interest cost of debt service, that is, the United States interest rate. Therefore, if borrowers are averse to exchange risk, the variation in the net inflow of portfolio capital should be explained more closely by the joint variation in CL and USL than by the variation in their differential.

40

Canadian term structure of interest rates. The Canadian term structure is defined here as the slope of the yield curve — that is, as the difference between CL and CS where CS is the rate on 91-day Treasury bills.[11] David Meiselman has demonstrated that the yield curve can be interpreted as expressing expected future short-term interest rates.[12] If long-term rates are currently higher than short-term, then future short-term interest rates will be expected to rise because profit-maximizing behavior on the part of borrowers and lenders, together with substantial arbitrage or portfolio substitution among all maturities, implies that long rates will be a geometric average of the current and expected short rates prevailing over the terms to maturity of securities underlying long-term rates. Thus, an upward-sloping yield curve implies that all interest rates are expected to rise in the future — the yield curve will shift upward. The variable CTS ($= CL - CS$) may serve as an indicator of interest-rate expectations: if CTS is positive, the level of interest rates is expected to rise in the future and capital losses can be expected on all maturities. The capital inflow would be negatively related to CTS.

If, in addition, the expectations reflected by the term structure are generally correct over a period of time, then CL would typically exceed CS when all rates are relatively low by historical standards, falling short of CS when interest rates are relatively high. The variance of the long-term interest rate about its mean would be less than that of the short-term rate. The avoidance of capital losses or pursuit of capital gains embodied in a negative covariation between inflows of portfolio capital and the term structure would amount to stabilizing speculation by foreign lenders in regard to Canadian interest

11. The rate on 91-day Treasury bills (CS) is measured in percent per quarter and is obtained from various issues of the *Bank of Canada Statistical Summary.*

12. David Meiselman, *The Term Structure of Interest Rates* (Englewood Cliffs, N.J.: Prentice-Hall, 1962).

rates, and lenders' expectations could be described as inelastic with respect to changes in the general level of Canadian interest rates.

Viewed in this manner, the hypothesis about the negative relation of portfolio capital inflows to *CTS* rests upon a theory of term structure determination through portfolio substitution and a hypothesis about the relative potency of disturbances affecting long-term and short-term interest rates. Either prop supporting the argument could prove empirically feeble. Even if expectations do determine the term structure, in which case the variability of long-term rates should be considerably less than the variability of short-term rates, random disturbances could render the long-term rate the more variable. As a matter of fact, the ratio of the variance of the short-term rate to its mean was .152 between the first quarter of 1952 and the second quarter of 1961, while the same ratio for the long-term interest rate was only .031. The qualification concerning random disturbances appears to be unimportant. With a few additional assumptions, it is possible to test the hypothesis that the yield curve moved as predicted by the neoclassical expectations theory — upward-sloping when interest rates are low, negatively-sloping when high. Specifically, we hypothesize that (1) the long-term rate is an average of expected future short-term interest rates plus a risk premium, and (2) expected future short-term rates are a weighted average of experienced short rates.[13] Using a Koyck distributed lag formulation, our hypothesis states that

$$CL_t = aX^0CS_t + aX^1CS_{t-1} + \cdots + aX^nCS_{t-n}.$$

This can be simplified to yield the stochastic equation

13. The approach used here is similar to that of Johnson and Winder in their study for the Royal Commission on Banking and Finance; see Harry G. Johnson and John W. L. Winder, *Lags in the Effects of Monetary Policy in Canada* (Ottawa: Queen's Printer, 1962), pp. 179–180.

$$CL_t = b + aCS_t + XCL_{t-1} + u_t$$

in which a tells whether short-term interest rates do enter significantly into the determination of the long rate and X gives the weight to be applied to past values of the short-term rate. This model explains 90 percent of the variation in the long-term rate between 1952-I and 1961-II. The estimated equation is

$$CL_t = .1972 + .1829CS_t + .6834CL_{t-1}.$$
$$\qquad (3.27) \qquad (4.05) \qquad\qquad (8.37)$$

The respective t-values appear beneath the regression coefficients. The sum of the coefficients for current and lagged values of the short-term interest rate is given by the coefficient of CS in the equilibrium equation

$$CL = .62 + .58CS.$$

Since the coefficient of CS is less than unity, it is consistent with the hypothesis stated above only if the hypothesis is restated to specify that the risk premium, $CL - CS$, varies inversely with the short-term interest rate. If we rewrite the equilibrium equation as

$$CL = .62 + CS - .42CS$$

then

$$CL - CS = .62 - .42CS.$$

As CS rises, so does CL, but in *smaller* proportion. The yield curve therefore apparently moved in the manner predicted by the neoclassical theory.[14]

14. This naive test of the expectations hypothesis was conducted primarily because Rhomberg's work implies that the yield curve moved in a divergent manner — upward-sloping when rates were relatively high, downward when low. Thus, in *our* notation, Rhomberg estimated

The equation above indicates that long-term securities pay a risk premium the size of which varies inversely with the overall level of interest rates. If liquidity preference considerations are important in determining the term structure — that is, if risk aversion is present in the sense that a lender prefers a sure return to one of equal actuarial value but greater variance — then an upward-sloping yield curve will reflect, not only the expectation of rising future rates, but also the risk premium that long-term lenders require if they are to be persuaded to hold long-term securities. The presence of risk aversion, then, implies that the yield curve will be steeper at any given level of interest rates than would be the case if liquidity preference were absent. Our interpretation of the slope of the yield curve is a measure of the market's interest-rate expectations, since interest rates could be expected to fall at a time when they were still low enough for risk aversion to keep $CL - CS$ positive. The theoretically negative relation between capital inflows and CTS remains intact, but any empirical estimate of the absolute value of $\partial PC/\partial CTS$ is biased downward. This consideration might be serious if the observed yield curve were always upward-sloping and the implied short rate at which the risk premium disappears well above recorded

---

$$CL_t = .03 + .31CS_t - .24CS_{t-1} + .96CL_{t-1}.$$

The implied equilibrium equation is

$$CL = .75 + 1.75CS$$

and the risk premium is

$$CL - CS = .75 + .75CS.$$

These results imply that the risk premium on long-term securities varies directly with the short rate: as the short rate rises, so does the long, but in *greater* proportion. Rhomberg notes that the series for Canada's long-term government bond yield in *International Financial Statistics* was changed after completion of his study so that data inadequacies are probably responsible for his odd results. Rudolf R. Rhomberg, "A Model of the Canadian Economy under Fixed and Fluctuating Exchange Rates," *Journal of Political Economy,* LXXII (February, 1964), 1–31.

short-term rates. In the Canadian case, however, the yield curve was often flat, and in the second and third quarters of 1959 the slope was negative. The implied short-term rate at which the risk premium disappears is

$$CL - CS = .62 - .42CS = 0$$

or $CS = 1.47$ percent per quarter. While this implied rate exceeds the highest recorded short rate of 1.39 percent per quarter, the difference does not appear large enough to destroy any mileage hoped for out of CTS as a measure of interest-rate expectations.

A more serious objection to the expectation of a negative relation between capital inflows and CTS arises if international capital movements are viewed as part of that process of arbitrage or portfolio substitution between short-term and long-term securities which the expectations theory requires. If portfolio substitution within Canada fails to dominate the term structure, then the flow of capital across the Canadian border might represent primarily this portfolio adjustment itself, rather than a response to expectations about future rates reflected in a term structure that already embodies a perfect portfolio adjustment. The assumption of imperfect arbitrage implies that markets for securities of different term are segmented: hedging behavior reflected in institutional preferences for particular maturities restricts portfolio substitution to securities of a given maturity group. The lines between different maturity groups — intermediate-term and long-term, for example — are not crossed, and the structure of yields must be explained by relative demands and supplies for securities of each maturity group. An upward-sloping yield curve would reflect an excess demand for short-term securities and an excess supply of long-term securities, and this would signal conditions favorable for the movement of investors from short- into long-term securities. Portfolio inflows would then be positively related to

CTS, provided, of course, that foreign investors do not have strong preferences for particular maturities.

At this point there is no firm theoretical prediction about the sign of the relation between the net portfolio inflow and the Canadian term structure. Although the market segmentation or hedging theory of term structure has received little support in the United States (where "operation twist" rests implicitly upon such theory), it might conceivably be relevant in the Canadian context. In that case, even though the yield curve were apparently to shift in the manner predicted by the neo-classical theory, this would not rule out the prediction that *PC* and *CTS* will be positively correlated. If this is true, then by the same token, short-term capital inflows will be negatively correlated with both the term structure and the net portfolio inflow. On the other hand, if *CTS* measures interest-rate expectations, then both short-term and long-term capital inflows should be negatively related to *CTS* and positively to each other, ceteris paribus. In the final analysis, the interpretation to be placed upon the role of *CTS* must await the empirical results.

Demand for loanable funds. The theory of competitive markets suggests that the Canadian interest rate should adequately proxy variations in Canadian demands for foreign funds unless the Canadian capital market is imperfect. If capital market imperfections typically forced the decision to borrow abroad, whatever the state of Canadian bond markets, then a demand-for-funds variable should capture the independent influence of thinness in the Canadian capital market on the volume of international capital flows. Although a logical demand variable would be a capital formation series, the link between borrowing and capital formation is weakened by the financing of capital expenditures with internal sources of funds. Even in 1956–1957, when the investment boom was at its height, internal funds were providing over two-thirds of gross business capital financing.[15] By excluding internal liquidity from the relevant capital formation series, we end up with a financial requirements variable, *FR*, which should measure the demand for outside funds — funds which must be borrowed from Canadian residents or foreigners or both. Specifically, the series *FR* is constructed by subtracting the sum of (1) corporation profits, (2) capital consumption allowances, and (3) miscellaneous valuation adjustments from current dollar investment in new machinery, equipment, and nonresidential construction.[16] Because some financial requirements are supplied by capital flows in the form of direct investment, an alternative "net" financial requirements variable, *NFR*, is constructed by subtracting direct investment in Canada from *FR*.

On the other hand, if the Canadian capital market is deep and smooth, variations in Canadian capital formation and financing might influence the portfolio inflow without any marked fluctuation in the Canadian interest rate. If this alternative hypothesis of a relatively perfect Canadian capital market is correct, an extra dollar of long-term funds sought should raise the net demand for foreign funds by the same amount, no matter who the seeker. In this case, net new issues of all long-term marketable securities (the ex post demand for funds), *NNS*, should perform better than *FR* and *NFR* in explaining the variation in net portfolio inflow.[17]

15. *Report of the Royal Commission on Banking and Finance* (Ottawa: Queen's Printer, 1964), p. 33.
16. The investment flows are from various issues of D.B.S., *National Accounts, Income and Expenditure by Quarters.* The corporate liquidity series is from Officer, unpub. diss., p. 264.
17. Although the Canadian government did not borrow in the U.S. during the 1950's, federal issues have been included in the variable *NNS* on the ground that new issues of governments to Canadian lenders may have cut some corporate and junior government borrowers out of the domestic market and forced them to resort more heavily to the U.S. capital market. Federal securities are also represented in the net capital inflow because the

The coefficients of *NNS*, *FR*, and *NFR* provide an estimate of the proportion of an increase in the demand for loanable funds that is supplied by the foreign capital market. The estimate will clearly be upward-biased in the case where *NNS* represents the demand for funds, because *PC* is correlated with a total that includes it. Therefore, a fourth demand-for-funds variable is constructed by subtracting portfolio inflows from net new issues to obtain a new series, *NNSC*, which represents net new issues sold to Canadians. It can finally be noted that *FR* and *NFR* also involve us in simultaneous equation bias because the financial counterparts of these flows are new security issues, some of which are sold to foreigners.[18]

Estimation of the Equations

Using the notation introduced above, the basic equation used to explain net inflows of portfolio capital may be written as

$$PC = a + b_1 CL + b_2 USL + b_3 CTS + b_4 \begin{bmatrix} NNS \\ NNSC \\ FR \\ NFR \end{bmatrix} + u.$$

The financial flows are measured in millions of dollars per quarter, the interest rates and term structure in percent per quarter (following Officer's practice). All equations presented in this chapter are estimated by the classical least-squares estimator, using data from the first quarter of 1952 to the

Canadian Government was retiring American-held securities during this period. The series for *NNS* (*S* in Officer's terminology) is in Officer, unpub. diss., p. 297.

18. Evidence about the relation of *PC* respectively to *CL* and to the demand-for-funds variables cannot, of course, be used independently for predictive purposes: a disturbance in *NNS* normally affects *CL* and vice versa. Rather, the two types of variables are included in equations explaining *PC* for the purpose of testing different hypotheses.

second quarter of 1961 inclusive. The cut-off points coincide with the termination of exchange control on December 14, 1951, and the renewal of interference with the free exchange market announced by the Minister of Finance on June 20, 1961. We therefore have 38 quarterly observations covering the period when the exchange market was most truly free. The seven additional observations covering the floating rate period were excluded because of the various erratic factors which took place at its beginning and end. Although dummy variables can be used to adjust for noise factors, most of the equations already include three seasonal dummies; and the ease with which regression results can be meaningfully interpreted tends to diminish as the number of dummy variables increases. Furthermore, the inclusion of dummy variables to eliminate erratic disturbances consumes the extra degrees of freedom gained by extending the observation period. Finally, experimentation produced the most stable regression results when the observations covered the period in which the free exchange rate was actually free.

In the presentation of empirical results, the t-values for the regression coefficients are shown immediately beneath each coefficient. Constant terms and seasonal dummies are not shown unless they are significant at the 5-percent level.[19] In cases where none of the seasonal dummies appear with a significant coefficient, the equation was estimated exclusive of the dummies. Every equation is further described by four summary statistics:

(1) *The coefficient of multiple determination* is denoted as *RSQC*. The statistic has been corrected for degrees of freedom,

19. Because we always have at least 30 degrees of freedom, a t-value greater than 2.04 indicates that the regression coefficient differs significantly from zero at the 5-percent level of significance — the variable has contributed significantly to the explanation of variation in the dependent variable. Similarly, a t-value greater than 2.75 indicates significance at 1 percent.

so *RSQC* can be used to compare equations having different numbers of independent variables.

(2) *The F-ratio*, denoted as *F* and shown with the relevant number of degrees of freedom for numerator and denominator, tests the significance of the overall relationship between dependent and independent variables against the null hypothesis of no significance — that is, that

$$b_1 = b_2 = \cdots = b_n = 0.^{20}$$

(3) *The Durbin-Watson d-statistic* is denoted as *DW*. If *DW* indicates the presence of significant autocorrelation, our regression coefficients will be unbiased, but the *t*-values and *F*-ratios are no longer strictly valid and their significance falls into doubt. The null hypothesis of no autocorrelation will be accepted if the computed value of *DW* lies between 1.6 and 2.4.

(4) *The standard error of estimate* is denoted as *SEE* and measures the closeness with which the estimated values of the dependent variable agree with the original values. The residuals can be expected to exceed double the *SEE* of an equation only 5 percent of the time and to fall short of the *SEE* about 67 percent of the time. The mean value of the dependent variable is also presented, to give some idea of the relative size of the standard error of estimate. Finally, the statistic has been adjusted so as to make it theoretically unbiased. Thus, *SEE* can be used to compare different equations.

The regression results can now be presented:

20. If the calculated *F*-ratio exceeds the relevant value of *F* tabulated below,

$$F(2,35) = 5.27 \qquad F(6,31) = 3.45$$
$$F(3,34) = 4.42 \qquad F(7,30) = 3.30$$
$$F(4,33) = 3.96 \qquad F(8,29) = 3.17$$
$$F(5,32) = 3.66 \qquad F(9.28) = 3.11,$$

then the null hypothesis that the observed relation arose by chance at the 1-percent level of significance can be rejected.

$$PC = \underset{(2.19)}{164} + \underset{(4.30)}{693CL} - \underset{(4.34)}{959USL} - \underset{(3.84)}{215CTS} + \underset{(5.16)}{.1995NNS}$$

$$RSQC = .58$$
$$F(4, 33) = 14.51$$
$$DW = 1.71$$
$$SEE = \$52.7 \text{ million.} \quad (2.1)$$

The mean value of *PC* equals \$74.3 million.

$$PC = \underset{(2.11)}{191} + \underset{(4.02)}{797CL} - \underset{(3.89)}{1073USL} - \underset{(3.62)}{249CTS} + \underset{(2.85)}{.1598NNSC}$$

$$RSQC = .40$$
$$F(4, 33) = 7.46$$
$$DW = 1.65$$
$$SEE = \$63.4 \text{ million.} \quad (2.2)$$

$$PC = \underset{(2.40)}{515CL} - \underset{(2.22)}{645USL} - \underset{(2.29)}{168CTS} + \underset{(2.21)}{.1997FR}$$

$$RSQC = .34$$
$$F(4, 33) = 6.21$$
$$DW = 1.70$$
$$SEE = \$66.1 \text{ million.} \quad (2.3)$$

$$PC = \underset{(2.37)}{516CL} - \underset{(2.07)}{618USL} - \underset{(2.43)}{177CTS} + \underset{(2.07)}{.185NFR}$$

$$RSQC = .33$$
$$F(4, 33) = 5.99$$
$$DW = 1.67$$
$$SEE = \$66.6 \text{ million.} \quad (2.4)$$

All independent variables are significant in all equations, and the signs of the regression coefficients agree with a priori expectations. Nevertheless, it is clear that variations in the net inflow of portfolio capital are explained best by equation 2.1, which uses net new security issues to represent the demand for funds. The superiority of security issues as the demand for funds variable is further confirmed by the fact that *NNSC* also yields a better explanation of the inflow than do either of the financial requirements variables. It may be recalled that *FR* and *NFR*, like *NNS*, tend to include *PC* and thus have simultaneity working for them, whereas there should be no spurious relationship between *PC* and *NNSC*. The two financial requirements variables yield virtually identical equations, so the subtraction of direct capital inflows from financial requirements is apparently an unnecessary refinement. Finally, it can be noted that the coefficients of *NNS* and *FR* are identical and suggest that about 20 percent of variations in the demand for funds — whether represented by the flow of expenditures or the financial flow of securities — was supplied by the foreign capital market.

If our time period is expanded to include the last two quarters of 1951 and the third quarter of 1961,[21] equations 2.1 and 2.3 become, respectively,

$$PC = 546CL - 723USL - 145CTS + .176NNS$$
$$\quad\quad (3.59) \quad\quad (3.73) \quad\quad (2.68) \quad\quad (4.46)$$

$$RSQC = .47$$
$$DW = 1.54$$
$$SEE = \$57 \text{ million}$$

and

$$PC = 405CL - 470USL - 110CTS + .20FR$$
$$\quad\quad (2.17) \quad\quad (2.00) \quad\quad (1.70) \quad\quad (2.27)$$

$$RSQC = .29$$
$$DW = 1.66$$
$$SEE = \$66 \text{ million.}$$

21. The equations were estimated during early experimental work for this study; since various lagged formulations were attempted at that time, the maximum period of observation was 1951 (third quarter) to 1961 (third quarter).

The addition of more observations picks up much more variation that is difficult to represent adequately in the equations. The overall fit deteriorates for both equations, and the individual explanatory variables are less significant. The probable explanation is the drastic fall in price of the Canadian dollar that took place in the third quarter of 1961: 3.7 cents, the largest single change during the entire period of the floating exchange rate. This can only have been regarded by borrowers and investors alike as the beginning of a persistent downward trend in the rate — the fulfillment of Finance Minister Fleming's promise on June 20, 1961, to bring the rate down by artificial means. Persistent exchange-rate depreciation is not conducive to capital inflows, and this is reflected in the smaller interest-rate coefficients. The poorer performance of *FR* does not seem to be due to the fact that vital information might have been ignored in the lopping off of a few observations at the beginning and end of the floating exchange rate period. The two equations above preserve the ranking noted previously — *NNS* continues to be superior to *FR* as the demand-for-funds variable.

Two other problems may affect our ability to discriminate between *NNS* and *FR*. The inferior performance of *FR* may be purely statistical and associated with the fact that the total variation in *FR* is less than the total variation in *NNS*: the standard deviation of *FR* is only $131 million, while that of *NNS* is $231 million, and the respective ratios of standard deviations to the means are .485 and .615. *FR* may therefore suffer from bringing a smaller amount of independent variation to the explanation of the dependent variable, *PC*. The covariance between *FR* and *PC* is only half as large as the covariance between *NNS* and *PC*. Another problem lies in the possible lag of investment expenditure behind its financing. The construction of our financial requirements variable assumes a mean lag between external financing and expenditure of less than half a quarter, yet today's investment expenditures may reflect the demand for funds in some earlier quarter. In this case, the best relation between PC and FR would be found by leading FR! [22] This problem does not arise with NNS. Subject to these qualifications, the performance of NNS is found to be superior to that of FR; it is therefore possible to lay aside the hypothesis that FR may capture an important independent influence of imperfection or thinness in the Canadian capital market on the volume of international capital flows.

Turning now to a discussion of the interest-sensitivity of portfolio inflows, note first that the joint variation in Canadian and United States interest rates explains the variation in the capital inflow more closely than does the variation in the Canadian-U.S. interest-rate differential. No matter what other variables are included in the equation, it is always true that (1) the regression coefficient of the interest-rate differential, DL, is smaller than the coefficients of the Canadian and U.S. rates, and (2) the interest differential has a less significant impact upon the net capital inflow. Thus, when DL replaces CL and USL in equation 2.1:

$$PC = 458DL - 123CTS + .177NNS$$
$$(2.97) \qquad (2.40) \qquad (4.23)$$

$$RSQC = .49$$
$$F(3, 34) = 13.49$$
$$DW = 1.39$$
$$SEE = \$58.2 \text{ million.} \quad (2.5)$$

22. Alternatively, if a lag occurs between marshalling the finance and making the capital expenditure, the financial requirements for period t might be constructed by subtracting internal liquidity at time t from capital expenditures at time $t + n$. In the early research referred to in n. 21, an alternative financial requirements series was constructed by subtracting internal liquidity, lagged one quarter, from capital expenditures. The variable did not perform as well as its unlagged counterpart, FR. The regression coefficient for the alternative series was .09 with a t-value of only 1.57. The overall equation deteriorated in all respects and the $RSQC$ dropped to .27.

This equation is inferior to equation 2.1 in every respect. The proportion of variation in *PC* that is explained falls by 9 percent, and all the independent variables are less significant. In fact, the variances of the regression coefficients are actually underestimated because the residuals are now positively autocorrelated.

It is interesting that the regression coefficient of the United States interest rate is always absolutely larger than the coefficient of the Canadian rate. This is a consistent pattern that appears no matter what other explanatory variables are included in the equation. The implication is that an increase in the interest differential caused by a fall in the United States rate will have a larger impact on the capital inflow than would the same increase in the differential caused by a rise in the Canadian rate. Because exchange risk is lower in the former case, the larger coefficient for *USL* supports the initial expectation that *CL* and *USL* convey more information than does *DL* alone. In addition, if the United States interest rate is serving as a proxy for the overall level of interest rates,[23] then the larger coefficient for *USL* may reflect the operation of an income effect. Thus, if the differential rises because the Canadian rate rises, an increased capital inflow represents a switch from Canadian to U.S. capital markets — the substitution effect. On the other hand, if the differential rises because the U.S. rate falls, borrowing costs are lower and an income effect may complement the substitution effect.

The information contained in equation 2.1 can be used to construct 95-percent confidence limits for the "true" coefficients, β_1, of *CL* and *USL*. Thus, for *CL* we have

23. Our reason for expecting that the U.S. interest rate may be serving as a proxy for the level of interest rates follows from the fact that U.S. long-term rates were always lower than Canadian long-term rates during the time period under investigation.

$$365 \leqslant \beta_1 \leqslant 1021$$

and for *USL*

$$508 \leqslant \beta_2 \leqslant 1410.$$

Because the two confidence intervals overlap for the range 508 to 1021, which includes both of our estimated coefficients, we cannot reject the hypothesis that the coefficient of (1) *CL* is as large as 959, the coefficient of *USL,* and (2) *USL* is as small as 693, the coefficient of *CL*. There may, therefore, be no significant difference between the estimated interest-rate coefficients. A more precise test would compute the statistic

$$t = \frac{b_1 + b_2}{\sqrt{\sigma_{b_1}{}^2 + \sigma_{b_2}{}^2 + 2 \, \text{cov}_{b_1 b_2}}}$$

where b_1 and b_2 are the algebraic values of the estimated regression coefficients. Unfortunately, the regression package used to estimate the equations for this study does not provide the covariance matrix of the regression coefficients, so there is insufficient data to complete the test. If we assume that cov $b_1 b_2 = 0$, we have

$$t = \frac{266}{\sqrt{161^2 + 221^2}} = \frac{266}{274} = 0.97$$

and can provisionally accept the null hypothesis of no significant difference. If, however, the covariance of the estimated regression coefficients is negative, as is likely, this will reduce the combined standard error and increase the probability that the difference is significant.

On the other hand, there is a statistical reason for the divergence in the estimated coefficients which reduces the probability that the difference is significant. Although our equations show clearly that an increase in *CL* will raise the net capital inflow, the true interest-sensitivity of portfolio investment is understated because the interest-induced capital inflow tends simultaneously to dampen the variation in the interest rate by increasing the demand for Canadian securities (increasing the supply of loanable funds). The simultaneous interaction between interest rates and capital flows imparts a downward bias to the coefficient of *CL* when the equation is estimated by ordinary least-squares. Portfolio inflows represent only a small fraction of total long-term borrowing, and, of course, many other factors enter into determination of the long-term interest rate. It can therefore be expected that the interest rate will have a larger effect on capital inflow than will capital inflow on the interest rate, and our equation does identify the correct direction of causation. The interest-rate coefficient is not a true partial derivative, however, and in Chapter 3 an attempt is made to estimate the extent of downward bias in *CL*. At this point it can simply be noted that the coefficient of *CL* is a minimum estimate — equation 2.1 shows that a rise in the Canadian interest rate by one percentage point will, ceteris paribus, increase the net capital inflow by at least $693 million. Alternatively, the interest elasticity of the net capital inflow is 9.08 [24] at the very least. By similar reasoning it can be stated that the coefficient of the United States interest rate is a maximum estimate, although the degree of upward bias is likely to be small because variations in capital flows to Canada constitute such a small portion of disturbances affecting the giant U.S. capital market. The chances of isolating empirically the effect of net flows of capital to Canada on the U.S. interest rate seem very slight, so the U.S.

24. The interest elasticities are evaluated at the means of the dependent and independent variables. In equations using security issues or a variant of security issues as the demand-for-funds variable, the elasticities are around 10 per *CL* and −11 for *USL*. When financial requirements are used to represent the demand for funds, the elasticities for *CL* and *USL* are approximately 7 and −7 respectively.

interest rate will continue to be regarded in this study as a predetermined variable.

Finally, it should be noted that the significantly negative coefficient for *CTS* supports the hypothesis that the term structure measures interest-rate expectations and that long-term capital flows were stabilizing as far as Canadian interest rates are concerned.

Further Specifications of the Model

The differential return on equity investments. Although bonds and debentures accounted for the largest part of total capital inflow between 1952 and 1962, common and preferred stocks comprised a minor portion of the capital movement; it seems desirable to introduce an additional yield variable which is more closely linked to this type of security transaction than are interest rates. A proxy for the differential return on capital invested in Canada over that invested abroad is constructed as the difference between (1) dividend payments / direct and portfolio investment in Canada on which dividends are paid and (2) dividend receipts / direct and portfolio investment abroad on which dividends are received. The resulting series is expressed in percent per quarter and is referred to as *DRK*.[25] When *DRK* is included in equation 2.1, the result is

$$PC = \underset{(2.63)}{195} + \underset{(4.47)}{695CL} - \underset{(4.61)}{986USL} - \underset{(4.25)}{234CTS}$$
$$+ \underset{(1.84)}{65DRK} + \underset{(5.35)}{.20NNS}$$

25. Dividend payments and receipts are from Officer, unpub. diss., pp. 271–272. The denominators of the two ratios (stocks, lagged two quarters) are from pp. 287–288. Official balance-of-payments publications indicate an approximate two-quarter lag between new issues of bonds and initial payment of interest. The construction of *DRK* builds in this same lag for equity transactions and dividend payments.

$$RSQC = \quad .61$$
$$F(5, 32) = \quad 13.12$$
$$DW = \quad 2.00$$
$$SEE = \$50.9 \text{ million.} \quad (2.6)$$

In spite of the fact that DRK is probably a very inaccurate representation of the actual yield differential on Canadian over foreign equities, the variable performs surprisingly well. Except for a slight fall in the F-ratio, the overall equation is improved in every respect. The coefficients of the previously included variables remain virtually unaltered, although each is slightly more significant. It is interesting that autocorrelation is completely nonexistent when DRK is included in the equation. Since DRK is significant at more than 10 percent, and the t-statistics are not biased upward by autocorrelation, DRK can be accepted as a net contributing factor in the explanation of net portfolio inflow. These comments hold, also, when DRK and NNSC are included in the same equation:

$$PC = \quad 229 \quad + 806CL - 1116USL - 273CTS$$
$$(2.54) \quad (4.19) \quad (4.15) \quad (4.01)$$
$$+ 75DRK + .168NNSC$$
$$(1.76) \quad (3.08)$$

$$RSQC = \quad .43$$
$$F(5, 32) = \quad 6.96$$
$$DW = \quad 1.93$$
$$SEE = \$61.5 \text{ million.} \quad (2.7)$$

The financial requirements variable, FR, becomes insignificant when DRK is included in the equation.

Exchange-rate speculation. An important objective of this study is to estimate the sensitivity of the capital account to changes in the exchange rate, because it has been shown above that exchange rate-induced capital flows have interesting implications for the relative leverages of monetary and fiscal policies. How strongly speculative considerations influence the international movement of capital depends largely upon the time horizon of the borrower or investor. The investor in short-term instruments needs to concern himself with behavior of the exchange rate in the near future because relatively small shifts in the rate can lead to considerable capital gains and losses. The long-term borrower or investor is less sensitive to a given expected change in the exchange rate, as illustrated in Table 2.1.

If the long-term investor will consider unloading his newly acquired securities quickly, then he will be interested in short-run fluctuations of the exchange rate, and speculative considerations could play some role in explaining net capital inflow. But this type of behavior is unlikely in the Canadian case because (1) new issues go mainly to large and typically long-term asset-holders like insurance companies and pension funds,[26] and (2) the Canadian borrower, a long-term debtor, has shouldered the major portion of the exchange risk because 80 percent of the inflow was in United States pay securities. As far as the borrower is concerned, the extra large interest coupons resulting from short-run dips in price of the Canadian dollar will be fairly well offset by the extra small interest coupons resulting from short-run upswings in the dollar, provided that these short-run fluctuations are fairly random. The major risk then concerns the redemption date, and this risk can be diminished through call privileges. Irreversible trends in the exchange rate would upset this reasoning, but there was no significant trend in the rate over the whole period. When the spot rate, RS,[27] is regressed upon a time trend, T, then:

26. Ronald A. Shearer, *Monetary Policy and the Current Account of the Balance of International Payments* (Ottawa: Queen's Printer, 1962), p. 182n.

27. The term "exchange rate" as used in this study refers to price of the Canadian dollar expressed in U.S. dollars; see Officer, unpub. diss., pp. 302–304.

$$RS = 1.0184 + .000394T$$
$$(221.41) \quad (1.92)$$

$$
\begin{aligned}
RSQC &= .04 \\
F(1, 36) &= 3.67 \\
DW &= 0.58 \\
SEE &= \$0.0139.
\end{aligned}
$$

(2.8)

The mean value of RS is $1.0261.

The overall relationship is not significant — indeed, the insignificant t- and F-statistics are upward biased because of the high degree of positive autocorrelation. The short-run volatility of the exchange rate, therefore, dominated any long-term trend. Unlike short-term capital flows, including the very active trade in outstanding securities, the net inflow through new issues and retirements should not be significantly influenced by speculative considerations concerning future rates. Canadian long-term borrowers may, however, have speculated in a different manner by adjusting the short-run timing of new issues to take advantage of savings in the exchange rate. Although consistent with the outlook of a nonspeculative long-term borrower, such behavior could not be distinguished empirically from that of a speculative borrower whose actions are governed by inelastic exchange-rate expectations. Evidence on the response of portfolio capital to movements of the spot rate and to various proxies for exchange-rate expectations can now be considered.

On the basis of reasonably detailed attempts to relate net and gross capital flows classified by type of international capital market transaction to interest- and exchange-rate factors, Helleiner has concluded that exchange-rate speculation was not of significant importance to Canadian borrowers.[28] He used the level of the spot rate itself as a proxy for long-run expectations because, in the absence of trend, a high absolute value

28. Helleiner, p. 398.

of the rate should lead to expectations of depreciation in the future. Helleiner restricted the use of this variable to the explanation of the trade in outstanding securities because changes in the volume of new issues loom large in the absolute total of international capital flows — thus, the net inflow via new issues has a large impact on the exchange rate itself. However, the lag from the borrower's perception of a favorable exchange-rate movement to contract to delivery of securities (the recorded item in the balance of payments) is probably as much as one quarter. This suggests that the equation is more correctly specified when the exchange rate enters in lagged rather than unlagged form and, at the same time, the simultaneity problem is avoided. When RS_{-1} is included in equation 2.1,

$$PC = 690CL - 935USL - 222CTS + .203NNS - 410RS_{-1}$$
$$(4.25) \quad (4.15) \quad (3.87) \quad (5.16) \quad (0.69)$$

$$RSQC = .58$$
$$F(5, 32) = 11.52$$
$$DW = 1.73$$
$$SEE = \$53.1 \text{ million.} \quad (2.9)$$

The sign of the exchange rate is in agreement with the hypothesis of inelastic exchange-rate expectations and the observed stability of the foreign exchange market, but the variable adds nothing to explanation of the capital inflow. When the unlagged spot exchange rate is included:

$$PC = 424CL - 620USL - 175CTS + 3549RS$$
$$(3.01) \quad (3.25) \quad (3.78) \quad (4.51)$$

$$- 2374RS_{-1} + .219NNS$$
$$(3.72) \quad (7.02)$$

$$RSQC = \quad .74$$
$$F(6, 31) = \quad 18.79$$
$$DW = \quad 2.31$$
$$SEE = \$41.9 \quad \text{million.} \quad (2.10)$$

The lagged rate becomes significant with the same sign, and the unlagged rate is significant with a sign consistent with the hypothesis that capital flow influences the unlagged rate, rather than vice versa.

Because of the importance of the extent of stabilizing behavior in capital flows under the flexible exchange rate, we have explored other evidence to test the interpretation that PC influences the spot exchange rate within the current quarter but is not significantly influenced by it. These explorations involved both single-equation and simultaneous estimations.

Single-equation approach: In discussing interest-rate effects, it has been noted that the regression coefficient of CL is downward biased because of the two-way relationship existing between capital inflows and Canadian interest rates. The problem arises from the fact that observed interest rates used to explain the inflow have already been dampened by that inflow. If the capital inflow were perfectly interest-elastic, there would be no variation in the Canadian interest rate and its coefficient would be zero in a least-squares regression.

Suppose now that the exchange rate is regressed upon the various components of the balance of international payments. If each component is defined as a net balance in favor of Canada — a net demand for Canadian dollars — the regression coefficients should all be equal in size, because all components are measured in the same units (millions of dollars), and a net demand for one Canadian dollar should have the same effect on its price whatever the source of the demand. If, however, the equation fails to identify the demand for Canadian dollars because of the presence of supply effects, then some components will appear to have an insignificantly positive, or even negative, effect upon the exchange rate. For example: a rise in the exchange rate induced by an increase in the net balance of payments on current account will tend to increase the supply of Canadian dollars if the foreign demand for Canadian exports and the Canadian demand for foreign imports are highly price-elastic. The upshot of this two-way relation may be reflected in a statistically insignificant regression coefficient for the net balance on current account. Similarly, net inflows of short-term and long-term capital will appear to have an insignificant effect on the exchange rate if they are each strongly affected by movements in the exchange rate itself. It all depends upon exchange-rate elasticities and historic sources of disturbance. Here is the result of this experiment:

$$RS = \begin{array}{cccc} 1.0057 & + .000055CA & + .000122PC & + .000034STK \\ (115.29) & (0.97) & (2.11) & (0.62) \end{array}$$

$$\begin{array}{cc} + .000182DIC & + .000077OR \\ (2.11) & (1.09) \end{array}$$

$$\begin{array}{rl} RSQC = & .19 \\ F(5, 32) = & 2.94 \\ DW = & 0.67 \\ SEE = & \$0.0128. \quad (2.11) \end{array}$$

Here CA is the net balance on current account, PC is the net inflow of portfolio capital, STK is the net inflow of short-term capital, DIC is direct investment in Canada, and OR is the change in official holdings of reserves.[29]

This equation yields a poor explanation of the exchange rate per se because it involves the fallacy that the statistical

29. All payments flows are in millions of dollars and were constructed from data in Officer, unpub. diss. CA is the sum of BM (p. 240) and BS (p. 243). DIC, PC, and OR are on pp. 276, 277, and 293, respectively. The construction of STK is discussed later.

balance of payments shows the demand and supply of foreign exchange and can explain observed movements in the exchange rate. Nevertheless, it gives an indication of which balance of payments components are themselves affected strongly by the exchange rate (the unidentified components) and which components are not strongly affected by exchange-rate movements (the identified components). The fact that equation 2.11 correctly identifies the effects of long-term capital inflows upon the price of the Canadian dollar suggests that these flows are not significantly affected by the exchange rate in the current quarter. Similarly, the failure of the equation to identify the effects of CA, STK, and OR upon the exchange rate suggests that these components are all strongly affected by the rate itself, as will be demonstrated later.

Simultaneous-equation approach: When simultaneous methods are used to estimate equations explaining portfolio investment, the exchange-rate variables become insignificant. When Officer estimates his portfolio investment equation by classical least-squares, the coefficient of $(RS - RS_{-1})$ is +2600 with a t-value of 3.29. When the two-stage least-squares (TSLS) estimator is applied to the exactly identified equation, its coefficient is −1400 with a t-value of −0.29. The latter sign is consistent with the hypothesis of inelastic exchange-rate expectations operating with a less than one-quarter lag; the insignificance of the variable is consistent with the theoretical and empirical evidence discussed earlier. Finally, when TSLS is applied to the overidentified equation, the coefficient of $(RS - RS_{-1})$ is +1600, but the t-value is only 1.33.[30] As would be expected, TSLS is less capable of breaking simultaneity when equations are overidentified, because too much variation in the current endogenous variables is explained in the first-stage regressions. Thus, the estimated variables used in second-stage regressions are similar to the original

30. *Ibid.,* p. 392.

current endogenous variables, and TSLS estimates will tend to reproduce the results achieved by classical least-squares.

In some of the exploratory research connected with the present study, we developed an overidentified model and applied TSLS estimation with similar results. When the portfolio investment equation was estimated by classical least-squares, the result was

$$PC = 799 + 483CL - 613USL + .199NNS - 168CTS$$
$$\quad\quad\;\;\; (3.20) \quad\;\; (3.21) \quad\;\;\; (5.19) \quad\;\;\; (3.10)$$
$$\quad\; + 1408RS - 2124RS_{-1} + .135PC_{-1}$$
$$\quad\quad\;\; (1.85) \quad\;\;\; (3.01) \quad\quad (1.17)$$

$$RSQC = .60$$
$$DW = 2.39.$$

(In subsequent work, the distributed-lag formulation of this model was abandoned because of failure of the lagged dependent variable to appear significantly.) When the equation is estimated by two-stage least-squares,

$$PC = 1071 + 450CL - 645USL + .173NNS - 234CTS$$
$$\quad\quad\;\;\; (2.99) \quad\;\; (3.69) \quad\;\;\; (4.17) \quad\;\;\; (2.78)$$
$$\quad\; - 43RS - 858RS_{-1} + .235PC_{-1}$$
$$\quad\quad (0.64) \quad\;\; (1.98) \quad\quad (1.92)$$

$$RSQC = .51$$
$$DW = 1.95.$$

The coefficients of exchange rates have fallen in size and significance and the signs are now consistent with the hypothesis of inelastic exchange-rate expectations. This incidental evidence generally confirms our interpretation of the relation between portfolio capital inflows and the exchange rate: stabilizing speculation operates strongly with a one-quarter lag, while the simultaneous relation between PC and RS reflects primarily the influence of the former upon the latter.

We have not, of course, exhausted the possible proxies for the influence of exchange-rate expectations on portfolio capital flows. The expectations variable used by Helleiner is the net forward premium on United States currency, defined as the percentage forward premium on the U.S. dollar minus the Canadian-U.S. short-term interest-rate differential. Helleiner argues that in view of the incompleteness of arbitrage between the Canadian and United States money and forward exchange markets, changes in the net forward premium should reflect changes in the market's estimate of the need to cover against the risk of capital loss due to exchange-rate movements.[31] In other words, the net forward premium is positive when the market expects the U.S. dollar to rise in value relative to the Canadian dollar — a view which would reduce net long-term capital flows to Canada. This hypothesis matches our institutional analysis, above, of this capital market rather poorly. Long-term exchange-rate expectations may wield only a weak influence on portfolio capital movements; the short-run net forward premium is not necessarily even a good proxy for long-run expectations. And if our argument about the speculative timing of new issues is correct, the net forward premium is not obviously a better proxy than the level of the spot rate or, perhaps, its deviation from long-term trend.

In any case, we have tried a variation of Helleiner's expectations variable in the portfolio investment equation, with similarly insignificant results. The net interest differential — employed successfully below to explain the short-term capital inflow — is defined as $DS - CFC$, where $DS = CS - USS$, the Canadian and United States short-term interest rates respectively, and CFC is the cost of forward cover (defined as the percentage forward discount on Canadian currency). This is

[31] Helleiner, p. 379.

essentially Helleiner's net forward premium with the sign reversed. An increase in the net interest differential should raise the capital inflow: if the differential is positive, the yield advantage of Canadian dollar assets is not outweighed by expectations of currency depreciation reflected in the forward discount. Apparently, the market then expects the currency to appreciate, and this might increase the long-term inflow. Empirically, the result is

$$PC = 557CL - 735USL - 211CTS - 86[DS - CFC]$$
$$\quad\;\,(2.93)\quad\;\;(2.65)\quad\;\;(3.80)\quad\quad\;\;(1.31)$$
$$\qquad\qquad\quad + .21NNS$$
$$\qquad\qquad\quad\;\;(5.37)$$

$$
\begin{aligned}
RSQC &= \quad .59\\
F(5, 32) &= \quad 12.19\\
DW &= \quad 1.82\\
SEE &= \$52.1 \;\text{ million.} \quad (2.12)
\end{aligned}
$$

The coefficient of the net interest differential has an incorrect sign according to the theoretical reasoning above, but the variable is insignificant. Helleiner's variable should perform the same except for a change in sign.[32] When the long-term rather than the short-term interest differential is used in the construction of the net interest differential, the regression coefficient is -89 with a t-value of 1.07.

The cost of forward cover alone was also employed as an expectations variable: an increase in its cost indicates an increase in hedging operations and, therefore, in the general expectation of currency depreciation. The result was

$$PC = 526CL - 714USL - 160CTS + 88CFC + .21NNS$$
$$\quad\;\,(2.34)\quad\;\;(2.23)\quad\;\;(2.07)\quad\;\;(1.05)\quad\;\;(5.26)$$
$$\qquad\qquad\qquad RSQC = \quad .58$$

32. The expected sign will, of course, be negative if Helleiner's variable is used.

$$F(5, 32) = 11.87$$
$$DW = 1.73$$
$$SEE = \$52.6 \text{ million.} \quad (2.13)$$

Again, the sign is incorrect and the coefficient insignificant.

The third expectations variable considered by Helleiner and other investigators is the quarter-to-quarter change in the exchange rate, CRS $(= RS - RS_{-1})$. It is subject to the same general doubts and objections as the net forward premium, even if we apply Officer's interpretation as a measure of deviation of the spot from the "normal" exchange rate when all the weight in determining the normal rate is placed upon the preceding quarter.[33] Furthermore, considering that CRS is the only practical statistical equivalent of the change in the exchange rate, reference to equation 2.10 and the surrounding discussion shows immediately that a completely different interpretation can be placed on any equation containing RS and RS_{-1}. If CRS proxies inelastic exchange-rate expectations, CRS should enter with a negative sign. However, we had earlier found convincing evidence to support a positive sign for RS and a negative one for RS_{-1} and would thus expect a positive sign for CRS on the basis of any reasonable assumption about the correlation between RS and RS_{-1}. Inserting CRS into equation 2.1 confirms the earlier argument, for it emerges with a significant positive coefficient. We continue to obtain approximately the same result, for the same reason, if we alter the hypothesis calling for CRS and insert the deviation of the spot rate from its trend, $DRST$:

$$PC = \underset{(2.24)}{158} + \underset{(3.42)}{556CL} - \underset{(3.66)}{801USL} - \underset{(3.38)}{184CTS}$$
$$+ \underset{(2.31)}{1530DRST} + \underset{(3.65)}{.21NNS}$$

33. Officer, *An Econometric Model of Canada*, p. 77.

$$RSQC = \quad .63$$
$$F(5, 32) = \quad 14.20$$
$$DW = \quad 1.76$$
$$SEE = \$49.5 \text{ million.} \quad (2.14)$$

It should be pointed out that the performance of $DRST$ will be almost identical to the performance of RS alone because there was no significant trend in the exchange rate. Therefore, the deviation in the spot rate from its "trend" is almost the same as the deviation of the spot rate from its mean. The subtraction of any constant from the spot rate will yield a series which is perfectly correlated with the spot rate series itself, and the use of either series in a multiple regression will yield the same slope coefficient.

In conclusion, for both economic and statistical reasons, none of the proxies for short-run exchange-rate expectations performs well in revealing the influence of the exchange rate on portfolio capital flows. Our own interpretation of the influence of RS and RS_{-1} supports the view that lenders and borrowers incurring exchange risks were either fairly insensitive to long-run exchange-rate expectations or believed the floating rate to be trendless and thus responded only to short-run deviations from the long-run average. In either case, speculative responses of long-term portfolio capital movements to the exchange rate tended strongly to be stabilizing.

NET INFLOWS OF SHORT-TERM CAPITAL

The balance on current and long-term capital accounts plus the net change in official gold and foreign exchange reserves is definitionally equal to the net inflow of short-term capital into Canada. Variations in this series (henceforth referred to as *STK*) are explained in this section. *STK* includes the following items:

the net capital inflow through trade in outstanding securities

the net balance of transactions in U.S. and Canadian Treasury bills

borrowings from nonresidents by finance companies

various loans made by the government of the United Kingdom to finance Canadian aluminum production in 1951–1953

U.S. Treasury bills and certificates held by Canadian banks that are excluded from item (2)

movements of United Kingdom Treasury bills

the change in the Canadian dollar deposit holdings of foreigners

bank balances and other short-term funds abroad excluding official reserves

the residual item "all other items," including changes in loans and accounts receivable and payable, and errors and omissions.[34]

---

34. Officer defines the net balance of payments on merchandise and services account as $BM + BS$. The balance of payments on long-term capital account, BLK, is defined as the sum of direct investment, net portfolio investment, net trade in outstanding securities, other long-term capital movements, and drawings on Canadian government loans. Finally, the net balance of transactions in Treasury bills with the U.S. and changes in official reserves are denoted as TBN and OR, respectively. These items do not sum identically to zero because of the exclusion of transactions numbers 3–9 in the text. If these excluded items are denoted as X, it is clear that

$$X \equiv - (BM + BS + BLK + TBN + OR).$$

Our net short-term capital inflow series is then defined as the sum of X, plus the net capital inflow via trade in outstanding securities, plus the net balance of transactions in Treasury bills with the U.S.

Our short-term capital series is clearly very aggregative, but this is unavoidable. With the exceptions of trade in outstanding securities, *NTOS*, and the net balance of transactions in United States and Canadian Treasury bills, *BTB*, quarterly breakdowns for the other components of short-term capital inflow are not available for the whole period.[35] Nevertheless, the series is quite suitable for our purposes. The primary concern of this study is to measure the responsiveness of capital movements to changes in domestic policy instruments and to ascertain the effects of these policy-induced or endogenous capital flows upon the ability of domestic policies to influence income — and for this we need to know the net movement of all funds across the border. Although economic policies might be drawn to discriminate among classes of short-term flows, our concern is with the sensitivity of an aggregative short-term capital series to turns of economic events and policies. The short-term capital inflow is, in fact, more fully explained statistically than the more homogeneous and probably more accurately measured portfolio inflows.

We have followed convention[36] by including the net trade in outstanding securities in the net inflow of short-term capital series. Explanation of the variation in portfolio inflow is slightly improved when trade in outstanding securities is included in the portfolio series, but a much larger improvement is obtained in the explanation of short-term inflow when trade in outstanding securities is included in that series. Further-

35. T. L. Powrie obtains better statistical results for the total short-term capital inflow than for its separate components; "Short-term Capital Movements and the Flexible Canadian Exchange Rate," *Canadian Journal of Economics and Political Science*, XXX (February, 1964), Table 1, p. 78.

36. This convention has been adopted by various economists such as Arthur I. Bloomfield, "The Significance of Outstanding Securities in the International Movement of Capital," *Canadian Journal of Economics and Political Science*, VI (November, 1940), 517; R. A. Radford, "Canada's Capital Inflow, 1946–53," *IMF Staff Papers*, IV (February, 1955), 226–227; and Paul Wonnacott, *The Canadian Dollar, 1948–1962* (Toronto: University of Toronto Press, 1965), p. 170.

more, if trade in outstanding securities alone is regressed upon the variables used above to explain portfolio inflows, and then upon the variables used below to explain short-term inflows, the results are far superior in the latter case. These experiments confirm our expectation that trade in outstanding securities responds more closely to short-term than long-term factors.

The Model: Explanatory Variables and Data

The net inflow of short-term capital is explained by the balance of merchandise trade with the United States, the Canadian-U.S. short-term interest-rate differential, an expectations variable involving the forward exchange rate, and an expectations variable involving the spot exchange rate. Each variable will be discussed in turn.

The balance of trade with the United States. If a Canadian importer purchases goods from the United States on credit, the resulting net import will be offset by a short-term capital inflow which takes the form of accounts payable. The balance of merchandise trade with the United States, *BMTUS*, is therefore included to test the hypothesis that short-term capital flows offset the basic balance because of the nature of institutional payments practices.[37] The expected sign of *BMTUS* is therefore negative, implying that United States exporters finance their own export sales to some degree by extending short-term trade credit.

The Canadian-United States short-term interest differential. An increase in the differential between Canadian and United States short-term interest rates (measured by 91-day Treasury bill rates) should increase the net inflow of short-term capital for a variety of reasons. Foreign exporters will be more willing to supply short-term trade credit or Canadian importers more

37. Officer, unpub. diss., p. 241.

willing to pay for it. American business firms may be induced to invest cash balances collected in anticipation of tax payment dates in Canadian Treasury bills or short-term commercial paper. Many of these transactions are probably unhedged in the forward market, either because the participants are insensitive to exchange risk or because they are unaware of the existence of forward exchange facilities.[38] Interest-arbitragers will be expected to move into short-term Canadian dollar assets, although the short-term interest rate differential alone is an imperfect variable for explaining short-term inflows on interest-arbitrage account. By definition, interest-arbitrage funds are covered in the forward exchange market because the arbitrager is interested in maximizing interest-arbitrage return, not in speculating on possible movements in the foreign exchange rate.[39]

In the explanation of long-term portfolio capital flows, Canadian and United States interest rates are included separately in order to pick up an income effect. In the case of short-term investment this seems unlikely, so the differential, DS, is used in order to gain a degree of freedom.

Thus far the argument assumes that short-term capital flows are uncovered in either the spot or forward markets. The remaining variables in the model emphasize the key role that speculation plays in the international money market, because hedging transactions cannot proceed unless some form of stabilizing speculation is present.

The quarter-to-quarter change in the exchange rate. If exchange rate expectations are inelastic, speculation will lead to

38. Young's study for the Royal Commission on Banking and Finance suggests that many firms misunderstand the working of the foreign exchange market; several corporations noted that they did not engage in forward exchange transactions because they were in the import and export, not the foreign-exchange speculation, business (Shearer, p. 174 n.2).

39. For analytical purposes it is useful to define any uncovered position in a foreign currency as speculative, whether or not assumption of the position was consciously motivated.

stabilizing flows of short-term capital — that is, short-term capital flows on speculative account will stabilize the exchange rate by countering movements in it. The use of CRS, defined as $RS - RS_{-1}$, to capture this type of capital account response proceeds from the argument that speculators base their judgments about future exchange rates on the relation between current and recent past values. Suppose that some disturbance results in a decline in the price of the Canadian dollar so that $RS_t < RS_{t-1}$. If expectations concerning future exchange rate movements are inelastic, speculators will believe that $RS_{t+1} > RS_t$; if expectations are perfectly inelastic, they will expect that $RS_{t+1} = RS_{t-1}$. In either case they will respond to depreciation in the value of Canadian currency by assuming uncovered positions in short-term Canadian dollar assets in order to take advantage of the expected exchange profit, and the recorded short-term capital flow will be negatively related to CRS. The strength of the relationship should increase with the inelasticity of expectations and the degree to which the expectations are actually realized; of course, expectations are partly self-fulfilling when this type of behavior exists.[40]

There are two problems in testing the influence of CRS on the short-term capital inflow. The first (noted above in con-

---

40. Two additional reasons for expecting a negative relation to hold between CRS and STK are given by Powrie, pp. 79–80. (1) There may be a group of speculators with various opinions about the future price of the Canadian dollar with individual forecasts scattered over a range surrounding the actual price. Those expecting a higher price will be speculative buyers; those expecting a lower price will be speculative sellers. A rise in the actual price carries it from below to above the levels forecast by some individuals who then switch from the buying to the selling side of the market. Compare with James Tobin, "Liquidity Preference as Behavior Towards Risk," *Review of Economic Studies*, XXV (February, 1958), 65–86. (2) A second reason arises from the timing of transactions with other primary purposes. A rise in imports tends to reduce RS, while the extension of trade credit to some importers increases accounts payable and hence STK. The resulting negative correlation between CRS and STK will be strengthened if the latter group of importers purchase foreign currency forward and outward arbitrage takes place.

nection with the relation of PC to RS) is the inexact identification of the relation. Equation 2.11 shows a positive but insignificant response of the exchange rate to changes in net short-term capital inflows. But the problem is not just one of unscrambling two directions of causation. If short-term flows tended strongly enough to stabilize the exchange rate, no significant variation of RS would be observed, and the regression coefficient of RS or CRS would be zero. In either case, an underestimate of the responsiveness of short-term capital flows to the exchange rate may be expected.

The second problem concerns the nature of the hypothesis that is tested by regressing short-term capital flows on CRS. A seemingly different hypothesis about speculators' responses to exchange-rate movements holds that they expect, on the basis of deep-seated and irrational feelings,[41] a parity relation between the Canadian and American dollars to prevail in the long run. Paul Wonnacott's test of this hypothesis failed to reveal the expected negative relation between the short-term capital inflow and deviation of the spot rate from parity.[42] What is worth noting here is the algebraic relation between CRS and the deviation of the spot rate from parity $(DRSP)$. CRS can be rewritten as

$$RS - RS_{-1} = (RS - \$1) - (RS_{-1} - \$1) = DRSP - DRSP_{-1}$$
$$= CDRSP.$$

Then it could be argued that speculators are not concerned about the deviation of the rate from parity per se, but that they do become increasingly concerned as the rate moves farther and farther from parity. The hypothesis is reasonable, but it does not prove much because CRS can also be interpreted

41. Egon Sohmen, *International Monetary Problems and the Foreign Exchanges,* Special Papers in International Economics, no. 4 (Princeton, N.J.: Princeton University International Finance Section, 1963), p. 27.
42. P. Wonnacott, *The Canadian Dollar,* pp. 178–179.

as the change in the deviation of the spot rate from the mean distance between Earth and Alpha Centauri. Good performance of CRS may lack a unique interpretation.

The forward premium. If Canadian imports are financed by trade credit and the price is quoted in United States dollars, the importer risks an increase in the Canadian dollar value of his U.S. currency liabilities because the Canadian dollar may depreciate before the debt matures. If he, or others with future U.S. dollar liabilities, believe that Canadian dollar depreciation is imminent or if they simply wish to avoid uncertainty, they can hedge risks by purchasing U.S. dollars forward while simultaneously selling Canadian dollars forward at the forward exchange rate, RF. An increase in these transactions will tend to reduce the forward relative to the spot rate, so that the forward premium, FP ($= RF - RS$), will tend to reflect the net demand for forward cover, influenced by the current balance of transactions normally hedged over the period in question. It will also, of course, reflect the net supply of forward cover, determined by speculators' expectations about the movement of future spot rates.

This analysis shows that FP may be influenced by nonspeculative factors, although it should also reflect the speculators' net assessment of the relation of the future to the present spot rate. A second nonspeculative group affected by — and affecting — movements of FP are interest arbitragers who find a hedged investment in Canadian-dollar assets more attractive, given the short-term interest-rate differential, as the forward premium rises. Thus, the net short-term capital inflow should be positively related to the forward premium, although the usual identification problem arises in that independent shifts in the capital inflow raise the net supply of forward Canadian dollars and thus tend to depress FP. The explanation of variations in the forward premium is covered in Chapter 3. We include the forward premium and the interest differential separately in the equation, rather than bundling them together into the net forward premium. Many short-term investors in Canada apparently take unhedged positions, so that lenders and speculators are not neatly segregated groups. Furthermore, considerable institutional differences exist among the various groups of short-term lenders and borrowers, and there is no reason to believe that they react homogeneously to changes in the components of the net forward premium, or with equal regularity and predictability. In any case, the prevalence of covered interest arbitrage will be tested below.

Regression Results

The basic model used to explain net inflows of short-term capital (including net trade in outstanding securities) may be written as

$$STK = a + b_1(DS) + b_2FP + b_3BMTUS + b_4CRS + u,$$

where the explanatory variables are, respectively, the differential between Canadian and U.S. 91-day Treasury bill rates, the forward exchange-rate premium, the balance of merchandise trade with the United States, and the change in the spot exchange rate from the previous quarter.

$$STK = 602DS + 31449FP - .4734BMTUS - 3512CRS$$
$$(7.82) \quad (4.30) \quad (3.63) \quad (3.61)$$

$$RSQC = .72$$
$$F(4, 33) = 25.85$$
$$DW = 2.64$$
$$SEE = \$68.5 \text{ million.} \quad (2.15)$$

The mean value of *STK* equals \$52.2 million. All of the independent variables enter with the theoretically correct signs, and every variable is significantly different from zero at better than one percent. Autocorrelation is significant in nearly all the short-term capital equations, but this is probably not too serious in view of the large t-statistics and F-ratios.

The coefficients of the interest differential and the forward premium are not comparable because the exchange-rate variables are measured in dollars. The coefficients can be made comparable by replacing the forward premium with an alternative series — the cost of forward cover (CFC) — which yields practically the same information as FP. CFC is defined as the percentage forward discount on the Canadian dollar, [100-$(RS - RF)/RS$]. A more obvious transformation would appear to be the precentage forward premium; but, for reasons given below, we wanted a series that would be positive whenever the cost of forward cover is positive — that is, whenever the forward rate lies below the spot rate. The percentage forward premium is simply CFC with the sign reversed. In addition to the change in sign, the coefficient of CFC will be 100 times smaller than the coefficient of FP. Thus, when CFC replaces FP:

$$STK = 600DS - 325.5CFC - .4740BMTUS - 3522CRS$$
$$(7.83) (4.32) (3.64) (3.63)$$

$$
\begin{aligned}
RSQC &= .72\\
F(4, 33) &= 25.96\\
DW &= 2.64\\
SEE &= \$68.4 \text{ million.} \quad (2.16)
\end{aligned}
$$

When we compare this equation with equation 2.15, it is clear that they are nearly identical. (The reason for slight discrepancies in the various regression coefficients arises because variation in the two series is not quite identical; we divided minus FP by RS to obtain CFC, and RS was not constant over the period.)

Examination of equation 2.16 shows that an increase in the interest differential by one percentage point has a larger impact on the short-term capital inflow than a decrease in the cost of forward cover by one percentage point. This result was to be expected from our discussion of interest-rate effects above, where it was suggested that many investors in short-term Canadian dollar assets probably look more closely at relative interest rates than at the specific configuration of spot and forward exchange rates. In other words, capital inflows on interest-arbitrage account do not tell the whole story, for then the coefficients of the interest differential and the forward discount would have the same absolute size.

As indicated above, international lenders engaging in covered interest arbitrage respond to net changes in the interest differential and the forward premium taken together, so that it should be possible to pick up the determinants of their behavior in a single variable without entering these two terms into the equation separately. On the other hand, if some arbitrage transactions are uncovered in practice, merging the two variables can be expected to reduce the overall explanatory power of the model. As a single variable, we use the net interest differential, defined as $DS - CFC$. It is well known that this expression only approximates the exact condition for determining the profitability of covered interest arbitrage. But the exact condition is more complicated, and its use renders extraction of the coefficient of interest-sensitivity very difficult.[43] Substituting the net interest differential into equation 2.16,

$$STK = 458.9[DS - CFC] - .4749BMTUS - 3220CRS$$
$$ (6.34) \qquad\qquad (3.21) \qquad\qquad (2.94)$$

43. Hedged investments in Canadian dollar assets are profitable if
$$RF - RS\left[\frac{1 + USS/100}{1 + CS/100}\right] > 0.$$

$$RSQC = \quad .64$$
$$F(3, 34) = \quad 24.04$$
$$DW = \quad 2.07$$
$$SEE = \$77.7 \quad \text{million.} \quad (2.17)$$

Although the overall fit is looser than in the case where the net short-term inflow is explained by the joint variation in DS and CFC, it is interesting to note that autocorrelation is virtually absent. Since all variables remain significantly different from zero at the one-percent level of significance, it can safely be assumed that our previous results are meaningful despite the fact that the t-statistics are biased upward by autocorrelation.

Further confirmation of our finding that interest rates have a larger impact on the capital inflow than has the forward premium is obtained if the inclusion of additional interest-rate variables to equation 2.17 improves the overall fit. Our discussion of portfolio capital inflows showed that the slope of the yield curve may serve as a proxy for the level of interest rates and as an expectations variable. Following this argument, an increase in the slope of the yield curve implies that all interest rates have fallen and are expected to rise in the future. Our portfolio equations were consistent with this view. Net inflows of short-term capital should therefore be negatively related to CTS. The result is

$$STK = \quad 118 \quad + 385.9[DS - CFC] - .3533BMTUS$$
$$(3.25) \qquad (5.61) \qquad \qquad (2.56)$$
$$- 206CTS - 3203CRS$$
$$(3.10) \qquad (3.27)$$

$$RSQC = \quad .71$$
$$F(4, 33) = \quad 24.98$$
$$DW = \quad 2.44$$
$$SEE = \$69.4 \quad \text{million.} \quad (2.18)$$

81

Alternatively, both the covered and uncovered interest-rate differentials can be included with the result that

$$STK = 326.2[DS - CFC] + 273DS - .4700BMTUS$$
$$\quad\quad (4.34) \quad\quad\quad\quad (3.31) \quad\quad (3.64)$$
$$- 3529CRS$$
$$(3.65)$$

$$
\begin{aligned}
RSQC &= \quad .72 \\
F(4, 33) &= \quad 26.05 \\
DW &= \quad 2.66 \\
SEE &= \quad \$68.3 \text{ million.} \quad (2.19)
\end{aligned}
$$

Equations 2.18 and 2.19 raise the proportion of explained variation and are just alternative ways to convey the information in equation 2.16. Thus, the interest-rate sensitivity implied by equation 2.18 is $385.9 + 206 = 591.9$, while the sensitivity implied by equation 2.19 is $326.2 + 273 = 599.2$. These values are not significantly different from the estimate of 600 produced by equation 2.16, and they serve to confirm the latter as the best specification of the short-term capital equation. In view of the fact that *CTS* adds nothing to the explanation produced by equations 2.16 and 2.19, which allow for differential interest-rate effects, it seems reasonable to conclude that the role of *CTS* in explaining short-term capital flows is primarily a statistical one as a proxy for the short-term interest rate. Variations in the term structure are due mainly to variations in the more volatile short-term interest rate — the correlation is $-.87$.

In conclusion, variations in the short-term capital inflow are explained more completely by the joint variation in the interest differential and the forward premium than they are by the variation in the net interest differential alone, because interest-arbitrage funds are not all covered in the forward exchange market. This finding holds some implication for monetary authorities choosing between control over short-term capital flows by manipulating short-term interest rates and the forward exchange rate.

Other Experiments

United Kingdom bill rates. Since movements in United Kingdom Treasury bills are included in the short-term capital flow, the differential between Canadian and British Treasury bill rates should improve the explanation of the inflow. When $(CS - UKS)^{44}$ is included in equation 2.15,

$$STK = 556DS + 88(CS - UKS) + 37514FP - .5307BMTUS$$
$$\quad\ (7.24) \qquad (2.03) \qquad\quad (4.94) \qquad\quad (4.15)$$
$$\qquad\quad - 3859CRS$$
$$\qquad\quad\ (4.08)$$

$$
\begin{aligned}
RSQC &= \quad .75 \\
F(5, 32) &= \ 23.47 \\
DW &= \quad 2.87 \\
SEE &= \$65.5 \ \text{million.} \quad (2.20)
\end{aligned}
$$

This equation provides our best overall explanation of the capital inflow in terms of significance of the independent variables. On the other hand, autocorrelation is more serious in this equation than in any of the others. One can probably conclude, therefore, that the regression coefficient for the Canadian-United Kingdom interest-rate differential is not truly significant.

Deviation of the spot rate from parity. It was argued above

44. The United Kingdom 90-day Treasury bill rate, *UKS*, is from various issues of the Bank of Canada's *Statistical Summary Supplement* and is measured in percent per quarter.

that the influence of deviation of the spot rate from parity cannot be distinguished statistically from that of the spot rate itself and that the interaction between the spot exchange rate and short-term capital flows might yield a relation with either sign, or perhaps no relation at all if short-term flows have indeed stabilized the exchange rate by countering movements in it. When $DRSP$ replaces CRS as the exchange-rate expectations variable, no significant relation is found:[45]

$$STK = 664DS - 383.4CFC - 0.46BMTUS - 680DRSP$$
$$(7.24)(4.19)(2.94)(0.62)$$

$$
\begin{aligned}
RSQC &= .62\\
F(4, 33) &= 16.48\\
DW &= 2.48\\
SEE &= \$80.4 \text{ million.} \quad (2.21)
\end{aligned}
$$

The net inflow of portfolio capital. Penner has suggested that the proceeds of long-term security sales abroad may not be repatriated immediately but may be held temporarily in foreign deposits. The long-term capital inflow will be offset by a short-term capital outflow.[46] This offsetting behavior appears confirmed when PC is included in equation 2.16:

$$STK = 649DS - 296CFC - .60BMTUS - 2808CRS$$
$$(8.33)(4.00)(4.25)(2.80)$$
$$- .3310PC$$
$$(1.93)$$

45. Powrie defines the "normal" exchange rate as a four-quarter centered moving average and finds the deviation of the actual exchange rate from the normal rate to have no significant influence on the net short-term inflow; see Powrie, pp. 81–82.

46. See Rudolph G. Penner, "The Inflow of Long-term Capital and the Canadian Business Cycle, 1950–1960," *Canadian Journal of Economics and Political Science,* XXVIII (November, 1962), 534.

$$RSQC = \quad .74$$
$$F(5, 32) = \quad 23.24$$
$$DW = \quad 2.59$$
$$SEE = \$65.72 \text{ million.} \quad (2.22)$$

PC is nearly significant at 5 percent. (Direct investment inflows are insignificant, however; the *t*-value is $+0.99$.)

Bias in the coefficient of CRS. The short-term capital equations all successfully identify the negative effect of changes in exchange rates on the short-term capital inflow.[47] Nevertheless, the absolute value of the estimated regression coefficient is almost surely smaller than the true value because the capital inflow has a positive effect on price of currency. It may also be true that the forward premium or percentage forward discount takes on some of the role of *CRS*. If *STK* is related to *CRS* alone,

$$STK = \quad 58 \quad - 5186CRS$$
$$\quad\quad (3.05) \quad\quad (3.27)$$

$$RSQC = \quad .19$$
$$F(1, 36) = \quad 10.70$$
$$DW = \quad 1.03$$
$$SEE = \$117.1 \text{ million.} \quad (2.23)$$

47. An alternative means of establishing the stability of the foreign exchange market is employed by Jerome L. Stein and Edward Tower in "The Short-Run Stability of the Foreign Exchange Market," *Review of Economics and Statistics,* XLIX (May, 1967), 173–185. In our notation, they estimate

$$RS = f(RS_{-1}, DS, USM/CM)$$

for periods when the Canadian dollar floated and for periods when it was officially stabilized. (*USM/CM* is the ratio of U.S. to Canadian money supply.) In both cases, the lagged dependent variable is the most significant of the explanatory variables, and its regression coefficient is significantly less than unity. In the context of their dynamic model, this finding implies that *RS* converges to its equilibrium value whenever a new short-run equilibrium price is established as a result of either government intervention or other causes. In essence, this is the same as our finding about the negative relation of *STK* to *CRS*.

This implies that an increase in the price of the Canadian dollar by one cent will lead to a net short-term outflow of $51.86 million. (It is interesting to note that *FP* or *CFC* alone has no significant impact on the net capital inflow, although the interest differential does.)

It could also be argued that the drop in size of the coefficient of *CRS* in equation 2.22 is due to the interaction between *PC* and *CRS* — specifically, if speculators believe that a high inflow of long-term capital pulls the exchange rate above its "normal" value, they may respond by moving out of short-term Canadian dollar assets. If *PC* does act as a proxy for exchange-rate expectations, the implied degree of exchange-rate sensitivity can be calculated as follows:

$$\partial STK/\partial PC = -.3310 \text{ (from equation 2.22)}$$
$$\partial RS/\partial PC = +.000122 \text{ (from equation 2.11)}$$

Therefore $\partial STK/\partial RS = -.3310/.000122 = -2707$, and when this is added to the directly-estimated exchange-rate coefficient, the implied exchange-rate sensitivity is $-2707 - 2808 = -5515$. Excluding *CRS* from the equation altogether,

$$STK = 710DS - 334.9CFC - .67BMTUS - .5078PC$$
$$(8.63) (4.19) (4.43) (2.90)$$

$$RSQC = .69$$
$$F(4, 33) = 22.43$$
$$DW = 2.45$$
$$SEE = \$72.2 \text{ million.} \quad (2.24)$$

Using the information contained in equation 2.11 again, the implied coefficient of exchange-rate sensitivity is -4160. These indirect estimates of exchange-rate sensitivity calculated from the regression coefficient of *PC* are probably maximum estimates: any speculative response to an increased inflow of portfolio capital could just as well be due to its expected influence on Canadian securities prices as on the exchange rate.

DIRECT INVESTMENT INFLOWS

To add empirical content to the theoretical analysis of Chapter 1, an estimate of the income-sensitivity of the capital account is required. We were unable to discover any significant relation between Canadian gross national product and either portfolio or short-term capital inflows. Variations in GNP do, however, explain 42 percent of the variation in direct investment in Canada.

$$DIC = .0183GNP - 40.5Q_3$$
$$\quad\quad (5.14) \quad\quad (3.31)$$

$$
\begin{aligned}
RSQC &= \quad .42 \\
F(4, 33) &= \quad 8.24 \\
DW &= \quad 2.14 \\
SEE &= \$25.02 \text{ million.} \quad (2.25)
\end{aligned}
$$

The mean value of DIC equals \$120.95 million. This simple equation is the best one we were able to develop as an explanation of capital inflows in the form of direct investment. Alternative specifications of the income variable, including lagged responses, and alternative demand-for-funds variables such as the financial requirements series referred to earlier, were all unsuccessful in explaining DIC.

The next most important explanatory variable appears to be the long-term interest-rate differential DL. Unlike portfolio and short-term capital flows, it is difficult to view the demand and supply of equity funds as cleared through any readily visible capital market. Decisions to make equity investments in Canada are probably associated directly with decisions to undertake real capital formation, or to accomplish some asset swap (see Chapter 4). Nevertheless, relative interest rates might influence the decisions of foreign-controlled corporations to raise funds in Canada or abroad, whether the latter involves floating securities in foreign capital markets or obtaining funds from corporate parents. In the latter case, the interest-rate effect might be swamped by established corporate financial practices, but, in principle, the effect should still be there. If Canadian long-term rates are relatively high, it is cheaper for the parent to arrange for funds in the foreign capital market, making available to the subsidiary such funds as are warranted by profitable capital expenditure opportunities. When the long-term interest differential is used to explain DIC,

$$DIC = \underset{(5.93)}{92} + \underset{(2.00)}{169\,DL}$$

$$
\begin{aligned}
RSQC &= .05 \\
F(1, 36) &= 4.01 \\
DW &= 1.59 \\
SEE &= \$32.14 \text{ million.} \quad (2.26)
\end{aligned}
$$

The calculated value of F along with the t-value for the regression coefficient do not permit us to reject the null hypothesis of no significant relation between DIC and the interest differential.[48] When Canadian and United States interest rates enter

48. One investigation of investment by U.S. parent corporations in established subsidiaries in Canada and elsewhere found gross investment in the subsidiaries positively related to the liquidity of the consolidated firm as a whole and negatively related to measures of alternative sales opportunities in the parent country (U.S.) or elsewhere. If high U.S. corporate liquidity coincides with low long-term interest rates in the U.S., as is very likely, this would help explain the observed relation between DIC and the Canadian-U.S. interest-rate differential. See Guy V. G. Stevens, "Fixed

the equation separately, as in the portfolio investment equations, they are completely insignificant.

If income sensitivity is important at all, it applies only to capital inflows in the form of direct investment. The absolute level of income sensitivity is small; an increase in the flow of income by $100 million per quarter would, ceteris paribus, increase the inflow of direct investment capital by only $1.83 million per quarter. However, the implied income-elasticity, evaluated at the means of the dependent and independent variables, is 1.1356.

SUMMARY OF ENDOGENOUS CAPITAL RESPONSES

In Table 2.2, the interest-rate, exchange-rate, and income-sensitivities derived from the equations estimated above are summarized. The estimated parameters are referred to as K_r, K_f, and K_y, respectively, as in Appendix A. The elasticity of the dependent variable with respect to the independent variable (η) is presented beneath each regression coefficient (β).

If we consider only the better equations, it seems reasonable to conclude that an increase in the long-term interest rate by one percentage point would raise the net inflow of long-term capital by at least $700 to $800 million per quarter. This calculation ignores the effect, if any, on direct investment inflows. The interest elasticity of long-term inflows varies between 9.1 and 10.6. Similarly, our best estimates for the interest-sensitivity of short-term capital inflows run from $600 to $700 million with elasticities of 7.4 to 8.7.[49] These estimates suggest

Investment Expenditures of Foreign Manufacturing Affiliates of U.S. Firms: Theoretical Models and Empirical Evidence," unpub. diss. (Yale University, 1967), chap. iv.

49. Elasticities are evaluated at the mean. Since they are expressed in terms of average net flows rather than average stocks, their absolute values are a little difficult to interpret because net inflows were negative in some quarters (8 for PC and 19 for STK). Negative net inflows reduce the algebraic value of Y and increase the apparent value of the elasticity coefficient.

TABLE 2.2. Summary of estimated responses of capital flows to changes in interest rates, the exchange rate, and gross national product

Equation	Dependent variable		K_r	K_f	K_y
2.1	PC	β	693	–	–
		η	9.0833		
2.2	PC	β	797	–	–
		η	10.4551		
2.3	PC	β	515	–	–
		η	6.7565		
2.4	PC	β	516	–	–
		η	6.7704		
2.5	PC	β	458	–	–
		η	6.0072		
2.6	PC	β	695	–	–
		η	9.1086		
2.7	PC	β	806	–	–
		η	10.5696		
2.9	PC	β	690	−410[a]	–
		η	9.0520	−5.6625	
2.10	PC	β	424	−2374[b]	–
		η	5.5603	−32.7496	
2.15	STK	β	602	−3512	–
		η	7.3987	−68.9871	
2.16	STK	β	600	−3522	–
		η	7.3741	−69.1835	
2.17	STK	β	459	−3220	–
		η	5.6400	−63.2512	
2.19	STK	β	599	−3529	–
		η	7.3618	−69.3210	
2.20	STK	β	644	−3859	–
		η	7.9149	−75.8033	
2.21	STK	β	664	−680[a]	–
		η	8.1607	−13.3574	
2.22	STK	β	649	−5515	–
		η	7.9763	−108.3325	
2.23	STK	β	–	−5186	–
		η		−101.8698	
2.24	STK	β	710	−4160	–
		η	8.7260	−81.7159	
2.25	DIC	β	–	–	.0183
		η			1.1356
2.26	DIC	β	169[a]	–	–
		η	1.3613		

[a] The variable is not significantly different from zero.
[b] The variable is lagged one quarter.

that an upward shift in the yield curve by one percentage point would improve the capital account by $1.3 to $1.5 billion, other elements remaining unchanged.

The best estimates of exchange-rate sensitivity imply that a one-cent reduction in the price of the Canadian dollar should raise the net inflow of short-term capital from $35 to $55 million per quarter. The corresponding elasticities run from -69 to -108. If we include the effects of exchange-rate movements on portfolio inflows, our estimates of K_f rise by an additional $24 million.

Finally, it might be noted that there is some empirical evidence that the Exchange Fund operated in a stabilizing manner during the period of the flexible exchange rate. If we follow Paul Wonnacott and take resistance to exchange-rate movements as the criterion of successful stabilizing activity, then an increase in the price of the Canadian dollar should induce the Exchange Fund to purchase United States currency. Since increases in official reserves, OR, are a negative or debit item in the balance of payments, we should expect a negative relationship to obtain between OR and CRS. Thus,

$$OR = 23.23 - 1029CRS$$
$$(3.31) \quad (1.76)$$

$$RSQC = .03$$
$$F(1, 36) = 3.11$$
$$DW = 1.99$$
$$SEE = \$43.1 \text{ million.} \quad (2.27)$$

The mean value of OR equals $22.03 million.

The sign of CRS is consistent with the hypothesis of stabilizing activity by the Exchange Fund, but the overall relationship is not significant at the 5-percent level. In view of the absence of autocorrelated residuals, however, it is safe to conclude that the relationship is significant at the 10-percent level. This raises our estimate of K_f (for a one-cent change in the price of the Canadian dollar) by a further $10.3 million.

BIFURCATION OF THE OBSERVATION PERIOD

Until 1957, the Canadian economy enjoyed seven years of prosperity interrupted only temporarily by the recession of 1953–1954. The ensuing swing into stagnation ended not only a single business cycle, but also a chapter in Canadian economic growth. Quarterly GNP increased by $128.9 million per quarter on the average before 1956, and by only $71.7 million thereafter. The real change is even smaller in the latter part of the period because of the greater degree of price inflation. The growth of real output, which averaged 5.3 percent per annum until the end of 1956, fell to 2.9 percent after 1956, and the average level of unemployment rose from 3.5 to 5.9 percent of the labor force.

Monetary policy was considerably tighter in the second half of the period. Although the average absolute change in the money supply was constant, the percentage increase fell from 1.3760 to 1.0961 per quarter after 1956. Quarterly short-term interest rates doubled to .8734 percent, while long-term rates increased from .8470 to 1.1155 percent. The average term to maturity of the outstanding public debt increased by 26 months.

Net inflows of short-term, portfolio and direct investment capital increased from an average of $145.7 million per quarter before 1956 to $360.5 million in the second period. The net deficit on current account more than doubled over the period to $358.4 million per quarter. The price of the Canadian dollar averaged $1.0336, or 1.43 cents higher than in the first period.

In view of these developments, we decided to re-estimate a few of our equations for two subperiods of the overall floating exchange-rate period — 1952-I to 1956-IV and 1957-I to 1961-II — in order to ascertain whether any significant changes occurred in our structural coefficients. When the portfolio investment equation 2.1 is re-estimated for the two subperiods,

1952-I–1956-IV

$$PC = 750CL - 739USL - 218CTS + .13NNS$$
$$\quad\;\; (3.34) \qquad (1.77) \qquad\;\; (2.12) \qquad\;\; (1.62)$$

$$RSQC = \quad .43$$
$$F(4, 15) = \quad 5.05$$
$$DW = \quad 1.85$$
$$SEE = \$52.3 \;\; \text{million.} \quad (2.28)$$

The mean value of PC equals $46.5 million.

1957-I–1961-II

$$PC = 606CL - 795USL - 235CTS + .25NNS$$
$$\quad\;\; (1.78) \qquad (1.71) \qquad\;\; (2.59) \qquad\;\; (2.84)$$

$$RSQC = \quad .49$$
$$F(4, 13) = \quad 5.63$$
$$DW = \quad 1.74$$
$$SEE = \$58.95 \;\text{million.} \quad (2.29)$$

The mean value of PC equals $105.2 million.

With the exception of the coefficient of NNS in equation 2.28, all variables are significantly different from zero at the 10-percent level or better. The general picture suggested by these representative equations is that interest rates were less significant during the second half of the period. Since the interest-rate coefficients remain similar in magnitude, the relative increase in their standard errors probably reflects the substantial collinearity that appears after 1956. The simple correlation between CL and USL increases from .6376 in the first half of the period to .9459 in the second half. Use of the differential will not circumvent this difficulty, of course, because DL is highly correlated with both CL and USL whereas, in the first part of the period, the correlation between DL and USL is only .0153. Hence, the variation in the interest differential is considerably smaller after 1956. The standard deviation of the differential falls from 44.63 percent of its mean in the first half of the period to only 25.36 percent after 1956. The smaller amount of independent variation in CL and USL provides a possible explanation for the superior performance of NNS which may be serving as a proxy for interest rates after 1956.

In order to test the null hypothesis that the structure of our equations did not alter significantly after 1956, we computed the statistic

$$F = \frac{Q_3/k}{Q_2/(m + n - 2k)}$$

Where Q_2 is the total of the sum of squared residuals from equations 2.28 and 2.29, Q_3 is the difference between the sum of squared residuals from equation 2.1 and Q_2, k is the number of explanatory variables (including the intercept), and m and n are the number of observations in each subperiod.[50] From equations 2.1, 2.28, and 2.29 we obtain $F(5, 28) =$ .3418. Since the calculated value of F does not exceed the

---

50. J. Johnston, *Econometric Methods* (New York: McGraw-Hill, 1963), pp. 136–137.

theoretical value of 3.76, the probability that the three sets of regression coefficients are significantly different from one another is less than one percent.

When we re-estimate the short-term capital equations, the general picture which emerges is that interest-arbitrage factors had a smaller absolute impact upon the net capital inflow in the first part of the period than in the second. On the other hand, speculative considerations seem to have been more important before 1956. Two equations, representative of our results, are reproduced below:

1952-I–1956-IV

$$STK = 500DS - 285.7CFC - .61BMTUS - 4140CRS$$
$$\quad\quad (4.89) \quad\quad (3.71) \quad\quad\quad (4.27) \quad\quad\quad (4.92)$$

$$\begin{aligned} RSQC &= \quad .84 \\ F(4, 15) &= \quad 27.15 \\ DW &= \quad 2.84 \\ SEE &= \$47.9 \text{ million} \end{aligned} \quad (2.30)$$

with the mean value of *STK* equal to $-\$8.95$ million.

1957-I–1961-II

$$STK = 607DS - 338.2CFC - .36BMTUS - 2032CRS$$
$$\quad\quad (2.94) \quad\quad (2.00) \quad\quad\quad (1.45) \quad\quad\quad (0.84)$$

$$\begin{aligned} RSQC &= \quad .23 \\ F(4, 13) &= \quad 2.84 \\ DW &= \quad 2.61 \\ SEE &= \$91.94 \text{ million} \end{aligned} \quad (2.31)$$

with the mean value of *STK* equal to $\$120.22$ million.

Although the coefficients of *DS* and *CFC* are larger after 1956, so are their standard errors. This again reflects the reduced amount of independent variation in these variables in the second half of the period. Canadian and United States short-term interest rates moved much more closely together after 1956, and the variation in their differential was correspondingly reduced. Furthermore, the correlation between the interest differential and the cost of forward cover increased from .4041 to .6166 in the second period, so that collinearity between the variables increases the difficulty of statistically untangling their separate influences.

Multicollinearity may also explain the inferior performance of *CRS* in the latter part of the period. The coefficient of correlation between *CFC* and *CRS* prior to 1956 is only .1229, but this triples to .3964 in the second period. Unlike the other variables, however, the absolute size of the regression coefficient has decreased while its standard error has increased. It may be true that the prolonged experience of a premium on the Canadian dollar gradually led to an upward revision of expectations concerning the "normal" level of its price. If this is the case, a given increase in the dollar's price would be expected to lead to a smaller capital outflow, since the expected exchange loss when the rate falls to its now higher normal level is smaller. We noted earlier that a unique interpretation of *CRS* may be impossible — it can be interpreted as the change in deviation of the spot rate from *any* "normal" value, whatever that might be.

The *F*-ratio again suggests that the structural coefficients of our equations did not change significantly from one period to the next — the calculated value of *F* is only .3883. The general conclusion that emerges from the foregoing discussion is that, although our relationships appear weaker in the latter part of the floating exchange rate period, no significant change in structural coefficients can be detected by the conventional tests of significance. The simultaneous nature of our relationships may suffice to explain the larger standard errors after 1956. If capital flows were especially sensitive to interest rates and exchange rates in the latter period, then the statistical counterpart of this increased responsiveness would be a reduction in the variation in our explanatory variables with a corresponding rise in the variances of the estimated regression coefficients. In this sense, our apparently inferior statistical results for the second half of the period may serve as indirect confirmation of highly interest-rate and exchange-rate stabilizing capital flows, although this is clearly a second-best method for establishing such a conclusion.

STOCK VERSUS FLOW FORMULATIONS

The empirical work presented in this chapter relates the flow, rather than the stock of financial assets, to the interest-rate differentials. This approach is based upon pragmatic considerations arising from the practical impossibility of discriminating between stock and flow theories in a world where desired stocks of securities are growing over time. It does not necessarily constitute a stand on the logical superiority of the flow over the stock theory.

Jerome Stein, in an influential article, attempted to resolve the issue of stock versus flow.[51] In an earlier study by P. W. Bell, the stock of capital was related to the interest-rate differential.[52] The implication of Bell's approach is that a given differential will be associated with a given stock of capital, so

51. Jerome L. Stein, "International Short-Term Capital Movements," *American Economic Review,* LV (March, 1965), 40–66.
52. P. W. Bell, "Private Capital Movements and the U.S. Balance-of-Payments Position," *Factors Affecting the United States Balance of Payments,* U.S. Congress, Joint Economic Committee, 87th Cong., 2nd sess. (Washington: Government Printing Office, 1962), pp. 399–481.

that a change in the differential leads to a once-and-for-all change in the stock — the flow is self-limiting. P. B. Kenen, on the other hand, related the flow to the differential, so that a given differential implies a given flow that will persist as long as the differential remains unclosed.[53] The policy implications of the two approaches are different. If, for example, Canada finances a persistent current account deficit by capital inflows, then the flow theory implies that a constant interest-rate differential will attract sufficient capital to cover the current account deficit. But if the stock theory is correct, stability in reserves or the price of the currency requires an increasing interest-rate differential.

In a comment on Stein's article, Patric Hendershott argues that the stock and flow approaches are really the logical extremes of a general stock adjustment process. The stock theory implicitly assumes complete adjustment of actual and desired stocks within a given time period, while the flow theory implies very slow adjustment — logically, adjustment of the stock to a given change in the interest differential is never completed.[54] The stock theory is clearly more reasonable the longer the time period; an annual model might be expected to yield results superior to those produced by a quarterly model. On the other hand, the never-ending process of adjustment implied by the flow theory, which grates on the sensibilities of some authors, such as H. P. Gray,[55] is easier to accept when one recognizes that the flow is theoretically self-limiting because the interest-rate differential is itself endogenous and will be negatively

53. P. B. Kenen, "Short-Term Capital Movements and the U.S. Balance of Payments," *United States Balance of Payments,* U.S. Congress, Joint Economic Committee, Hearings, 88th Cong., 1st sess. (Washington: Government Printing Office, 1963), pp. 153–191.

54. Patric H. Hendershott, "International Short-Term Capital Movements: Comments," *American Economic Review,* LVII (June, 1967), 562.

55. H. Peter Gray, "International Short-Term Capital Movements: Comments," *American Economic Review,* LVII (June, 1967), 549–550.

related to the net capital inflow (this is discussed in Chapter 3).

The flow theory has received unanimous empirical support while attempts to discriminate between the stock and flow approaches have been unsuccessful or, at best, inconclusive. If the stock of assets is denoted by S and the interest-differential by R, then the stock theory asserts that

$$S_t = a_0 + a_1 R_t + a_2 S_{t-1}$$

where a_2 is a crucial parameter. If a_2 differs significantly from unity, the stock equation is a variant of a standard stock adjustment model where the change in the stock in any period (the flow) is some proportion of the difference between desired and actual stocks at the beginning of the period. Thus, if k is the "reaction coefficient,"

$$S_t - S_{t-1} = k(S_t^* - S_{t-1})$$

where the desired stock, S_t^*, depends upon the interest differential (and other variables subsumed under R). Thus,

$$S_t^* = \alpha_0 + \alpha_1 R_t$$

and

$$S_t - S_{t-1} = k\alpha_0 + k\alpha_1 R_t - kS_{t-1}.$$

Comparing the two equations, it is clear that

$$(1 - k) = a_2.$$

The faster the speed of adjustment, the closer a_2 tends toward zero, so that

$$S_t = a_0 + a_1 R_t,$$

99

and the interest-rate differential determines the allocation of a stock rather than a flow of capital among countries. On the other hand, as the speed of adjustment tends toward zero, the second equation tends toward a third,

$$S_t - S_{t-1} = b_0 + b_1 R_t,$$

in which case the differential explains the flow of capital. Exactly the same information is conveyed by the first equation, which approaches

$$S_t = a_0 + a_1 R_t + S_{t-1}$$

as k becomes close to zero. Since Stein's estimates of the coefficient of the lagged stock variable in the stock equation differ insignificantly from unity, the stock theory merges into the flow theory. In other words, the stock theory fails this test.[56]

An alternative test considered by Stein takes first-differences of the variables in the stock equation, yielding

$$S_t - S_{t-1} = a_1(R_t - R_{t-1}) + a_2(S_{t-1} - S_{t-2}),$$

and compares the resulting explanation of the flow with that yielded by the third equation. If the first-differenced variables yield the better explanation of the flow, the stock theory may be accepted as the correct one. The stock theory also fails this test because the level variables are more significant.[57]

Unfortunately, this test is inconclusive: on the basis of prior evidence that there is no significant relation between the lagged flow and the flow, Stein drops the lagged flow variable in his regressions. Our research confirms this finding. Thus,

56. Gray, "International Movements," p. 549, and Stein, "International Short-Term Movements," p. 569.
57. *Ibid.*

$$STK = 666DS - 364.6CFC - .50BMTUS - 3460CRS$$
$$(5.97) \qquad (4.08) \qquad\quad (3.72) \qquad\quad (3.54)$$
$$- .10STK_{-1}$$
$$(0.83)$$

$$
\begin{aligned}
RSQC &= .72 \\
F(5, 32) &= 20.70 \\
DW &= 2.49 \\
SEE &= \$68.7 \text{ million.} \quad (2.32)
\end{aligned}
$$

It is not cricket to conclude that the stock theory is invalid when the lagged flow variable is dropped as an explanatory variable, for this is tantamount to setting up the test to support the flow theory in the first place — that is, it amounts to assuming that $a_2 = 1$ in the first of the three equations above.

An important difficulty — perhaps the most important — involved in discriminating between the stock and flow theories is not recognized in the literature. The hypothesis that the interest-differential determines the allocation of a stock of international capital among countries is not easily transferred from a static and timeless world to a dynamic one where stocks of securities and planned real savings are growing. If desired stocks are growing over time, a given interest-rate differential may well be associated with an increasing stock. Even if the stock theory is correct, it would be difficult to disentangle the two theories when desired stocks depend, not only upon interest differentials, but also upon other factors correlated with time itself.[58] In this case, the flow theory will yield better predictive results, and it is really this consideration which backs our pragmatic approach via a flow theory.

58. Black relates STK to both change in and level of the covered interest-rate differential, which, in our notation, is approximately equal to $[DS - CFC]$. Black finds that the equation

$$STK = 7.1 + 605.9 \, \Delta \, [DS - CFC]$$
$$(4.24)$$

explains 38 percent of the variation in STK, whereas

$$STK = 95.8 + 554.9 \, [DS - CFC]$$
$$(5.97)$$

explains 53 percent of the variation in net short-term flows to Canada. The flow formulation therefore gives better results than the stock formulation, although a slightly better explanation is obtained when both the level and the first difference of the covered interest differential are included in the equation. The level of the differential remains the more important explanatory variable — in fact, the increase in percentage of the explained variation due to inclusion of the first-difference variable is not statistically significant at the 1-percent level. See Stanley W. Black, "Theory and Policy Analysis of Short-Term Movements in the Balance of Payments," *Yale Economic Essays,* VIII (Spring, 1968), 42–44.

3 Interactions between Capital Flows and Interest Rates

An exogenous disturbance that raises the Canadian interest rate induces an increased inflow of interest-sensitive capital. The interest-induced capital inflow simultaneously damps the swing in the interest rate caused by the disturbance. Chapter 2 reported some success in detecting the first of these causal linkages despite the identification problem. That very success foretells difficulty in measuring the reverse impact of a capital-flow disturbance on the rate of interest. The theoretical discussion in Chapter 1 readily illustrates the importance of the second relation for the leverage of domestic policy instruments on interest rates and, through them, aggregate demand. At the extreme, perfectly interest-elastic international capital movements would swamp the effects of all domestic disturbances on the interest rate and peg it at the "world" rate of interest. With elasticity imperfect, or perfect but subject to slow adjustments, the effect of disturbances is merely damped. In either case, these connections render the leverages of domestic policy instruments on domestic policy targets much different from a world where capital flows are not interest-elastic.

On the basis of quarterly data, international capital flows did not appear perfectly interest-elastic during Canada's experience with a floating exchange rate. The results summarized in Table 2.2 indicate, for example, a range of interest elasticities for portfolio capital flows that runs from 9.1 to 10.6. It is clear that some scope remains for independent short-run variation in the Canadian interest rate; the question is, how much?

PROBLEMS OF ESTIMATION

To seek a quantitative answer to this question is to confront most of the estimation problems known in empirical research. This section explains our choice of simple procedures, having known biases over theoretically more sophisticated but empirically less tractable methods.

The use of quarterly data facilitates ignoring a good deal of the simultaneity depicted in a general equilibrium model and assists the identification of some relations through lags in causation. The monetary variables (net new issues of securities, interest rates, and international capital flows) interact with real variables, of course, but the latter generally lag behind monetary disturbances by at least one quarter. For instance, recent research on the determinants of capital formation in Canada has detected some interest sensitivity, but none or almost none makes its appearance within a quarter.[1] By the same token, a change in international capital flows affects the price of the Canadian dollar and hence the balance of trade; but this linkage also requires more time, as does the subsequent effect of a change in the trade balance on levels of domestic income and employment. The real sector can be largely lopped off from the financial variables that are our first concern as un-

1. Thomas A. Wilson, *Capital Investment and the Cost of Capital: A Dynamic Analysis,* Studies of the Royal Commission on Taxation, no. 30 (Ottawa: Queen's Printer, 1967).

likely to produce simultaneous correlation between predetermined and omitted variables, that would lead to biased and inconsistent estimates.

There is no such refuge in identifying relations among the financial variables themselves. In early experiments we developed small simultaneous systems covering up to a half-dozen financial variables. These were either exactly identified, and estimated by indirect least-squares, or overidentified and estimated by two-stage least-squares. All attempted to break out the effect of capital-flow disturbances on Canadian interest rates directly, and all failed.

We then altered our approach to the specification of determinants of the Canadian interest rate. Liquidity-preference theory views the interest rate as the price that lenders demand for holding the existing stock of securities. It suggests the following strategy: consider the Canadian interest rate to be determined by the stock of securities held by Canadians. The stock of Canadian securities held by foreigners is determined by the Canadian interest rate (in relation to foreign rates). The sum of the domestic and foreign-held stocks equals the total stock, which can be treated in various ways (including as an exogenous variable). The impact of a disturbance affecting foreign holdings of Canadian securities on the Canadian interest rate can be read directly from the reduced-form relations of this system, because any of the total stock of securities not held by foreigners must be held by Canadians and changes in the interest rate must leave them content with that stock. All results reported below concerning the long-term interest rate and capital flows rest on some version of this strategy. It would not work for the short-term interest rate and capital flows because of data problems, but we have been able to employ a similarly conceived approach utilizing the interaction between short-term international capital flows and the forward exchange rate.

LONG-TERM CAPITAL FLOWS AND
INTEREST RATES

Models of the sort described in the preceding paragraph can be developed for long-term capital flows and interest rates and estimated by various techniques. In this section we present two approaches. First, the ordinary least-squares (OLS) method is used to develop two estimates of the impact of capital-flow disturbances on the Canadian interest rate. Since the OLS biases in the two calculations run in opposite directions, they provide bracketing minimum and maximum estimates of the "true" relation. More important, as we shall see, the two OLS estimates embody differing economic as well as statistical approaches to the relation. We also present two-stage least-squares (TSLS) estimates, which naturally fall within the OLS brackets.

Immediately upon tackling the estimation of determinants of the Canadian long-term interest rate, CL (using liquidity-preference theory for guidance), we confront the same problem of stock versus flow relations that arose in Chapter 2. The theory calls for a relation between the *level* of the Canadian interest rate and the *stock* of long-term securities held in Canada. However, as is hardly surprising, the relation between the interest rate and the stock in domestic portfolios refuses to show up in our subsector models of a steadily growing economy, either in its crude form or when first-differenced to relate changes in the interest rate to net new issues of securities. Therefore, we retreated to relating the *level* of the interest rate to the *flow* of net new issues, a procedure consistent with that of Chapter 2 and rationalized in the same way.[2] Even the re-

2. In a sense, this is a logical if imprecise reformulation of the theoretically correct approach in analyzing time series for a growing economy. Both the supply (stock) of securities and the demand grow steadily. A regression of the interest rate on the size of the stock thus naturally fails to pick up the liquidity-preference relation, because the exogenous variable

finement of a nonlinear relation between the interest rate and the flow of new securities, to rescue something of the liquidity-preference approach, produced nothing superior to a linear relation between the variables.[3]

It turns out that variations in the Canadian interest rate, *CL,* can be explained tolerably well by net new issues of securities retained in Canada (*NNSC*) plus other monetary variables. Also employed are the percentage change in the money supply, *PCMS,* and the average term to maturity of the outstanding public debt, *ATM.* The latter variables provide the basis for measuring the impact of domestic interest-rate policies in subsequent calculations. They should also reduce bias in the estimates caused by correlating predetermined variables with the error terms, especially if our argument about lags in the influence of real variables is accepted.

Fitting this equation over the same time period covered by the equations in Chapter 2, we obtained

$$CL = .4600 + .0002138NNSC - .06125PCMS$$
$$ (5.64) (2.29) (4.83)$$
$$ + .005379ATM - .1469Q_1 + .08321Q_3$$
$$ (7.47) (2.85) (1.80)$$

$$RSQC = .71$$
$$F(7, 30) = 16.84$$
$$DW = 1.02$$
$$SEE = .0922 \text{ percent}, \quad (3.1)$$

is correlated with excluded variables governing the growth of the demand for securities. Substituting the flow of new securities for the stock goes some distance toward purging the variable of this unwanted correlation, i.e., reflecting deviations in the growth of the securities stock from the growth patterns of the excluded variables. This is to say less than that the result is an unbiased estimate.

3. One other reason for this quest was the significantly positive autocorrelation which plagued the interest-rate equations. An intensive search for omitted variables failed to raise the Durbin-Watson statistics, thus a nonlinear relation seemed a likely possibility.

with the mean value of CL equal to .9742 percent per quarter.

The equation is interpreted as follows. Net new issues sold to Canadians is measured in millions of dollars. A one billion-dollar increase in $NNSC$ will therefore tend to raise the interest rate by .2138 percent. An increase in ATM by one month will raise the interest rate by .005379 percent. Finally, an increase in the rate of change of the money supply by one percent will decrease the interest rate by .06125 percent. This interpretation rests upon the assumption that the regression coefficients are partial, not total derivatives. The coefficients of the explanatory variables are total derivatives only when the equation is reduced, that is, when the interest rate is expressed as a function of exogenous variables alone.

Equation 3.1 implies that an exogenous increase in the inflow of portfolio capital by one billion dollars will tend to lower the interest rate by 21.38 basis points, because $NNSC \equiv NNS - PC$ and $\partial CL/\partial PC = -.0002138$. This partial impact excludes the damping effect that the induced fall in interest rate would have on the total portfolio inflow, exogenous disturbance and all. The desired total differential can be obtained with the aid of any equation explaining PC reported in Chapter 2. Since we are interested in the interactions between capital flows and Canadian interest rates, not in developing an overall econometric model of the Canadian economy, only truncated versions of the portfolio capital equation are reproduced here. To generate a range of estimates, we have selected five portfolio equations to combine with our interest-rate equation. Detailed calculations using portfolio equation 2.6 are presented below to illustrate our methodology. The estimates generated by the other portfolio equations are summarized in Table 3.1.

The truncated version of equation 2.6 is $PC = 695\ CL - 986\ USL$ where the United States interest rate is included so that changes in Canadian monetary conditions can be linked to exogenous changes in U.S. monetary conditions. In the reduced-form equations, we ignore the constant terms and seasonal dummies but allow for exogenous disturbances in CL and PC by using shift parameters denoted as CL^* and PC^*, respectively. Substitution of equation 2.6 into equation 3.1 yields

$$
\begin{aligned}
CL = CL^* &+ .0002138NNS \\
&- .0002138(PC^* + 695CL - 986USL) \\
&- .06125PCMS + .005379ATM \\
= .8707CL^* &- .0001861PC^* - .05333PCMS \\
&+ .004683ATM + .1835USL + .0001861NNS.
\end{aligned}
\tag{3.2}
$$

This result implies than an exogenous increase in capital inflows by one billion dollars will lower the Canadian interest rate by 18.61 basis points. If capital flows were completely unresponsive to relative interest rates, an exogenous inflow of this magnitude would lower the interest rate by 21.38 basis points. Interest-elasticity therefore limits the fall in interest rates to 87.07 percent of the effect that would be realized in the absence of endogenous capital flows.

Since part of the capital inflow is endogenous, we can turn the preceding analysis around and conclude that an exogenous inflow of one billion dollars will not increase the total net inflow by the same amount. When the portfolio equation is expressed in reduced form:

$$
\begin{aligned}
PC = 605.1CL^* &+ .8707PC^* - 37.06PCMS + 3.255ATM \\
&- 858.4USL + .1293NNS.
\end{aligned}
\tag{3.3}
$$

As expected on the basis of the preceding analysis, only 87.07 percent of an exogenous increase in capital inflows will be maintained in the final equilibrium because of the reduction by 12.93 percent in net inflow of interest-sensitive capital.

A slightly larger estimate of the damping effect of capital flows on the long-term interest rate is generated when the Mc-Leod-Weir 40-bond average, *MWL,* is used to represent the Canadian interest rate.[4] Regressing *MWL* upon the same variables employed to explain *CL* yields

$$MWL = .6476 + .0003789NNSC - .05518PCMS$$
$$\quad\;\, (6.25) \qquad\quad (3.20) \qquad\qquad\;\; (3.43)$$
$$+ .005308ATM - .1670Q_1 + .0670Q_3$$
$$\quad\;\, (5.80) \qquad\quad (2.55) \qquad (1.14)$$

$$RSQC = .60$$
$$F(6, 31) = 10.84$$
$$DW = .88$$
$$SEE = .1172 \text{ percent.} \quad (3.4)$$

The mean value of *MWL* equals 1.1908 percent per quarter.

This equation is clearly inferior to 3.1 in all but one respect: the significance of the variable *NNSC* is considerably improved, and this may more than offset the lower value of the Durbin-Watson statistic. (Or, the apparent rise in significance may simply be a reflection of the increased degree of positive autocorrelation.) The larger coefficient for *NNSC* is consistent with the previous chapter's argument that the market with the greatest "depth, breadth, and resiliency" is the market for governments. For the same reason, we have found that the interest sensitivity of portfolio inflows is smaller when *MWL* is used to represent the Canadian interest rate. Three representative equations are

$$PC = 87.25 + 573.4MWL - 835.5USL - 225.5CTS$$
$$\quad\;\, (1.14) \qquad (3.90) \qquad\quad (3.93) \qquad\quad (3.84)$$

4. *MWL* is the average yield on 40 bonds (municipal, provincial, public utility, and industrial) published by McLeod, Young, Weir and Company and expressed in percent per quarter.

$$+ .1290NNS$$
$$(2.96)$$

$$
\begin{aligned}
RSQC &= .55 \\
F(5, 32) &= 13.03 \\
DW &= 1.63 \\
SEE &= \$54.45 \text{ million} \quad (3.5)
\end{aligned}
$$

$$PC = 89.61 + 710.0MWL - 993.9USL - 249.1CTS$$
$$\quad (1.06) \qquad (4.66) \qquad (4.41) \qquad (3.84)$$

$$+ .0605NNSC$$
$$(1.14)$$

$$
\begin{aligned}
RSQC &= .46 \\
F(5, 32) &= 9.23 \\
DW &= 1.69 \\
SEE &= \$60.09 \text{ million} \quad (3.6)
\end{aligned}
$$

$$PC = 129.2 + 609.1MWL - 651.2USL$$
$$\quad (1.74) \qquad (3.58) \qquad (2.74)$$

$$
\begin{aligned}
RSQC &= .25 \\
F(3, 34) &= 7.78 \\
DW &= 1.11 \\
SEE &= \$70.66 \text{ million.} \quad (3.7)
\end{aligned}
$$

The simultaneous solution of each of these equations with the interest rate equation reduces the latter to, respectively,

$$
\begin{aligned}
MWL = .8215MWL^* &- .0003113PC^* + .0003113NNS \\
&- .04533PCMS + .004361ATM \\
&+ .2601USL \quad (3.8)
\end{aligned}
$$

$$
\begin{aligned}
MWL = .7880MWL^* &- .0002986PC^* + .0002986NNS \\
&- .04348PCMS + .004183ATM \\
&+ .2968USL \quad (3.9)
\end{aligned}
$$

$$
\begin{aligned}
MWL = .8125MWL^* &- .0003079PC^* + .0003079NNS \\
&- .04483PCMS + .004313ATM \\
&+ .2005USL. \quad (3.10)
\end{aligned}
$$

These equations imply that interest-sensitive capital flows reduce the effectiveness of domestic policies aimed at changing the interest rate by 17.85 to 21.20 percent, more than was indicated by the equations using *PC*. Alternatively, the effectiveness of domestic interest-rate policies is reduced to about 80 percent of what it would be in the absence of endogenous capital flows.

Implications for Monetary Policy

The model can be used to demonstrate the loss in effectiveness of domestic policies employed to manipulate the interest rate when capital flows are interest-elastic. Equation 3.1 indicates that, when the rate of capital inflow is constant, a one-percent reduction in the rate of increase in the money supply will raise the interest rate by 6.125 basis points. When the interaction between capital flows and the interest rate is taken into account, however, the induced capital inflow limits the rise in the interest rate to 5.333 basis points. The effectiveness of the given policy action is therefore reduced by 12.93 percent. The same conclusion holds for the loss in effectiveness of debt-management policy. In the absence of interest-sensitive capital flows, an increase in the average term to maturity of the outstanding debt by one year will raise the interest rate by .06455 percent. In actuality, however, the influx of interest-sensitive capital will limit the rise in the interest rate to only .05620 percentage points. Alternatively, we can say that the change in the money supply or term to maturity required to provide any given change in interest rates will have to be 14.85 percent greater when capital flows are interest-sensitive than when they are not.

It is noteworthy that the interest-rate equation implies that a reduction in the rate of increase of the money supply by one percent will have the same effect upon the interest rate as an increase in the maturity of long-term debt by 11.39 months. To calculate this trade-off, we note that the interest rate will be unchanged if

$$dCL = -.05333dPCMS + .004683dATM = 0$$

or if

$$dATM = \left(\frac{.05333}{.004683}\right) dPCMS = 11.39dPCMS.$$

Degree of Interest-Rate Independence

Considerable interest attaches to one possible source of disturbance in PC, variations in the United States long-term interest rate (USL). Interest-elastic capital flows raise squarely the question of how much scope exists for independent variation in Canadian interest rates.[5] This case also permits the development of two independent OLS estimates bracketing the relation between PC and the Canadian long-term rate, as promised above.

First, the results implied by the equations already presented can be summarized. If the United States rate rises by one percentage point, the shrunken Canada-U.S. differential reduces the capital inflow and, in turn, limits the adverse movement of the interest-rate differential from Canada's point of view. In equilibrium, equation 3.2 indicates that the Canadian interest rate will have risen by 18.35 basis points. Net movement of the interest differential against Canada will therefore be 81.65

5. In Chapter 2 we noted the reduction over the 1950's of the variance in differential between Canadian and U.S. long-term interest rates, suggesting a declining trend in the independence of Canadian interest rates. See David W. Slater, "International Factors in Canadian Credit Conditions," *The Canadian Banker*, LXXV (Spring, 1968), 5–14.

basis points, and from this it can be inferred that the net reduction in the rate of capital inflow will be

$$dPC = \left(\frac{\partial PC}{\partial CL}\right) dCL + \left(\frac{\partial PC}{\partial USL}\right) dUSL$$
$$= 695(.1835) - 986(1.00) = -858.4,$$

or \$858.4 million. If the equations employing the McLeod-
Weir interest-rate series are used, the independence of Canadian from foreign interest rates appears somewhat further reduced. Something between 20 and 30 percent of any change in
the U.S. rate will be fed into the Canadian rate through the
induced change in capital flows.

The Canadian monetary authorities could prevent the tighter
monetary policy of the United States from feeding into Canada
through the change in capital inflows by increasing the rate of
change in the money supply by .1835/.05333 = 3.441 percent. Shortening the maturity structure of outstanding debt by
roughly three years would accomplish the same result.

When our interest-rate equation is combined with other
portfolio investment equations, the estimated reduction of independent variations in the Canadian long-term interest rate
because of the effects of capital flows upon the rate ranges
from 8.31 to 14.69 percent. These numbers indicate the reduction in effectiveness of domestic interest-rate policies directed at the long end of the market. The reduced form equations are summarized in Table 3.1.

The interaction between capital flows and interest rates
therefore provides a partial explanation for the observed
similarity in Canadian and United States interest-rate movements. Without reviewing all the possible sources of bias leading up to the reduced interest-rate equations, it seems clear that
they lead to an underestimate of the response of the Canadian
interest rate to a change in the U.S. rate. This is so even if the

TABLE 3.1. Reduced interest-rate and portfolio investment equations

Portfolio equation	Dependent variable	Independent variables					
		CL^*	PC^*	NNS	PCMS	ATM	USL
2.7	CL	.8530	−.0001823	.0001823	−.05225	.004588	.2035
2.6	CL	.8706	−.0001861	.0001861	−.05333	.004683	.1835
2.3	CL	.9008	−.0001925	.0001925	−.05517	.004845	.1242
2.5	CL	.9108	−.0001947	.0001947	−.05579	.004899	.0892
2.10	CL	.9169	−.0001960	.0001960	−.05616	.004932	.1215
[a]	–	1.0000	−.0002138	.0002138	−.06125	.005379	–
2.7	PC	687.5	.8531	.1469	−42.11	3.698	−952.0
[a]	–	806.0	1.0000	–	–	–	−1116.0
2.6	PC	605.1	.8707	.1293	−37.06	3.255	−858.4
[a]	–	695.0	1.0000	–	–	–	−986.0
2.3	PC	463.9	.9009	.0991	−28.41	2.495	−581.0
[a]	–	515.0	1.0000	–	–	–	−645.0
2.5	PC	417.2	.9108	.0892	−25.55	2.244	−417.2
[a]	–	458.0	1.0000	–	–	–	−458.0
2.10	PC	388.8	.9169	.0831	−23.81	2.091	−568.5
[a]	–	424.0	1.0000	–	–	–	−620.0

[a] These rows provide the unreduced regression coefficients.

relation is viewed as a predictive device that embodies simultaneous relations excluded from our model, rather than as a structural estimate. On the other hand, linkage of the Canadian and U.S. interest rates need not operate wholly through international capital movements. In Canada, the expectational forces which Keynes described as governing the interest rate may well be triggered by changes in the U.S. rate, with expectations rather than actual capital flows doing most of the work of keeping the two rates in line. (The sympathetic movements of the two countries' stock markets are suggestive.[6]) In Chapter 2 we examined the hypothesis that the Canadian long rate is determined by expected future short rates where expectations are based upon experienced short rates. The empirical result is repeated here for convenience.

$$CL = .1972 + .1829CS + .6834CL_{-1}$$
$$(3.27) \quad (4.05) \quad\quad (8.34)$$

$$
\begin{aligned}
RSQC &= .90 \\
F(3, 34) &= 107.4 \\
DW &= 1.04 \\
SEE &= .05535 \text{ percent.} \quad (3.11)
\end{aligned}
$$

If the neoclassical expectations hypothesis is replaced by the Keynesian hypothesis that the Canadian long-term rate is determined by directly held expectations of what its normal long-run level should be, then using the United States long-term rate as a measure of prevailing opinion concerning the level of

6. Grubel has shown that the correlation between average returns per year (dividends plus appreciation) in U.S. and Canadian share prices is much higher than that for the U.S. and any of nine other countries. See Herbert G. Grubel, "Internationally Diversified Portfolios: Welfare Gains and Capital Flows," *American Economic Review,* LVII (December, 1968), 1299–1314. The parallel movement of Canadian and U.S. interest rates has been investigated by William Poole, "The Stability of the Canadian Flexible Exchange Rate, 1950–62," *Canadian Journal of Economics and Political Science,* XXXIII (May, 1967), 215–216.

North American interest rates that is viable in the long run gives us

$$CL = -.03534 + .7568USL + .4176CL_{-1}$$
$$\quad\quad (0.81) \quad\quad (6.91) \quad\quad\quad (4.87)$$

$$RSQC = .94$$
$$F(3, 34) = 179.56$$
$$DW = 1.07$$
$$SEE = .04365 \text{ percent.} \quad (3.12)$$

This equation suggests that the Keynesian hypothesis explains variations in the Canadian interest rate with somewhat more precision than does the neoclassical expectations hypothesis. If the short-term rate is included as an explanatory variable, it is especially interesting to note that it adds nothing at all to the explanation of the long-term rate. Thus,

$$CL = .008422 + .04534CS + .6683USL + .4156CL_{-1}$$
$$\quad\quad (0.14) \quad\quad (0.99) \quad\quad (4.71) \quad\quad (4.84)$$

$$RSQC = .94$$
$$F(4, 33) = 134.7$$
$$DW = 1.03$$
$$SEE = .04365 \text{ percent.} \quad (3.13)$$

Our results suggest that the level of the Canadian long-term interest rate is at times much more strongly influenced by expected United States monetary conditions than by expected Canadian monetary conditions reflected in the Canadian short-term rate. They also lend support to such Canadianisms as "Canadian interest rates are determined by the Federal Reserve Board," and "Canada is the thirteenth Federal Reserve District." The apparent significance of CS in equation 3.11, coupled with its insignificance when USL is included in the equation, suggests that CS may simply proxy the U.S. short-term rate in equation 3.11. We shall argue later in this chapter that independent variations in Canadian short-term rates from their U.S. counterparts were severely limited by induced variations in interest-elastic capital flows, so that the short end of the Canadian yield curve was more or less anchored to the short end of the U.S. yield curve.

The only other variable that entered significantly into the explanation of the long-term interest rate when the specification included *USL* was the percentage change in the money supply. Thus,

$$CL = .007360 + .7938USL - .01018PCMS + .3558CL_{-1}$$
$$\quad\;\; (0.17) \qquad\; (7.69) \qquad\quad (2.50) \qquad\qquad (4.25)$$

$$
\begin{aligned}
RSQC &= \quad .95 \\
F(4, 33) &= 156.2 \\
DW &= \quad 1.07 \\
SEE &= \quad .04071 \text{ percent.} \quad (3.14)
\end{aligned}
$$

Various combinations of security issues and net capital inflows, lagged and unlagged, invariably turned up with theoretically incorrect (though insignificant) signs; *USL* remained dominant throughout.

At this stage, we have the basis for two estimates of the action Canadian authorities must take to ward off the effects of an increase in United States long-term interest rates. One estimate is a minimum and the other a maximum, for both economic and statistical reasons; they should thus bracket any "true estimate" of this policy leverage. If expectations are on the side of the authorities, our initial calculations designate the minimum action Canadian authorities must take in order to insulate the interest rate from the effects of a U.S. interest-rate change on capital inflows, because we have probably underestimated the induced change in the capital inflow. Our equations indicate that the rate of change in the Canadian money supply would have to be increased by at least 1.60 to 3.90 percent per quarter in order to insulate the interest rate on Canadian governments from an increase in the U.S. rate by one percentage point. (To neutralize the effects on the industrial average, *MWL,* the rate of change would have to be increased by at least 4.47 to 6.83 percent per quarter.) On the other hand, if the authorities must combat domestic expectations that the Canadian rate will follow the United States rate, equation 3.14 implies that the required change in the rate of monetary increase would be 11.42–48.77 times as large as in the case where induced changes in capital flows alone connect the Canadian to the U.S. rate. This is a maximum estimate in the statistical sense as well: *CL* and *USL* are very likely to be positively correlated with variables omitted from equation 3.14, so that the partial coefficient is overestimated. Thus there are brackets around the relation; the range of these estimates may seem dismaying, but most of the variation is probably due to the ineluctable economic significance of the state of interest-rate expectations.

The indirect consequences of monetary policy under a flexible exchange rate will also differ substantially depending upon the state of expectations. With expectations on the side of the Canadian authorities, the induced change in international capital flows will be smaller, as will the effect on the exchange rate and current-account balance. With expectations against the authorities, the induced capital-account disturbance needed to accomplish any given protection to the domestic interest rate is larger, as are the consequent indirect effects through the exchange rate and current account.

Estimation by Two-Stage Least-Squares

Because our calculations are based upon a simultaneous equation system, the validity of the exercise hinges crucially upon identification of the relevant parameters. If, for example, an exogenous disturbance that raises the net capital inflow simultaneously increases the demand for funds, the damping effect of the capital inflow on long-term interest rates will be understated by our calculations. The omission of a common explanatory variable that causes the demand and supply schedules to shift more or less together should be reflected in a significantly positive degree of correlation between the residuals of the equations explaining portfolio inflows and interest rates. The correlation coefficient for the residuals of equations 2.1 and 3.1 (which employ *CL* to represent the interest rate) is .2058. The correlation of the residuals of equations 3.4 and 3.5 (which use *MWL* as the interest rate) is practically nil — the coefficient is only .0698. A coefficient of .3220 or larger is required for significance at the 5-percent level.[7] We

7. We based our test concerning ρ — the "true" correlation coefficient — on the statistic

$$1/2 \ln \frac{(1 + r)}{(1 - r)},$$

which is approximately normal with mean

$$1/2 \ln \frac{(1 + \rho)}{(1 - \rho)}$$

and variance $1/(n - 3)$. Therefore, the distribution of

$$z = \left[1/2 \ln \frac{(1 + r)}{(1 - r)} - 1/2 \ln \frac{(1 + \rho)}{(1 - \rho)} \right] \sqrt{n - 3}$$

is approximately standard normal. See John E. Freund, *Mathematical Statistics* (Englewood Cliffs, N.J.: Prentice-Hall, 1965), p. 311. For the null hypothesis that $\rho = o$, we computed

$$z = \frac{\sqrt{n - 3}}{2} \left[\ln \frac{1 + r}{1 - r} \right] = 2.958 \ln \frac{(1 + r)}{(1 - r)}$$

for $n = 38$. If r is significantly different from zero at the 5 percent level ($\alpha = .05$), we require

$$z \geq 1.96 \text{ or } \ln \frac{(1 + r)}{(1 - r)} \geq \frac{1.96}{2.958} = .6626.$$

Therefore $r \geqslant .322$. For $\alpha = .01$, r must exceed .410.

cannot, therefore, reject the null hypothesis of no correlation, so this test for identifiability is passed.

We also experimented with the construction of models which could be estimated by two-stage least-squares (TSLS) as a check on our a priori reasoning about the nature and direction of the biases in our regression coefficients. At the simplest level, we estimated the model:

$$CL = f(NNSC, ATM, PCMS, Q_1, Q_2, Q_3)$$
$$PC = g(\widehat{CL}, USL)$$

where $\widehat{CL}$ was estimated by regressing CL upon the predetermined variables: $NNSC$, ATM, $PCMS$, USL, Q_1, Q_2, and Q_3. The equation explaining CL is, of course, the same as 3.1 because the explanatory variables are all assumed to be exogenous. But two-stage least-squares yielded larger estimates for the interest sensitivity of portfolio inflows than did ordinary least squares (OLS) and this is what would be expected if independent variations in interest rates were partially removed by induced capital flows. The TSLS equation was

$$PC = -34.72 + 803.6CL - 840.9USL$$
$$(0.47) \quad (1.93) \quad (1.63)$$

$$SEE = \$74.7 \text{ million,} \quad (3.15)$$

which can be compared with the OLS equation:

$$PC = -36.27 + 550.2CL - 530.9USL$$
$$(0.48) \quad (2.40) \quad (1.80)$$

$$RSQC = .12$$
$$F(3, 34) = 4.06$$
$$DW = 1.05$$
$$SEE = 76.5 \text{ million.} \quad (3.16)$$

We experimented with models in which the interest rate was regressed upon *NNS* and *PC* separately instead of on *NNSC*. In all cases, the regression coefficients of *PC* and *NNS* turned up with theoretically incorrect, though insignificant, signs. We therefore moved on to the construction of three sector models which assumed the variable *NNSC* to be endogenous. Our best result for explanation of the interest rate was generated by the model:

$$CL = f(\widehat{NNSC}, PCMS, ATM, Q_1, Q_2, Q_3)$$
$$PC = g(\widehat{CL}, USL, \widehat{NNSC}, Q_1, Q_2, Q_3)$$
$$NNSC = h(\widehat{CL}, USL, PCMS, Q_1, Q_2, Q_3)$$

The interest-rate equation is specified exactly as it was when estimated by ordinary least-squares. The specification of the remaining equations was conditioned by our desire to have an exactly identified model, and this means that each equation of the model must itself be exactly identified. We therefore included seasonal dummies in the portfolio investment equations even though prior experimentation with ordinary least-squares failed to show their relevance. The variable *CTS*, which adds significantly to the explanation of *PC,* was excluded to avoid either having to add an equation to explain the short-term interest rate or cause overidentification of the remaining equations. Finally, we assume that the supply of securities, *NNSC*, is negatively related to the Canadian-United States interest differential. *PCMS* is also included, with an expected negative sign as an alternative indicator of monetary ease and, partly, as an aid to identification. Our TSLS estimates of this model are:

$$CL = .4570 + .001062N\widehat{NSC} - .1028PCMS + .004113ATM$$
$$(2.92) \qquad (2.71) \qquad (3.46) \qquad (2.79)$$

$$- .3333Q_1 - .1285Q_2 + .1246Q_3$$
$$(2.67) \qquad (1.24) \qquad (1.38)$$

$$SEE = .1767 \text{ percent} \quad (3.17)$$

$$PC = 10.14 + 3323\widehat{CL} - 4210USL + .9082N\widehat{N}SC$$
$$(0.04) \quad (1.15) \qquad (1.11) \qquad (1.03)$$

$$- 140.9Q_1 - 157.0Q_2 + 18.85Q_3$$
$$(0.67) \qquad (0.73) \qquad (0.19)$$

$$SEE = \$205.3 \text{ million} \quad (3.18)$$

$$NNSC = 1355 - 22730\widehat{CL} + 26690USL - 448.5PCMS$$
$$(0.19) \qquad (0.23) \qquad (0.24) \qquad (0.20)$$

$$- 147.5Q_1 + 702.9Q_2 + 479.6Q_3$$
$$(0.08) \qquad (0.29) \qquad (0.20)$$

$$SEE = \$1158 \text{ million.} \quad (3.19)$$

Our TSLS estimate for the Canadian interest rate supports our previous argument that the initial calculations set forth in this chapter provide minimum estimates of the loss in independence of Canadian interest-rate policies directed at the long-term end of the market. Comparison of equations 3.1 and 3.17 shows that the coefficients of the predetermined variables are left relatively unchanged by the TSLS estimator, while the coefficient of *NNSC* is increased greatly in size and rises in significance. The overall goodness of fit deteriorates when the interest-rate equation is estimated by TSLS (the standard error of estimate is almost twice as large as for the OLS estimate), but this is to be expected. Ordinary least-squares has the property of minimum variance, but it is, of course, minimum variance around a biased mean. The portfolio equation is clearly inferior to all of those estimated in Chapter 2, although the signs are correct. As expected, the measured interest sensitivities are strikingly large, but large standard errors render this result uninteresting. The equation explaining *NNSC* is not

123

worthy of comment, although the regression coefficients turn up with the signs they were expected to have.

Although we have presented the entire model here, in the interest of completeness, our relatively poor TSLS results for *PC* and *NNSC* are not essential for the purpose of analyzing the question of interest-rate independence. The estimator employed above is a single-equation estimator, the sole purpose of which is to purge the endogenous explanatory variables of any stochastic components associated with the disturbance term. We can therefore use our TSLS interest-rate equation with any portfolio investment equation used previously. The results are summarized in Table 3.2.

TABLE 3.2. Reduced two-stage least-squares equations determining long-term interest rate (*CL*)

Portfolio equation	Predetermined variables					
	*CL**	*PC**	*NNS*	*PCMS*	*ATM*	*USL*
2.7	.5388	−.0005722	.0005722	−.05539	.002216	.6386
2.6	.5753	−.0006110	.0006110	−.05915	.002366	.6025
2.3	.6464	−.0006865	.0006865	−.06645	.002659	.4428
2.5	.6728	−.0007145	.0007145	−.06916	.002767	.3272
2.10	.6895	−.0007323	.0007323	−.07088	.002836	.4540
[a]	1.0000	−.001062	.001062	−.1028	.004113	−

[a] This row provides the unreduced regression coefficients.

The increased sensitivity of the Canadian interest rate to the supply of securities sold domestically implies a corresponding increase in the damping effect of capital inflows upon the rate. The coefficient of *CL** in Table 3.2 indicate that the effectiveness of domestic policies aimed at changing the level of the long-term interest rate was reduced to 53.88–68.95 percent of what it would have been in the absence of endogenous capital flows. Alternatively, it can be said that induced changes in capital flows eliminated 31.05–46.12 percent of independent variations in the Canadian interest rate. These estimates are a little more than three times as large as those based upon our ordinary least-squares regressions.

Turning to the question of independence from foreign interest-rate policies, Table 3.2 indicates that 32.72–63.86 percent of any change in the United States interest rate will be fed into the Canadian rate through the induced change in rate of capital inflow. To insulate the Canadian rate from an increase in the U.S. rate by one percentage point, the monetary authorities would have to increase the rate of change in the money supply by 4.73–11.53 percent per quarter. These offsetting monetary requirements are three times as large as those estimated in our initial calculations.

Our two-stage least-squares results therefore suggest that we have fairly bounded our estimates of Canadian interest-rate dependence. In round numbers, our calculations suggest that one-fifth to three-quarters of any change in the United States interest rate would be passed on to Canada in the absence of offsetting actions by the monetary authorities. The upper estimate is based on the hypothesis that expected U.S. monetary conditions link the Canadian rate directly to the U.S. rate, but the relation also picks up the indirect relation through capital flows. The estimate is subject to some upward bias because an exogenous disturbance that raises CL will, in theory at least, have some impact on the U.S. rate through the resulting increase in rate of capital outflow from the United States. Our TSLS calculations, on the other hand, indicate that the lower estimate of interest-rate dependence is downward biased and that up to 60 percent of changes in the U.S. rate may be fed into the Canadian rate through induced variations in the rate of capital inflow.

SHORT-TERM CAPITAL FLOWS AND INTEREST RATES

If the short-term interest rate is considered a key tool of monetary policy, then the importance of international capital flows in damping changes in the rate is clear even without knowledge of the theory of internal and external balance. This section develops such estimates. Its presentation parallels the preceding section on the long-term interest rate. We could not employ liquidity-preference theory in the same fashion as before because no satisfactory measure exists for changes in the stock of assets to which the short-term rate might be related. Instead, we use the interaction between the short-term capital market and forward exchange market, through covered interest arbitrage, to provide bracketing estimates (using OLS estimation) of the impact of *STK* on *CS*. As before, the brackets embody both opposite statistical biases and differing economic assumptions. Then two-stage least-squares is employed to develop what we hope is an unbiased estimate.

Short-Term Flows, the Interest Rate and the Forward Exchange Rate: Ordinary Least-Squares Estimates

The net inflow of short-term capital, *STK*, is well explained by equations 2.15 and 2.16. Consider equation 2.15,

$$STK = 602 \ DS + 314.5 \ FP - .4734 \ BMTUS - 35.12 \ CRS,$$

where balance-of-payments variables are measured in millions of dollars, interest rates are in percent, and exchange-rate variables have been converted to cents. The equation indicates that an exogenous disturbance that raises the interest differential by one percentage point tends to increase the net inflow of short-term capital by $602 million per quarter. This is only a partial effect, of course, because the induced capital inflow will tend to reduce the interest differential by increasing the supply of loanable funds in Canada. If part of the capital inflow is covered in the forward market, the increased supply of Canadian dollars forward combined with upward pressure on the spot rate will reduce the forward premium. It is conceivable that money market and exchange market adjustments could completely eliminate the increase in net capital inflow.

In order to gain some idea of the reverse impact of capital flows on the Canadian interest rate, an estimate of $\partial CS/\partial STK$ is needed. Direct regressions of interest rate upon net capital inflow and other variables failed to pick up the desired negative relationship we were looking for, so we resorted to an indirect procedure. The most important variable explaining the capital inflow, outside of the interest differential, is the forward premium. An increase in the forward premium should, by raising the net inflow of capital, be associated with a decline in the Canadian interest rate. We therefore include the forward premium as a variable in our interest-rate equation. Because we are interested in our ability to change the Canadian interest rate relative to the United States rate, the level of the U.S. short rate is also included in the equation. Finally, income is included as a measure of economic activity and the percentage change in the money supply as a monetary policy variable. The resulting equation is

$$CS = -.7820 - .4691FP + .5426USS - .03893PCMS$$
$$(7.50) \quad (4.98) \quad (4.37) \quad (3.24)$$
$$+ .0001477GNP - .1548Q_3$$
$$(7.60) \quad (3.65)$$

$$RSQC = .93$$
$$F(6, 31) = 66.03$$
$$DW = 1.15$$
$$SEE = .09046 \text{ percent.} \quad (3.20)$$

The mean value of CS is equal to .64197 percent per quarter.

The two equations together imply that a one-cent increase in the forward premium tends to raise the net capital inflow by $314.5 million and lower the interest rate by .4691 percentage points. An indirect estimate of the reverse impact of capital inflows on the Canadian interest rate, $\partial CS/\partial STK$, is therefore provided by the quotient $(\partial CS/\partial FP)/(\partial STK/\partial FP) = -.001492$. Thus, an exogenous disturbance that raises the Canadian interest rate by one percentage point tends to increase the net capital inflow by $602 million, which in turn reduces the interest rate by $(602)(.001492) = .8979$ percentage points. Similarly, about 90 percent of the effects of changes in the forward premium upon net capital flows is wiped out by the offsetting change in relative interest rates induced by the capital flow. This is seen most clearly by noting that, although a rise in the forward premium by one cent tends to increase the net capital inflow by $314.5 million, the reduced form coefficient of FP is only 32.1. This implies that the interest rate has fallen sufficiently to eliminate $282.4 million, or 89.79 percent, of the inflow induced by the initial rise in the forward premium.

According to these calculations, exogenous variations in the Canadian short-term interest rate are practically eliminated by the reverse impact of interest-elastic capital flows upon the interest rate. If this is true, the Canadian monetary authorities will find it difficult to conduct an independent interest-rate policy in "bills only," and monetary policy will operate indirectly on the level of income by changing the currency price and the net balance of payments on current account. But our calculations must be interpreted as maximum estimates of the damping effects of capital inflows upon relative interest rates. The indirect estimate of $\partial CS/\partial STK$ is biased upward because it is derived by dividing $\partial STK/\partial FP$ into $\partial CS/\partial FP$. The denominator is biased downward because capital inflows on interest-arbitrage account will tend to lower not only the interest differential, but also the price of the foward relative to the spot dollar. The numerator, on the other hand, is biased upward. A rise in FP tends to raise STK and lower CS; the reduction in CS, however, mitigates the rise in STK and places further upward pressure on FP. If FP should in fact prove to be unaffected by disturbances in CS or STK, these biases would go to zero and the maximum estimate would be the correct one. Evidence on the actual behavior of FP can supply a lower-bound estimate for the effect of STK disturbances on CS.

The theory of interest parity indicates a relation among the spot and forward exchange rates and domestic foreign interest rates that must hold (within the limits of transactions costs) in order to render further covered interest arbitrage unprofitable. It is

$$RF = RS \left[\frac{1 + USS/100}{1 + CS/100} \right].$$

This relation does not suggest that the forces of interest-arbitrage alone determine the price of the currency forward, but rather that any discrepancy between RF, however determined, and its interest-parity level will be eliminated as interest-arbitragers fully exploit the guaranteed interest advantage. Interest-parity is achieved by adjustments of all four variables, not by interest rates alone, as has been assumed thus far. The formulation above suggests the RF changes in the same proportion as RS with the factor of proportionality equal to

$$1 - \left[\frac{CS - USS}{100 + CS} \right].$$

Officer's estimates for the coefficient of the spot rate adjusted for this proportionality factor, as a determinant of RF, run very close to unity and are highly significant.[8]

8. See unpub. diss. by Lawrence H. Officer, "An Econometric Model of the Canadian Economy under the Fluctuating Exchange Rate" (Harvard University, 1964), p. 384.

Although Officer's formulation of the interest-parity relation is precise, it is difficult to use his results to extract the effect of a change in the interest differential upon the forward rate, since $\partial RF/\partial DS$ itself depends upon the level of both the spot rate and the Canadian interest rate. We have therefore adopted a looser version of the interest-parity relation by regressing the forward rate upon both the interest differential and the spot rate in order to measure their separate influences. The balance of merchandise trade with the United States is included in order to ascertain whether hedging by traders had a significant impact on the price of the forward dollar. The result is:

$$RF = 4.428 - .2818DS + .9553RS + .0004195BMTUS$$
$$\quad (2.07) \quad (1.57) \quad (45.95) \quad\quad (1.15)$$

$$
\begin{aligned}
RSQC &= .99 \\
F(7, 30) &= 368.35 \\
DW &= .53 \\
SEE &= .1602 \text{ cents.} \quad (3.21)
\end{aligned}
$$

The mean value of RF equals 102.39 cents.

All variables appear with theoretically correct signs. The coefficient of the interest differential picks up the negative relation between the forward premium (or the forward rate, given the level of the spot rate) and the interest differential predicted by the interest-parity theory. This provides an indirect route for establishing the effect of interest-arbitrage inflows upon the forward rate. Direct regressions of RF upon STK fail to identify this negative relationship because STK is itself strongly influenced by changes in the forward relative to the spot rate. As indicated above, $BMTUS$ is included to measure the responsiveness of the forward rate to transactions whose primary purpose is other than speculation on foreign exchange or the pursuit of an interest advantage. An exogenous change in the trade balance should affect the forward rate in the same direction. If all transactions are on a cash basis, a rise in *BMTUS* raises the spot rate and the resulting reduction in covered inflows raises the forward rate. If some transactions are on a credit basis, *RF* may be affected directly if traders hedge by selling foreign exchange forward for future delivery of Canadian currency. If the exchange market is stable, the spot rate will be stabilized by speculators. Discrepancies between forward and spot rates will tend to be eliminated by the purchases of forward speculators, and the forward rate will be locked in relation to the spot rate. Despite the high degree of autocorrelation, resulting in underestimates of the standard errors of the regression coefficients, the very high *t*-value for *RS* suggests that speculative factors are of key importance in determining the relation of the forward to the spot rate.[9]

Some more recent contributions to the empirical literature make the speculative supply of forward exchange a distributed-lag function of the spot rate: the expected spot rate is a function of its own past values.[10] The addition of the lagged dependent variable does improve equation 3.21 slightly; thus,

9. An institutional cause of this extremely close tie between the forward and current spot rates exists in the banks' practice of matching forward sales of foreign exchange immediately with spot purchases. Shifts in demand for forward exchange are thus transferred immediately to the spot market, although the banks, of course, unwind their short forward and long spot positions to some degree in subsequent transactions; *Report of the Royal Commission on Banking and Finance* (Ottawa: Queen's Printer, 1964), p. 298.

10. See Sven W. Arndt, "International Short Term Capital Movements: A Distributed Lag Model of Speculation in Foreign Exchange," *Econometrica*, XXXVI (January, 1968), 61, and Hans R. Stoll, "An Empirical Study of the Forward Exchange Market under Fixed and Flexible Exchange Rate Systems," *Canadian Journal of Economics*, I (February, 1968), 65. One problem in basing speculation on an expected exchange rate derived from distributed past spot rates is that the heavy weight carried by the current spot rate in determining the forward rate suggests great difficulty in untangling speculative supply adjustment processes from other factors influencing the time path of the spot rate.

$$RF = 3.469 - .3150DS + .9222RS + .0003479BMTUS$$
$$\quad (1.64) \qquad (1.82) \qquad (34.85) \qquad\qquad (0.99)$$

$$+ .04242RF_{-1}$$
$$(1.91)$$

$$RSQC = \quad .99$$
$$F(8, 29) = 349.76$$
$$DW = \quad 0.78$$
$$SEE = \quad .1538 \text{ cents.} \quad (3.22)$$

A disadvantage of this type of formulation is that it applies the same lag structure to all variables in the equation. Except for decision and perception lags, it is difficult to understand why present capital flows should respond to interest differentials prevailing n quarters in the past.[11] Zvi Griliches has developed a simple test to discover whether the apparently superior performance of the distributed-lag formulation indicates a more accurate specification of the underlying economic behavior or whether it merely reflects autocorrelation. If RS_{-1} is included in the equation, and its regression coefficient is insignificantly different from the negative product of the coefficients of RS and the lagged dependent variable, it can be concluded that the superior performance of the distributed-lag formulation is spurious.[12] Applying the test to equation 3.22 gives

$$RF = -1.965 - .2534DS + .9708RS + .0002858BMTUS$$
$$\quad (1.05) \qquad (1.98) \qquad (44.85) \qquad\qquad (1.10)$$

$$+ .7053RF_{-1} - .6573RS_{-1}$$
$$(5.42) \qquad\quad (5.14)$$

11. Arndt implicitly makes this assumption by regressing the capital inflow upon its own lagged value. The lagged interest differential is not statistically significant. See Arndt, pp. 64–65.

12. Zvi Griliches, "Distributed Lags: A Survey," *Econometrica,* XXXI (January, 1967), 33–34.

$$RSQC = \quad .99$$
$$F(9, 28) = 576.33$$
$$DW = \quad 1.64$$
$$SEE = \quad .1132 \text{ cents.} \quad (3.23)$$

The negative product of the coefficients of RS and RF_{-1} is $-.6847$. To test whether the coefficient of RS_{-1} differs significantly from this value, we constructed the t-statistic

$$\frac{\beta(RS)(RF_{-1}) - \beta(RS_{-1})}{\delta(RS_{-1})}.$$

Since the calculated value of t is only $.2143$, we cannot reject the null hypothesis of no significant difference between the coefficients. This implies that the performance of equation 3.22 simply reflects autocorrelation.

In the search for omitted variables that might be the cause of the autocorrelated residuals in equation 3.21, we discovered that GNP and $PCMS$ produced a marked improvement in the equation. The level of income is included as a proxy for the confidence factors affecting the forward rate. $PCMS$ is included as a policy variable. An increase in the rate of change of the money supply implies the need for less reliance upon foreign financing and a consequent easing of pressure on the forward relative to the spot price of the dollar. Both variables are therefore expected to have positive signs. The result is

$$RF = 4.307 - .6288DS + .9483RS + .0002401BMTUS$$
$$\quad (2.85) \quad (3.97) \quad (64.16) \quad (0.90)$$
$$\quad + .0001069GNP + .03673PCMS$$
$$\quad (5.18) \quad (2.31)$$
$$\quad + .1815Q_1 - .1368Q_3$$
$$\quad (2.97) \quad (2.32)$$

133

$$
\begin{aligned}
RSQC &= \quad .99 \\
F(9, 28) &= 588.26 \\
DW &= \quad 1.21 \\
SEE &= \quad .1120 \text{ cents.}
\end{aligned}
\quad (3.24)
$$

With the exception of the trade balance,[13] all variables are significant. The interest differential and the spot rate are increased in significance and autocorrelation has been considerably reduced. If a distributed-lag formulation gives superior performance solely because of autocorrelation, the reduction in severity of this problem in equation 3.24 implies that the lagged dependent variable will add nothing to the overall explanation. This is, in fact, what is discovered. The t-value for the coefficient of RF_{-1} is only .35. When RS_{-1} is also included, the difference between its coefficient ($-.3965$) and the negative product of the coefficients of RS and RF_{-1} ($-.4055$) is not statistically significant.

Although exchange rates failed to show any significant trend over the period, we attempted to eliminate any possibility of spurious correlation by subtracting the spot rate from both sides of the equation. The explanation of the forward premium is:

13. As indicated previously, the role of $BMTUS$ is to pick up the effects on the forward rate of transactions whose primary purpose is other than to speculate on foreign exchange or to pursue a favorable interest-rate differential. The variable fails consistently to show up with a significant coefficient, although the sign is as predicted. We also experimented with the use of the trade balance in first-differenced form, basing this formulation on some of the ideas presented in Bent Hansen, *Foreign Trade Credits and Exchange Reserves,* Contributions to Economic Analysis, no. 23 (Amsterdam: North-Holland Publishing Co., 1961), chap. iii. If we assume that the proportion of imports and exports financed by trade credit of given maturity is equal and constant, a constant nonzero trade balance will be associated with a constant net stock and no net flow of trade credit. A shift in the trade balance to a new level then implies a one-shot flow of credit to adjust to the new stock level. Experiments with first-differenced variables continued to yield insignificant regression coefficients, and in some cases the coefficients were incorrectly signed.

$$FP = -.9492 - .7469DS + .0001550BMTUS$$
$$(5.14) \quad (4.11) \quad\quad (0.49)$$
$$+ .00009630GNP + .04311PCMS$$
$$(4.02) \quad\quad (2.33)$$
$$+ .2110Q_1 - .1406Q_3$$
$$(2.98) \quad (2.03)$$

$$RSQC = .54$$
$$F(8, 29) = 4.30$$
$$DW = 0.85$$
$$SEE = .1314 \text{ cents.} \quad (3.25)$$

The mean value of FP is equal to $-.2174$ cents.

The interest-differential becomes most significant when the forward premium is explained, but autocorrelation also becomes more serious. On the other hand, autocorrelated residuals do not lead to bias in the estimated regression coefficients, and the good performance of equation 3.24 suggests that a nonspurious relation does exist between the interest differential and the forward premium.[14] Since our short-term capital equations employ the forward premium rather than the spot and forward rates jointly, we will use equation 3.25 to take into

14. Using various instrumental-variables estimation techniques, Helliwell shows that the forward premium is related most strongly to the differential on finance paper and implies almost exact interest parity. Our coefficient for the interest-rate differential is less than unity (significantly different at the 10-percent level but not at the 5-percent level), and this may reflect the fact that the most common instrument for interest-arbitrage transactions is commercial paper. Nevertheless, our primary interest lies in the problem of interest-rate independence, and the Treasury bill rate is the prime policy variable which the Bank of Canada and the U.S. Federal Reserve Board attempt to manipulate when they conduct short-term interest-rate policies. Although TSLS experiments reported upon later in this chapter failed to eliminate the bias in our estimate (if, indeed, it is biased), we do allow for the possibility of perfect interest arbitrage in our estimates of interest-rate independence. See John Helliwell, "A Structural Model of the Foreign Exchange Market" *Canadian Journal of Economics,* II (February, 1969), 100.

account the fact that the forward premium plays a part in accommodation of the money and exchange markets to changes in the rate of net capital inflows.

An indirect estimate of the response of the forward premium to changes in the net capital inflow is provided by the quotient

$$\frac{\partial FP/\partial DS}{\partial STK/\partial DS} = -.001241.$$

Thus, while an increase in the forward premium by one cent tends to increase the capital inflow by $314.5 million, the resulting inflow simultaneously reduces the forward premium by $(314.5)(.001241) = .3902$ cents. In other words, 39.02 percent of exogenous changes in the forward premium are eliminated by the induced capital movement.

This information can be substituted into the relations developed above to revise the indirect estimate of $\partial CS/\partial STK$. Because 39.02 percent of any change in the forward premium is eliminated by the resulting change in net capital inflow, an unbiased estimate of $\partial STK/\partial FP$ is obtained by revising the estimated regression coefficient upward from 314.5 to 314.5/ .6098 = 515.7. This reduces our indirect estimate of $\partial CS/ \partial STK = -.4691/515.7 = -.0009096$, and from this we can conclude that $(602)(.0009096)$ or 54.76 percent of any exogenous change in the Canadian interest rate will be eliminated by the resulting change in capital flow.

If we assume, as a limiting case, that interest-arbitrage transactions proceed to the point where interest parity is achieved, so that the forward market is always in equilibrium, then

$$RF = RS\left[\frac{1 + USS/100}{1 + CS/100}\right]$$

and

136

$$FP = -RS\left[\frac{CS - USS}{100 + CS}\right].$$

Substitution of this expression into the short-term capital equation gives us

$$STK = \left[602 - 314.5\frac{RS}{100 + CS}\right](CS - USS)$$
$$- .4734BMTUS - 35.12CRS.$$

The partial derivative, $\partial STK/\partial CS$, is now a complex function of RS, CS and USS; as expected from the criterion for profitable interest arbitrage, it is larger the greater the interest differential and the lower the price of Canadian currency. If these variables assume their mean values, then

$$\frac{\partial STK}{\partial CS} = 602 - \left[\frac{314.5RS}{(100 + CS)^2}\right](100 + USS) = 281.6.$$

The assumption that the forward market is in continuous equilibrium implies that $(281.6)(.001492)$, or 42.01 percent, of independent variations in Canadian interest rates are eliminated by the induced change in net capital flows. The reduction in size of the effective interest-rate coefficient implies that 53.22 percent of the adjustment process is borne by the forward market.

In summary, the calculations above indicate that the two-way relation between interest rates and capital flows removed something like 42 to 90 percent of independent variations in the Canadian interest rate during Canada's experience with a floating exchange rate. The larger estimate is clearly a maximum, since it assumes that capital flows, exogenous or endogenous, have no effect whatsoever upon the relationship between the spot and forward exchange rates. Hence, there is no feedback to the capital flow via this route, and the inflow continues until eliminated or practically eliminated by an adverse shift in the interest differential. The lower estimate may be fairly regarded as a minimum, as it assumes continuous equilibrium of the forward market in response to the process of covered interest arbitrage. Our statistical evidence on the behavior of the forward premium and the forward rate suggests that the latter was not quite this responsive to disturbances in the Canadian interest rate. It typically absorbed enough of the adjustment to leave the reduction in variability of Canadian interest rates from those abroad near the lower end of our range, at roughly 55 percent. In other words, the efficiency of interest-rate policy directed at the short end of the market was reduced to about 45 percent of what it would have been in the absence of endogenous capital flows.

Other Ordinary Least-Squares Estimates

Similar experiments, substituting the cost of forward cover (*CFC*) for the forward premium, were also conducted. As noted in Chapter 2, the former variable is almost perfectly but inversely correlated with the latter; it is slightly easier to work with because it is expressed in percent rather than cents and thus becomes directly comparable to the interest-rate differential. Equations employing or explaining *CFC* differ only insignificantly from those involving *FP,* except for the reversal of signs; one that explained *CFC,* specified exactly as 3.25, was used to calculate limits on the damping of interest-rate disturbances by short-term capital flows. Corresponding to the minimum, best-guess, and maximum estimates of 42, 55, and 90 percent using *FP,* we secured 41, 55, and 89 percent using *CFC.*

Although the interest-sensitivity of capital flows to Canada increases when they are related to both the Canada-United States and the Canada-United Kingdom differentials, the sensi-

138

tivity of the Canadian interest rate to changes in the rate of capital inflow is reduced. Equation 2.20 was

$$STK = 556DS + 88\,(CS - UKS) + 375.14FP \\ - .5307BMTUS - 38.59CRS.$$

When this equation is the basis of our calculations, the indirect estimate of $\partial CS/\partial STK$ falls to $-.001250$, implying that at most only $(644)(.001250)$, or 80.53 percent of independent variations in the interest-rate differential are eliminated by the resulting capital flow. When the capital flow is permitted to feed back into the forward premium, the damping effect of capital flows upon the interest rate alone is reduced to 45.49 percent. The assumption that the forward market is in continuous equilibrium (the forward exchange rate is equal to its interest parity) further reduces, to 32.74 percent, our estimate of the reduction in variability of the Canadian interest rate due to capital flows. These somewhat larger estimates of interest-rate independence arise from the fact that the proportion of capital flows covered in the forward market increases when the Canadian-United Kingdom interest-rate differential is included in the equation.

In summary, using both sets of estimates, it is reasonable to conclude that during Canada's experience with a floating exchange rate, interest-elastic capital flows cut roughly in half the effectiveness of interest-rate policy directed at the short end of the market.

We also experimented with determining the interest-rate differential itself and found that the effect of capital flows upon the differential is slightly greater than their effect upon the Canadian interest rate alone. This may mean that the United States interest rate also plays a part in the process of adjusting to international capital movements; but if it does, its role is very limited in view of the negligible divergence in the two sets of estimates. On the other hand, the divergence may be merely a statistical artifact, because the U.S. interest rate was included in our equation explaining the Canadian rate level. Our best equation explaining the differential is specified the same as that which explains the Canadian rate alone, except for deletion of the U.S. rate as an explanatory variable. The result is:

$$DS = -.7897 + .5044CFC + .0001GNP + .006443PCMS$$
$$(5.60) \quad (4.15) \quad (6.32) \quad (0.42)$$
$$+ .1008Q_1 - .1262Q_3$$
$$(1.76) \quad (2.60)$$

$$RSQC = .63$$
$$F(6, 31) = 8.82$$
$$DW = 0.90$$
$$SEE = .1055 \text{ percent.} \quad (3.26)$$

The mean value of DS is equal to .071553 percent per quarter.

This equation is decidedly inferior to the one that explains CS alone. The coefficient of the money-supply variable now appears insignificant and wrongly signed. The other coefficients are, however, in line with our previous results. If STK equation 2.16 is considered, it appears that short-term capital flows reduced the variability of the interest-rate differential by 92.98 percent in the case where the cost of forward cover is assumed to be wholly exogenous. This estimate is reduced to 57.35 percent when the forward discount is permitted to respond to the capital inflow, and to 42.53 percent when it is assumed that interest-arbitrage transactions proceed until the net interest differential is eliminated.

The estimates derived in this section are based on our best equations for the net capital inflow, the interest rate (and interest-rate differential), and the forward premium (and cost of forward cover). Further estimates could be generated, but they would be based upon capital inflow equations estimated in Chapter 2 and rejected there as inferior to those used here. Our results are summarized in Table 3.3.

TABLE 3.3. Percentage loss in the independence of Canadian interest-rate policy, using alternative short-term capital equations and alternative assumptions about adjustment of forward exchange rate

Equation explaining *STK*	Assumption about forward exchange rate		
	FP (*CFC*) is exogenous	*FP* (*CFC*) is endogenous	*FP* (*CFC*) is endogenous and interest parity prevails
2.15	89.79	54.76	42.01
2.16	88.96	54.87	40.71
2.20	80.53	45.49	32.74
2.16[a]	92.98	57.35	42.53

[a] These estimates use the equation explaining the interest-rate differential.

Estimates Using Two-Stage Least Squares

In discussing the preceding calculations, we have indicated various types of simultaneous equation bias in our least-squares regression coefficients. In an attempt to reduce this, we have applied the TSLS estimator to the basic model employed above:

$$STK = f(\widehat{DS}, \widehat{CFC}, BMTUS, CRS)$$
$$DS = g(\widehat{CFC}, GNP, PCMS, Q_1, Q_3)$$
$$CFC = h(\widehat{DS}, GNP, PCMS, Q_1, Q_3).$$

The two-stage least-squares results are:

141

$$STK = -11.42 + 683.1\widehat{DS} - 292.0\widehat{CFC} - .4770BMTUS$$
$$\quad (0.30) \quad\quad (6.22) \quad\quad\quad (2.06) \quad\quad\quad\quad (3.54)$$
$$- 35.57CRS$$
$$(3.31)$$

$$SEE = \$70.58 \text{ million} \quad (3.27)$$

$$DS = -.7745 + .4785\widehat{CFC} + .00009907GNP$$
$$\quad (1.33) \quad\quad (0.50) \quad\quad\quad (2.59)$$
$$+ .004772PCMS + .09615Q_1 - .1235Q_3$$
$$(0.75) \quad\quad\quad (0.53) \quad\quad (1.14)$$

$$SEE = .1055 \text{ percent} \quad (3.28)$$

$$CFC = 1.215 + 1.271\widehat{DS} - .0001402GNP - .03138PCMS$$
$$\quad (1.12) \quad\quad (0.59) \quad\quad\quad (0.79) \quad\quad\quad\quad (0.53)$$
$$- .1932Q_1 + .1967Q_3$$
$$(2.55) \quad\quad (1.13)$$

$$SEE = .1450 \text{ percent} \quad (3.29)$$

These results indicate that the regression coefficients generated by the two estimators are not substantially different. As should be expected the TSLS estimate of the interest sensitivity of short-term capital flows is larger than the OLS estimate; but sensitivity to the percentage forward discount (CFC) is numerically smaller, contrary to expectation. The explanation of the interest-differential is virtually unaltered, but GNP alone remains significant. The coefficient of the interest-differential in the equation explaining CFC is almost twice as large when the TSLS estimator is used, but the variable lacks significance. Nevertheless, if our calculations are based upon these equations, it appears that 51.12 percent of independent variations in the Canadian interest rate were removed by the resulting induced change in capital inflow. Calculations based upon the

OLS estimates of the same equations indicate that 54.87 percent of independent interest-rate variations were eliminated.

A direct estimate of $\partial DS/\partial STK$ is provided by the model

$$STK = f(\widehat{DS}, \widehat{CFC}, BMTUS, CRS, Q_1, Q_3)$$
$$DS = g(\widehat{STK}, GNP, PCMS, BMTUS, Q_1, Q_3)$$
$$CFC = h(\widehat{STK}, GNP, PCMS, BMTUS, Q_1, Q_3),$$

where $BMTUS$ is included in the equation explaining the interest differential solely as an aid to identification. Theoretically, this model is exactly identified. The results for STK and DS are:

$$STK = 674.2\widehat{DS} - 299.9\widehat{CFC} - .4032BMTUS - 31.08CRS$$
$$ (6.26) \qquad (2.16) \qquad\quad (2.84) \qquad\qquad (2.88)$$

$$SEE = \$68.89 \text{ million} \quad (3.30)$$

$$DS = -.5916 - .0002259\widehat{STK} + .00009783GNP$$
$$ (1.46) \qquad (0.34) \qquad\qquad (1.81)$$

$$- .02539PCMS + .00002332BMTUS$$
$$(1.38) \qquad\qquad (0.64)$$

$$SEE = .1426 \text{ percent.} \quad (3.31)$$

Insignificant intercepts and seasonal dummies have been ignored, as has the equation explaining CFC that fails to identify correctly the relation between CFC and STK. Equations 3.30 and 3.31 imply that the reduction in variability of the differential due to interest-elastic capital flows is only 15.23 percent, and this hardly seems plausible in the light of previous calculations.

Our best explanation for STK was yielded by the overidentified model

$$STK = f(\widehat{DS}, \widehat{CFC}, BMTUS, CRS, Q_1, Q_3)$$
$$DS = g(\widehat{CFC}, GNP, PCMS, ATM, Q_1, Q_3)$$
$$CFC = h(\widehat{DS}, GNP, PCMS, BMTUS, Q_1, Q_3).$$

Again we fail to explain the interest differential and the cost of forward cover when two-stage least-squares is used. The only significant variable affecting the differential is *GNP*, and none of the explanatory variables for *CFC* are significant. But some of the downward bias in the coefficients of *DS* and *CFC* in the capital inflow equation has been removed, and this is the result that should ideally be obtained; the equation is

$$STK = 38.85 + 659.0\widehat{DS} - 379.4\widehat{CFC} - .4086BMTUS$$
$$\quad\quad (1.02) \quad\;\; (6.26) \quad\quad\; (3.20) \quad\quad\quad\; (2.93)$$
$$\quad\quad - 28.52CRS - 25.99Q_1 - 53.07Q_3$$
$$\quad\quad\;\;\; (2.74) \quad\quad\; (0.97) \quad\;\; (1.76)$$

$$SEE = \$67.87 \text{ million.} \quad (3.32)$$

If we use the information contained in this equation in conjunction with that generated by the OLS estimates of *CFC* and *DS*, it appears that 51.99 percent of independent variations in the interest differential were eliminated by induced capital flows.

A brief recapitulation of the main findings of this chapter is in order. Depending upon the long-term interest rate that we use, it appears that at least 10–20 percent of any exogenous or policy-induced variation in the Canadian rate will be eliminated by the change in capital flow caused by the movement of the interest rate. The use of two-stage least-squares to better sort out the demand and supply relationships increases this range to 31–46 percent. Looking at the connection between Canadian and United States interest rates, our estimates indicate that at least 10–30 percent of any change in the U.S. rate will be passed on to Canada through induced variations in the rate of capital flow. This range of estimates is increased to 33–64 percent when the TSLS estimator is employed, and up to 80 percent when expectational influences are allowed for.

A slightly greater loss in the independence of short-term interest-rate policy is implied by our calculations. As an outside estimate, we found that up to 90 percent of policy-induced variations in the short-term rate can be eliminated by induced capital flows; but when the impact of capital flows upon the relation between spot and forward exchange rates is allowed for, the range of estimates is reduced to 46–57 percent. If we assume, further, that interest parity holds more or less continuously, the implied loss in interest-rate independence is reduced to only 33–43 percent.[15] Our TSLS estimates did not alter these conclusions to any substantial degree. It can thus be concluded that interest-rate policy directed at the long-term end of the market enjoyed a slightly greater degree of success than policies conducted in "bills only."

15. During the 1950's and early 1960's a decrease was noted in the frequency with which the Canadian forward rate departed from the value that would correspond to interest-arbitrage parity. This would imply an increasing trend in the effectiveness of monetary policy through the short-term interest rate.

4 Direct Investment and Capital Formation

Foreign direct investment provides resources and inducements for expanding gross domestic capital formation in Canada. In this chapter, a statistical model to isolate this critical link between capital flows and domestic expenditure is developed. We consider theories of the determinants of capital formation and construct and test an investment model for Canada which takes account of direct investment. The model is tested first on the economy as a whole, then it is applied separately to periods of prosperity and recession and to individual sectors of the economy.

A recurring complaint heard among Canadian critics of United States direct investment has been that U.S. companies do what Canadians would do if left alone; they argue, or imply, that American capital formation in Canada is merely a substitute for Canadian investment and that it provides no net addition to the Canadian capital stock.

Such an offset can occur in several ways. First, if we abstract from their effects on domestic expenditure, the investment inflows cause a flexible exchange rate to appreciate and hence will have a deflationary impact. Secondly, any outlay for capital formation, even under conditions of less than full employment, may cause scarcities of some resources needed for other investments and in that way delay, reduce, or exclude those investments. For example, bottlenecks may occur in the construction industry or in the building materials or machinery industries. Finally, foreign-financed investments may have various effects on the investment plans of other firms in the same industry, or in other industries from which the firm buys or to which it sells. These relations may be very powerful, because an individual firm's capacity and output levels affect many others tied to it in the marketplace. Such linkages warrant further consideration.

Foreign investment may be complementary with as well as substitutable for domestic investment, both within and among different industries. The argument that direct investment will substitute for home investment in the same industry assumes that a given amount of investment is waiting to be performed in the industry and that Canadian and United States companies are both able to perform it. Thus, U.S. investment may simply replace Canadian. This argument ignores the widely recognized concomitants of foreign investment — access to foreign skills, trained personnel and technology. Also, much direct United States investment in Canada is for very large projects that may well be beyond the capacity of Canadian companies to undertake. Even where large Canadian companies exist and do have the necessary resources, they may be less likely to undertake a project than would a U.S. firm which enjoys larger sources of internal liquidity relative to the project's capital cost. Furthermore, if the U.S. investment is intended to serve as a source of supply for the parent company, the risks facing a Canadian company contemplating the same investment are greater and the probability of its making the investment lower.

Interindustry substitution on a large scale is not very likely;

147

only if the good produced as a result of foreign direct investment is a strong substitute in final consumption, or as a factor input, will another industry's investment be adversely affected. And it is very possible that strong complementarity effects exist: foreign direct investment may cause the demand for domestic firms' outputs to rise and thereby stimulate investment. In Canada, foreign investment in petroleum leading to pipeline construction is an example. If the foreign investment is in a producer's good, it may stimulate the industries using that input. The "pecuniary external economies" [1] made familiar in development economics are relevant here — complementarities abound in such a field. The investment that U.S. companies undertake in Canada which would not have occurred otherwise gives rise to further domestic investment. Such complementary investment may be one of the most important effects of United States direct investment.

The main intention of this chapter is not to trace the interrelations stemming from foreign direct investment, but only to construct a simple single-equation aggregate model that will indicate the association between aggregate foreign direct investment and total domestic capital formation. In order to do this, a model of investment behavior is required that identifies and distinguishes the domestically financed component of capital formation.

THEORIES OF INVESTMENT BEHAVIOR

A large and contentious literature has developed on the subject of investment behavior. The two main hypotheses that have emerged may be called the "acceleration theory" and the

1. One treatment of this concept can be found in Tibor Scitovsky, "Two Concepts of External Economies," *Journal of Political Economy*, LIII (April 1954), 143–151.

"residual funds theory." Recently some writers, especially Dale Jorgenson,[2] have tried to restate and test investment theory, casting it in a neoclassical model. But the acceleration and residual funds approaches, although lacking the theoretical precision of the neoclassical analysis, offer empirical generalizations readily extendable into a model that is particularly useful for our purposes.

The acceleration principle states that the demand for capital goods is given by the relation of output to capacity. Earlier and simpler versions of the theory identified capacity needs with changes in output. In more recent work, a capacity-output variable is employed to allow for the influence of demand, as well as output, on investment. In its most extreme form the acceleration theory ignores the role of finance. It is assumed that if firms are bent on investing, finance will be forthcoming, either internally or externally, and that either the cost of funds is of no consequence or the supply schedule is infinitely elastic.

Residual funds theorists accept the role of the capacity-output variable in explaining the demand for capital, but argue that the supply of funds to the firm is also a major determinant of investment behavior. This approach is found in the writings of Meyer, Kuh, Glauber, and Duesenberry,[3] who argue that after certain prior claims on funds — including dividend payments — are satisfied, a firm will devote the remaining funds to capital projects, the demand for which could be

2. Dale W. Jorgenson, "Anticipations and Investment Behavior," *Brookings Quarterly Econometric Model of the United States,* ed. J. S. Duesenberry *et al.* (Chicago: Rand McNally, 1965).

3. The relevant writings are: John R. Meyer and Edwin Kuh, *The Investment Decision* (Cambridge, Mass.: Harvard University Press, 1957); John R. Meyer and Robert Glauber, *Investment Decisions, Economic Forecasting and Public Policy* (Boston: Division of Research, Graduate School of Business Administration, Harvard University, 1964); Edwin Kuh and John R. Meyer, "Investment, Liquidity and Monetary Policy" in Commission on Money and Credit, *Impacts of Monetary Policy* (Englewood Cliffs, N.J.: Prentice-Hall, 1963); James S. Duesenberry, *Business Cycles and Economic Growth* (New York: McGraw-Hill, 1958).

explained in terms of the acceleration principle taken in a long-run context. In this model the investment demand schedule of the firm, reflecting the capacity-output relation, together with the supply of funds schedule, determines the level of investment. It is also assumed that the firm faces a rising supply price of funds as it undertakes increasing amounts of investment, particularly after switching from internal to external sources of finance. This model is used in our work.

A satisfactory investment model should specify not only the variables determining capital formation, but also the time pattern of the investment process. Two lags are discernible: first, in Locke Anderson's terminology,[4] a "decision lag" between the change in value(s) of the variable(s) determining the investment decision and the time when a decision is made to invest. In addition, there is a lag between the investment decision and the actual expenditure of funds, the expenditure lag. The expenditure lag itself can be subdivided into several stages: the letting out of contracts, issuing of orders, and so forth.[5]

Given the lags in the process, it is important to know their length and nature — whether they are simple or distributed over time and, if the latter, how they are distributed. A simple lag of the form $Y = f(X_{t-a})$ assumes that the effect of an event X has all its influence on Y in period a after time t. A distributed lag assigns the effect of a change in X over several periods, with a different weight usually assigned to each time period. From theoretical reasoning, as well as available empirical evidence, it is fairly clear that distributed lags provide a better description than do simple lags of the time pattern of the investment process, at least when quarterly data are used.

4. W. H. Locke Anderson, *Corporate Finance and Fixed Investment* (Boston: Division of Research, Graduate School of Business Administration, Harvard University, 1964).
5. Jorgenson, "Anticipations," pp. 38–39.

Considerable work has been done recently on distributed lags, and a number of fairly sophisticated forms of distributed-lag functions have been developed.[6] The results of their statistical application are often impressive. However, when a wide range of theoretical investment models employing distributed lags do well statistically, it is hard to avoid the suspicion that some part of the success stems from use of the distributed lags, not from the underlying model. These models often involve using earlier values of the dependent variables as explanatory variables. Given the autocorrelated nature of time series, the possibility of obtaining high spurious correlations is much increased.

In addition, there is an important theoretical objection to the use of distributed-lag functions. The explanatory variables may be thought to enter the equations with different lags. The problem is illustrated by using a Koyck lag: let Y_t be the dependent variable, X_t and Z_t the independent variables, and assume that X_t enters with a lag and Z_t without a lag. We might have an equation such as

$$Y_t = a_0 X_t + a_1 X_{t-1} + \cdots + a_n X_n + t Z_t + u_t \quad (4.1)$$

Koyck then assumes that the a's decline geometrically — by the factor k where k is less than 1. Rewrite 4.1:

$$Y_{t+1} = a X_{t+1} + a k X_t + a k^2 X_{t-1} + \cdots + b Z_{t+1} + u_{t+1} \quad (4.2)$$

and

6. For example, see *ibid.;* also Shirley Almon, "The Distributed Lag Between Capital Appropriations and Expenditures," *Econometrica,* XXXIII (January, 1965), 178–196; Frank de Leeuw, "The Demand for Capital Goods by Manufacturers: A Study of Quarterly Time Series," *Econometrica,* XXX (July, 1962), 407–423; John Kareken and Robert Solow, "Lags in Monetary Policy: A Summary," in Commission on Money and Credit, *Stabilization Policies* (Englewood Cliffs, N.J.: Prentice-Hall, 1963); L. M. Koyck, *Distributed Lags and Investment Analysis* (Amsterdam: North-Holland Publishing Co., 1954).

$$kY_t = \qquad akX_t + ak^2X_{t-1} + \cdots + bkZ_t + u_t.$$

Then

$$Y_{t+1} - kY_t = aX_{t+1} + bZ_{t+1} - bkZ_t + (u_{t+1} - ku_t)$$

or

$$Y_{t+1} = kY_t + aX_{t+1} + bZ_{t+1} - bkZ_t + (u_{t+1} - ku_t) \quad (4.3)$$

In Koyck's model there is no problem because $Z = 0$. But when a second variable is assumed as entering with a different lag (if all variables enter with the same lag there is no difficulty), we find that it has two different coefficients. The bkZ_t is subtracted to remove the lagged influence it has if it is left embodied in the kY_t. If we went ahead and estimated equation 4.3, we would arrive at estimates of k and b (the coefficient of Z_{t+1}) that would be inconsistent with the estimate of bk. An iterative process might arrive at consistent values of b and k.

Rather than deal with this and other problems in distributed-lag formulations, we shall use much less sophisticated lag models — equally weighted moving averages — that allow experimentation with the lag structure. As will become clear shortly, we wish to show that direct investment has an independent influence on capital formation. Yet, it is not a variable controlling the investment decision in the same way as do conditions in the domestic economy; therefore, its relation to capital formation may well operate with a different lag structure. By using different lags for direct investment and the other independent variables, our ability to isolate the association between capital formation and direct investment is increased.

The question of specific statistical content of the independent variables in the investment model can be considered now. In a simple accelerator model, changes in output can be represented by changes in sales deflated by a price index. The chief virtue of the sales figure is its availability and straightforward meaning. The more realistic capacity-output variables are difficult to construct. Output series can sometimes be secured, but reliable capital stock figures are, unfortunately, not available. A proxy for the capacity-output variable is often used: for example, the past peak of an industrial production series can be taken as indicating capacity output and deviations from this output as an index of pressure on capacity.[7]

Fewer difficulties attend the construction of flow-of-fund variables. The main components are profits (before or after taxes), undistributed profits, and depreciation allowances. The series should measure liquid assets remaining after inflexible prior claims have been satisfied. Profits after taxes, rather than before, are generally included. Depreciation allowances are really a part of the funds available for gross investment and should also be included; moreover, since recorded depreciation costs reflect accounting practices and tax considerations, a truer measure of business cash flows is provided by profits plus depreciation. Because it can be strongly argued that dividend distributions also comprise a prior claim on business funds,[8] undistributed profits, rather than simply profits after taxes, should be included in the flow-of-funds variable. Meyer and Glauber tend to obtain best results with undistributed profits plus depreciation, from among the possibilities given here. The liquidity figure may also be deflated if it is used to explain real investment.

CONSTRUCTING AN INVESTMENT MODEL

The question with which this discussion began was one of the association between United States direct investment and

7. For a discussion of the shortcomings of this and other capacity measures, see A. Phillips, "An Appraisal of Measures of Capacity," *American Economic Review,* LIII (May, 1963), 275–292.

8. John Lintner, "Distribution of Incomes of Corporations Among Dividends, Retained Earnings and Taxes," *American Economic Review,* XLVI (May, 1956), 97–113.

Canadian capital formation. The ideal model provides a measure of the marginal contribution, positive or negative, of direct investment to domestic capital formation. To achieve this, we shall reverse the usual regression equation[9] in which direct investment is *explained* by Canadian capital formation and use direct investment as the explanatory variable.

For purposes of exposition, assume that there is no direct investment in Canada. Then a model can be constructed that explains Canadian capital formation along the lines of the investment theory outlined above. Capital formation is a function of some combination of accelerator and financial variables. It is not our concern to know what "really" explains investment — in terms of a previously specified model — as long as our equation as a whole gives a good explanation. The accelerator and financial variables should tell what Canadian businesses would invest, in terms of the economic variables relevant to their decisions. If there remained a significant residual in the regression equation that could be explained by direct investment inflows, one could argue that these inflows were a net addition to Canadian capital formation. This two-stage process can be collapsed into one equation: $I = f(A,F,D)$, where I = Canadian capital formation, A = accelerator or capacity pressure, F = flow of funds, D = United States direct investment in Canada. A positive and significant coefficient for D would indicate the contribution of direct investment to domestic capital formation.

The argument that direct investment has not contributed to capital formation employs two prongs: first, that this financial flow often does not lead to the creation of physical capital by the United States subsidiary — in other words, that there is not even an initial contribution to capital formation; second,

---

9. Lawrence H. Officer, *An Econometric Model of Canada under the Fluctuating Exchange Rate* (Cambridge, Mass.: Harvard University Press, 1968), pp. 73–75.

that offsets to the initial rise in capital formation occur elsewhere in the host economy. If the regression coefficient for direct investment is equal to one, this argument is, on balance, met: either a dollar of direct investment leads to a dollar of capital formation with no leakage into simple liquidity accumulation by U.S. or other companies, or any shortfall is offset by external effects on other investors that are positive on balance. Actually, no specific value for the partial effect of variations in direct investment, with everything else held constant, can be predicted theoretically. But we shall regard strong, systematic relationships with coefficients "close to" one (or greater than one) as an indication that some of the impact of direct investment on capital formation has been captured.

Before proceeding further with discussion of the investment equation, it is worth noting the omission of interest-rate variables from that equation. It is true that the earlier view of rate of interest as having virtually no effect on investment has recently been modified; however, in an equation in which we are trying to capture the main domestic determinants of Canadian investment in order to isolate the contribution of direct investment, there seemed little reason to include what still appears to be a weak influence on capital formation for the period in question. R. Rhomberg and Thomas A. Wilson have found that the interest rate has some effect on Canadian capital formation;[10] Johnson and Winder, on the other hand, report no success at all with the interest rate in their investment equations and also raise several strong objections to Rhomberg's results.[11] They point out that the interest-rate series he

10. R. Rhomberg, "A Model of the Canadian Economy under Fixed and Fluctuating Exchange Rates," *Journal of Political Economy*, LXXII (February, 1964), 1–31; Thomas A. Wilson, *Capital Investment and the Cost of Capital: A Dynamic Analysis,* Studies of the Royal Commission on Taxation, no. 30 (Ottawa: Queen's Printer, 1967), pp. 76–79.
11. Harry G. Johnson and John W. L. Winder, *Lags in the Effect of Monetary Policy in Canada* (Ottawa: Queen's Printer, 1962), pp. 122–125.

employs moves differently from the typical Canadian long-term rates and that the lags he uses do not seem plausible.

Further discussion of our investment equation will be facilitated by writing it in linear form, as:

$$I = aA + fF + dD + u \tag{4.4}$$

In order for d to be interpreted as the net additional contribution to capital formation of direct investment, certain conditions must be satisfied: D must not be closely influenced by A or F if it is to represent an additional influence on capital formation; the variables A and F must act on I more strongly than on D or act with a different lag. This means that we must consider the sizes of correlations among the independent variables and the lag structure with which they affect the dependent variable.

There is another way to deal with the problem of identifying the effect of direct investment. We can construct an alternative model in which the residuals from the equation

$$I = a'A + f'F + u' \tag{4.5}$$

are regressed upon D. If the predetermined variables of equation 4.4 were linearly independent, then the coefficient of D in the residual equation (d') should equal d. In addition, a' and f' would be equal to a and f respectively. Furthermore, the constant term of equation 4.4 would equal the sum of the constant terms of 4.5 and the residual equation. This last point can be seen by writing the residual equation as

$$u' = c'' + d'D + u'' \tag{4.6}$$

and letting c and c' represent the constant terms for equations 4.4 and 4.5. Then, substituting 4.6 into 4.5, the latter can be rewritten with the constant term:

$$I = c' + c'' + a'A + f'F + d'D + u''$$

Since the coefficients of the independent variables in this equation are the same as in 4.4, it follows that $c = c' + c''$. Our assumption of low collinearity between D and the other two independent variables can be checked by comparing our results with those predicted on the assumption of linear independence.

So far we have been considering the possibility that A and F may influence D as well as gross capital formation in Canada. Another possibility is that D may represent the influence of the United States export market (or other external markets) on Canadian investment. This component of investment could just as well be carried out by Canadian as U.S.-owned firms. Then d would not represent a net contribution of foreign investment to capital formation because it could still be operating to displace the efforts of Canadian-owned firms. In fact, however, most sales by U.S.-controlled companies go to the Canadian market.[12] Moreover, even those investments destined to produce goods for the United States market may be more likely to be undertaken by a U.S. subsidiary supplying its parent company than by an independent Canadian enterprise.

Another noteworthy feature of this model is that, for an economy like Canada's, the theory of investment may have less explanatory power than in a more highly industrialized country. Specifically, when investment is directed toward import substitution, as in the cases of petroleum and automobiles, past changes in output or even in the present capacity-output relation may not be very important. Furthermore, when investment serves to exploit newly discovered natural resources — as in the cases of petroleum and some mineral ores — conventional investment theory, which assumes an established indus-

12. See R. Lubitz, "United States Direct Investment in Canada and Canadian Capital Formation, 1950–1962," unpub. diss., (Harvard University, 1966), p. 24.

try producing for a steadily growing market, may be less useful. Much of the "development" type investment in Canada is financed by outside capital, so direct investment may reflect the behavior of investment in new fields, while the other independent variables may control its pattern in established Canadian industries.

Estimation of the investment equation presents some of the familiar problems of econometrics. Before dealing with specific problems of data, some conceptual difficulties will be considered. The major difficulty that econometricians will immediately note is the use of a single equation to deal with a simultaneous world. Investment not only depends upon, for example, output and profits, but also helps determine them; the estimated coefficients are therefore biased. While not denying the seriousness of the charge, several things may be said to suggest that this point is less important than it may at first appear to be. First, in most forms of the equation used, the independent variables are lagged and therefore predetermined. The simultaneity problem is not completely removed in this case, since the investment variable is likely to be autocorrelated, and its earlier values will both influence the predetermined variables and be correlated with the current value of the endogenous variable. Second, the sign and the "reasonableness" of size of the coefficients may enable us to check on the presence of simultaneity — although it is possible, if the coefficient of determination ($RSQC$) is high, to have both "reasonable" coefficients and simultaneity. Finally, our primary aim is to isolate the capital formation-direct investment relation, and this can be done even though simultaneity is present in the rest of the equation. It is true that capital formation and direct investment are also mutually related because direct investment is made to finance capital formation. But the assumption we make is only that such a relationship is present

158

and strong; for our purposes the direction of causation is not vital.

Two more familiar problems in time-series analysis are autocorrelation and collinearity among the independent variables. The model will be tested using quarterly time series, which almost invariably means that autocorrelation is present. We have avoided trying to improve the Durbin-Watson statistic by such mechanical devices as first-differencing. In interpreting our results, it is important to remember that the variances are understated because of autocorrelation. The multicollinearity problem was usually not serious because the independent variables are so constructed that collinearity among them is unlikely. The alternative residuals model provides another check on the seriousness of the problem of multicollinearity.

The interpretation of d requires caution. The coefficient of direct investment will reflect (1) what United States companies do, (2) what Canadians do in response to U.S. investment, and (3) statistical (but not economically relevant) covariation between total capital formation and direct investment. There is a danger that omitted influences and the consequences of mis-specification will show up in the direct investment term — that d may simply be a proxy for these other influences. Fortunately, because direct investment originates outside the Canadian economy, it is less likely to play the role of a proxy variable.

STATISTICAL SERIES AND THEIR DEFICIENCIES

The data which are currently available for Canadian capital formation do not permit an exact test of the investment model elaborated above. However, inadequacies of the data should not prevent drawing some conclusions based on the model. Quarterly data are employed throughout; to deal with seasonal variations, we use the method of seasonal dummy variables. The capital formation, accelerator, financial, and direct investment variables will be discussed in turn.

There is only one *quarterly* series for capital formation: total gross capital formation subdivided into the usual three categories of residential construction, nonresidential construction, and new machinery and equipment expenditure. These data are not disaggregated into public and private, or into any industrial groupings. Such subdivisions are available on an annual basis only. The capital-formation variable we use therefore includes some public investment expenditures in the form of government-enterprise capital formation. Remaining government investment is included in the national accounts under government expenditure on goods and services, but the investment component is not available separately on a quarterly basis. The quarterly investment series we use, denoted as *IB*, excludes residential construction and combines nonresidential construction and new machinery and equipment expenditure; it is taken directly from the *National Accounts*. Residential construction is excluded because its behavior and determinants are quite different from other forms of capital formation, and because direct investment is of little importance to it. The decision was also made to express capital formation in a real rather than a monetary form. The price deflator used was derived from the seasonally adjusted, currently weighted implicit price deflators used in the GNP series.

Constructing the accelerator variable presented the most difficult statistical problem. At the time of analysis, no satisfactory data on Canadian capital stock were available. The accelerator used in the equations below was, simply, changes in real GNP. Three attempts were made to construct a capacity-output index; the results generally were not considered very satisfactory.[13]

The flow-of-funds variable presented fewer problems. Three reasonably adequate versions were used:

1. The source for profits after taxes and for depreciation allowances is Dominion Bureau of Statistics, *Quarterly Corporation Profits*. The depreciation and profits figures therein cover only incorporated private companies, but these undertake most of the capital formation. The first funds variable is simply the sum of profits after taxes and depreciation — again seasonally unadjusted, and deflated by the capital goods price index. This deflation was done because it was thought that real investment decisions are probably closely related to the real value of corporate funds.

2. The variable more generally used in this work subtracts dividend distributions from profits after taxes; the source for undistributed corporate profits is the *National Accounts*. This second variable, then, is undistributed profits plus depreciation, seasonally unadjusted and in constant dollars.

3. The third variable was constructed as a gamble and will be explained after direct investment is discussed. It required the removal from undistributed profits plus depreciation of certain influences related to foreign-owned companies. This variable gives a more "purely" Canadian funds figure.

The last variable to consider is direct investment. Here the problem is the existence of two data sources — the D.B.S. and the United States Office of Business Economics — which give very different numbers for U.S. direct investment to Canada. The differences, explained elsewhere,[14] generally favor use

13. For details on these variables: see *ibid.*, pp. 76–77, for the variables used and pp. 86–88 for the results obtained.
14. *Ibid.*, pp. 78–82.

of the Canadian series; furthermore, the other variables are based on Canadian data. Consequently, using Canadian data for direct investment improves the chances for consistency in the underlying series used in the analysis.

We have investigated only direct investment from the United States to Canada and ignored other foreign flows. It seemed inappropriate to lump all direct investment together. The direct investment decision is taken on the basis of both domestic and Canadian factors; and the domestic factors for the United States and Europe differ enough so that "all direct investment" could be a very heterogeneous variable. On the other hand, if a separate variable for non-U.S. direct investment were included, the same problems of heterogeneity (within this quantity) would exist; yet there might be sufficient similarity, although not exact correspondence, between U.S. direct investment and non-U.S. direct investment to create serious collinearity problems in the statistical estimation. Furthermore, the United States accounts for a very large share of total foreign investment in Canada, hence the ignored portion of foreign is small. Nonetheless, in interpreting the direct investment coefficient, one should be aware of the possibility that it may have picked up some variation that is more properly attributable to non-U.S. direct investment.

The direct-investment variable then, is the Canadian figure (except when stated otherwise) deflated by the capital goods price index. The deflation was performed for the same reasons as for internal funds. This is a flow to be spent on real investment; even if spent on existing assets, the price deflation would still be necessary. The variable is used both in simple lag form and in the form of moving averages of different time spans.

Another direct investment variable was created as a partial check on the validity of the regression model. This variable is direct investment *plus* retained earnings of foreign companies in Canada; it is used in an equation run with internal funds *less* these same retained earnings as the independent variable. The purpose was to create more homogeneous variables and to show that internal funds and direct investment make different contributions to investment — that United States and Canadian companies behave differently. The series for retained earnings leaves much to be desired. It is available only on an annual basis. To create a quarterly series, we assumed that the quarterly pattern of retained earnings was the same as the quarterly pattern for direct investment in a given year and then distributed the annual retained earnings figure by this quarterly pattern. The other choice was to distribute it by the pattern of Canadian profits, but we wanted to maintain the hypothesis that the decision by United States companies to retain earnings is made on the same grounds as the decision to undertake direct investment. And, since the pattern of retained earnings results more from corporate decisions than from economic forces imposed on the firm, it seemed legitimate to use the direct investment pattern that is also a decision variable.

The regression equations were run on data extending from 1950 to 1962 inclusive. The first date is dictated by the introduction of flexible exchange rates in 1950, the really significant rise in direct investment at this time, and the lack of quarterly direct investment data for earlier years. Often the dependent variables start after 1950–1951 because earlier observations were needed to allow for lags in independent variables. The last date was chosen because the end of the flexible exchange rate was accompanied by sufficient disorder and confusion to render subsequent years incomparable with the earlier ones.

QUANTITATIVE RESULTS

In early discussion of the empirical estimates we shall present the basic equation and its variants; we shall then consider the meaning of the evidence.

The first equation, which displays our basic results, is:

$$IB = 177 + 1.72D_{t-2} + 1.21U_{t-2} + 0.06A_1 + 0.09A_2$$
$$(2.54) \quad (8.07) \quad (1.07) \quad (1.36)$$
$$RSQC = .75$$
$$DW = .98 \quad (4.7)$$

The symbols are defined as follows:

IB: investment in plant and machinery, deflated
D: direct investment, deflated
U: undistributed profits plus depreciation, deflated
A_1: change in GNP, $t - 5$ to $t - 1$
A_2: change in GNP, $t - 9$ to $t - 5$.

The numbers in parentheses refer throughout to the *t-statistic* and *not* to the standard error. Seasonal dummy variables are not shown.

The direct investment variable will be discussed in detail later. Clearly, the coefficient for U is highly significant statistically; this was true of all equations including U. The accelerator performed badly — no surprise in view of our theoretical discussion. In much of our work the variable was run as A; the six-period change in output lagged two periods.

The investment variable IB includes both government and private activity, whereas direct investment and internal funds refer only to private investment. Several regressions were run with investment scaled down to include only "private" investment. As noted previously, only annual breakdowns of private and public capital formation are available, so that the quarterly series for private investment is only an approximation. A typical result for private investment, PIB, follows:

$$PIB = 240 + 1.19D_{t-2} + 0.86U_{t-2} + 0.075A_1 + 0.08A_2$$
$$\qquad\quad (2.49) \qquad (8.18) \qquad (1.72) \qquad (1.68)$$
$$RSQC = .79$$
$$DW = 1.04 \quad (4.8)$$

This equation is directly comparable with equation 4.7. The size of the regression coefficients is reduced as one would expect: PIB/IB is usually slightly above 0.8. However, the coefficients fall by more than the reduction in the dependent variable, and the constant term rises in value. It is possible to explain D's superior performance in equation 4.7 on theoretical grounds by arguing that it is more appropriate to relate D to IB than to PIB — this would mean, presumably, that public investment complements the direct investment-induced capital formation. A statistical explanation is also possible: change in the size of the coefficients and the constant term may occur because multiplication of IB by a near-constant fraction reduces its variance more than proportionately. PIB is "explained" more by the constant term in the regression and less by variation of the independent variables than is the case for IB. Thus, IB has a mean of 1160.8 and a standard deviation of 208.8, whereas PIB has a mean of 953.8 and a standard deviation of 157.0. Comparing the means and standard deviations of PIB and IB,

$$95/116 \simeq .82$$
$$157/208 \simeq .75$$

and we see that the means fall less than the standard deviations. If a quarterly investment series were available, there might be more fluctuation and possibly a smaller reduction in the regression coefficients. In later work IB is used. It

165

should be remembered that the coefficients of U and D may be overstated, which is probably more serious for U than for D: the public investment in IB probably moves similarly to the private investment induced by U so that the coefficient of U is increased.

A third equation is based on United States data on direct investment. For the equation comparable to equation 4.7:

$$IB = 214 + 0.737D + 1.25U + 0.06A_1 + 0.10A_2$$
$$(2.53) \quad (8.44) \quad (1.00) \quad (1.45)$$

$$RSQC = .76$$
$$DW = 1.00 \quad (4.9)$$

The most important difference occurs in the coefficient of D, which is much smaller in the present case. This is a result of the larger size of D in the U.S. figures (a mean of 103.1 with a standard deviation of 56.9, compared to 85.0 and 25.1 for the D.B.S. data). In terms of significance there is little difference.

Another comparison involves the flow-of-funds variable. Several equations used profits after taxes plus depreciation, rather than undistributed profits plus depreciation. The latter was always superior, bearing out the theoretical expectations developed by Meyer, Kuh, and Glauber.

In addition to the use of simple lags, different moving averages were employed for D and U. These averages extended from two to four quarters and assumed influences to operate for as long as six quarters. Different lag structures for D and U were often tested. Without listing all the combinations tried, once can say that most equations were very similar, though some were somewhat more satisfactory than others. Simply trying out different combinations of moving averages is undoubtedly a crude technique. Nevertheless, once the decision to eschew Koyck-Solow distributed lags is made, and given that simple lags are inadequate and that no other lag structure can be assumed to be correct on a priori grounds, something like this makeshift procedure is all that remains.

The use of moving averages improved the equations over the simple lag equations given before.[15] As an example:

$$IB = 377.6 + 1.1861U^* + 2.400D^* + 0.0818A$$
$$(8.8181) \quad (2.8498) \quad (2.1222)$$
$$RSQC = .82$$
$$DW = .76 \quad (4.10)$$

Here U^* is a moving average for periods $t-1$ to $t-4$, while D^* is a moving average for periods $t-2$ and $t-3$. First, note that the coefficient of U, whether in simple lag or averaged lag, displays a very consistent behavior. It is usually between 1.0 and 1.2, with a mode of 1.1, and its t-value is usually around 7 or 8 and sometimes reaches 9. In short, it is stable and highly significant. Even when investment is regressed simply on U and the seasonals, the same general values persist for the regression coefficient and its t-value. It is this strong behavior of undistributed profits plus depreciation — whether as the "true" cause of investment or as a proxy for such a cause — which yields a degree of confidence that a good part of the "Canadian" portion of investment has been explained. On this assumption, the direct investment coefficient represents an additional and separate contribution.

Before discussing direct investment, the accelerator term needs comment. The coefficient for this variable is also fairly stable, taking values around 0.07 to 0.09 and generally having t-values above 2.00, making it significant at the 5-percent level. When one considers all the reasons why the accelerator variable should perform unsatisfactorily, these results are fairly impressive.

15. The change in degrees of freedom from equation 4.7 to equation 4.8 is 42 to 39.

The coefficient of D raises more serious questions, especially as it is the coefficient in which we are particularly interested. Its estimated values are shown in Table 4.1, as calculated in

TABLE 4.1. Values of regression coefficient of capital formation on direct investment for alternative formulations of direct-investment lag

Periods averaged	d	t	Constant term
D_{t-1} (simple lag)	1.1036	(1.6942)	504.4073
D_{t-2} (simple lag)	1.1297	(1.7743)	473.6894
D_{t-3} (simple lag)	1.2331	(2.0290)	495.5424
D^*_1 (1, 2)	2.5108	(2.7364)	367.1174
D^*_2 (2, 3)	2.4000	(2.8498)	377.6212
D^*_3 (3, 4)	1.7148	(1.9528)	454.6436
D^*_4 (1, 2, 3)	3.2889	(3.3702)	313.6730
D^*_5 (2, 3, 4)	2.5849	(2.5887)	367.5594
D^*_6 (1 − 4)	3.3886	(2.8113)	385.9020

different equations run with A and the same U^* (moving average for $t - 4$ to $t - 1$). For simple lags the coefficient is around unity, for two-period averages about two, and for three-period averages three. There is no clear way of determining what the "true" coefficient is from these results. The t-values rise as the number of periods included in the average increases up to a three-period average; for the four-period average that value falls off. This may mean that our results do not simply reflect the process of averaging.

One can try to explain the results in terms of their statistical properties and their economic significance. A result of taking a moving average is to reduce the scatter of observations without reducing its mean. In a simple regression model the regression line would become steeper and its intercept would fall due to a compression of observations in a horizontal direction; the mean and the values of the dependent variable would not change. As a consequence, the equation would have a higher regression coefficient and a smaller constant term. In Table 4.1 this inverse relation between constant term and slope is evident. Furthermore, although the means of D do not change, the standard deviations fall from 23.3 (D_{t-1}) to 12.34 (D^*_6).

The economic explanation may be that direct investment is too volatile for a simple lag to show its true relation to capital formation. Direct investment is not always very large and may be influenced by a few large transactions. A simple lag loses the distributed expenditure effect coming from a direct investment flow in a given period; by using a moving average, the effect on investment can be spread over several periods. Also, companies often build up funds before spending; if the buildup extends over several periods, it would be correct to average before applying it to investment. It may be significant that the coefficient of undistributed profits does not change when an average is used. This number is much less sensitive to single transactions because the number of transactions in a single quarter is large. Thus, the best estimate of d may well exceed that for unaveraged values of D.

As a check on our investment equation, we estimated the residual correlation model discussed earlier. The equation without the direct investment term is:

$$IB = 587 + .1021A + 1.2377U^* \qquad (4.11)$$
$$(2.48) \qquad (8.56)$$

where U^* is the same as in equation 4.10. The residuals from 4.11, R, were then run against various estimates of D. Using the same estimate of D^* as in 4.10:

$$R = -200 + 2.2638D^* \qquad (4.12)$$
$$(2.92)$$

It is apparent that the regression coefficients in equations 4.11 and 4.12 agree with those in 4.10. It follows that the coefficient estimated in the original direct investment model represents the net additional effect of direct investment. This result reflects the very low collinearity between D and the other independent variables; the simple correlation coefficients are shown on p. 173. Additional coefficients (which can be compared with Table 4.1) from the residual model are shown below:

Period averaged	d	t
D_{t-2}	.9357	(1.7044)
D^*_4	2.997	(3.3744)
D^*_6	3.1906	(3.1625)

Another prediction based on the assumption of linear independence of the independent variables was that the constant term of the complete equation would equal the sum of the two other constant terms. For equations 4.10, 4.11, and 4.12 this is also roughly true ($378 \simeq 587 - 200$). It should also be pointed out that the constant terms are significant at 5 percent.

But, can regression coefficients of the magnitude of three be accepted? This would mean that $1 of direct foreign investment is associated with $3 of capital formation. The number may in a sense be overstated because depreciation allowances and retained earnings of United States-controlled firms also finance capital formation, and direct investment may be a proxy for these sources of funds. This line of argument cannot be pushed far, however, since the internal funds of U.S.-controlled companies are in the funds variable (U) and should not require D as a proxy. Still, some of the investment financed by these funds may affect the estimated coefficient of D. If these internal funds moved more like direct investment than like Canadian profits, D could be expected to act as a proxy for them. To test for this possibility, two new variables, described earlier, were created: DR, direct investment *plus* retained earnings distributed by the quarterly direct investment pattern, and UR, liquidity *less* these same retained earnings. Here is an example of the results:

$$IB = 283.70 + 2.52DR^* + 1.14UR^* + 0.0835A$$
$$\qquad\quad (7.200) \quad\; (10.0385) \quad (2.5167)$$
$$RSQC = .87$$
$$DW = 1.05 \quad (4.13)$$

The equation comparable in lag structure to 4.7 is:

$$IB = 326.55 + 3.2809D^* + 1.1562U^*_7 + 0.0899A$$
$$\qquad\quad (3.3656) \quad\; (9.0331) \quad\; (2.422)$$
$$RSQC = .84$$
$$DW = .82 \quad (4.14)$$

The t-value for direct investment changes from 3.4 to over 7. The performance of UR^* also improves, from $t = 9$ to $t = 10$.[16] The regression coefficient form DR changes very little, while the coefficient for D^* falls substantially. If one could add depreciation allowances to D, the coefficient for D might very well be reduced even more to further improve the equation.

What this exercise shows is not that the coefficient for D

16. $UR^* =$ moving average UR ($t-1$ through $t-3$); $DR^* =$ moving average DR ($t-1$ through $t-3$). Helliwell's research on the effect of credit tightness upon investment confirms this by showing a lesser effect of scarce liquidity on foreign subsidiaries than on domestically owned firms; John F. Helliwell, *Public Policies and Private Investment* (Oxford: Clarendon Press, 1968), pp. 150–156.

is "really" unity, but rather that $1 of direct investment will generally be used in conjunction with other finance. Moreover, the influence of this finance is indistinguishable from "Canadian" investment behavior. In other words, an equation in which we segregate Canadian from United States influence as much as possible will provide a better total explanation of Canadian capital formation than one in which we do not. In this way a specific U.S. net contribution can be identified.

Collinearity between U and D may lead to an overstatement of the coefficient of D (but see the intercorrelation coefficients below). The existence of third-country direct investment may be another factor tending to raise it, although the low correlation of United States and third-country direct investment in Canada ($R = .33$) probably means that this is not very important. A third factor is public capital formation, which for statistical reasons cannot be excluded from IB. We shall treat three as a maximum figure for the true value. Taking account of the three factors mentioned that make for overstatement, two may be a better estimate. It could be argued that if complementarity of investment does exist, then $d = 2$ is a perfectly reasonable value. But this number is not a constant in the Canadian economic structure; rather, it would depend on the kind of direct investment undertaken, as well as on many other influences. Thus, even if the analysis presented is accepted, it cannot predict the future magnitude of responses to direct investment with any great degree of accuracy. All one can say is that the equations show a relation between investment and direct investment which is of such a magnitude as to indicate strongly that most direct investment is associated with capital formation.

One serious statistical problem that invariably arises in time-series analysis — autocorrelation — does exist here, as seen by the Durbin-Watson statistics. Given the degrees of freedom available, a Durbin-Watson value less than 1.6 is sufficient to reject the null hypothesis of no positive autocorrelation; and with Durbin-Watson values of less than one, strong positive autocorrelation is indicated. If first differences are employed, most of the relationships are insignificant statistically and negative autocorrelation is introduced. The method of first differences is incapable of dealing with this problem. In defense of our procedure, it may be said that enough satisfactory relations were found so that, even if the standard errors are understated, some confidence in the results is warranted. Also, when our variables were adjusted for retained earnings, the t-values increased as did the Durbin-Watson statistics.

As indicated earlier, a not serious problem was multicollinearity. Although there is no accepted measure of multicollinearity, the intercorrelations between the independent variables give some idea of how "serious" it is. Some of these correlation coefficients are given below:

Variables	R
D, U	.0102
D, A	$-.0627$
U, A	.2649
DR, UR	$-.2280$
U^*_6, D^*_6	.1582
UR^*_2, DR^*_2	$-.1074$

The low correlation between direct investment and internal funds provides some assurance that D was not simply a proxy for it, and also that it was not picking up the influence of omitted variables that reflect the general level of economic activity.

173

EFFECTS OF PROSPERITY AND RECESSION

During our sample period, the level of economic activity in Canada varied considerably, ranging from periods of full and overfull employment to periods of substantial unemployment. In order to test the stability of estimates derived for the period as a whole, it is important to re-estimate the equations for periods of "prosperity" and "recession" separately. The aim of such a bifurcation is to see how the explanatory variables fare for the two subperiods and, particularly, how direct investment behaves over the cycle. One would expect, according to residual funds theories, that as the pressure on internal funds grows during the upswing, direct investment funds are directed more toward real capital formation. In the aggregate, direct investment provides real resources; to the individual firm it provides the means to command resources. During the downswing, when the pressure of demand is low, one would expect the additional funds provided by direct investment to be less likely to lead to capital formation.

It is not very obvious how to divide the full sample period. First a variable must be chosen to serve as an index to identify the timing and extent of the upswing and the downswing. The variable selected can be some index of business activity or a proxy for it. If a cyclical series is used as the index, the turning points may provide a way of deciding where to subdivide the period. The objection to a straightforward application of turning points arises when we look at another problem, that of the timing of investment in relation to the business cycle. There is no need to repeat the earlier discussion of lags to see the difficulty. One could divide the time series for I_t on the basis of some index, X_t, but the determinants of I_t may change in an earlier period. Since these determinants, or explanatory variables, can have various lag structures, it may not be feasible to subdivide the period on the basis of their values. Instead of relying on some precise statistical definition of the "upswing" and "downswing," very loose definitions were employed, identifying long enough stretches of "prosperity" and "recession" partly to avoid the worst aspects of the timing problem. This procedure lacks objectivity, but at least it avoids spurious precision.

Canada, in our period, presents especially great difficulties for identifying cyclical swings. The years from 1950–1962 can be classified roughly into three subperiod categories: (1) recession and (2) prosperity until 1957, then (3) high-level stagnation afterward. After 1957, capital formation hovered around $5 billion a year, although in 1956 it had already reached the annual rate of $6 billion; unemployment remained mostly within the range of 6–8 percent. To take the little ripples in this period as turning points in the business cycle would be pointless; economically they were all of a piece and have been treated as such.

Using for guidance the seasonally adjusted Gross Domestic Product index, and taking unemployment data and capital formation into account,[17] we have defined the two subperiods — which for want of a better term will be called upswing and downswing — as follows:

I. Upswings: 1951-I to 1953-III   11 quarters
                       1955-I to 1957-I   9 quarters

II. Downswings: 1953-IV to 1954-IV   5 quarters
                       1957-II to 1962-IV 23 quarters.

Three equations were estimated, one for the whole period and two for each subperiod. Several versions of the funds and direct investment variables were tried; there were marked dif-

17. D.B.S., *Indexes of Real Domestic Product by Industry of Origin, 1935–61* (Ottawa: Queen's Printer, 1963).

ferences in the equations. Typical patterns occur in the following equations for the case $U = U^*_6$ and $D = D^*_1$:

Entire period: $IB = 321.8 + 2.8953D + 1.2119U + 0.0834A$
$$(3.5074) \quad (9.9192) \quad (2.1952)$$
$$RSQC = .8330$$
$$DW = .77 \qquad \text{(4.15a)}$$

Upswing: $IB = 18.2 + 4.7851D + 1.4746U + 0.0809A$
$$(5.5735) \quad (9.4375) \quad (1.7414)$$
$$RSQC = .9336$$
$$DW = 1.75 \qquad \text{(4.15b)}$$

Downswing: $IB = 512.3 + 0.7988D + 1.1846U + 0.829A$
$$(0.6029) \quad (4.7865) \quad (1.4951)$$
$$RSQC = 0.8000$$
$$DW = .73. \qquad \text{(4.15c)}$$

The equation for the upswing period is very good — not only is $RSQC$ over .9, but the Durbin-Watson statistic (1.75) indicates no autocorrelation. This equation is representative of all the others, in the sense that the upswing period always did "best" in terms of statistics relating to the equation as a whole and also to D and U.

For fuller discussion of the results, it is useful to introduce the results from the residuals model. The variables are the same as those in equations 4.15.

Entire period: $IB = 558 + 0.1009A + 1.2829U$
$$(2.3783) \quad (8.7404)$$
$$R = -243 + 2.7611D$$
$$(3.6109) \qquad \text{(4.16a)}$$

Upswing: $IB = 465 + 0.1208A + 1.5525U$
$$(1.4829) \quad (5.6235)$$

176

$$R = -375 + 4.2835D$$
$$(5.5844) \qquad\qquad (4.16b)$$

Downswing: $\quad IB = 569 + 0.0877A + 1.2148U$
$$(1.6201) \quad (5.0771)$$

$$R = -63 + 0.7198D$$
$$(0.6574) \qquad\qquad (4.16c)$$

The residuals model again shows that D performs better during the upswing. The regression coefficients for D are consistent for the two models, and the constant terms roughly obey the pattern predicated on the independence assumption, with the upswing period more out of line in this respect.

In equations 4.16 the accelerator has its highest t-value for the entire period but its highest regression coefficient for the upswing period. In the complete equations (that is, in 4.15), the t-value is again higher for the full period, but here the regression coefficients do not differ much. A survey of all the equations computed shows that the accelerator does better (higher t-value and coefficient) for the downswing more frequently than in the upswing (although in the particular equations 4.15 above this is not the case).

It may be that A's performance is worsened by its interactions with other variables. Where they (especially D) perform well — and D does perform well in the upswings — A's impact seems to weaken. This conjecture is partly confirmed in that, as longer-lagged values of D and U are used, A loses its explanatory powers in the upswings (where it might be expected to perform well) than for the downswings (where one would expect poorer performance). The longer the lag and the longer the period over which D is averaged, the better its own performance. Thus, for $U = U^*_6$ and D going from D_{t-2} to D^*_1, D^*_4, D^*_6, the coefficient for A falls in the upswing period from 0.12 to 0.08, 0.05 and 0.06; the same coefficient over the same range of equations for the downswing period hovers around 0.08. Moreover, it is clear from equations 4.16 that it is the upswing accelerator which is most affected by the addition of D in the complete equation.

But this is not the complete story. The simple correlation between D and A moves from negative to positive as D is lagged further and averaged over more quarters; thus, the higher coefficient for A in equations with shorter lags for D may be an offset to this negative correlation. In any case, the correlation between A and D is uniformly so low (for the upswing, $R[A, D^*_1] = -.10$) that interaction between these variables cannot really account for much of A's performance. A more plausible explanation is that upsurges in Canadian investment are tied more to long-run growth prospects than to short-run changes in final demand as represented by the accelerator relation.

The residual funds variable performs best for the full period and worst for the downswing. The size of the t-value is much smaller in the downswing. The patterns in equations 4.15 and 4.16 are similar: the difference in the size of the coefficient is never great, but if the difference has an economic interpretation it may be that liquidity is not a constraining force during the downswing. That is, a dollar of liquid funds is less likely to lead to a dollar of investment in the downswing than during the upswing. The lower t-value for the downswing may indicate that it is a less significant influence on investment during such periods, or that other influences are relatively more important.

The coefficient for D shows the widest variation between periods of upswing and downswing. In equation 4.15b its value is 4.79 for the upswing with a t-value of 5.57 — a much better performance than for the period as a whole. We are again faced, more pressingly this time, with the large size of the impact of direct investment. Here there is a strong case for believing that the complementarity of investments is important: for example, large projects like the pipeline construc-

178

tion undertaken during the mid-1950's were complementary to investment in oil wells. Another possibility is that other omitted factors were important and that D serves as a proxy for these other factors: for instance, the external financing of business investment rose sharply in this period.[18] But if the model is accurate, such influences should be subsumed under the inducement to invest as reflected in the accelerator and residual funds variables. External financing merely enables investment decisions reached on other grounds to take place. It is also possible that D is a proxy for the generally good prospects of resource-related investment in Canada during the period; such prospects have influenced investment decisions by both foreign investors and domestically owned companies. The weakness of the accelerator variable may be especially troublesome here. Also, if D were simply a proxy, A and U might be expected to pick up some of the influence of these omitted variables.[19] The meaning of the equation for the upswing is that a larger part of total investment can be explained by direct investment for the upswing than for the entire period. In such periods, purely Canadian factors provide a weaker explanation or fail to reflect all inducements to invest. The vigor of the Canadian boom and the high capital formation rates had external causes.

The enormous difference between the coefficients of D for the upswing and for the downswing has important implications. It partly bears out allegations that direct investment in the late 1950's and early 1960's did not contribute to capital formation. Perhaps the reasons were not those that Canadians complained of — takeovers — but rather that the economy, running at a low level, just did not need extra resources, so

18. *Report of the Royal Commission on Banking and Finance* (Ottawa: Queen's Printer, 1964), pp. 33–35.
19. The good value of the Durbin-Watson indicates the smaller likelihood that systematic influences were omitted.

that the "displacement" theory had some validity. In the mid-1950's the inflow added substantially to investment funds and, if the equations can be trusted, led to substantial capital formation.

INDIVIDUAL INDUSTRIAL SECTORS

The relationship of capital formation to direct investment will now be disaggregated, employing regression equations that are similar (in intent, if not results) to those reported in the earlier part of the chapter. Before doing so, some descriptive statistics are presented on direct investment and capital formation.

The lack of certain basic data seriously restricts the analysis at a disaggregated industry level. No quarterly data of any sort exist on direct investment or capital formation at this level, hence the analysis must be on an annual basis. Direct investment figures are available for only eight industrial categories. The industrial classifications used for direct investment are based on the *enterprise* (the organization consisting of a group of firms), whereas capital formation data (and other figures like profit and production) are on either a *plant* or *firm* basis. This means that true comparability is impossible, and whatever adjustments are made are largely arbitrary. Other data problems will be discussed as they arise.

Tables 4.2 and 4.3 present most of the available data on direct investment and capital formation at the industry level.[20] Table 4.2 gives direct investment flows, both in the Canadian

---

20. The capital formation variables are explained in Lubitz, "Direct Investment in Canada," p. 125.

TABLE 4.2. United States and Canadian statistical estimates of direct investment flows, by industry

A. Canadian data[a] (millions of dollars)

Year	Petro-leum	Mining	Pulp, paper	Manufac-turing	Utili-ties	Merchan-dising	Fi-nance	Miscel-laneous
1950	116	30	9	–	–	90	–	–	–
1951	140	37	31	–	–	107	–	–	–
1952	180	99	7	76	2	6	2	4
1953	175	108	1	59	6	32	15	4
1954	190	69	23	49	4	8	17	10
1955	198	57	35	87	9	24	21	12
1956	254	76	43	135	2	20	24	18
1957	262	81	48	121	4	33	25	19
1958	209	81	19	95	3	14	8	16
1959	203	141	18	158	8	35	34	16
1960	180	209	26	138	14	20	40	23
1961	156	157	13	149	7	32	49	41
1962	156	165	13	178	18	55	30	22

Source: Dominion Bureau of Statistics, *The Canadian Balance of International Payments, A Compendium of Statistics from 1946 to 1965* (Ottawa: Queen's Printer, 1967), table 6.1.

[a] The statistics above are *gross* and will add to a greater amount than net direct investment in the balance of payments.

B. United States data (millions of dollars)

Year	Petroleum	Mining, smelting	Manufacturing	Trade	Other
1950	122	29	88	32	17
1951	125	41	39	6	24
1952	125	142	135	7	22
1953	185	118	45	31	24
1954	194	94	73	8	40
1955	161	42	84	10	56
1956	302	46	149	24	80
1957	250	60	184	−2	186
1958	237	78	72	−2	37
1959	115	120	146	−6	43
1960	138	202	30	15	84
1961	99	12	122	– 65	–
1962	132	75	23	– 82	–

Source: United States Department of Commerce, Office of Business Economics, *Balance of Payments: Statistical Supplement*, rev. ed. (Washington: Government Printing Office, 1962).

TABLE 4.3. Gross business capital formation by industry, Canada, 1950–1962 (millions of dollars)

Year	Mining	Iron mining	Manufacturing	Petroleum
1950	60	—[a]	502	87
1951	98	—[a]	793	131
1952	102	30	973	171
1953	145	48	969	189
1954	143	44	822	221
1955	131	36	947	311
1956	280	30	1394	345
1957	334	49	1479	368
1958	121	32	1095	325
1959	127	57	1144	314
1960	171	79	1178	269
1961	190	90	1085	214
1962	274	148	1269	349

Source: Canada, Department of Trade and Commerce, *Public and Private Investment* (various issues); Dominion Bureau of Statistics, unpublished data.
[a] Not available.

Dominion Bureau of Statistics and the United States Office of Business Economics versions. The D.B.S. figures include any return of capital and are therefore *gross* flows, as no disaggregation of return capital flows is available; thus, they sum to a larger number than aggregate direct investment as given in the balance of payments statistics. The large role played by petroleum and mining stands out in the data. Manufacturing, while important, is a very heterogeneous group, and United States investment is concentrated in certain manufacturing industries.

The concentration of direct investment in two industries led us to compare direct investment with capital formation in the two areas. In petroleum, capital formation moves clearly in phase with direct investment (the capital formation figure used is for oil wells and refining but not pipelines, which are generally financed by methods other than direct investment). Although the direct investment and capital formation series are not directly comparable, it is still noteworthy that direct investment is a very large proportion, absolutely, of investment in this industry. Thus, in 1955–1956, direct investment in petroleum accounted for 65–75 percent of a large amount of capital formation.

Postwar experience in the Canadian petroleum industry offers a case study in the pattern of direct investment. As its investment started to pay off, the industry relied more on internal financing and commenced to repatriate earnings — this is evident in Table 4.4, which also shows O.B.E. figures on earnings, repatriations, and undistributed earnings. As earnings rose, repatriations changed from negative amounts to steadily rising positive amounts. Undistributed earnings, however, did not grow substantially because direct investment remained the major source of finance for capital formation. Another interesting point is that investment expenditure grew steadily in the period 1950–1957 and thus did not reflect the 1953–1954 recession. Two possible reasons for this are that, first, new industries are less likely to suffer the ordinary vicissitudes of the business cycle — it is one of the signs of newness that an industry will ride out recession phases; second, petroleum output was directed to an existing market, hence it was import-replacing investment and therefore did not simply depend on an expanding domestic market, but could also displace alternative supplies. It can be said that petroleum was a natural area for direct investment: a new activity that would not automatically be exploited by existing domestic companies.

Explaining the investment pattern for the mining sector is much less straightforward. Mining is a very heterogeneous industry with some parts (coal mining, for example) in decline and other parts (like iron) at new and rapidly expanding

TABLE 4.4. Capital formation in Canadian petroleum industry and direct investment, earnings, undistributed subsidiary earnings, and repatriated income of United States petroleum companies in Canada (millions of dollars)[a]

Year	Direct investment[b]	Capital formation[b]	Earnings[c]	Undistributed subsidiary earnings[c]	Repatriated income[c]
1950	116	87	17	20	−3
1951	140	131	3	20	−17
1952	180	171	12	31	−20
1953	175	189	14	36	−22
1954	190	221	10	25	−11
1955	198	311	39	41	4
1956	254	345	91	67	29
1957	262	368	112	67	56
1958	209	325	57	40	27
1959	203	314	74	44	41
1960	180	269	97	46	60
1961	156	214	121	51	74
1962	156	249	121	33	90

Source: Canada, Department of Trade and Commerce, *Public and Private Investment*; Canada, Dominion Bureau of Statistics, *Canadian Balance of International Payments and International Investment Position;* United States Department of Commerce, Office of Business Economics, *Survey of Current Business*, and *Balance of Payments: Statistical Supplement*.

[a] The definition of the petroleum industry differs for the capital formation and direct investment series; see Raymond Lubitz, "United States Direct Investment in Canada and Canadian Capital Formation, 1950–1962," unpub. diss. (Harvard University, 1966), p. 117.

[b] Canadian dollars.

[c] U.S. dollars.

stages. It is evident from Tables 4.2 and 4.3 that no pattern emerges if we simply compare direct investment and capital formation in mining. For 1951–1955, the two series move together in the minimal sense that direction of change is the same.[21] But an enormous investment surge in 1956–1957 is not at all reflected in the direct investment figures (nor in the O.B.E. figures on plant and equipment expenditure of United States companies in Canada).[22] This must mean that Canadian or non-U.S. foreign companies did the investing then. Finally, in 1959–1960, direct investment rose sharply and investment expenditure rose but not to its previous peak.

A clearer picture is obtained by looking at a particular mining industry in which the importance of United States investment is known, for example, the iron ore industry. When investment expenditure in iron ore is isolated, it behaves quite differently from that for nonferrous metals. Also, it does follow the pattern of direct foreign investment: it does not rise in 1956–1957 but does in 1958–1962, the period of large investment in the Labrador iron mines. It seems that the upsurge in direct investment was the buildup in investment funds needed to finance heavy investment in this industry.

The Dominion Bureau of Statistics commentary in various issues of *The Canadian Balance of International Payments* supports our speculations about the mining pattern. The 1954 report states that the falling off in direct investment in 1954 "coincided with the commencement of operations by some of the major new developments." [23] Possibly, then, United States companies did not need to participate in the general 1956–1957 mining boom. The 1956 report mentions that continental investors were then active.[24] The 1960 and 1961–1962 reports

21. An example of the difficulty of using data from the balance of payments on direct investment with capital formation is provided by the fact that in some years direct investment appears greater than total capital formation. At least part of the reason for this is that direct investment includes smelting and other ancillary activities of the mining companies, while capital formation does not.

22. See Lubitz, "Direct Investment in Canada," p. 143.

23. D.B.S., *The Canadian Balance of International Payments and International Investment Position, 1954* (Ottawa: Queen's Printer), p. 16.

24. *Ibid., 1956*, p. 20.

confirm the relationship between iron ore projects and direct investment in ancillary facilities and mining.[25] In manufacturing, the general outlines of movements of investment are similar; but here the earnings of U.S. companies are much more important than direct investment as a source of investment financing.

We now present sectoral regression equations for petroleum, mining, manufacturing, and utilities: the first three because they are the three important disaggregated sectors receiving direct investments flows, the fourth to see if any offsets to foreign-financed capital formation occurred in a sector not receiving significant direct investment. For purposes of comparison, corresponding aggregate annual equations were also run.

The equations take the same form as in the basic model outlined earlier, except that annual observations are now used; data problems are particularly vexing.[26] The variables are defined as before. The accelerator is the annual change in value of the production index. Direct investment, as already explained, is a gross figure. It must be emphasized that the data used are very unreliable and that the results should be treated with caution.

Five sets of equations, given in Table 4.5, were run. In each

25. *Ibid., 1960,* p. 32; *1961–62,* p. 47.

26. Rather than explain details of their construction here, the reader is referred for description of the statistical series to Lubitz, "Direct Investment in Canada," pp. 124–133. The sources used included various issues of the following: (Canada) Department of Trade and Commerce, *Public and Private Investment*; Department of National Revenue, *Taxation Statistics*; D.B.S., *The Canadian Balance of International Payments and International Investment Position*; D.B.S., *Quarterly Corporate Profits*; D.B.S., *National Accounts, Income and Expenditure by Quarters*; D.B.S., *Index of Industrial Production*; D.B.S., *Revised Index of Industrial Production, 1935–1957* (Ottawa: Queen's Printer, 1959); D.B.S., *Indexes of Real Domestic Product by Industry of Origin, 1935–1961* (Ottawa: Queen's Printer, 1963).

TABLE 4.5. Equations relating capital formation to direct investment, manufacturing, petroleum, mining, utilities sectors: 1950–1961 and 1951–1962

Sector and period[a]	Con-stant	Independent variables			Significance indicators		
		D	U	P'	F[b]	RSQC	DW
Aggregate							
1950–1961	1405	9.02 (2.26)[c]	–	–	5.11	.34	.65
	−102	6.15 (2.38)	1.18 (6.28)	−44.83 (1.88)	11.39	.81	1.53
1951–1962	2381	6.60 (1.79)	–	–	3.21	.24	.99
	−923	8.11 (2.16)	1.06 (3.79)	57.93 (1.69)	9.18	.78	1.71
Manufacturing							
1950–1961	666	3.61 (2.44)	–	–	5.97	.37	1.00
	450	2.65 (1.32)	0.36 (0.84)	−6.18 (−0.57)	2.07	.44	1.34
1951–1962	868	2.21 (1.66)	–	–	2.75	.22	1.41
	443	1.21 (0.72)	0.50 (1.42)	8.21 (.91)	1.74	.39	1.32
Petroleum							
1950–1961	−28	.98 (2.45)	–	–	5.66	.36	.41
	−154	.88 (7.30)	.54 (8.83)	−.09 (.69)	60.80	.96	2.31
1951–1962	23	.76 (2.01)	–	–	3.97	.28	.79
	75	.70 (2.60)	.39 (3.50)	−.004 (.018)	6.89	.72	1.30
Mining							
1950–1961	169	.15 (.59)	–	–	0.07	.007	1.11
	123	−.09 (.12)	.37 (.88)	.11 (.02)	0.32	.11	.42
1951–1962	163	.39 (.56)	–	–	0.48	.046	1.23
	84	−.06 (−.12)	.65 (2.10)	−.37 (.18)	1.74	.40	.86

TABLE 4.5 — *Continued*

Sector and period[a]	Con- stant	Independent variables			Significance indicators		
		D	U	P'	F[b]	RSQC	DW
Utilities[d]							
1950–1961	387	3.36 (1.45)	–	–	2.12	.18	.72
	363	−.08 (−.05)	4.13 (4.18)	−14.65 (1.37)	7.73	.74	1.43
1951–1962	127	4.20 (2.22)	–	–	4.94	.33	.80
	−308	2.74 (1.32)	2.56 (2.49)	13.04 (.99)	5.04	.65	.96

[a] In equations for 1950–1961 current values are used for D and U; in those for 1951–1962 one-year lags are used.

[b] Significance levels: $F(1, 10) = 4.96$ (5 percent), 10.04 (1 percent). This applies to the equations with D as the sole independent variable. $F(3, 8) = 4.07$ (5 percent), 7.59 (1 percent) for the equations with three independent variables.

[c] The values in parentheses are the values of t.

[d] In the utilities equations, direct investment is aggregate direct investment, not direct investment in utilities.

set, two time periods were covered: 1950–1961 and 1951–1962. Direct investment data by industry were not available before 1950 or for 1962. In the equations for 1950–1961, the liquidity and direct investment variables are unlagged; in those for 1951–1962, these variables are lagged one period. The accelerator is always $P_t − P_{t-1}$, where P is the index of production. F-ratios are reported so that the reader may see which equations are significant. For F (3, 8) the 5-percent and 1-percent significance levels are 4.07 and 7.59. The results are mixed: the estimates are unsatisfactory for mining and marginal for manufacturing; it is difficult to know what to make of the equations for utilities and the aggregate equations.

The one really encouraging estimate is for petroleum. The value of $RSQC$ for the first equation is high, as are the D and

U coefficients. The accelerator term enters with the wrong sign, but at least it is not significant. It may not be damaging that the accelerator performs badly, since market demand is not geared to previous output in a case like this where import substitution is important; consequently, one would not expect the assumptions of the acceleration model to apply. Rather one would expect (assuming a smooth flow of oil discoveries) that, as funds became available, they would be invested. This hypothesis at least is consistent with the better performance of the unlagged D and U variables. In such an industry, residual funds are not an inducement to invest but an enabling factor. The small size of the coefficient for U is puzzling, and no explanation is apparent.

The coefficient for D is also smaller than one would expect on the basis of its size in the aggregate equations in both its quarterly and annual forms. Three explanations are possible: (a) the role of internal financing (retained earnings and depreciation) is minor in this young industry, and the large coefficients for D occur in the aggregate equation partly because they may act as a proxy for retained earnings; (b) complementary investments will not occur to the same extent in a single industry as in the economy as a whole; and (c) aggregate investment contains some capital formation that is unaffected by direct investment but is not fully explained by the other two variables — D picks up some of this effect. If these explanations are valid, the coefficient of direct investment in the petroleum equation is the "true" effect of direct investment within a given industry, uncontaminated by the other effects mentioned. The magnitude is sensible. We would expect it to be less than one because direct investment in the sectoral equations is *gross* investment, and some expenditure from direct investment proceeds goes for noncapital expenditures (for example, licenses) and takeovers. The satisfactory results for the petroleum equation — which is our closest approximation to a well-defined industry with reasonably comparable figures for direct investment (balance of payments data) and the other variables — constitutes strong evidence on the role of direct investment. Moreover, petroleum was the major field of direct investment in our period. Thus, to explain it is to explain much of what happens in the postwar period.

There is little to be said about the aggregate equation (covered in the previous section). The switch in the sign of P may be an artifact resulting from the very high negative correlation of D_{t-1} and P ($R = -.78$).

The estimates for manufacturing are not very satisfactory. Although the coefficient for D is of the right order of magnitude, it is not significant, nor are any of the F ratios. There is a high D_t, U_t correlation ($R = 63$), and this may spoil the performance of both. Also, the accelerator should be important in an established field like manufacturing, and its dismal performance may weaken the entire equation. Finally, the direct investment series is very shaky, and this may have caused more trouble.

The most disappointing, although not surprising, result is in the mining sector. The coefficient for direct investment has the wrong sign and is virtually without any influence in the equation. In simple regressions (not shown), D had coefficients of 0.15 and 0.39, but these were far from significant. Even the liquidity variable is disappointing, although it is almost significant at 5 percent in the second equation ($t = 2.10$; 5-percent significance with 8 degrees of freedom requires $t \geqq 2.31$). Finally, the sign of the accelerator term is wrong in the second equation and far from significant in both. Given the heterogeneity of the mining production index, this was expected. The poor performance of the liquidity variable, as well as direct investment, raises other issues. The explanation for direct investment probably follows the one given earlier in this chapter: in 1956 and 1957 large mining investments were made by other than United States companies. The two observations are far out of line, as their residuals show. The mining sector is small enough to be influenced by a few special investment projects that do not react to the independent variables as the others might and therefore throw the equation off. The behavior of liquidity is very puzzling. The only thing that makes sense is that lagged U performs better than current U. This is perhaps due to the lumpiness of mining investment, which requires a prior buildup of funds.

The utilities sector provides a most intriguing result. The direct investment variable here is aggregate direct investment; the test is whether aggregate direct investment acted as an offset to capital formation in fields like utilities that do not attract direct investment. The coefficient of D would be expected to be negative if there is an offset. In fact, the coefficient is negative but quite insignificant in the first equation; although not significant in the second, it is positive and has a t-value greater than one. This is a superficial test, but as far as it goes it provides no evidence of an offset. Much of the explanation of utility investment seems to come from U, but its coefficient is much too large to be credible. This probably reflects the large amount of external finance used in the utilities sector for which U serves as a proxy.

Why should D have a positive effect in the utilities equations? This may simply be a spurious result. Or, it may be that utilities and direct investment are complementary and that the better performance of lagged D would be expected. It may be complementary in the sense that investment in petroleum especially would have linkages to pipelines and other transportation investment. Finally, the peak direct investment came when utilities investment also boomed, in 1956–1958, and this may explain the correlation without meaning that it is spurious. The great burst of capital formation in the mid-1950's intensified by direct investment, gave rise to comple-

191

mentary social-overhead investment to which direct investment can be partially tied. Table 4.6 illustrates this, with investment

TABLE 4.6. Capital formation in utilities, petroleum and natural gas, and transportation: Canada, 1950–1962 (millions of dollars)

Year	Utilities[a]	Petroleum and natural gas; transportation
1950	759	55
1951	939	11
1952	1194	95
1953	1254	80
1954	1164	65
1955	1136	46
1956	1762	177
1957	2308	310
1958	2153	238
1959	1842	59
1960	1772	99
1961	1698	165
1962	1601	72

Source: Canada, Department of Trade and Commerce, *Public and Private Investment*; Dominion Bureau of Statistics, unpublished data.
[a] Rail, water, pipelines.

in transportation and utilities in 1956–1958 showing the impact of investment in oil and natural gas transportation. Such investment can reasonably be called complementary to direct investment in petroleum.

Discussion of the effect of direct investment in Canada cannot avoid consideration of the takeover problem. Some evidence in a study done for the Economic Council of Canada on the subject is now available (see Table 4.7); it indicates

TABLE 4.7. Value of cash payments for firms acquired in international mergers, relative to total direct investment, and value of acquired firms in relation to total foreign-controlled enterprises: Canada, 1950–1961 (percentages)

Year	Value of cash payments for acquired firms as percentage of total direct investment		Value of firms acquired in foreign mergers as percentage of total foreign-controlled enterprise
	Series I[a]	Series II	
1950	2%	4%	2%
1951	11	11	7
1952	3	4	2
1953	7	7	4
1954	19	20	11
1955	25	31	15
1956	21	21	14
1957	3	15	7
1958	6	7	13
1959	13	13	7
1960	22	25	29
1961	14	18	20

Source: G. L. Reuber and Frank Roseman, *The Takeover of Canadian Firms, 1945–61: An Empirical Analysis*, Economic Council of Canada, Special Study no. 10 (Ottawa: Queen's Printer, 1969), table III.3.

[a] Series I and II represent separate estimates of the value of cash payments; it appears impossible to settle on one as preferable.

that the value of acquired firms rose over the period 1950–1962. The value of takeovers was clearly larger in the second half of the period than in the first. More relevant to our purposes, the ratio of cash paid for acquisitions to total direct investment also rose. Although the data present problems, this ratio was clearly highest for 1954–1956, 1960, and 1961. The peak years were 1955, when it ranged between 31 and 25 percent depending on the cash payment series used, and 1960, when it was between 25 and 22 percent. Manufacturing and trade were the leading industrial divisions for takeover. The large role of takeovers in manufacturing may help explain its dismal performance in the regression equations.[27]

That direct investment in the latter half of our period apparently went more to takeovers and less to capital formation would agree with the picture suggested by the equations for subperiods: the direct investment-capital formation link weakened when the economy stagnated. This may be because the rate of return on the purchase of existing assets fell less than on assets constructed by purchasing current productive services. A possible explanation is that the prices of assets can adjust downward more quickly, to compensate for the falling present value of their future income streams, than can prices of productive services.

The conclusions of this chapter can be briefly stated. We have found strong and systematic relationships between direct investment and capital formation, suggesting, in the aggregate and in average circumstances, that a dollar's worth of direct investment can be associated with about two dollars of capital formation. The impact of the inflow is particulary marked during periods of vigorous domestic activity; its influence during periods of recession is much weaker. This suggests that direct investment is a net addition to capital formation when the Canadian demand for capital generates strong pressures on her own resources. The relation operates with a lag that may average about two quarters. The results on a sectoral

27. Reuber and Roseman give estimates of the fraction of the value of assets controlled by nonresidents in 1962 comprised by the assets of firms acquired by foreigners during the period 1945–1961: manufacturing 12.3 percent; mining 1.7 percent; construction 4.9 percent; transportation 38.0 percent; trade 5.9 percent. Allowance was made for the effect of price changes on asset values. See their table III.4.

level were mixed; but in the petroleum industry, an industry accounting for about one-half of the inflow, significant relations were discovered between capital formation and direct investment.

5 Direct Foreign Influences on Canadian Prices and Wages

The modern theory of economic policy, discussed briefly in Chapter 1, generally identifies the objective of internal balance with the equation of aggregate demand to aggregate supply. Some models assume rigid internal money prices and associate internal balance with full employment. Others assume prices to be flexible and equate domestic balance with stability of the general price level. The economist making empirical use of these models faces the problem that in the usual case the levels of prices and employment both respond to shifts in aggregate demand. The consequences of failing to hit the desired internal balance include an undesired rate of change in the price level, as well as an inappropriate aggregate-demand balance. If inflation and employment rates are locked into this "Phillips curve" relation, independent policy objectives for the levels of employment and prices are precluded unless some policy instrument can be found to shift the curve.[1]

1. For a theoretical analysis of the Phillips curve relation in this framework, see A. M. C. Waterman, "Some Footnotes to the 'Swan Diagram' — or How Dependent is a Dependent Economy?" *Economic Record*, XLII (September, 1966), 447–464.

The Phillips curve embodies one popular view of determinants of the price level. If it were a *sufficient* view, this study of the effects of exogenous and endogenous capital flows on internal balance in Canada could proceed without more than passing reference to the subject of inflation. Income adjustments to exogenous capital disturbances could be treated as some normal bundle of price and output adjustments occurring in the narrow range of unemployment rates observed in the postwar period. Endogenous capital flows could similarly be related to aggregate-demand disturbances involving some standardized mix of price and output changes. Inflationary disturbances outside of Canada, if associated with exogenous changes in capital flows to the country, would require consideration only by dint of their influence on the net demand for Canadian goods — the balance of trade — and thus on aggregate demand, employment and prices in Canada.

There are two problems with this procedure for passing off inflationary influences on the adjustments surrounding international capital flows. First, it assumes product and factor prices to be flexible, rather than cost-determined, and that any influence of foreign inflation on the Canadian price level results strictly from its "macro" influence on internal balance (and its price- and output-level components). Second, it ignores the probability that inflationary disturbances may be concentrated in particular sectors rather than spread evenly over the whole economy.

That money prices and wages are to some extent cost-determined is widely accepted in discussions of inflation in closed economies. Oligopolistic industries may base their selling prices on unit money costs, marked up to yield a target rate of return. With wages and input prices largely controlling money cost levels, changes in selling prices may show little sensitivity to short-run changes in the rate of capacity utilization or the level of inventory holdings. By the same token, the supply price of labor, especially in strongly unionized sectors, may be sensitive to the general cost of living but relatively insensitive to the tightness of the labor market of the sector or industry in question. These elements of sectoral cost determination may affect movements of the price level in several ways. Reviewing United States experience in the 1950's, Charles Schultze suggested that shifts of demand among industries may contribute to inflation. If some prices or wages are more flexible upward than downward in response to changes in sectoral excess demand, then changes in the composition of aggregate demand pull prices or wages upward in the sectors favored by the shift, to a greater extent than they are reduced in those that are disfavored. Likewise, efforts of a few major unions to improve their relative wage position, or of a few major oligopolies to raise their target profit rates, can supply a disturbance that augments the general inflation rate.

Sectoral and markup elements of this sort could also operate in the international economy. They would consist of changes in Canadian product or factor prices occurring in *direct* response to changes in particular foreign (hereafter, United States) prices and to some degree independent of Canadian market forces. As we shall argue below, the price of a particular Canadian product, or the wage in a Canadian industry, might for several reasons be related directly to the price of the same product or the wage of the same industry in the United States. (In principle, Canadian prices could be keyed in this way to the prices of dissimilar products or factors in the United States, but we shall neglect this possibility.) Consider the effect of such linkages on the models used in this study. The price and employment ingredients of internal balance may respond to exogenous capital disturbances in ways that depend heavily on what is happening to the foreign price level. For example, the impact of a rise in United States interest rates on the Canadian interest rate, and thereby the Canadian level of aggregate demand and employment, will not be the same when the United States disturbance is associated with U.S. inflation as when higher American interest rates stem from some other cause.

In short, we need assurance that these direct price and wage linkages are not so important that they undermine our efforts to estimate policy leverages (and the like) from "macro" models and data. This chapter seeks to test for "micro" linkages between Canadian and United States prices and wages and to detect the channels through which they operate. Its function is thus negative, and (to anticipate our conclusions) it is successful in turning up no strong evidence of these potentially disruptive micro linkages.

Before turning to the design of our statistical investigation, it may help to put this hypothesis of international price linkages into a broader theoretical perspective. Most theoretical models of inflation omit mention of the international sector of the national economy entirely,[2] and how these elements of cost determination, through their influence on aggregate internal balance, relate to external equilibrium in the open economy is anything but clear. If we ignore the influence of product differentiation, transport costs, and the like, the money prices of traded goods within a country must equal their international prices multiplied by the exchange rate. As the proposition is often put in Canada, Canadian wholesale prices are equal to world (United States) prices plus the tariff. When foreign

2. As an exception, the study for the Economic Council of Canada by Bodkin and others develops a simple method for showing the effect of inflation in the prices of imported inputs on the level of product prices. Implicitly, however, this approach is based on changes in the *domestic* prices of imported goods, or in their foreign prices with a fixed exchange rate. The heart of the problem is joint determination of the exchange rate and the domestic price level. See Ronald G. Bodkin *et al.*, *Price Stability and High Employment: The Options for Canadian Economic Policy*, Economic Council of Canada, Special Study no. 5 (Ottawa: Queen's Printer, 1966), pp. 16–18.

money prices change, either the domestic price level must change in the same proportion (possibly excepting nontraded goods) or the exchange rate must alter. In any system of macroeconomic relations applicable to the Canadian economy, the price level and the exchange rate must be jointly determined. If the exchange rate is fixed, changes in the world prices of traded goods alter their domestic prices by the same amount. In turn, the price changes affect the balance of income claims in the domestic-goods sector, and thereby the current-account balance, in rather complicated ways. Rising money prices of exportables or importables disturb the domestic sector through both cost and demand channels (assuming cost-determined pricing to be present), and the net outcome for domestic-sector excess demand is not clear in the absence of more detailed assumptions.[3]

What about the mechanism with a flexible exchange rate? The pure theory of this case suggests that general inflation abroad, which would normally increase the demand for Canadian currency at a given exchange rate, might simply induce an appreciation of the Canadian exchange rate that would leave the Canadian price level unaffected. This independence would require only that the money value of Canadian aggregate demand be unaffected by the exchange rate so long as the current-account balance remains equal to zero. Alternatively, a flexible exchange rate might be expected to respond to domestically generated inflation, which would then proceed as in a closed economy because of the absence of a current-account leakage.

Unfortunately for simple views of the optimality of a flexible exchange rate, both theory and fact suggest that it

3. J. D. Pitchford, *A Study of Cost and Demand Inflation,* Contributions to Economic Analysis, No. 33 (Amsterdam: North-Holland Publishing Co., 1963), chap. ix. Also see D. Cavalieri, "Stabilisation des prix et rééquilibre de la balance des paiements en periode d'inflation," *Economie Appliquée,* XX, no. 3(1967), 347–388 (esp. 352–375)

might readily fail to provide this independence for the domestic price level. If elements of cost determination are present in either domestic prices or wages, the assurance that foreign inflation need not influence aggregate demand no longer guarantees that it cannot affect domestic prices. It is the essence of cost-determined prices that they may be shifted to positions that do not involve equilibrium (zero excess demand) in the market in question. Especially if industry wages and selling prices are rigid downward, new equilibrium values for home price level and exchange rate, after a disturbing bout of foreign inflation, may not be predictable solely from the average change in foreign prices. Since time rates of adjustment in the various goods and foreign exchange markets become decisive, composition of the aggregate inflationary disturbance must also be known.

Some aggregate statistical evidence on the Canadian economy confirms these theoretical propositions about inter-relations of the price level and the exchange rate. In exploring the determinants of the change in the Canadian consumer price index (percentage change in a given quarter from a year earlier), Ronald Bodkin and others have found that the corresponding unlagged United States price index alone explained 62 percent of the variance of the Canadian index, with a highly significant regression coefficient of 1.008. The time period considered, 1953–1965, was mostly that of the flexible exchange rate. On the other hand, both the regression coefficient and the significance of the United States price level dropped when Canadian domestic determinants were added: lagged price changes, wage changes, and/or changes in the implicit deflator for imports of goods and services.[4] The last of these might well comprise the channel whereby the foreign price level wields its influence on Canadian prices and thus displaces

4. Bodkin *et al.*, *Price Stability*, pp. 147–151. This study summarizes most of the other relevant empirical investigations.

the statistical influence of the U.S. price level.[5] In any case, the high simple correlation between Canadian and U.S. price movements suggests that the theoretical prediction of price independence with a flexible exchange rate falls wide of the mark. Furthermore, the determinants of changes in average hourly earnings in Canadian manufacturing turn out to include changes in the corresponding United States wage series, in this case with the U.S. percentage changes averaged over the current and three preceding quarters. Canadian wages seem to respond by 30 to 40 percent of current and recent past changes in U.S. wages.[6] Because the mobility of labor between the Canadian and U.S. markets hardly seems large enough to account for this link, it must operate either through some circuitous market channel or through "demonstration" effects on Canadian wage demands.

To explore this dependence of Canadian on foreign price and wage movements further, a number of tests could be devised. One might dig intensively into the determinants of the Canadian aggregate price level, to sort out the influence of foreign prices operating through macro and micro channels. Second, the relation between changes in the prices of traded and nontraded goods, and their respective influence on Canadian factor costs, might be explored. A third approach would call for disaggregation, to investigate the differential sensitivity of various Canadian product and factor prices to their United States counterparts; this last approach is the one we have employed. Industry disaggregation is also used in one of the few extant studies of the sensitivity of Canadian to

5. Vanderkamp's results also attribute a strong role to import prices in determining movements of the Canadian consumer price index, and excess-demand proxies do not enter significantly into his best price equation; John Vanderkamp, "Wage and Price Level Determination: An Empirical Model for Canada," *Economica*, XXXIII (May, 1966), 194–218.
   6. Bodkin *et al.*, *Price Stability*, table 5.1.

foreign price changes. R. J. Wonnacott sorted the sectors of the Canadian economy into those with prices determined externally and those with prices determined on the domestic market, then employed interindustry analysis to measure the effect on the Canadian price level of a rise in the prices of foreign-priced final and intermediate goods.[7] Our strategy complements Wonnacott's: we investigate empirically the sensitivity of Canadian to United States wholesale prices and wages at the industry level, then seek to identify those characteristics which make this industry-level sensitivity strong or weak.

INTERDEPENDENCE OF INDUSTRY
WHOLESALE SELLING PRICES

Restricting our inquiry to the Canadian manufacturing sector (about 25 percent of total value added), we secured data on the largest possible number of comparably defined Canadian and United States industries at the four-digit level of the Standard Industrial Classification. These were employed, in two stages, to answer the following two questions. (1) How closely were annual changes in Canadian industry wholesale prices during the period 1957–1966 related to wholesale price changes in comparable United States industries? (2) Could differences in the closeness of this relation from industry to industry be associated with characteristics of the Canadian

7. Ronald J. Wonnacott, *Canadian-American Dependence: An Inter-industry Analysis of Production and Prices,* Contributions to Economic Analysis, no. 24 (Amsterdam: North-Holland Publishing Co., 1961), chaps. viii–x. If all foreign prices rise by 1 percent, Wonnacott finds that the Canadian cost of living rises by 0.39 percent; if only U.S. prices rise, by 0.36 percent. These estimates assume that Canadian factor costs remain constant. If Canadian wages rise by the same amount as the Canadian cost of living, then an increase of 1 percent in foreign prices raises Canadian prices and the wage rate by about 0.55 percent.

industries? It may be helpful to consider the general rationale of this two-part design before turning to the details.

Previous research cited above has related changes in Canada's general level of wholesale or retail prices (with lags) to such customary determinants as changes in money costs, the utilization of capacity, and the level of prices of imports. The same sort of investigation of the short-run dynamics of price adjustment could be developed for individual industries, employing these and perhaps other independent variables to explain changes in Canadian industry selling prices. Various industry or sectoral studies, more or less matching this description, can be found in the literature. Undertaking a series of detailed industry studies was an unattractive prospect, however, considering the focus of our general concern on macro variables and the problems of data collection and estimation involved. Therefore, we began by exploring the relation of Canadian industry price changes solely to price changes in the corresponding United States industries and ignoring the other putative determinants of Canadian industry price movements. Some unsuccessful attempts to take account of other factors are reported below.

Knowledge of the closeness of this simple relation between price changes in individual Canadian and U.S. industries holds some predictive interest, although it bears little relation to the general concern of this study in the leverage of broad policy instruments. But the connection becomes evident if the common characteristics of industries which transmit foreign price changes promptly and strongly can be detected. Then one can consider policies which might disconnect the linkage, or at least anticipate its action in transmitting general foreign price changes.

Price data employed in the analysis were the Industry Selling Price Indexes for Canada and the Industry and Sector

Price Indexes for the United States.[8] These series represent
the best available indicators of selling prices actually charged
at wholesale by enterprises in the various industries; the fact
that they represent list rather than market prices is not especially damaging for our purposes. Because they are collected on an enterprise rather than a product basis,[9] the data
can more readily be used in conjunction with the variables included at the second stage of the analysis, which are also
gathered on an enterprise basis. Finally, and most important,
the Canadian industry selling price indexes cover only the
prices of Canadian outputs and not competing imports (they
are, of course, affected by variations in the prices of imported
inputs). The data have, unfortunately, been collected only
since the mid-1950's and thus fail to cover the whole period
of the fluctuating exchange rate. There was no reason to cut
off the investigation of industry price relations, however, at
the demise of the flexible exchange rate, so the period covered
is 1957–1966. A serious difficulty arose because the United
States Standard Industrial Classification does not correspond
to the Canadian SIC, even in the latter's revised form, and
neither one matches the United Nations system. Judgment
had to be exercised about whether or not to include a Canada-
United States pair of industries when they did not appear exactly comparable in definition. In some cases a match could
be worked out by combining either United States or Canadian

8. D.B.S., *Industry Selling Price Indexes, 1956–59* (Ottawa: Queen's
Printer, 1961), and subsequent issues of *Prices and Price Indexes*; U.S.
Department of Labor, Bureau of Labor Statistics, *Wholesale Prices and
Price Indexes* (Washington: Government Printing Office, 1967).

9. As an exception, data for several U.S. industries (generally in the
wood products and chemicals sectors) are based on prices collected on a
commodity basis. Indexes for them were reassembled using product weights
outlined in the appendix to D.B.S., *Industry Selling Price Indexes*. Before
the U.S. Industry and Sector Indexes became available, we used this type
of index generally to represent U.S. price changes. The results showed much
the same pattern as those in Table 5.1, although the fits were poorer.

industries. Proceeding in this way, we arrived at a sample of 50 industries; this provides reasonably even coverage for most major sectors of Canadian manufacturing, although consumer durables are rather lightly represented.

Several questions about the nature of the influence of United States on Canadian industry prices affected the forms in which we tested the relation. What would constitute a reasonable unit period of observation? Changes occurring from quarter to quarter are likely to be quite small and thus subject to rounding error. Lags in the relation might not be particularly stable, especially considering that each industry typically produces a mixture of products, so that the basic data would be indexes with shifting weights. Finally, quarterly data might generate spurious correlations due to common patterns of seasonality in the United States and Canada. These considerations point to the superiority of annual over shorter period data. We checked this conjecture with experiments using both quarterly and monthly data: quarterly generally performed no better than annual data. Using information on month-to-month changes, for the two years in which they are available, we got quite poor results. Because the influence of world (United States) prices probably operates with a lag that varies from industry to industry, we tried both coincident Canadian and U.S. changes and experiments with lagging the Canadian changes by three and six months.

Should allowance be made for movement in the exchange rate? Several lines of argument present themselves. Consider a purely competitive international market for a single homogeneous product. At any point in time a single price ought to prevail in all countries, after national currencies are converted to a common basis by the prevailing exchange rate. This theoretical model implies that the best explanatory relation between Canadian and world prices should result if changes in Canadian prices are related to changes in United States prices adjusted for changes in the exchange rate. On the other hand, once differentiated products and administered prices in imperfectly competitive markets are considered, the influence of the exchange rate becomes more dubious. Canadian sellers might not react to a 3-percent rise in the price of competing U.S. goods as they would to a rise of 3 percent in price of the U.S. dollar. The stability (in other words, inelasticity) of expectations about the exchange rate, documented in Chapter 2, contrasts with expectations about movements in the general price level that were widely held over the period of this study and suggests that the influence of foreign prices and the exchange rate as determinants of Canadian industry price changes should be tested independently. Finally, the operation of administered prices in conditions of differentiated oligopoly might cause Canadian price changes to be more closely related to U.S. price changes without an exchange-rate adjustment than with such an adjustment. All three approaches to the role of the exchange rate were explored.

It is clear that we might fail to pick up the influence of United States on Canadian prices through failing to take into account the assorted domestic influences operating on the Canadian industry's selling prices. Attempts to include influences on individual industries are reported below. At this stage we experimentally inserted the Canadian Gross National Expenditure deflator or the aggregative selling price index[10] as independent variables to provide rough proxies for the general pressure of inflationary forces in Canada on the individual industry's prices.

Table 5.1 summarizes our principal regression results for this first stage of the analysis. Columns 1, 2, and 3 show the regression coefficients of annual Canadian on United States industry price changes, 1957–1966, with the Canadian prices respectively unlagged, lagged one quarter, and lagged two

10. This unpublished index was supplied by the D.B.S.

TABLE 5.1. Regression coefficients of Canadian on United States wholesale price changes, by industry, 1957–1966 (including standard errors)

	Simple regressions			Multiple regressions[a]	
Industry	No lag (1)	One quarter lag (2)	Two quarter lag (3)	Including exchange rate (4)	Including general price index (Canada)[b] (5)
Slaughtering and meat-packing	0.2009 (0.1853)	0.7401[c] (0.0845)	0.7232[c] (0.1372)	0.2061 (0.1992)	1.2636[c] (0.6276)
Poultry	1.1228 (0.6692)	0.4137 (0.8565)	0.2098 (0.6974)	1.1604 (0.7380)	1.4795 (0.8835)
Fish processing	−0.0460 (0.0658)	−0.0105 (0.0618)	−0.0135 (0.0748)	−0.0227 (0.0878)	−0.0517 (0.0701)
Fruit and vegetable preparations	−0.2439 (0.4290)	−0.0103 (0.4014)	0.1603 (0.4561)	−0.2958[d] (0.3635)	0.1551 (0.6344)
Feed mills	0.2400 (0.2560)	0.4625[c] (0.1684)	0.6681[c] (0.1751)	0.0624 (0.4138)	0.2911 (0.2828)
Bread and other bakery products	−0.1640 (1.0323)	−0.4641 (0.8721)	−0.6507 (0.8426)	−0.6366 (0.9811)	1.0185[c,e] (0.4298)
Carbonated beverages	0.0321 (0.4147)	0.0869 (0.4296)	0.1374 (0.4466)	0.0015 (0.4501)	0.7526[c] (0.1272)
Distilled liquors	0.8282 (1.3030)	0.6907 (1.0396)	0.1094 (0.6739)	1.4839[d] (1.1572)	0.7815[c] (0.0600)
Breweries	−0.2917 (0.6581)	−.1442 (0.4351)	0.8221 (0.5481)	−0.7699 (0.7186)	−0.2364 (0.7702)
Wines	0.0516 (0.0660)	0.0956 (0.0641)	0.1006 (0.0860)	0.0475 (0.0795)	0.0558 (0.0743)
Chewing gum	−0.0190 (0.2784)	−0.0572 (0.2344)	−0.1197 (0.2361)	0.1215[d] (0.2331)	−0.1731 (0.3599)
Sugar refining	2.5704 (2.0160)	3.2640[c] (1.6578)	3.1227[c] (1.2461)	2.5704 (2.0160)	0.8332 (0.4608)
Cigarettes	−0.0751 (0.3605)	0.0409 (0.4248)	0.4112 (0.6012)	−0.2129 (0.3496)	−0.3870[e] (0.2265)
Tobacco, cigars and cigarettes	0.1730 (0.3199)	0.3612 (0.3521)	0.7885 (0.4873)	−0.0013 (0.3730)	−0.3780[e] (0.2081)
Rubber goods	0.7094 (0.5243)	0.6723 (0.5303)	0.4785 (0.6162)	0.4685[d] (0.3560)	0.7461 (0.4960)[e]
Gloves and mittens	0.7643 (0.9704)	1.0682 (1.0357)	0.4330 (1.1219)	0.7643 (0.9704)	1.0570[c,e] (0.4372)
Leather tanning	1.3309[c] (0.0957)	1.2472[c] (0.1154)	0.6516 (0.3377)	1.3327[c] (0.1102)	1.2855[c] (0.0995)
Woolen cloth	1.1952[c] (0.5014)	1.7678[c] (0.4958)	1.0238 (0.6082)	1.1780[c] (0.5797)	0.5790[c] (0.0750)
Woven filament rayon	0.5089[c] (0.2018)	0.4134 (0.2237)	0.2722 (0.2468)	0.5757[c] (0.1757)	0.7288[c,e] (0.1253)
Clothing (men's factory)	0.4470 (0.2446)	0.5029 (0.2528)	0.5918 (0.3210)	0.4804 (0.2744)	0.3253[e] (0.2630)
Hosiery	−0.0939 (0.6100)	−0.2599 (0.4249)	−0.6613 (0.4276)	−0.3232 (0.6027)	0.6350[c] (0.0754)
Veneers and plywoods	0.8180 (0.5116)	0.9864 (0.5368)	0.8150 (0.4445)	0.8141 (0.5557)	0.9449[c] (0.1918)

TABLE 5.1 — *Continued*

Industry	Simple regressions			Multiple regressions[a]	
	No lag (1)	One quarter lag (2)	Two quarter lag (3)	Including exchange rate (4)	Including general price index (Canada)[b] (5)
Lumber mills	0.7550[c]	0.7590[c]	0.5941[c]	0.7528[c]	0.8485
	(0.1179)	(0.1007)	(0.2035)	(0.1222)	(0.4728)
Shingle mills	0.8018[c]	0.7965[c]	0.6774[c]	0.8118[c]	0.1528
	(0.0564)	(0.1122)	(0.1986)	(0.0583)	(0.2375)
Furniture	1.1841	0.5996	0.2982	1.1730	1.5411
(wooden office)	(0.8434)	(0.6709)	(0.5748)	(0.9553)	(0.9048)
Pulp mills	0.5169	0.2948	0.0857	1.0343[e,d]	0.2290
	(0.2767)	(0.2481)	(0.2980)	(0.2082)	(0.2172)
Agricultural implements	0.5717[c]	0.5387[c]	0.4401[c]	0.5887[c]	0.1623
	(0.0742)	(0.0862)	(0.1371)	(0.0771)	(0.4656)
Iron castings	0.8431	1.0573[c]	0.7174[c]	1.2454[c]	2.0833[c]
	(0.4888)	(0.3997)	(0.3486)	(0.5889)	(0.8013)
Pig iron	0.6201[c]	0.5373[c]	0.3158[c]	0.6712[c]	0.3306
	(0.0614)	(0.0696)	(0.0809)	(0.0667)	(0.9371)
Steel ingots and castings	−0.0492	0.1113	0.4472	−0.4047	−0.0487
	(0.6509)	(0.7229)	(0.5586)	(0.6387)	(0.7106)
Rolled iron and steel	0.3089	0.2333	0.2472	0.0837	0.3066
products	(0.2873)	(0.3872)	(0.3267)	(0.3180)	(0.3092)
Trucks	0.3422	0.1071	0.0469	0.2667	0.2909
	(0.4823)	(0.2857)	(0.3591)	(0.5959)	(0.4686)
Brass and copper	0.9210[c]	0.6844[c]	0.4359	1.1904[e,d]	0.7551[c,e]
products	(0.1458)	(0.1424)	(0.2238)	(0.1591)	(0.1471)
Brass ingots	1.1320[c]	0.6793	0.1587	1.5561[c]	1.2455
	(0.3561)	(0.4014)	(0.4687)	(0.4852)	(0.6382)
Faucets and	−0.0547	−0.0165	−0.0204	−0.1519	−0.2509
combinations	(0.5875)	(0.5891)	(0.5708)	(0.6956)	(0.5206)
Nonferrous metal	0.9186[c]	0.8872[c]	0.7284[c]	0.9194[c]	0.0197
smelting and refining	(0.1969)	(0.2047)	(0.2546)	(0.1729)	(0.4515)
Batteries	0.4922	0.6252	0.5040	0.4759	0.4056
	(0.4656)	(0.5056)	(0.5295)	(1.0356)	(0.4642)
Refrigerators, vacuum	0.9884[c]	0.6189	0.5041	0.8620	1.5103[c]
cleaners and appliances	(0.4227)	(0.4712)	(0.4456)	(0.4819)	(1.0418)
Cement (hydraulic)	−0.1047	−0.1491	−0.3784	−0.0966	0.3620
	(0.5677)	(0.5584)	(0.5644)	(0.6252)	(0.5543)
Clay products from	0.2809[c]	0.2941[c]	0.3107[c]	0.2393	0.2776[c]
imported clay	(0.1187)	(0.0882)	(0.0844)	(0.1946)	(0.1304)
Glass and glass	0.0485	−0.0536	−0.0922	0.1471	0.0779
containers	(0.2032)	(0.2734)	(0.2026)	(0.1950)	(0.2344)
Gypsum products	0.1351	0.1262	0.0005	0.1779	0.2461[c,e]
	(0.1226)	(0.1535)	(0.1801)	(0.1284)	(0.1151)
Blocks, gravel	1.3885	1.0321	1.0008	0.7869	1.2993
	(1.0831)	(1.0441)	(1.0177)	(1.3451)	(1.1313)
Concrete (ready-mixed)	1.0414	−0.2238	−0.8232	1.3158	−0.3683[c]
	(1.8014)	(1.8527)	(1.4221)	(1.9453)	(0.9889)
Clay products from	1.3840[c]	1.3899	1.2052	1.1646	1.3740
domestic clay	(0.5854)	(0.8275)	(0.7194)	(0.7232)	(0.7260)
Petroleum products	0.1297	0.2530[c]	0.2784[c]	0.1315	0.0986
	(0.1578)	(0.0707)	(0.1249)	(0.1711)	(0.1834)

TABLE 5.1 — *Continued*

Industry	Simple regressions			Multiple regressions[a]	
	No lag (1)	One quarter lag (2)	Two quarter lag (3)	Including exchange rate (4)	Including general price index (Canada)[b] (5)
Acids, alkalies and salts	0.7678[c]	0.7357[c]	0.7400[c]	0.7312[c]	2.5562
	(0.2110)	(0.2390)	(0.2615)	(0.2674)	(2.0283)
Fertilizers	−0.0988	−0.1775	−0.0233	−0.0317	−0.1061
	(0.5245)	(0.4890)	(0.5500)	(0.5477)	(0.5534)
Paints, varnishes and lacquers	0.1548	0.1846	0.2723[c]	0.1072	0.7924[e]
	(0.2058)	(0.1551)	(0.1289)	(0.2262)	(0.2442)
Vegetable oils	0.4939[c]	0.4066[e]	0.1916	0.4705[c,d]	0.5817[e]
	(0.1228)	(0.1090)	(0.1125)	(0.0948)	(0.0918)

[a] U.S. price-change variable entered with no lag.

[b] Both GNP deflator and aggregative selling price index were tried; the regression coefficient in col. 5 comes from the equation in which the general price indicator was more significant.

[c] Regression coefficient significant at 5-percent level.

[d] Exchange-rate coefficient in this equation significant at 5-percent level.

[e] Coefficient of the general price index significant at 5-percent level.

quarters. Column 4 gives the regression coefficient of the Canadian on the U.S. price change when the exchange rate (price of the U.S. dollar) is added as a separate predetermined variable, and indicates those industries for which the exchange rate was significant. Likewise, column 5 gives the regression coefficients when some measure of aggregate wholesale price change in Canada is added to the equation,[11] and indicates those industries for which aggregate Canadian price movements significantly affected the Canadian industry selling price.

The most striking finding that emerges from Table 5.1 is

11. Both the GNP deflator and the aggregative selling price index were added in separate regressions. The regression coefficient on the U.S. price change in col. 5 comes from the equation in which the aggregate Canadian price index was more nearly significant.

that the influence of foreign on Canadian prices, variable though it may be from industry to industry, is seldom improved by making any adjustment for variations in the exchange rate. As column 4 shows, only in one case is the United States price-change variable made significant by addition of the exchange rate to the equation; the exchange rate itself is significant at the 5-percent level in only seven cases, and in four of them its sign is perverse. In the typical case it contributed nothing to the portion of the variance explained by the U.S. price alone. This result cannot be explained by a lack of variability in the exchange rate (it would have been more variable, though, if quarterly data were employed). Although our period covers four and a half years in which the rate was pegged at $0.925, it also includes the pegging of the rate and its devaluation from a high of $1.0786. Because of the negative results in this test, we performed the alternative experiment of adjusting the United States price-change series for changes in the exchange rate in a sample of five industries (slaughtering and meat-packing; rubber products, including footwear; furniture; agricultural implements; and acids, alkalies, and salts). The pattern remained the same, in that multiplying changes in U.S. industry prices by exchange-rate changes failed to improve the fits based on U.S. prices alone.[12]

The influence on industry prices of general movements of

12. Although the data seem to establish the weak role of the exchange rate, two qualifications should be kept in mind. First, the variability of the exchange rate was relatively low (and rendered smaller by the use of quarterly data). Second, the role of changes in raw materials prices might upset our method of distinguishing between foreign-price and exchange-rate influences. Suppose that for any given industry, changes in U.S. product prices and world raw materials prices are highly correlated, and that the Canadian prices of raw materials are much more responsive to the exchange-rate-adjusted world prices of raw materials than are the Canadian prices of final goods to U.S. final goods prices. (This is plausible because of the undifferentiated character of raw materials.) Then part of the influence of movements in the exchange rate would be picked up by the U.S. price variable.

Canadian prices, expressed by changes in the aggregate price deflator of GNP or aggregate selling price index, proved only a little stronger than that of the exchange rate, producing a significant coefficient with the right sign in only seven cases. Its addition generally left the coefficient of the United States price change unaltered. It did convert insignificant price coefficients to significant ones in six cases, but it demolished previously significant relations in twelve cases. Collinearity between U.S. industry price changes and general Canadian price movements may thus account for a portion of our findings on price linkages at the industry level between the two countries. Some further evidence of collinearity appears below when we examine other determinants of price changes in individual Canadian industries.

Our experiment of lagging the Canadian price changes behind the United States by zero, three, and six months produced significant regression coefficients in respectively 16, 18, and 13 cases. Moving from zero to three months, significant coefficients became insignificant in only three cases. Thus, it seems that three months is the best estimate of the median lag in the effect of U.S. on Canadian wholesale prices of manufactured goods, although the margin of superiority is thin. The existence of this lag tends to support an implication of the insignificant role of the exchange rate: the typical Canadian price reaction picked up in our sample behaves like an administrative rather than a market reaction to a U.S. price change, since it occurs only with a lag and responds to the foreign currency price more strongly than it does to the exchange rate or the exchange-rate-adjusted price.

It is clear from Table 5.1 that the industries sampled vary widely in both size and statistical significance of response to foreign price changes. Nonsignificant regression coefficients are invariably small, but the significant ones vary considerably. Taking those that are significant at roughly the 10-percent level, and using the regressions summarized in column 1 of Table 5.1, the range is from 1.38 down to 0.28, with a median of 0.84 and quartile observations of 1.13 and 0.57. Employing a lag of three months in the Canadian response (column 2), the median drops slightly to 0.74, the quartiles to 1.06 and 0.50. These price sensitivity coefficients provide the inputs for the next stage of our calculations, in which we seek factors that explain high or low Canadian price response.

The first differentiating factor suggested by economic theory is the extent of an industry's participation in international trade, measured by the sum of exports and imports divided by the value of domestic production.[13] The presence of competitive imports provides a clear link between Canadian and world market prices. The same should hold for the existence of substantial export sales. A competitive industry should charge the same prices at home and abroad and thus reflect export price changes on the home market. In the case of concentrated export industries that dump abroad, some linkage will remain if the margin between the world and domestic prices stays reasonably constant.[14] These arguments deduce

13. The international trade variable is a gross index, with exports defined as a percentage of domestic output and imports as a percentage of sales. The data, until recently collected only on a product basis in Canada, were reassembled on an industry basis using the weights included in D.B.S., *Industry Selling Price Indexes.* Calculations were performed for 1956, 1961, and 1965, then averaged. The basic source of data was D.B.S., *Trade of Canada* (various issues). Although there is some case for using only Canadian trade with the U.S., rather than total trade (especially where products are differentiated), we have employed data on total trade because of the theoretical importance of price linkages through third-country trade.

14. Anne Romanis, "Cost Inflation and Incomes Policy in Industrial Countries," *IMF Staff Papers,* XIV (March, 1967), 169–206, notes evidence of the extent of openness of industrial economies on the institutional structure of domestic price and wage determination. Openness tends to be associated with the formation of powerful centralized employers' federations for wage bargaining with trade unions (p. 196). Also, David Schwartzman indirectly confirms the relevance of trade participation in showing that it seems to limit the extent to which highly concentrated Canadian industries

price linkage from the *presence* of trade participation, yet our formulation hypothesizes that the price linkage increases with the *extent* of trade participation. The importance of trade participation lies in assuring significant elasticities of substitution between foreign and domestic output (in either foreign or domestic markets). In the international market for a single homogeneous product there would be no reason to expect a correlation between the extent of trade participation and the size of such elasticities of substitution; one needs only "some trade" to guarantee against a corner solution. Nonetheless, a pragmatic argument can be made. Our product categories are in fact anything but homogeneous, so that an industry with a higher trade-participation variable is likely to encounter significant international price competition for a higher proportion of its subproducts. This would justify the hypothesis as stated.

The second variable that might explain the extent of transmission of United States price changes to Canada is the extent of foreign ownership in an industry.[15] In 1965, residents of the United States owned 44 percent and controlled 46 percent of capital invested in Canadian manufacturing industry.[16] Foreign ownership is not spread randomly across manufactur-

---

can exploit potential monopoly profits; see his "The Effect of Monopoly on Price," *Journal of Political Economy*, LXVII (August, 1959), 352–362.

15. The direct investment variable is defined in D.B.S., *The Canadian Balance of International Payments, 1960, and International Investment Position* (Ottawa: Queen's Printer, 1962), pp. 62–63. It is based on book-value data and relates to the aggregate investment in Canada in companies whose principal owners are nonresidents. Data pertaining to control rather than ownership were used — although, of course, the variable suggests only potential, not actual exercise of control. Most of the data refer to the year 1964 and some to 1962; they were taken from *ibid., 1963, 1964, and 1965.* Some general impressions were also gained from A. E. Safarian, *Foreign Ownership of Canadian Industry* (Toronto: McGraw-Hill, 1966).

16. Task Force on the Structure of Canadian Industry, *Foreign Ownership and the Structure of Canadian Industry,* prepared for the Privy Council Office (Ottawa: Queen's Printer, 1968), p. 199. Hereafter cited as Watkins Report.

ing industry but typically concentrates in those trades producing branded (trademarked), patented, or otherwise differentiated articles. Makers of such goods control the prices of their own brands — to whatever degree that control is influenced and constrained by oligopoly and the existence of close substitutes. Although the link has received little attention among the many Canadian suspicions concerning the behavior of foreign subsidiaries, price adjustments by subsidiaries in the Canadian market may sometimes follow mechanically upon price changes by their parents in the United States market, or at least be subject to some parental influence beyond that of Canadian market conditions. Thus, we predict that higher levels of foreign ownership are associated with closer dependence of Canadian on U.S. price changes. This might be either because of centralization of decision-making in the parent or it might be a result of oligopolistic pricing patterns in an industry dominated, in both Canada and the United States, by the same firms.[17]

The third discriminant variable that we propose is seller concentration in the Canadian industry.[18] One might argue that a purely competitive market would be blind to developments not embodied in domestic supply or demand shifts and thus would take no account of foreign price changes until they fed through foreign trade or into Canadian macroeconomic variables. In a concentrated industry, however, where sellers exercise some control over both their individual prices

17. The authors of the Watkins Report mention but do not describe an unsuccessful test of this hypothesis (*ibid.*, pp. 81–82).

18. Concentration, measured by the percentage of employment accounted for by the three leading firms, is taken from G. Rosenbluth, *Concentration in Canadian Manufacturing Industries* (Princeton, N.J.: Princeton University Press, 1957). Rosenbluth's estimates rest on 1948 data. Some data and qualitative observations based on 1962 were supplied by Mr. Max Stewart, of the Economic Council of Canada. The results reported below do not appear to have been altered by this more recent information.

and, collectively, over the industry's average price level, foreign developments may be taken directly into account and may furnish excuses for the elevation of list prices even before a disturbance in excess demand is felt. The higher the concentration, the more closely do we expect Canadian to follow United States prices.

From discussion of these three hypotheses about the determinants of Canada-U.S. industry price linkages, it is clear that interaction among the independent variables is to be expected. High levels of foreign trade, if they correspond to high substitution elasticities, ought to weld tight price linkages irrespective of the other variables. It may not interact statistically with them, but influence of the other two variables may be apparent only in industries where trade participation is not too high.[19] Foreign ownership and concentration might interact positively because the higher the concentration, the greater the freedom of the individual firm (subsidiary) to make its individual price preferences stick in the market. Turning the proposition around, and noting that industries which are highly concentrated in Canada are usually also highly concentrated in the United States, high concentration raises the chance that firms in industries with heavy foreign ownership will employ the same pattern of mutual price adaptation in Canada as they do in the United States.

To test these hypotheses about the determinants of industry price linkages we employed an analysis of variance procedure on the regression coefficients in column 1 of Table 5.1, splitting them into three classes: below 0.20, between 0.20 and 0.60, and above 0.60. (Other splits were tried and gave somewhat less significant results.) We tried both restricting the

19. Evidence summarized in the Watkins Report suggests that foreign ownership may predispose a firm to somewhat higher trade participation, as we define it, then a comparable domestically owned firm would display (pp. 199–205). Also note Schwartzman's results on the effect of trade on monopoly (n. 14 above).

analysis to regression coefficients significant at the 95-percent level and also throwing in all coefficients regardless of significance. Since the insignificant coefficients almost always had low absolute values, the choice between these procedures might be expected to make little difference; that was in fact the case. Data on all three of the classificatory variables outlined above were unfortunately available for only 17 of the 50 industries listed in Table 5.1, reducing the available degrees of freedom seriously.[20]

First we tested the three classificatory variables separately. Foreign trade participation and foreign ownership proved to be significant at the 95-percent level, but concentration did not. In view of the relatively weak rationale for the hypothesis concerning concentration, this result accords well with theoretical predictions. Next we employed a two-way analysis of variance layout to check for interactions between pairs of the classificatory variables. Only a dichotomous classification of the regression coefficients was used because of the shortage of degrees of freedom. It turns out that foreign trade and foreign ownership vary together, that is, that price transmission is stronger when foreign trade and foreign ownership are both high than would be expected from the additive combination of their effects. There is no significant interaction of concentration with either of the other two variables. The quantitative results of this analysis of variance are presented in Table 5.2.

20. Slaughtering and meatpacking, fruit and vegetable processing, feed mills, bread and bakery products, distilled liquors, tobacco, rubber goods (footwear), leather goods (tanning), men's factory clothing, wooden furniture, lumber and shingle mills, pulp mills, primary iron and steel, agricultural implements, motor vehicles, petroleum refining and products, acids, alkalies and salts.

TABLE 5.2. Analysis of variance of price-sensitivity coefficients

Source of variation	Degrees of freedom	F	$F_{.95}$
Tests for significance of individual discriminant variables			
Trade participation	(2, 13)	5.0	3.8
Foreign ownership	(2, 13)	4.2	3.8
Seller concentration	(2, 13)	1.6	3.8
Tests for interaction of discriminant variables			
Trade participation and foreign ownership			
Trade participation	3	3.4	2.8
Foreign ownership	2	3.7	3.2
Interaction	13	2.6	2.3
Foreign ownership and concentration			
Foreign ownership	3	2.3	2.8
Concentration	2	2.4	3.2
Interaction	6	1.1	2.3
Trade participation and concentration			
Trade participation	3	2.6	2.8
Concentration	2	2.5	3.2
Interaction	6	1.3	2.3

Source: Calculated from price-sensitivity coefficients in Table 5.1, col. 1.

INTERDEPENDENCE OF INDUSTRY AVERAGE HOURLY WAGES

The preceding section shows that relatively strong direct linkages exist between wholesale price changes in Canadian industries and their United States counterparts. Yet there has been little or no outcry in Canada about this shackling of the price level to external developments — a silence exemplified by the lack of any substantial discussion in the Watkins Report on foreign ownership. In the case of industry-level wage linkages between the two countries, we shall find the situation essentially reversed. On the one hand, recent Canadian demands for wage parity with U.S. workers have prompted the voicing of much concern about the dominant influence of U.S. wage bargains; but our statistical investigation shows industry wage linkages between the two countries to be much weaker than price linkages.

This conclusion is not surprising in reference to a model of competitive markets. In the labor market there is very little mobility between the two countries, in contrast to the extensive role of commodity trade in the manufacturing sector. Any industry-level linkage must result either from imported bargaining factors influencing the Canadian wage-determination process or from indirect linkages operating through common Canada-United States industry profit rates, rates of technological change, and the like. The former might include economic and social institutions that would provide the vehicles for effective transmission of income aspirations — fraternal clubs, the communications media, and, of course, trade unions.

To test the strength and sources of industry wage linkages, we used the same two-stage procedure as for price linkages, beginning by establishing a sample of 27 comparably defined Canadian and United States industries for which data are available on average hourly wages. The period covered is 1958–1966, its shortness forced by the lack in some cases of suitably disaggregated U.S. data before 1958.[21] Neither series includes fringe benefits, but the Canadian data include overtime.

Table 5.3 summarizes the results of regressing the annual

21. D.B.S., *Man-Hours and Hourly Earnings* and *Review of Man-Hours and Hourly Earnings* (various issues); U.S. Department of Labor, Bureau of Labor Statistics, *Employment and Earnings Statistics for the United States, 1909–66* (Washington: Government Printing Office, 1966).

TABLE 5.3. Regression coefficients of Canadian on United States money wage changes, by industry, 1958–1966 (including standard errors)

Industry	U.S. change unlagged (1)	U.S. change lagged six months (2)
Slaughtering and meat-packing	−0.0311	1.4201[a]
	(0.6365)	(0.5219)
Canned fruit and vegetables	−0.8005	0.7919
	(0.7591)	(0.6618)
Bread and other bakery products	−0.9421[a]	0.3058
	(0.4393)	(0.6085)
Feed mills	−0.5324	0.1713
	(0.4894)	(0.4448)
Breweries	0.9024	2.0079
	(1.3372)	(1.6477)
Tobacco, cigarettes and cigars	−1.3020[a]	0.0548
	(0.6368)	(0.7369)
Rubber goods, including footwear	1.0076[a]	−0.6407
	(0.4942)	(0.8631)
Leather tanning	1.0000	−0.0965
	(1.0367)	(0.5607)
Woolen goods	0.0609	0.4016[a]
	(0.2407)	(0.1791)
Synthetic fabrics	0.6059[a]	0.2561
	(0.2759)	(0.3669)
Clothing (men's factory)	−0.2050	−0.0792
	(0.2787)	(0.4114)
Plywoods and veneers	−0.6681	−0.0077
	(0.7640)	(0.9477)
Furniture	0.4656	0.2531
	(0.2762)	(0.2509)
Pulp and paper	0.4371	−1.0823
	(0.9254)	(0.8126)
Agricultural implements	0.6061	−0.1992
	(0.3752)	(0.4692)
Fabricated and structural steel	0.7984	0.5470
	(0.4475)	(0.4637)

TABLE 5.3 — *Continued*

Industry	U.S. change unlagged (1)	U.S. change lagged six months (2)
Primary iron and steel	0.2910	3.2296[a]
	(0.6334)	(1.0436)
Motor vehicles	1.0164[a]	0.1983
	(0.3781)	(1.0293)
Brass and copper	−0.4791	0.1621
	(0.2783)	(0.3804)
Nonferrous metal smelting and refining	0.1265	−0.0609
	(0.6151)	(0.6177)
Refrigerators	0.2554	0.4554
	(0.5642)	(0.5447)
Clay products	0.7784	0.5774
	(0.4043)	(0.3663)
Glass and glass containers	0.4961	−0.1771
	(0.2911)	(0.3364)
Petroleum refining	0.2032	−0.1530
	(0.2732)	(0.3316)
Acids	0.4305	0.0510
	(0.2303)	(0.4873)
Fertilizers	−0.5121	0.4453
	(0.9049)	(0.9028)
Paints and varnishes	0.0749	−0.1906
	(0.1832)	(0.2626)

[a] Regression coefficient significant at 5-percent level.

percentage changes in Canadian wages on their United States counterparts. Following the results of the price equations, no adjustment is made for changes in the exchange rate. As could be expected, the relations are typically much less close than in the price equations, and negative regression coefficients are not uncommon. The table shows the results both of assuming no lag (using annual data) for the Canadian wage response and of inserting a six-month lag. The inclusion of a lag of one year yields estimates fairly similar to those for six months. Unlike the price equations, no strong central tendency appears in the length of the lag. If we select as superior the lag giving the more (nearly) significant regression coefficient, the unlagged relation appears better in 18 cases, the six-month lag in nine. If, on the other hand, we rule out negative signs as nonsensical and select the more nearly significant positive-signed coefficient, the score indicates no lag in 15 industries, a six-month lag in 10, and a tie in two (that is, both coefficients negative).[22] There is some evidence of similar patterns prevailing in related industries: for example, six-month lags are quite common in the textile and clothing sectors, no lags in the durable goods industries. Because of the prevailing lack of statistically significant relations, however, the chances are quite high that these patterns really reflect random behavior.

Despite the evidently thin results at the first stage, we continued to seek for classificatory variables that might explain instances of direct wage linkage between Canadian and United States industries. The first variable selected is the presence of an international union in the industry. One of the charges brought by opponents of international unions is that they may force U.S. patterns of wage settlement on Canadian industry. Whatever the truth of this charge, U.S. organizations of international unions often provide information and bargaining expertise to their Canadian affiliates, and this could provide the transmission belt.[23] Data were secured from a number of

22. Because wage bargaining tends to occur in key industries in rounds from one to four years apart, causing discrete shifts in some cases, it is not obvious that the negative signs are nonsensical; they might represent incorrectly identified lag structures. See Otto Eckstein and Thomas A. Wilson, "The Determination of Money Wages in American Industry," *Quarterly Journal of Economics,* LXXVI (August, 1962), 386–387.

23. J. H. G. Crispo, *The Role of International Unionism in Canada* (Washington and Montreal: Canadian-American Committee, 1967), pp. 5–6, 29–30.

sources, including reports filed under the Corporations and Labour Unions Returns Act and reports of the several major international unions involved.[24] These data were generally presented on the basis of type of work or product produced rather than on the basis of industrial classification. Consequently, they were reorganized and assembled using the product weights outlined in the appendix of D.B.S., *Industry Selling Price Indexes, 1956–59.*

A second variable included in the analysis of variance test was foreign ownership, using the same data as in the price linkage test. International corporations might be expected, for a variety of reasons, to employ industrial relations practices on both sides of the border that could lead to similar rates of wage increase. Furthermore, this variable should interact with the presence of international unions, which to some extent would result in the presence of the same people at both Canadian and United States bargaining tables.[25]

The third variable was geographical proximity of the Canadian and United States portions of a North American industry. Proximity should make workers on the Canadian side more immediately and accurately conscious of U.S. wage levels. In some cases, it may result in limited amounts of direct competition in the labor market across the border. Either way, it would tend to increase industry wage linkages. To measure proximity, we secured rough estimates of the percentage of enterprises in an industry concentrated in adjacent regions of the two countries. For most manufacturing industries this meant exploring the extent of concentration in the

24. The international union variable was expressed as the percentage of workers in a Canadian industry who are members of an international union. Most relevant information came from the Canadian Department of Labour, *Labour Organizations in Canada* (Ottawa: Queen's Printer, annual). The year 1962 was used in the analysis because that was the first year for which reports were made under the Corporations and Labour Unions Returns Act.

25. Crispo's discussion (e.g., p. 41) suggests that this phenomenon occurs but is not common.

Great Lakes industrial region;[26] proximity for the lumber and pulp sectors is associated with concentration in the Pacific Northwest.

The final variable was seller concentration, employed above in investigating price linkages. The rationale was that increased industrial concentration gives greater scope for industrywide bargaining, which in turn favors the influencing of Canadian wage settlements by contemporary United States developments. The failure of the concentration variable in the price linkage tests, however, coupled with Eckstein's and Wilson's negative results in a related inquiry,[27] gave little basis for expecting positive results.

In view of the small portion of significant regression coefficients in Table 5.3, we decided to employ in the analysis of variance whichever coefficient is more (nearly) significant. The justification for this practice is perhaps less clear than it was for the price relations, where insignificance was nearly always associated with low positive values for the regression coefficients; in Table 5.3, a few significant negative coefficients appear. But with such a small harvest of significant coefficients, the analysis of variance could not be confined to them alone. First, the wage-sensitivity coefficients were divided into two groups (below and above 0.50) and tested for significant intergroup differences against the four classificatory variables,

26. Various industry manuals and the *Census of Manufactures* were used, and some general impressions came from Ronald J. Wonnacott and Paul Wonnacott, *Free Trade between the United States and Canada: The Potential Economic Effects* (Cambridge, Mass.: Harvard University Press, 1967).

27. Eckstein and Wilson, "Determination of Money Wages," p. 400. Investigating a related question, Schwartzman found no significant differences between the ratios of Canadian to U.S. wages for industries in which Canadian concentration exceeds that in the U.S., and the ratios for those industries in which concentration is about the same; David Schwartzman, "Monopoly and Wages," *Canadian Journal of Economics and Political Science*, XXVI (August, 1960), 428–438.

one at a time. Each proved insignificant at the 95-percent level, but international unionism accounts for an intergroup difference nearly significant at the 75-percent level. Extensive experiments at subdividing the coefficients in different ways did not bring the results closer to significance, although international unionism continued to emerge the strongest. Two-way analysis of variance was also attempted, using each of the possible pairs of discriminant variables, but no significant classifications or interactions were found. Degrees of freedom are again insufficient for a three-way layout. The details of this analysis are shown in Table 5.4 on page 226.

OTHER DETERMINANTS OF CANADIAN PRICE AND WAGE CHANGES

A possible reason for the relatively poor statistical results reported here is the exclusion of many possible determinants of Canadian industry price and wage changes from the statistical analysis. In the case of Canadian industry prices, these might include changes in Canadian wages and productivity, operating either independently or through their joint influence on unit labor costs. (Courchene has shown that the relation between actual and desired inventories also wields a major influence on price changes, but data limitations make it impossible to extend his results to our larger sample of industries.[28]) Canadian wage changes might be influenced by productivity growth, or by United States product price changes for the industry in question (through expectational factors not reflected wholly in U.S. wage changes).

28. Thomas J. Courchene, "An Analysis of the Price-Inventory Nexus with Empirical Application to the Canadian Manufacturing Sector," *International Economic Review*, X (October, 1969), 315–336.

225

TABLE 5.4. Analysis of variance of wage-sensitivity coefficients

Source of variation	Degrees of freedom	F	$F_{.95}$
Tests for significance of individual discriminant variables			
International unionism	(1, 24)	2.9	4.3
Foreign ownership	(1, 24)	1.7	4.3
Geographic proximity	(1, 24)	1.1	4.3
Tests for interaction of discriminant variables			
International unionism and foreign ownership			
International unionism	3	1.0	2.5
Foreign ownership	2	1.6	2.7
Interaction	13	0.9	1.9
Foreign ownership and geographic proximity			
Foreign ownership	3	1.6	2.5
Geographic proximity	2	1.4	2.7
Interaction	13	1.2	1.9
International unionism and geographic proximity			
International unionism	3	1.1	2.5
Geographic proximity	2	1.2	2.7
Interaction	13	1.2	1.9

Source: Wage-sensitivity coefficients from Table 5.3.

We attempted to relate our Canadian price and wage changes to these additional determinants, first taking them separately and then in addition to the influence of United States prices and wages, respectively. We hoped this procedure would clarify the preceding results in either of two ways. First, insignificant relations between the Canadian and U.S. variables might conceivably become significant when other Canadian domestic variables were added. Second, the putative U.S. determinants of Canadian price and wage changes might turn out to be highly collinear with their Canadian domestic determinants, throwing the conclusion in the other direction by calling into question the simple linkages found above between Canadian and U.S. industry price changes.[29]

The results tend toward the latter conclusion, although the extent of statistically significant findings is small enough to warrant only a brief summary. Data were obtained on changes in productivity by dividing an index of labor supply (number of hours worked) into an index of total output for each industry. (The use of value added rather than total output would have been preferable, but indexes of value added could not be readily assembled at this level of disaggregation.) Our annual series of Canadian industry price changes were run successively on annual Canadian wage changes (unlagged and lagged six months), productivity changes, and the product of the two — changes in unit labor costs. The simple regressions on wage changes produced three significant coefficients using unlagged wage changes and five significant coefficients using wage changes lagged six months (plus two more with perverse signs). Simple regressions of annual price changes on productivity changes (unlagged) produced only five significant coefficients and a predominance of perverse signs over the whole sample of 24 industries. Unit labor costs worked rather better, however, yielding ten significant relations with correct signs. Furthermore, analysis of the variance of the regression coefficients on unit labor costs showed that their influence on

29. Courchene's results (*ibid.*) suggest this latter finding. Adding United States price changes to a quarterly analysis of the determinants of price changes in Canadian iron and steel, leather, and total manufacturing, he finds that the U.S. change reduces the significance of other determinants (wage changes, desired minus actual inventories) without being very significant itself.

227

prices is stronger where labor costs are a large proportion of total costs and where the industry's participation in international trade is small.

The important question is whether these domestic cost variables tended either to create or to destroy significant relations between Canadian and United States price changes. One would not necessarily expect much interaction, since the influence of U.S. prices registers most heavily in areas where trade participation is high, and the influence of unit labor costs where it is low. Adding U.S. price changes to the simple regressions of prices on Canadian unit labor costs, a significant coefficient for the U.S. price change emerged in only four industries and the significance of Canadian unit labor costs generally fell. Looked at the other way, adding changes in unit labor costs to the simple regressions of Canadian on United States price changes, the significance of the U.S. changes was lost in eight industries and created in three. These findings give some basis for suspecting that collinearity between U.S. prices and Canadian domestic variables might account for some of the results reported in the preceding section, but the case is not very clear-cut.

The analysis of Canadian industry wage changes was developed in a similar way. Productivity changes proved to be a significant determinant of wage changes, taking those of the United States into account, in only four cases out of 23 (two with perverse signs), and its inclusion did not affect the dependence of Canadian on U.S. wage changes discernibly one way or the other. Our wobbly conclusions about the impact of U.S. wages through international unionism thus seem to stand no more shakily than before.

Probably the most important finding of this chapter is the apparently direct linkage between United States and Canadian industry selling prices. The fact that this linkage appears closer *without* adjusting for changes in the exchange rate, and the fact that movements in general Canadian price indicators help only moderately to explain Canadian industry price variations after U.S. variations are taken into account, argue for "micro" industry price influence working independently of the "macro" forces that, it is ordinarily felt, determine the Canadian price level. Operating within the limits of tolerable rates of unemployment, it cannot be assumed that Canadian policy-makers hold great power over the wholesale price level,[30] and our results show that even such a strong measure as varying the exchange rate seems to have little effect, at least over the range observed in the period under study. To put the same proposition another way, with either a fixed or flexible exchange rate, Canada can attain a rate of money price increase lower than that abroad only by incurring heavy unemployment.[31] But this conclusion should not be ridden too hard. Our findings in Chapters 2 and 3 concerning the importance of stabilizing expectations about the exchange rate probably apply in some degree to its influence on commodity prices as well, and these expectations would not hold in the face of every sort of exchange-rate variation. The stability of exchange-rate expectations, the instability of price expectations (that is, anticipation that mild inflation would continue), and the small range of movements in the flexible exchange rate that actually occurred may account for more of our results than the implied pattern of imperfect market behavior.

One source of this price linkage, the channels of international trade, comprises a market force working in any highly

30. This confirms the results of Grant L. Reuber, "The Objectives of Canadian Monetary Policy, 1949–61: Empirical 'Trade-Offs' and the Reaction Function of the Authorities," *Journal of Political Economy,* LXXII (April, 1964), 116–119.

31. See Vanderkamp, "Wage and Price Level Determination," pp. 208–209. Vanderkamp finds (p. 207) that even an unemployment rate of 8 percent only holds the increase of Canadian consumer prices down to 1 percent if prices are rising by 2 percent annually.

open economy; presumably it must be lived with as a price paid for the real gains from trade. Remembering that our extent-of-trade-participation variable represents only a poor proxy for the height of international substitution elasticities, there is no reason for thinking that small changes in the extent of Canadian trade participation — by raising or lowering tariffs, for example — would perceptibly alter the independence of the Canadian price level. The positive association of foreign ownership with the direct transmission of foreign price disturbances, however, can probably not be excused in this way. Reducing the degree of foreign ownership in an industry would probably increase its price independence, although our study provides no basis for concluding that this benefit would offset any associated real costs.

The statistically significant results of our wage linkage investigation are sufficiently thin that the best conclusion may well be that there are no conclusions. Certainly the negative finding that no significant industry wage linkages can be found for 1958–1966 holds some interest in light of current Canadian concern over the influence of international unionism. On the other hand, our results suggest that, so far as such linkages can be found, international unionism is the only apparent explanation for them. These findings contrast with those of studies using a higher degree of aggregation: the more one disaggregates the data, the less do wage changes in Canada appear related to those in the United States.[32] This negative result gives comfort both to users of macro models such as those underlying Chapters 7 and 8 of this volume and to

32. Bodkin et al., Price Stability, found a significant linkage in the aggregate data. Also, a subsequent analysis at a two-digit level of disaggregation, based on the standard international industrial classification system, by one of the authors suggests the existence of direct links between U.S. and Canadian wages for the period 1953–1956, particularly in the paper, transportation equipment, electrical apparatus, and chemicals industries; Grant L. Reuber, "Wage Adjustments in Canadian Industry, 1953–66," Review of Economic Studies XXXVII (October, 1970), Table 3.

makers of Canadian financial policy. The determination of Canadian money price and wage levels may take place in a structure of macro relations that tends to tie them closely to the United States economy. But Canadian wages are not also tied at the industry level, and the linkage of industry selling prices, although clearly evident, is not overwhelmingly strong.

6 Lag Patterns in the Process of Adjustment

During the 1950's the view was commonly taken that Canadians imported more than they exported, then borrowed enough capital abroad to make up the difference.[1] Apart from the emotional concern over "living beyond our means" associated with this proposition, it embodies a plausible sequence of economic events starting with a disturbance that increases domestic aggregate demand and thus worsens the current account and, at the same time, begins to raise interest rates and expected yields on new projects, thus prompting a capital inflow. A variant of this view, time-honored in the staple theory of Canadian economic growth, is that exogenous changes in exports are the moving force in the economy, with changes in the capital account and in domestic spending fol-

1. One of the most prominent official expositors of this view during the 1950's was the Governor of the Bank of Canada James E. Coyne, who developed the theme in a number of his speeches and annual reports. Among the more prominent academic economists whose statements implied essentially the same view was Clarence L. Barber, in *The Canadian Economy in Trouble: A Brief to the Royal Commission on Banking and Finance* (privately printed, 1962), and "On Surplus Budgeting," *Canadian Tax Journal*, XIII (July-August, 1965), pp. 319–322.

lowing in the wake of changes in exports. On the other hand, the theory of balance of payments adjustments to autonomous capital inflow disturbances identifies a series of reactions that would go the other way if the primary source of disturbance to the economy lay in the capital accounts. At issue between these views of the causal connections in the process of adjustment are questions both of the distribution of disturbances (domestic demand versus capital inflows) and the strength of the respective mechanisms of adjustment.

Some attention has already been given to these causal relations and to the dynamic properties of the balance-of-payments adjustment process in previous chapters. Chapter 2 investigated lags in the response of capital flows to changes in interest rates and the exchange rate and Chapter 4 measured the lagged response of capital formation to inflows of direct investment. Here we explore these matters further and more directly with two objectives. The first is to cast additional empirical light on the lag patterns and reaction times between the more important variables of the adjustment process. The second is to study the relevant lag patterns for further information about causal links between the variables. The results not only supply evidence for the calculations developed in Chapters 7 and 8, but also help establish the relative importance of the exogenous and endogenous components of capital flows to Canada — the subject matter of Chapters 7 and 8 respectively.

The evidence presented below on lags is based mainly on simple correlation coefficients (r) calculated for pairs of variables (x and y), lagging and leading one of these variables by quarters over a two-year period, $t = -7$ to $t = +7$, from the base period, $t = 0$: $r(x_{-7}, y_0)$, $r(x_{-6}, y_0)$ . . . $r(x_{+6}, y_0)$, $r(x_{+7}, y_0)$.[2] This procedure corresponds to plotting both varia-

2. The simple procedure used here is also employed by Milton Friedman

bles over time on a graph and attempting to identify the lag relationships by visual inspection. A series of more complicated techniques for examining lag structures was also employed; these techniques are summarized in Appendix B. The evidence obtained by applying these procedures is quite consistent with and reinforces the picture indicated by the simple correlation evidence. At the same time, this supplementary evidence does not add substantially to the information obtained by applying the simple correlation procedure. Accordingly, the statistical evidence based on these other procedures is not included in the discussion that follows, though it is referred to where it clarifies and amplifies the information obtained by simple correlation.[3]

Two questions arise in connection with the simple correlation coefficients reported below. One concerns their sensitivity to changes in the number of observations and to slight variations in the sample period. Although we have not undertaken an extensive series of tests on this point, numerous coefficients were calculated varying the number and period of observa-

and David Meiselman in "The Relative Stability of Monetary Velocity and the Investment Multiplier in the United States, 1887–1957," *Stabilization Policies: A Series of Research Papers Prepared for the Commission on Money and Credit* (Englewood Cliffs, N.J.: Prentice-Hall, 1963), pp. 209–213.

3. This supplementary evidence has been particularly useful in evaluating the effect of seasonality on the simple correlation evidence. If either x or y has a significant seasonal pattern and at least one of them shows serial correlation, then a high $r(x_t, y_0)$ is likely to show up with a periodicity of four making it impossible to distinguish between a one-year lag and no lag at all. The methods described in Appendix B explicitly allow for seasonality. The consistency between the evidence obtained by applying these techniques and that obtained from simple correlations suggests that seasonality does not impair the validity of the latter evidence. For example: when the step-wise regression procedure used in connection with the first method outlined in Appendix B was applied to the variables shown in Table 6.1 and 6.2, a seasonal variable was selected for inclusion in the relation on the first step only three times in the 22 trials run. These three exceptions relate to the link between short- and long-term capital flows, on which our evidence may be regarded as relatively weak.

tions slightly. These tests suggest that the lag patterns indicated below are not very sensitive in these dimensions.

A second issue relates to the pattern of the correlation coefficients and the significance of differences between the various correlation values given below. As is apparent from the tables, the difference between the highest value of r and other values is sometimes small and not statistically significant,[4] a difficulty further compounded by the seasonal cycles observable in many of the series. Although the discussion below draws particular attention to the highest value of r, it is important to consider as well the pattern of the coefficients, noting how they build up and decline as alternative assumptions are made about the lag relationship.

LAG RELATIONSHIPS AMONG BROAD AGGREGATES

Statistically, the current-account balance is by definition equal to the capital-account balance. In simple statistical terms, therefore, there can be no lag in overall adjustment between these two accounts: the net adjustment in both is necessarily simultaneous. Moreover, this balance of payments

4. It is possible to test the statistical significance of differences between alternative leading or lagging relations for a given pair of variables on the basis of the hypothesis $r(Y_t, X_{t-i}) = r(Y_t, X_{t-j})$. Because our emphasis is on patterns of correlation coefficients that supply more a priori information than the test supposes, and because of the difficulty of computing it for all the relevant pairs of coefficients, we have used it only for general guidance. The test depends not only on the sample size, $r(Y_t, X_{t-i})$ and $r(Y_t, X_{t-j})$, but also on $r(X_{t-i}, X_{t-j})$. Nonetheless, the reader may find the following examples helpful. For our sample size, if all three correlation coefficients average 0.75, the difference $r(Y_t, X_{t-i}) - r(Y_t, X_{t-j})$ must be approximately 0.16 for significance at the 5-percent level; as the autocorrelation coefficient $r(X_{t-i}, X_{t-j})$ approaches zero, however, so does the required difference. If all three correlation coefficients average 0.45, the required difference rises to approximately 0.35, and reducing the autocorrelation of X no longer necessarily reduces it.

235

identity imposes a significant constraint on the lag patterns within each account in that, on balance, lags and leads in each must cancel one another out in order to maintain the identity.

The first level of disaggregation considered relates to the lag patterns among the following broad subaggregates of the balance of payments from the beginning of 1951 to the end of the first quarter of 1962.[5]

BM = balance of merchandise trade
CA = current-account balance
$CB = CA - ID$
ID = net balance of interest and dividend payments
K = net balance of total long-term capital flows
SK = net balance of total short-term capital flows
STK = net balance of total short-term capital flows, including net trade in outstanding securities

Table 6.1 shows the simple correlation coefficients between the current account and the balance of trade on the one hand, and long- and short-term capital flows on the other. The highest coefficient in each row with the correct sign is shown in parentheses.[6] These figures, together with those obtained from supplementary tests based on Appendix B, provide no evidence for believing that changes in the current-account balance or the balance of trade from 1951 to 1962 followed long-term capital movements. They suggest, rather, that

5. The data for these variables were obtained from the following sources. *BM* and *CA:* D.B.S., *The Canadian Balance of International Payments and International Investment Position* (Ottawa: Queen's Printer, annual); *ID:* Lawrence H. Officer, "An Econometric Model of the Canadian Economy Under the Fluctuating Exchange Rate," unpub. diss. (Harvard University, 1964), pp. 271–273 ($= PINT_{-1} + DIVP - DIVR$ using Officer's notation); *K:* Officer, unpub. diss., pp. 275–283 ($= DIC + PNIR + PTOS + OLK - DLGC,$ using Officer's notation); *SK:* as defined in Chapter 2, p. 71.

6. With 30 observations, all coefficients of about .35 or greater are statistically significant at a 95-percent level of statistical significance.

changes in the current-account balance, CA and $CB,$ and net long-term capital movements coincided, and that changes in the balance of trade preceded or coincided with changes in long-term capital flows. The difference in lag patterns with CA and BM can probably be explained in terms of a lag in changes in the balance of invisible trade and, particularly, interest and dividends behind changes in the balance of merchandise trade. If changes in capital flows coincide with changes in the balance of trade and start yielding interest and dividends within the next year, changes in the current-account balance might appear to lag up to a year behind changes in the trade balance. The pattern of the correlation coefficients relating ID to K bears out this picture, suggesting that variations in K led variations in ID by some two quarters during the period in question.

This picture is completed by the coefficients relating to net short-term private capital flows. The distinction between long- and short-term capital flows is imprecise conceptually as well as statistically. Conceptually, the distinction is based mainly on a difference in the investor's motivation and the responsiveness of the capital flow to existing interest and exchange rates and expectations about future rates. Short-term flows can be defined statistically in terms of the term to maturity of the financial instrument bought and sold. The variable SK follows this convention. But it is generally recognized that transactions in longer-term instruments, especially outstanding securities, may reflect capital flows that — in terms of motivation and responsiveness to interest and exchange rates — may be more closely akin to short- than long-term capital flows. For this reason, studies of capital flows have frequently classified trade in outstanding long-term securities as short-term capital flows,[7] a practice supported by the evi-

7. For example, Charles P. Kindleberger, *International Short-Term Capital Movements* (New York: Columbia University Press, 1937), pp. 3–4. Rudolph G. Penner, in "The Inflow of Long-Term Capital and the Canadian Business Cycle, 1950–1960," *Canadian Journal of Economics and Po-*

TABLE 6.1. Lead-lag relations among current- and capital-account aggregates (simple correlation coefficients)

	Leads (by quarters)								Lags (by quarters)							n^a
	−7	−6	−5	−4	−3	−2	−1	0	+1	+2	+3	+4	+5	+6	+7	
	Leading values of K								Lagging values of K							
CA_0	−.19	−.05	−.23	−.38	−.39	−.42	−.60	(−.72)	−.52	−.46	−.47	−.52	−.26	−.04	−.07	31
CB_0	−.23	−.13	−.27	−.43	−.44	−.49	−.63	(−.73)	−.56	−.50	−.45	−.49	−.28	−.11	−.04	31
BM_0	.09	.27	.07	−.05	−.11	−.20	−.42	−.59	−.39	−.45	−.54	(−.60)	−.19	.06	.01	31
SK_0	.14	.16	.19	.12	.08	.03	.04	.00	.16	.17	.30	(.38)	.30	.17	.11	31
STK_0	.18	.12	.19	.10	.11	.11	.16	.15	.27	.27	.39	(.45)	.30	.17	.07	31
ID_0	.30	.47	.35	.42	.49	(.57)	.48	.39	.50	.40	.17	.09	.22	.41	.10	31
	Leading values of SK								Lagging values of SK							
CA_0	−.42	−.43	(−.74)	−.38	−.19	−.14		−.54	−.14	−.01	−.04	−.28	.16	−.05	−.07	30
CB_0	−.44	−.53	(−.73)	−.41	−.30	−.13		−.54	−.15	−.11	−.05	−.31	.11	−.11	.00	30
BM_0	−.22	−.26	(−.67)	−.17	.00	−.17		−.43	.01	.20	.08	.04	.36	.02	−.15	30
K_0	.33	.35	(.59)	.40	.28	.23		.00	−.02	−.01	.16	.20	.14	−.01	.18	31
	Leading values of STK								Lagging values of STK							
CA_0	−.46	−.47	(−.77)	−.45	−.29	−.26		−.65	−.24	−.04	−.06	−.30	.16	−.02	−.03	30
CB_0	−.49	−.56	(−.77)	−.50	−.41	−.26		−.65	−.25	−.15	−.07	−.33	−.12	−.09	.03	30
BM_0	−.23	−.27	(−.63)	−.21	−.08	−.26		−.54	−.09	.16	.04	.02	.39	.06	−.14	30
K_0	.34	.37	(.64)	.49	.37	.35		.15	.09	.03	.13	.16	.12	−.06	.16	31

Leading values of CA | Lagging values of CA

				Leading values of CA								Lagging values of CA					n
K_0	−.26	−.26	−.42	−.61	−.62	−.59	−.60	(−.72)	−.57	−.34	−.30	−.31	−.09	.12	−.04	31
SK_0	−.17	−.05	−.25	−.45	−.09	−.04	−.27	−.57	−.10	−.21	−.28	(−.67)	−.13	−.21	−.14	31
STK_0	−.21	−.11	−.31	−.51	−.18	−.15	−.39	−.68	−.22	−.30	−.36	(−.69)	−.17	−.22	−.16	31

				Leading values of CB								Lagging values of CB					n
K_0	−.29	−.34	−.50	−.65	−.61	−.62	−.65	(−.73)	−.60	−.42	−.40	−.41	−.18	.03	−.13	31
SK_0	−.14	−.12	−.24	−.45	−.11	−.13	−.28	−.57	−.10	−.31	−.31	(−.64)	−.16	−.35	−.21	31
STK_0	−.19	−.18	−.31	−.51	−.20	−.24	−.40	−.68	−.23	−.40	−.41	(−.68)	−.22	−.37	−.23	31

				Leading values of BM								Lagging values of BM					n
K_0	−.23	−.27	−.35	(−.65)	−.60	−.55	−.46	−.59	−.34	−.09	.03	.09	.28	.47	.33	31
SK_0	−.21	.05	−.11	−.32	−.07	.13	−.12	−.48	−.10	−.03	−.07	(−.58)	−.10	.02	.15	31
STK_0	−.22	.01	−.15	−.38	−.14	.02	−.24	(−.58)	−.18	−.09	−.11	.53	−.07	.05	.18	31

[a] n = number of observations.

dence presented in Chapter 2. In accordance with this practice, a second statistical series, *STK,* that includes trade in outstanding securities, has been used to indicate short-term capital flows.

Whichever indicator of short-term capital flows is chosen, the correlation coefficients in Table 6.1 indicate that, during the period in question, short-term capital flows led long-term flows, the current account, and the balance of trade by about a year. This result is somewhat puzzling and uncertain. It is conceivable, but not very plausible, that autonomous movements in short-term international capital flows predominantly cause adjustments in other balance-of-payments variables. The pattern might appear, however, because short-term capital flows accompany changes in income and associated actual or expected changes in interest rates and respond more quickly to income disturbances than do *CB, BM,* and *K.*[8] If the result cannot be rationalized in this fashion, one could alternatively discount the evidence that *SK* and *STK* led *CA, CB,* and *BM* by as much as a year on several grounds: first, *SK* is calculated as a residual and consequently incorporates various residual error terms that may distort the statistical picture; second, the difference in seasonal pattern between the current and capital accounts, combined with strong autocorrelation (especially in *CA, CB,* and *BM*), may distort the correlation pattern; third, given the constraint of the balance of payments identity referred to earlier and the evidence of coincident changes in *K* and *CA,* the plausibility of *SK* leading *CA* by as much as a year is open to question.

The evidence gleaned from our experiments with distributed

---

litical Science, XXVIII (November, 1962), 536, defines Canadian short-term flows to include trade in outstanding securities — as do Paul Wonnacott, *The Canadian Dollar, 1948–1962* (Toronto: University of Toronto Press, 1965), pp. 62–64, and R. A. Radford, "Canada's Capital Inflow, 1946–53," *IMF Staff Papers,* IV (February, 1955), 237–242.

8. The evidence in Table 6.4 supports this view.

lag formulations is generally consistent with the picture indicated by the simple correlation evidence: changes in K, according to most tests, lagged behind — or, in a few tests, coincided with — changes in BM and CA; changes in SK led changes in BM, CA, and K.

LAG RELATIONSHIPS AMONG MAJOR COMPONENTS

Table 6.2 shows the simple correlation coefficients among various capital-account components and the current account and the balance of trade. These estimates suggest some significant differences in lag patterns among the major capital-account components and the current-account variables. The estimates for net new issues indicate the same lag pattern as that between the aggregate long-term capital account, K, and CA, CB, and BM: changes in the capital-account variable coincide with changes in CA and CB and lag four quarters behind changes in BM. The lag patterns for trade in outstanding securities and direct investment are substantially different, however. Changes in trade in outstanding securities lead changes in CA by one quarter and coincide with changes in CB and BM; changes in direct investment lead changes in CA, CB, and BM by two quarters.

The supplementary evidence based on distributed lag formulations, as before, supports the evidence on lag patterns presented in Table 6.2. Tests based on a Koyck-type formulation (method [c] in Appendix B) suggested that changes in CA and BM may have lagged as much as a year behind changes in PC. Also, this evidence supports the view that changes in $NTOS$ and in DIC led changes in CA and BM.

In a further set of tests, consideration was given to the lag patterns between current- and capital-account variables relating to Canada's trade and investment with the United States

TABLE 6.2. Lead-lag relations among current-account variables and the components of net long-term capital flows (simple correlation coefficients)

	Leads (by quarters)								Lags (by quarters)							n^a
	−7	−6	−5	−4	−3	−2	−1	0	+1	+2	+3	+4	+5	+6	+7	
	Leading values of *PC*								Lagging values of *PC*							
CA_0	−.11	.17	−.15	−.24	−.27	−.18	−.50	(−.59)	−.41	−.31	−.42	−.46	−.26	.01	.07	31
CB_0	−.18	.01	−.19	−.25	−.33	−.24	−.54	(−.59)	−.46	−.33	−.40	−.41	−.28	−.31	−.05	31
BM_0	.16	.46	.09	.03	−.02	.00	−.32	−.51	−.32	−.34	−.55	(−.63)	−.26	.00	−.01	31
	Leading values of *NTOS*								Lagging values of *NTOS*							
CA_0	−.19	−.33	−.39	−.48	−.44	−.49	(−.60)	−.53	−.44	−.25	−.16	−.14	.04	.11	.08	31
CB_0	−.23	−.37	−.44	−.53	−.51	−.55	(−.62)	−.61	−.45	−.25	−.17	−.12	.03	.04	.08	31
BM_0	.02	−.16	−.12	−.21	−.22	−.35	−.49	(−.49)	−.42	−.28	−.22	−.12	.14	.22	.00	31
	Leading values of *DIC*								Lagging values of *DIC*							
CA_0	−.24	−.42	−.25	−.32	−.25	(−.56)	−.37	−.50	−.36	−.53	−.32	−.37	−.13	−.17	−.03	31
CB_0	−.26	−.46	−.24	−.41	−.23	(−.60)	−.38	−.54	−.39	−.58	−.32	−.42	−.15	−.22	−.03	31
BM_0	−.12	−.22	−.09	−.12	−.16	(−.45)	−.32	−.34	−.23	−.43	−.23	−.21	.02	.08	.06	31

[a] n = number of observations.

only. Not surprisingly perhaps, the results of these tests agreed closely with the results of the tests based on data relating to Canada's trade and investment with the world as a whole.

The lag pattern between changes in *DIC* and *CA, CB,* and *BM* conforms with the classical picture of the current account adjusting to autonomous movements of long-term capital as described in Chapters 1 and 7. Autonomous flows initiate an adjustment process that leads to accommodating changes in the current account. Where changes in *DIC* are directly matched by changes in capital goods imports, as sometimes occurs with direct investment, the transfer is automatic and no lag occurs between changes in *DIC* and *CA* or *CB*. On the other hand, where the transfer is accomplished indirectly through price (including interest and exchange rates) and income adjustments, a lag between the initiating disturbance and the accommodating changes in *CA* or *CB* is to be expected. According to our evidence, the bulk of the adjustment will have occurred within half a year of the initial disturbance.

The lag patterns between changes in *PC* and *CA, CB* and *BM,* on the other hand, conform more closely to the modern emphasis on accommodating foreign capital flows in response to domestic disturbances giving rise to changes in prices (including interest and exchange rates) and incomes. Short-term capital flows might be expected to accompany or possibly precede these adjustments in response to actual and expected changes in interest and exchange rates and in response to changes in the demand for trade credit to finance imports. Because of the difference in motivation underlying long-term capital flows and the longer term of such investments, one would expect induced changes in *PC* to lag behind changes in *SK* as well as changes in income, *CA, CB,* and *BM.*

Autonomous versus Induced Investment

One difficulty with the foregoing tests is that no explicit distinction is made between autonomous and induced changes in foreign investment — a key distinction for purposes of this study. To derive results that relate more directly to these two categories of variation in foreign investment within each of the three main statistical classifications — *DIC, PC,* and *NTOS* — an attempt has been made to estimate autonomous and induced variations within each category of investment. This has been done by fitting linear regression equations by ordinary least-squares to explain variations in each category of capital flow as a function of (1) explanatory variables that reflect domestic disturbances in Canada, including domestic policy changes, and (2) the current-account balance, *CA.* Variations in capital flows as estimated by these relations have been classified as induced, and variations in the residual flows (actual minus estimated) have been classified as autonomous.

Taking an extreme view, one might argue that everything is so closely inter-related with everything else that it is impossible to identify capital flows that are totally independent of the structure and institutions of the Canadian economy. Empirically, however, enough current and leading causal influences seem likely to be operative to make such a distinction both feasible and interesting. The specification of the estimated relationships outlined above is based on two considerations. First, any balance-of-payments component is related to any other without a lag because of the constraint that the overall balance at any time must sum to zero. Hence it is necessary to remove variations in capital flows associated with the pressure imposed by this constraint if autonomous variations in capital flows are to be isolated. Second, it is also necessary to delete variations in capital flows associated with the major domestic determinants of capital flows, whether they arise from shifts in market schedules or from shifts in policy. Removal of these induced changes is subject to the constraint that the domestic determinants of induced capital flows do not also influence the current account closely and concurrently; if they do, the rationale for including the current-account balance in the equation breaks down. In other words, our specification assumes that changes in CA may have an independent influence on capital flows and do not simply mirror the variations in capital flows induced by a common set of domestic disturbances.

Direct investment. The estimates of induced direct investment are based on the following equation:

$$DIC = 81.138 + 144.80DL - 0.09446CA - 21.191Q_1$$
$$(6.75) \quad (2.29) \quad\quad (3.68) \quad\quad (2.24)$$
$$RSQC = .32$$
$$DW = 2.11. \quad (6.1)$$

This relationship assumes that direct capital flows are induced by: (1) the differential in long-term interest rates between Canada and the United States, serving as a proxy for differences in the rate of return on capital in the two countries; (2) the current-account balance, reflecting changes in the level of Canadian demand, direct connections between direct investment and trade flows and the capital-inducing effect of changes in the current account via pressures on the exchange rate and inelastic exchange-rate expectations; and (3) a quarterly seasonal dummy variable. In total, these three variables explain about a third of the variation in DIC.

When the residuals from equation 6.1 (DIC', reflecting autonomous variations in DIC) are correlated against CA'_0 and BM_0, the lag pattern shown in Table 6.3 is indicated. This evidence tends to corroborate our earlier evidence that most of the variation in direct investment flows into Canada during the period in question was autonomous and that autonomous changes in these flows led adjustments in the current account by about half a year.

Investment in net new issues. When a similar procedure was followed in connection with private net new issues, *PC,* the following relationships were fitted:

$$PC = 49.179 + 379.61DL + 252.07DS_{-1} + 28.600UM$$
$$(1.49) \quad\quad (3.40) \quad\quad\quad (4.54) \quad\quad\quad\quad (4.92)$$
$$ + .23044NNS$$
$$ (6.56)$$

$$RSQC = \ .68$$
$$D.W. = 1.93 \quad (6.2)$$

$$PC = -13.346 + 422.78DL + 18.522UM - 0.13486CA_{-1}$$
$$(0.38) \quad\quad (3.22) \quad\quad\quad (3.06) \quad\quad\quad\quad (2.22)$$
$$ + 0.20553NNS$$
$$ (4.83)$$

$$RSQC = \ .56$$
$$D.W. = 1.60 \quad (6.3)$$

where *DL* is the long-term interest differential between Canada and the United States, DS_{-1} is the short-term interest differential lagged one quarter, *UM* is the unemployment rate in Canada expressed as a percentage, *NNS* is the net new issue of Canadian long-term securities, and CA_{-1} is the current-account balance lagged one quarter. Equation 6.2 explains over 68 percent of the variation in *PC,* and equation 6.3 over 56 percent. The only difference between the two is the substitution of CA_{-1} for DS_{-1}.

Variations in *NNS* can be expected to reflect changes in domestic policies, particularly in fiscal and debt-management policies. The inclusion of both interest-rate variables and *NNS* can be justified on the ground that, in the short run at least, adjustments in financial markets are less than perfect and, as a consequence, variations in *NNS* may have an influence on *PC* even after the effect of changes in interest rates has been taken into account.

Changes in *UM* may be regarded as primarily determined domestically, in large part by domestic policies geared to the regulation of domestic demand. The coefficient of *UM* is positive — which is open to some doubt, as one might expect the demand for foreign capital to be inversely related to *UM*. However, the demand for funds has already been taken into account by *NNS*. Consequently, *UM* may be serving as a proxy for the supply of new domestic savings which can be expected to be positively related to the level of employment: the lower the level of *UM,* the higher the level of domestic saving and liquidity and the less the call on foreign capital, given the demand for funds. On this view the sign of the parameter may be regarded as plausible.[9]

Given the supply price of foreign capital and domestic demand and supply conditions for credit, it is plausible to expect that variations in short-run interest differentials between Canada and the United States should induce a positive response in long-term net new issues for several reasons. First: under these assumptions, a rise in the short-term differential, given the long-term differential, will induce borrowers to substitute long-term borrowing for short-term borrowing. Second: if, as some of our earlier evidence suggests, current-account changes lead changes in long-term portfolio investment flows, changes in the current account will have an immediate impact on short-term borrowing and short-term interest rate differentials,

9. Variables that more directly reflect the supply of new domestic savings might be preferable to *UM*, but it is not obvious what they should be. Changes in the supply of new domestic savings may not be fully reflected in interest rates, particularly in the short run, thus affording some scope for the supply of domestic savings to have an independent effect on *PC* even after interest-rate changes are taken into account.

given the exchange rate. This is because the lag between current-account changes and long-term capital changes must inevitably be financed through short-term capital flows. And as short-term differentials change, given the supply price of foreign capital, the change in short-term will in time be reflected in long-term differentials through interest-rate arbitrage between the long and short sectors of the market. Third: on a free rate of exchange, the change in the current account will tend to induce an accommodating change in the exchange rate. If exchange-rate expectations are inelastic, the *effective* rate of return on long-run investment will have altered as a consequence, and lenders and borrowers will have an incentive to adjust their lending and borrowing.

The third consideration suggests that changes in short-term interest rates and exchange rates to some degree are substitutes from the standpoint of inducing capital flows.[10] This may explain why, when DS_{-1} is omitted from the equation, the coefficient of CA_{-1} shows up as statistically significant. Apart from serving as a proxy for the cost of funds, there seems to be no rationale for including CA with a lag. The coefficient for neither DS nor CA is significant when current rather than lagged values of these variables are included in the equation. It cannot be argued that lagged values of these variables serve as proxies for lagged values of PC, because when PC_{-1} is added to these equations as an explanatory variable, its coefficient is insignificant and the coefficients of DS_{-1} or CA_{-1} remain significant.

Equation 6.2 suggests that about 70 percent of the variation in PC may be regarded as induced. Moreover, these induced changes apparently lag behind changes in short-term interest rates. When the residuals from equation 6.2 (PC', reflecting autonomous changes in PC) are correlated with CA_0, the lag

10. For further elaboration see G. L. Reuber and R. J. Wonnacott, *The Cost of Capital in Canada* (Washington: Resources for the Future, 1961), pp. 57–65.

pattern shown in Table 6.3 is obtained. On this showing, autonomous variations in *PC* led current-account adjustments by one quarter during the sample period.

All the statistics on net new issues used for estimation purposes are defined as relating to deliveries — that is, the figures account for the actual amount of new portfolio securities delivered by the borrower to the lender in each quarter. But decisions about lending and borrowing are made at the time when new issues are offered, rather than when they are delivered. If one wishes to examine the lag structure between the current account and *PC* as a means of exploring their causal connections, the relation between the current account and offerings may be more significant than between the current account and deliveries of new issues as reported in official statistics. If for institutional and technical reasons deliveries lag behind offerings, *PC* may in fact lag behind *CA* and *BM*, but decisions about new issues may lead *CA* and *BM*. Consequently, the evidence adduced above could be misleading. If, on the other hand, it can be established that there is little or no lag between offerings and deliveries, the evidence presented above may be regarded as more significant.

The information available on offerings and deliveries is incomplete but gives no reason for believing that the lag between offerings and deliveries of new issues is long enough to qualify seriously the evidence presented earlier on lag patterns. Official data on offerings and deliveries are available by quarters from 1957.[11] When simple correlation coefficients $r(D_1, O_0)$ are calculated to estimate the lag between offerings, O, and deliveries, D, the value of $r(D_0, O_0)$ is substantially greater than the value of other correlation coefficients that allow for a lag.

	D_0	D_{+1}	D_{+2}	D_{+3}
O_0	(.83)	.52	−.32	−.11

11. D.B.S., made available privately.

The second set of data available on this question relates only to new issues payable in United States currency[12] and shows the date of issue and delivery, as well as the amount of each issue since 1951. Unfortunately, most dates for the earlier years are unavailable and sometimes they are missing even for more recent years. Nevertheless, the data can be used to obtain quite a clear notion of the lag between offerings and deliveries. For purposes of this study, an average lag for the year 1964 has been calculated on the basis of a mean weighted by the size of the issue, the median, and the mode (estimated in terms of monthly intervals).[13] The mean estimate indicates an average lag of two months; the mode and median indicate an average lag of one month. As these estimates suggest, the frequency distribution is highly skewed in the direction of a shorter lag than that suggested by the weighted mean. This estimate is consistent with the preceding estimate of the lag derived from D.B.S. data.

Investment in outstanding securities. Our attempt to estimate induced variations in net trade in outstanding issues was less successful than our attempt to estimate induced changes in net new issues. The best estimates, judged by the portion of variance explained, derived after considerable experimentation, follow.

$$NTOS = -10.433 + 105.18DL + 52.223DS_{-1} - 0.14878BM$$
$$(1.02) \quad\quad (1.82) \quad\quad (2.17) \quad\quad\quad (4.18)$$

$$RSQC = .44$$
$$D.W. = 1.88 \quad (6.4)$$

12. Bank of Canada, made available privately.
13. The estimated average lag between offerings and deliveries of new Canadian issues payable in U.S. dollars in 1964 follows: mean, weighted by size of issue, 59 days; median, 32 days; mode, based on 30-day intervals, 30 days. In cases where precise dates were missing but months or quarters were given, either the offering date or the middle of the month or quarter, whichever was later, was assumed.

$$NTOS = 6.5729 + 57.173DS_{-1} - 0.15149BM$$
$$\quad\quad (1.53) \quad\quad (2.32) \quad\quad\quad (4.13)$$

$$RSQC = .40$$
$$D.W. = 1.99 \quad (6.5)$$

The difference between equation 6.4 and 6.5 is the inclusion of *DL* in the former. These equations explain about 44 percent at most of the variation in *NTOS*.

The most significant variables entering all equations fitted for *NTOS* are the current-account variables, and of the two the balance of trade is more significant than the current-account balance. It may be noted that, if one regards *NTOS* as short-term capital, the foregoing estimates for *NTOS* support the interpretation given earlier to the equations relating to *PC*. In explaining the role of DS_{-1} and CA_{-1}, it was suggested that the lag between *PC* and the current account was compensated for by short-term capital flows. This is consistent with the equations for *NTOS* into which *CA* and *BM* enter without a lag.[14]

When the residuals from equation 6.4 (*NTOS'*, reflecting autonomous changes in *NTOS*) were rerun against CA_0, the lag pattern shown in Table 6.3 was indicated. These estimates leave the lag pattern uncertain because there is not much to choose from between $r(NTOS'_{-2}, CA_0)$ and $r(NTOS'_{+4}, CA_0)$. In summary, it can be said that induced variations in *NTOS* seem to account for the smaller portion of total variation in *NTOS* during the period in question, and that these induced variations appear to have coincided with current-account changes and to have lagged one quarter behind short-term interest rate changes. The lag pattern for autonomous variations in *NTOS*, which evidently were more important

14. The coefficients of *CA* and *BM* are insignificant at the 5-percent confidence level when these variables are included in these equations with a lag. When *CA* is substituted for *BM* in equation 6.5, the regression coefficient for *CA* is statistically significant. The value of *RSQC* becomes .35.

TABLE 6.3. Lead-lag relations among current-account variables and estimates of the components of net long-term autonomous capital flows (simple correlation coefficients)

	Leads (by quarters)								Lags (by quarters)							n^a
	-7	-6	-5	-4	-3	-2	-1	0	$+1$	$+2$	$+3$	$+4$	$+5$	$+6$	$+7$	
	Leading values of DIC'								Lagging values of DIC'							
CA_0	.12	$-.28$	$-.17$	$-.22$	.07	$(-.32)$	$-.22$	$-.01$	$-.03$	$-.16$	$-.10$	.01	.20	.09	.07	28
BM_0	.03	$-.36$	$-.18$	$-.25$	$-.11$	$(-.44)$	$-.29$	.08	.11	$-.17$	$-.03$	.10	.29	.27	.20	28
	Leading values of PC'								Lagging values of PC'							
CA_0	$-.02$	$-.02$	$-.25$	$-.09$	$-.22$	$-.12$	$(-.33)$	$-.16$	$-.25$	$-.09$	$-.01$	.07	$-.08$	.09	.11	26
	Leading values of $NTOS'$								Lagging values of $NTOS'$							
CA_0	.02	$-.33$	$-.29$	.07	$-.17$	$(-.38)$	$-.14$	.19	.04	.13	.12	.34	.17	.00	.02	27

[a] n = number of observations.

than induced variations, is uncertain; but there is some suggestion that autonomous variations in *NTOS* led changes in *CA* by two quarters.

SUPPLEMENTARY EVIDENCE

In order to clarify further some of the time relationships between the variables considered in previous pages, several supplementary relationships were considered, some of which are shown in Table 6.4. It seemed particularly worthwhile to compare the lag patterns between changes in *CA* and various categories of investment flows, on the one hand, with changes in long-term interest rate differentials, exchange rates (X), and gross national product (*GNP*) on the other. Such comparisons provide some check on the rationale advanced earlier for including *CA* in the equations used to estimate autonomous changes in capital flows — in particular, the influence of changes in *CA* on adjustments in the capital account via exchange-rate movements.

Table 6.4 provides further evidence that the time characteristics of the main categories of foreign investment are quite different. Moreover, the lagged or coincident movement in *DIC, NTOS,* and *PC* with changes in *DL* is consistent with evidence presented earlier that *DL* is a significant determinant of changes in investment flows in these categories.[15]

Third, this evidence has some bearing on the question of what relation, if any, exists among variations in income, investment flows, and the current account. Changes in *GNP* seem both to lag a quarter or two behind changes in *CA* and to lead changes in *CA* by two or three quarters; there is no significant

15. The wrongly signed values of r can be ignored in Table 6.4.

TABLE 6.4. Lead-lag relations between current- and capital-account variables and GNP, interest rates, and exchange rates (simple correlation coefficients)

	Leads (by quarters)								Lags (by quarters)							n^a
	-7	-6	-5	-4	-3	-2	-1	0	$+1$	$+2$	$+3$	$+4$	$+5$	$+6$	$+7$	
	Leading values of *GNP*								Lagging values of *GNP*							
CA_0	$-.69$	$-.69$	$-.36$	$-.37$	$-.77$	$-.79$	$-.46$	$-.45$	$-.81$	$(-.81)$	$-.45$	$-.42$	$-.75$	$-.77$	$-.41$	31
CB_0	$-.57$	$-.61$	$-.52$	$-.44$	$-.77$	$-.80$	$-.56$	$-.51$	$-.82$	$(-.82)$	$-.55$	$-.49$	$-.76$	$-.79$	$-.51$	31
SK_0	$.54$	$.40$	$.10$	$.11$	$.45$	$.40$	$.11$	$.15$	$.53$	$.48$	$.21$	$.22$	$(.58)$	$.52$	$.18$	31
$NTOS_0$	$.39$	$.36$	$.36$	$.42$	$.43$	$.44$	$.44$	$(.50)$	$.48$	$.49$	$.45$	$.47$	$.46$	$.40$	$.42$	31
PC_0	$.35$	$.50$	$.33$	$.30$	$.47$	$(.60)$	$.41$	$.35$	$.46$	$.52$	$.30$	$.27$	$.38$	$.46$	$.29$	31
DIC_0	$.33$	$.35$	$.42$	$.32$	$.43$	$.46$	$(.49)$	$.42$	$.44$	$.46$	$.46$	$.32$	$.38$	$.40$	$.43$	31
	Leading values of *DL*								Lagging values of *DL*							
CA_0	$-.12$	$.07$	$.12$	$.20$	$.34$	$(.40)$	$.36$	$.17$	$.13$	$-.07$	$-.03$	$-.02$	$-.16$	$-.26$	$-.31$	31
CB_0	$.01$	$.12$	$.12$	$.18$	$.29$	$.12$	$-.18$	$-.32$	$-.43$	$-.48$	$(-.58)$	$-.53$	$-.41$	$-.30$	$-.28$	31
SK_0	$.15$	$.09$	$-.04$	$-.25$	$-.29$	$-.26$	$-.21$	$-.23$	$-.02$	$-.04$	$.16$	$.23$	$.30$	$.34$	$(.39)$	31
$NTOS_0$	$-.12$	$-.20$	$-.36$	$-.51$	$-.46$	$-.27$	$.00$	$.30$	$.34$	$.40$	$(.41)$	$.39$	$.25$	$.25$	$.11$	31
PC_0	$-.55$	$-.43$	$-.37$	$-.15$	$.05$	$.13$	$.32$	$(.55)$	$.49$	$.44$	$.42$	$.35$	$.11$	$.02$	$.11$	31
DIC_0	$-.22$	$-.47$	$-.39$	$-.23$	$-.23$	$-.02$	$.21$	$.38$	$.41$	$.27$	$(.43)$	$.31$	$.31$	$.07$	$-.16$	31
ID_0	$.06$	$-.02$	$-.01$	$-.10$	$.02$	$.06$	$.12$	$.20$	$.41$	$.34$	$.34$	$.36$	$(.50)$	$.42$	$.24$	31

	Leading values of X								Lagging values of X							n
CA_0	.42	.22	.01	−.08	.05	.22	.33	.27	.41	(.51)	.41	.27	.11	.03	.07	28
CB_0	.36	.21	.04	−.06	.08	.26	.40	.35	.47	(.52)	.43	.28	.35	.33	.25	28
SK_0	(−.34)	−.28	−.18	−.12	−.28	−.29	−.12	.13	−.07	−.03	.04	.09	.00	−.11	−.11	28
$NTOS_0$	−.52	−.28	−.13	.28	.32	.19	−.03	−.14	−.37	−.50	(−.61)	−.57	−.19	.11	.17	28
PC_0	−.04	−.04	.03	.16	.07	−.02	−.20	−.51	(−.60)	−.57	−.42	−.36	−.21	−.09	.07	28
DIC_0	−.20	−.06	.08	.11	−.02	−.15	−.28	(−.34)	−.23	−.14	−.25	.00	.14	.31	.38	28
DS_0	−.32	−.11	−.03	.00	−.17	−.25	−.30	−.49	(−.68)	−.66	−.43	−.11	.00	.10	.30	28
DL_0	.06	.11	.11	.16	−.12	−.33	−.47	(−.64)	−.62	−.50	−.36	−.12	.15	.40	.45	28
GNP_0	−.30	−.17	−.09	−.22	−.36	−.36	−.42	−.53	(−.53)	−.42	−.34	−.33	−.09	.09	.08	28

[a] n = number of observations.

difference between the strength of these linkages.[16] At the same time, changes in *GNP* lead changes in *DIC* by one quarter and changes in *PC* by two quarters. The pattern for *SK* and *NTOS* is somewhat obscure, but there is some suggestion that changes in *GNP* lag behind changes in short-term capital flows.

Fourth, this evidence also sheds some light on the lag patterns between movements in the exchange rate, X,[17] and other variables. Variations in X appear to coincide with variations in *DL* and *DIC* and to lag one quarter behind variations in *GNP, DS,* and *PC*. Variations in X lag about two quarters behind changes in *CA* and three quarters behind variations in *NTOS*. The estimates may also suggest that X leads *SK*, though the extent of the lead is uncertain. A lead of X ahead of *SK* suggests equilibrating short-term capital movements.

Finally, the figures in Table 6.4 provide indirect evidence that changes in the current account induced adjustments in the capital account via exchange rates during the free-rate period. Given inelastic exchange-rate expectations, one would expect a reduction in X to be associated, ceteris paribus, with a larger interest-rate differential. Accordingly, one would expect a significant negative correlation between X and *DS* and *DL* with little or no lead or lag. This is because a change in the exchange rate, given inelastic expectations about a normal exchange rate, is equivalent to a change in the cost of foreign funds; hence, it can be expected that a change in the exchange rate will be followed by a corresponding adjustment in Canadian interest rates. Further, since foreign interest rates can be taken as given, the differential between Canadian and foreign rates can be ex-

16. The bimodal pattern of *CA* on *GNP* suggests the obvious two-way relation through the foreign trade multiplier and the marginal propensity to import, with changes in *GNP* lagging behind changes in exports and changes in imports lagging behind changes in *GNP*.

17. $X = 100$ U.S. cents — spot price of Canadian dollar in U.S. cents = $-DRSP$ in Chapters 2 and 3.

pected to rise and fall with the exchange rate. The figures given in Table 6.4 are consistent with this picture.

Although the evidence that has been presented on lag patterns is imperfect and somewhat impressionistic in a number of respects, it is generally consistent with the following propositions for the period in question.

(1) There were significant lags in the process of balance-of-payments adjustment between the current and the capital account, and the lead-lag relations between various categories of the capital account and the current account differ.

(2) On an aggregative basis, changes in long-term capital flows coincided with or lagged behind changes in the current-account balance and did not lead such changes, as one would expect from classical discussions of the transfer process.

(3) The evidence from more detailed analysis suggests that changes in capital flows associated with net new portfolio issues of securities lagged behind changes in the current account and the balance of trade. Changes in direct investment, on the other hand, led changes in the current account by about half a year, conforming with the classical picture of the adjustment process. The evidence on short-term capital movements and trade in outstanding securities is somewhat uncertain. Taken at face value, it suggests that short-term capital movement led changes in the current account during the sample period. This more detailed picture of the lag patterns is consistent with the picture derived from aggregative data, since changes in net new issues during the period in question were larger than changes in trade in outstanding securities, thereby giving heavier weight in the aggregate figures to the lag associated with new issues.

(4) As for the mechanism of adjustment, the evidence adduced is consistent with the view that the lag in reaction of the current account and the capital account in response to domestic

income and financial disturbances differed. Changes in the current account and short-term foreign investment evidently led changes in income; changes in the major long-term categories of foreign investment lagged behind changes in income. Thus, though changes in the current account and the long-term capital account may be partly explained in terms of differences in the response of each to domestic disturbances, rather than in terms of one account inducing a reaction in the other, the observed pattern is also consistent with the view that during the period in question changes in the current account induced changes in the capital account via changes in the exchange rate, as elaborated earlier. Empirical support for this interpretation is provided by the positive and significant correlation between changes in the exchange rate and simultaneous changes in interest differentials between Canada and the U.S.

7 The Mechanism of Adjustment to Exogenous Capital Flows

In Chapter 1, theoretical models dealing with the macroeconomic effects of capital inflows on the economy were reviewed. The next five chapters filled gaps in the evidence on various structural features of the Canadian economy that assume strategic importance in these models. In this and the following chapter our own statistical evidence is combined with that from other sources to generate numerical estimates of the theoretical elasticities and propensities and assess their implications. We distinguished earlier between two sets of theoretical models, those treating international capital movements as disturbances and those assuming their variations to be induced by changes in other variables. Here we collect data bearing on the first group of models; endogenous capital movements are dealt with in Chapter 8.

EXOGENOUS AND ENDOGENOUS CAPITAL MOVEMENTS

Fundamental to this analysis is a theoretical distinction between capital flows caused by developments within the Canadian economy and those occurring independent of the domestic situation. A corresponding empirical separation would show to what extent Canada was forced to adapt to capricious changes in capital flows due to external factors or, on the other hand, to what extent these changes were brought on by policy actions within the Canadian economy. Procedurally, the distinction is important for establishing the relative significance of the analyses of this chapter and the next. Later in this chapter the separation is used to determine whether or not exogenous disturbances tend to stabilize the current-account balance.

The logic of distinguishing exogenous and endogenous components of capital flows through regression analysis has been discussed. But the nature of the exogeneity sought in Chapter 6 differs from that called for in this chapter. Earlier concern was with the variation of capital flows that is independent of *all* major sources of disturbance within the Canadian economy, whether originating in shifts of market schedules or in policy actions. Now only the variation associated with policy instruments (and not Canadian market parameters) will be treated as endogenous. This distinction, clear in principle, of course proves weak in practice. Without an elaborate effort to develop indexes of policy action or decision, it is necessary to settle for measuring the impact of policy changes through their impact on market variables — which of course reflect, as well, the market's response to the policy changes and private-sector disturbances generally. The interest rate supplies the central example of this problem. The predetermined variables specified below should thus be interpreted as those which *might have been* influenced by policy, not those whose variation has entirely or predominantly reflected the choices of policymakers.

The extent to which variations in Canadian capital inflows were dominated by policy influences, defined in this broad sense, is shown by coefficients of determination when the flows are regressed upon the policy instruments. We have used a regression program indicating net contribution of each independent variable to total explained variance, when they are added in the order of greatest contribution, to gain some additional evidence on sources of the endogenous pulls. What independent variables should be included as embodying the possibility of control through Canadian domestic policy during the 1951–1962 period? In the case of long-run portfolio (PC) and short-run capital flows (SK), the long and short interest rates (CL and CS) are obvious candidates. For long-term flows we also included net new issues of securities (NNS), a factor which clearly could be influenced by investment taxes and the like, although this type of instrument has not been used substantially in Canada; also, the unemployment rate (UM), on the ground that it may affect the uncertainty with which foreign investors view the yields promised by current Canadian new issues. For short-term flows, the differential between spot and forward exchange rates (FP) has also been employed on the ground that authorities can (if they wish) enter the forward market to influence the volume of covered interest arbitrage.[1] The following list shows the proportion of variance explained by these chief policy variables (adjusted for degrees of freedom) for net new issues of securities, trade in outstanding securities, and other short-term capital movements, respectively:

PC / NNS, CL, CS, FB, UM	34%	
$NTOS$ / CS, CL, FP	16%	
SK / CS, CL, FP	26%	

1. Such an intervention would, of course, have been relatively pointless during the period of the fluctuating exchange rate and does not in fact seem to have occurred; see Ronald A. Shearer, *Monetary Policy and the Current Account of the Balance of International Payments,* working paper prepared for the Royal Commission on Banking and Finance (Ottawa: Queen's Printer, 1962), p. 180.

In the case of net new issues, the variable with the greatest explanatory strength is the stock of new securities issued, which alone explains 30 percent of the variance of *PC*. The long-term interest rate (CL) would obviously do better if included as a differential over the United States rate, but what we want is a crude measure of its independent significance. Perverse signs may occur in regressions such as these, when independent variables of known significance are omitted. Also, the included variables may serve as proxies for them, possibly causing an overestimate of the portion of the variance explained. A case in point is the sign of the long-term interest rate in the equation for trade in outstanding securities. The Canadian short-term interest rate, however, conventionally performs reasonably well in making the greatest contribution to the explained variance of both trade in outstanding securities (18 percent) and other capital movements (15 percent).

Analyzing the extent of endogenous variation in direct investment (*DIC*) poses a special problem. Theory suggests including the long-term interest rate as a proxy for anticipation of returns on equity capital created by public policy, the unemployment rate as a proxy for unused capacity, and an accelerator term (*FSP2*).[2] Including these variables gives the following:

$$DIC \: / \: CL, \: FSP2, \: UM \qquad 40\%$$

Of this, 38 percent is due, rather surprisingly, to the long-term interest rate; and indeed, the sign of the accelerator coefficient goes wrong is seasonal dummy variables are introduced into the equation. The positive sign of *CL* strongly suggests that the long-term interest rate serves as proxy for the level of and

2. This term, borrowed from Lawrence Officer's model, consists of the slope of a regression equation of real final output on time, over the seventh through the second periods prior to the current quarter.

outlook for general prosperity in the Canadian economy, since equity and debt capital are to a degree complementary; such a relation could hardly be expected to predict accurately the response of direct investment to a policy-induced change in Canada's long-term interest rate. Of the other variables in the equation, the accelerator term is not subject to policy control during the current period, and one may doubt whether it is practically controllable in any case. Therefore, it seems wise to regard direct investment as largely, if not totally, exogenous to current macroeconomic policy variables.

We can expand these results slightly by examining the residuals from the preceding equations in comparison with the actual inflows of capital during the period. Theoretically, one would expect a random pattern over time in the residuals of the regression equations analyzed above; indeed, the Durbin-Watson statistics indicate in each case only a slight degree of positive autocorrelation of the residuals or none at all. Nonetheless, it is only in the case of other short-term capital movements (SK) that the annual totals of the (quarterly) residuals fail to show significant patterns when compared with the actual annual figures for capital flows. The great bulge in the inflow of portfolio capital of 1956–1958 is not particularly under-estimated — that is, it can be viewed largely as a market response to Canadian policy variables. Major overestimates occur for 1953, 1955, and 1961, however — all years of relatively sharp declines in the portfolio inflow. Only in the last year is the residual clearly associated with Canadian policies not represented in the regression equation; the others presumably reflect exogenous disturbances. Likewise, the equation for trade in outstanding securities rather accurately explains the large inflow of 1956–1959 except for the initial burst in 1956, but notably fails to explain the net outflows of 1952 and 1955. Thus, the exogenous components of international capital flows can be seen both in the total unexplained variance in regressions on variables controllable by domestic policy and in large disturbances occurring at particular times. But these exogenous bursts do not generally correspond to high or low absolute values of the capital series in question.

Direct investment may best be viewed as totally exogenous to current Canadian policy variables, although we shall make use below of the series minus its "endogenous" component. During the period under study, portfolio and short-term capital inflows seem to have contained large exogenous elements, both in the sense of total unexplained variance and substantial unexplained fluctuations at particular points in time; nonetheless, they were markedly affected by Canadian policy variables.

CAPITAL INFLOWS AND AUTONOMOUS DOMESTIC EXPENDITURE

Now the quest begins for measurements of induced changes in Canadian domestic income and the balance of payments associated with disturbances in international capital flows. These relations are best assembled in several stages. We shall next review evidence on the association between variations in capital inflows and "autonomous" changes in components of domestic expenditure — autonomous in the sense of not being induced by changes in total income and expenditure; then we shall turn to the subsequently induced effects on total expenditure and the balance of payments.

In Chapter 1 it was stressed that economic theory allots a crucial role to the coefficients describing how the proceeds of a transfer are financed and spent, yet empirical work on national income relations has so far neglected them almost entirely. Chapters 3 and 4 presented the main results of our own inquiry, reviewed here briefly along with some supplementary evidence. We take up first the link between inflows of direct investment and gross domestic capital formation.

Direct Investment and Capital Formation

Direct investment in Canada (as measured in the balance of payments statistics) and certain domestic investment projects stem from the same decisions made by foreign entrepreneurs, particularly those in the United States. The existence of a link between the two is not in doubt, but its magnitude cannot be narrowed down much by a priori analysis. A dollar's worth of direct investment might lead to less than a dollar's worth of capital formation if the direct inflow is partly for takeovers of going firms, or if domestic entrepreneurs are thereby frightened out of investing. It might lead to more than a dollar's worth if direct investment finances capital formation together with funds from other sources, such as retained earnings, or if complementary investments are made by governments or Canadian-owned firms. Our procedure was to regress the total of nonresidential construction and plant and equipment investment — including that by government enterprises — on direct investment and also on the chief domestic determinants of investment, corporate liquidity and accelerator or output-capacity relations. In the absence of multicollinearity among the independent variables, we argued that the regression coefficient for capital formation on direct investment should provide the desired estimate.

We experimented with various lags in the equations, including the use of moving averages of past quarters' values of direct investment. The range of results for the regression of capital formation on direct investment generally suggested that, on the average over the 1950–1962 period, one dollar of direct investment was associated with between $1.50 and $3 of capital formation. If one accepts our argument that using a moving average of past quarters' values for direct investment is economically superior to employing simple lags, then our conclusion is that $1 of direct investment in a given quarter is associated with a total of $2 or more of capital formation over roughly the succeeding three quarters. Part of this leverage of direct investment seems due to the simultaneous use of retained earnings to finance expansion of the Canadian subsidiaries of foreign firms; part, however, must be ascribed to net complementary investments, both public and private, in other firms or industries.

We also sought to discover how the relation between direct investment and capital formation may have varied with the level of Canadian employment (or phase of the business cycle), industry composition of investment, extent of capital inflow for takeover purposes, and the like. We divided the period 1951–1962 into 20 quarters of upswings (the whole of 1951–1957 minus the 1953–1954 recession) and 28 quarters of recession or stagnation (that recession plus the second quarter of 1957 to the end). In the upswing phase the influence of direct investment appeared particularly large and significant; in the "downswing" phase both the value of the coefficient and its significance dropped sharply, as did the explanatory powers of the other variables. The weaker influence of direct investment in years of recession or stagnation seems to have been due both to an increased incidence of inflows for takeover purposes and to the smaller amount of complementary investment stimulated at such times. Our study of investment determinants for disaggregated sectors — manufacturing, petroleum, mining, and utilities — showed that the industry mix is also influential. When direct investment flows to a new and rapidly growing sector such as petroleum, one would expect it to have less leverage on capital formation because of the absence of support from retained earnings, and that seems to have been the case with petroleum. On the other hand, the positive relation (not statistically significant) between total direct investment and utilities investment, which does not draw on direct capital inflows, weakly suggests the typical presence of a complementary rather than competing relation between capital formation financed by direct investment and that undertaken by domestically controlled sectors of the economy.

One dollar of direct investment has been associated with a lag averaging about half a year, with $2 or more of domestic capital formation under average conditions. When the Canadian economy is in a highly prosperous phase, or when direct investment flows toward older industrial sectors where it is supported by retained earnings, the value might rise to $3 or more. It may fall to $.80 during phases of recession or stagnation, when takeovers are being encouraged by these or other forces, or when direct investment goes primarily to new sectors of those unusually weak in stimulating complementary investment.

Portfolio Investment, Interest Rates, and Capital Formation

The influence of direct investment in capital formation can be determined in what is a relatively straightforward manner if our view is correct that the two are linked in the first instance by a common set of administrative decisions. No question then arises of mutual causation, and the single-equation approach employed in Chapter 4 seems relatively trouble-free. To measure the effect of other sorts of capital inflow, the more complex procedures of Chapter 3 become necessary. Although we have argued that Canadian interest rates influence capital formation only with a lag, the interest rate and the capital inflow are simultaneously determined, and the effect of a capital flow

267

disturbance on the interest rate can be measured without bias only in a reduced-form system. How large an initial disturbance in portfolio capital inflows would be necessary to reduce the Canadian long-term interest rate by ten basis points? The least-squares estimates summarized in Table 3.1 suggest $132 million (mid-point of a range running from $128 to $137 million). The biases in least-squares estimation of the underlying parameters tell us that this is a maximum estimate. Using two-stage least-squares to supply a best guess, the value falls considerably to about $39 million (range of $34 to $44 million, based on Table 3.2). Finally, if the disturbance arises because of a fall in United States interest rates, the direct expectational effect on Canadian rates substitutes in large measure for the actual capital inflow, which might then be as small as $13 million (using equation 2.6). As noted in Chapter 3: although these estimates of the capital flow-interest rate relation lie rather far apart, all are relevant because each possesses its own economic interpretation.

A different simultaneous procedure was used in Chapter 3 to estimate the impact of capital-flow disturbances on Canadian short rates. In this case the interaction between the short-term capital and forward exchange markets supplied the necessary information, providing three estimates, each based on a different assumption about behavior of the forward rate. If the forward rate is unaffected by an exogenous disturbance in the short-term inflow, an increase of as little as $17 million quarterly might reduce the Canadian short rate by ten basis points. If, at the other extreme, the forward rate adjusts fully to eliminate the possibility of profitable covered interest arbitrage, $36 million is needed. If the forward rate behaves in the fashion typical over the 1951–1962 period, the associated inflow is $27 million.

To link these effects on interest rates to changes in Canadian domestic expenditure, estimates are needed of the interest sensitivity of the major expenditure categories. Here we settle for drawing together the findings of other scholars. Although pessimism has reigned over the possibility of finding measurable influences of the interest rate on investment, and this determinant was omitted from our own incidental analysis of investment determinants (Chapter 4), several recent studies have produced significant results. For example, Rudolf Rhomberg found that a decline of one percentage point in the interest rate on Canadian long-term government bonds would increase residential construction by $62 million one and a half quarters later,[3] nonresidential construction by $173 million three quarters later, and machinery and equipment $122 million four quarters later.[4] Rhomberg notes that the implied elasticities (evaluated at the mean) lie between -0.5 and -1.0. Apparently the lags were chosen to optimize the results of the equations in terms of theoretical expectations; in any case, those for business fixed investment are not unreasonable in the light of other studies of investment determinants, including the results presented in Chapter 4.

Statistical work undertaken by Thomas A. Wilson for the Royal Commission on Taxation uncovered a substantial response of Canadian manufacturing investment to the corporate bond rate.[5] Using four-quarter moving totals of the investment series, and assuming that Canadian manufacturing invest-

3. Rudolf R. Rhomberg, "A Model of the Canadian Economy under Fixed and Fluctuating Exchange Rates," *Journal of Political Economy,* LXXII (February, 1964), 9–10. His equation for residential construction was estimated in first differences, including as the predetermined variable the change in the long-term bond rate lagged one quarter. The figure in the text ignores the difficulty of getting from first differences to undifferenced variables and places the lag at the middle of the period in which the change that enters Rhomberg's equation occurs.

4. These figures are in constant 1957 prices, converted from Rhomberg's 1949 values using GNP implicit deflators.

5. Thomas A. Wilson, *Capital Investment and the Cost of Capital: A Dynamic Analysis,* Studies of the Royal Commission on Taxation, no. 30 (Ottawa: Queen's Printer, 1967), pp. 76–79.

ment lags behind decisions (and capital appropriations) in the same pattern found by Shirley Almon for the United States,[6] Wilson found that a decline of 1 percent in the interest rate would raise the annual rate of manufacturing investment in plant and equipment by $530 million (1957 prices), corresponding to an elasticity of — 0.67.[7] If Almon's U.S.-derived weights are applicable to Canada, about one third of this increase in expenditures would take place within three quarters after the interest-rate decline, two thirds within five, and nearly all within seven. Using the older, Koyck-type distributed-lag formulation, T. Russell Robinson found a slightly stronger ultimate impact of the Canadian corporate bond rate on gross domestic investment, quarterly data seasonally adjusted, for the period 1952–1965.[8] His estimates imply that 41 percent of the effect of a decline in the corporate bond rate would be felt within three quarters, 59 percent after five, 75 percent after two years. Certain general deficiencies of the distributed-lag technique due to the pervasive autocorrelation of economic time-series, plus disagreement with the de Leeuw-Almon results and those of Chapter 4 above on the shape of the lag of investment expenditures, render this result somewhat suspect.

6. That is, using the best set of weights generated by Mrs. Almon's polynomial method; see her "The Distributed Lag Between Capital Appropriations and Expenditures," *Econometrica,* XXXIII (January, 1965), table 2. Compare Frank de Leeuw, "The Demand for Capital Goods by Manufacturers: A Study of Quarterly Time Series," *Econometrica,* XXX (July, 1962), 407–423.

7. Other predetermined variables in the equation giving these results were corporate depreciation plus retained earnings, as a liquidity variable, and an index of real gross domestic product as a measure of capacity requirements. Wilson's equations deteriorated (lower $RSQC$, interest-rate coefficient insignificant) when a more sophisticated variable was introduced to represent capital requirements — potential minus actual net final output.

8. T. Russell Robinson, "Foreign Trade and Economic Stability: The Canadian Case," unpub. diss. (Yale University, 1966), table 4.2. Also see his "Canada's Imports and Economic Stability," *Canadian Journal of Economics,* I (May, 1968), 401–428.

Other studies of the interest-sensitivity of investment have elaborated on the behavior of residential construction. Johnson and Winder, using a distributed-lag model, failed to pick up any influence of interest rates in business fixed investment. Residential construction, however, appeared significantly related to the differential between the National Housing Act effective lending rate (the rate obtainable to lenders on N.H.A.-guaranteed mortgages) and the McLeod, Young, and Weir index of bond yields, with an elasticity of mortgage approvals to the differential of 0.99.[9] But this is a supply elasticity for funds, not a demand elasticity for housing. It reflects the response of lenders to a change in the relative attractiveness of mortgage yields over a period when there was generally a backlog of would-be borrowers at the N.H.A. maximum rate. A thorough investigation by Lawrence B. Smith of the magnitude and lag structure of the response of residential construction expenditures to long-term interest rates indicates that a decline of one percentage point in the long-term interest rate would increase residential mortgage approvals by $42 million; in the first quarter after the rise in approvals, residential construction would rise about $10.9 million and in the second quarter further to $27.7 million, with peak expenditures coming about seven or eight months after the interest-rate change.[10]

9. Harry G. Johnson and John W. L. Winder, *Lags in the Effects of Monetary Policy in Canada,* working paper for the Royal Commission on Banking and Finance (Ottawa: Queen's Printer, 1962), chap. xi and pp. 196–197. The estimate is based on monthly observations running April, 1954–December, 1961.

10. Lawrence Berk Smith, "The Postwar Canadian Residential Mortgage Market and the Role of Government," unpub. diss. (Harvard University, 1966), pp. 168, 200–209. These computations were based on current dollar data over the 1951–1963 period. The average price level for the period should correspond well to the 1957 values used in our own calculations; but because of the upward trend in prices over the period, there is likely to be a slight upward bias in the underlying regression coefficients when the results are interpreted in real terms. We have not tried to correct for this.

271

These figures will be used below, although they represent a supply response in the face of a backlog of demand at the N.H.A. maximum lending rate. Because of the dominance of special conditions and policies in the Canadian mortgage market since the war, no one has extracted an estimate of the elasticity of demand for housing with respect to either interest rates or the relative price of residential construction; general evidence suggests that these elasticities would be reasonably high.[11]

Other Capital Inflows and Categories of Domestic Expenditure

Fixed investment is obviously the chief component of Canadian domestic expenditure that is influenced by international capital movements. It may not be the only one, however; so we performed a series of experiments to check for various other plausible links between categories of domestic expenditure and categories of capital inflow during the 1951–1962 period. Our method was to re-estimate the least-squares versions of Lawrence Officer's equations for each of these expenditure classes, adding selected independent variables which might indicate an influence for international capital flows.

First, expenditure on consumers' durable goods might be influenced by inflows of short-term capital in two ways. Short-term inflows might increase the liquidity of finance companies and banks, raising the availability of installment credit or lowering its cost to the borrower. Households might on balance

---

Later research by Smith, published after our own calculations were completed, suggests a somewhat smaller response; see his "A Model of the Canadian Housing and Mortgage Markets," *Journal of Political Economy,* LXXVII (September-October, 1969), 795–816.

11. *Ibid.,* pp. 44–46, 220–223. Housing demand is clearly elastic to changes in down payment requirements and to reductions in monthly payments by increasing the maximum period of repayment.

sell off financial assets to finance increases in their purchases of durable goods. Indeed, these possibilities provide about as meaningful embodiment as can be given to the charge, popular during the period of high capital inflows in the late 1950's, that Canadians were "living beyond their means." The first hypothesis implies a positive relation of quarterly purchases of consumers' durables to unlagged short-term capital inflows (*SK*), the second to unlagged trade in outstanding securities (*NTOS*). Re-estimating Officer's equation for consumer durables, including these two variables separately, we obtained correct signs for both variables with the former significant at the 10-percent level. There seemed no important gain in keeping separate these two hypotheses about the influence of short-term capital inflows on durables purchases, and so we also experimented with entering a single variable covering the whole of the short-term capital inflow (*STK*). When a slight alteration is made in the other variables in Officer's equation,[12] this variable is significant at the 5-percent level. It indicates that an additional inflow of $1 million of short-term capital leads to an increase of $159,000 in expenditure on consumers' durable goods; the implied elasticity of durables purchases, evaluated at the mean, is 0.01.

In experimenting with Officer's equation for nonfarm business inventories, we tried adding the short-term interest rate, as well as direct investment and total short-term capital inflows — the latter two as possible sources of inventory financing. No

---

12. Officer had employed a principal component in lieu of two income variables (disposable wage and nonwage income), each divided by a base-weighted price index of consumer durable goods, in order to eliminate the collinearity introduced by their use. We found that the correlation between the two series was barely significant, however, and that the two income variables introduced separately are more significant than the principal component. See Lawrence H. Officer, *An Econometric Model of Canada under the Fluctuating Exchange Rate* (Cambridge: Harvard University Press, 1968), p. 287.

significant relations were found; only the short-term capital flow entered with the right sign, and the adjusted *RSQC* for Officer's equation was reduced in the process.[13]

Finally, to supplement the evidence cited above concerning the influence of long-term interest rates (and through them long-term capital flows) on residential construction, we checked for a direct effect. Households may sell off outstanding securities in order to finance their equity in new residential construction; one would expect that trade in outstanding securities might thus influence residential construction expenditures with a lag that is probably less than one quarter. Adding trade in outstanding securities, and also appropriately lagged interest-rate variables, to Officer's equation, we found an influence, correctly signed and significant at 5 percent. It indicates that an increase of $1 million in capital inflows through trade in outstanding securities corresponds to an increase of $523,-000 in expenditures on residential construction during the current quarter; the implied elasticity, evaluated at the mean, is 0.03.[14]

13. Significant responses of manufacturing inventories are reported by Courchene, but the absolute values of his coefficients are too small for their inclusion in the following calculations to make any difference; T. J. Courchene, "Inventory Behavior and the Stock-Order Distinction: An Analysis by Industry and by Stage of Fabrication with Empirical Applications to the Canadian Manufacturing Sector," *Canadian Journal of Economics and Political Science,* XXXIII (August, 1967), 325–357.

14. These experiments probably exhaust the short-term direct responses of expenditure categories to capital inflows, but not the longer-term ones. For instance, T. R. Robinson and T. J. Courchene have found a systematic response of provincial and municipal expenditures to private gross fixed business investment. Their results suggest that an increase of $1 in private investment might lead to a total increase of provincial and municipal expenditure of about $0.25, spread over the third through fifth succeeding quarters and peaking in the fifth. It will be seen below that including such longer-term responses in our own calculations would compound dubious arithmetic without altering our qualitative conclusions. T. R. Robinson and T. J. Courchene, "Fiscal Federalism and Economic Stability: An Examination of Multi-Level Public Finance in Canada," *Canadian Journal of Economics,* II (May, 1969), 697–715.

TABLE 7.1. Impacts of exogenous disturbances in international capital flows on categories of Canadian domestic expenditure (millions of 1957 dollars, quarterly rates)

International capital flow — Variable	Amount of change[a] ($ million)	Interest rate — Variable	Amount of change (percentage points)[b]	Expenditure variable	1	2	3	4	5	6
U.S. direct investment	$100	—	—	Business fixed investment	100[c] 27[d]	100 27	100 27	0 0	0 0	0 0
Net portfolio[e]	132 39 13	Corporate	−0.1	Business fixed investment	1.2[f] 0[g]	2.2 0	2.8 17.3	3.0 12.2	2.8 0	2.3 0
Net portfolio[e]	132 39 13	Long-term government	−0.1	Residential construction	1.8[h]	2.7	4.2	2.5	0.8	0
Total short-term	36 27 17	Short-term government	−0.1	Consumer durables	2.9	0	0	0	0	0

[a] Where multiple estimates appear they correspond to differences in assumed economic conditions, or differing statistical biases in the estimates, or both. See text here, and Chapter 3.

[b] Here interest rates are measured in the conventional fashion of percent per year. The equations presented in Chapters 2 and 3 employed Officer's series, in which interest rates are expressed in percent per quarter. Allowance for this was made in calculating the change in capital flows associated with the assumed interest-rate change.

[c] This line pertains to periods of full employment.

[d] This line pertains to periods of less than full employment.

[e] Net new issues of securities plus trade in outstanding securities.

[f] This line uses T. A. Wilson's estimates of the response of manufacturing investment to changes in the corporate bond rate; it assumes the applicability of Shirley Almon's lags for the U.S. to Canada; also that the elasticity estimated for the manufacturing sector applies to the whole of gross business capital formation.

[g] This line uses Rudolf Rhomberg's estimates of the response of nonresidential construction and machinery and equipment investment to the government bond rate.

[h] Residential construction expenditures in the first period are associated with the financing of construction through trade in outstanding securities; the remaining expenditure changes reflect the impact of a lower interest rate on mortgage approvals, taking the lag between approval and construction into account.

Table 7.1 summarizes the associations outlined above between categories of capital inflow and domestic expenditure. Where applicable, the implied change in the appropriate Canadian interest rate is included, and the size of the disturbance is arbitrarily selected as that which would produce a change of 0.1 percent (ten basis points) in the interest rate. These results will be utilized further after we have explored the relation between changes in capital formation in Canada and changes in gross national product and the current-account balance.

EXPENDITURE CHANGES AND NATIONAL INCOME MULTIPLIERS

The next step in analyzing the effects of exogenous disturbances in capital flows on the Canadian economy is to link the exogenous expenditure changes discussed in the preceding section to changes in total Canadian income or expenditure and its endogenous components, in particular, the level of demand for imports. This linkage is, of course, one of central interest in all applied studies of income determination; it has often been investigated previously for the Canadian economy, the investigations showing the full range of sophistication from the simplest least-squares estimates to complex econometric models. This section assembles and interprets the results of some of these investigations.

Large-scale econometric models, such as those of Officer and Rhomberg, can be manipulated to yield matrices of impact and dynamic multipliers showing the response of each endogenous variable in the system to a change in any predetermined variable. (Rhomberg presents a large array of impact and dynamic multipliers for his own model; dynamic multipliers were calculated from Officer's model in connection with our study, and the method of calculation and the general dy-

276

namic properties of the model are discussed in Appendix C.) Impact multipliers amount to a generalization of the familiar Keynesian simultaneous multiplier. In principle, they supply the answers to the question raised in the preceding paragraph, taking into account in the process the full range of interdependencies in the economy that are included in the model. In practice, however, their use is subject to serious constraints.

Both Rhomberg and Officer treat as endogenous all categories of private expenditure labeled exogenous in simple models of income determination, listed in Table 7.1 as the Canadian expenditure categories likely to show significant direct effects of variations in the rate of capital inflow. We therefore lack multiplier values based on exogenous disturbances in these variables; it is necessary to resort to proxies and especially to accord government purchases of goods and services, wholly exogenous in both the Officer and Rhomberg models, their traditional status as "honorary investment." [15] But this is not a very satisfactory procedure. The commodity composition of government expenditures, in particular their import content, differs greatly from that of private investment (including consumer durables). These differences are reflected in the structures of the econometric models — especially Officer's which distinguishes four separate categories of commodity imports. Using substitute impact multipliers for government expenditure will supply us with biased estimates of the induced changes in income and imports.

Another problem stems from the short-run nature of these models, both of which are based on quarterly observations. Only a modest portion of the income adjustments associated

15. Goods only, in the case of Officer's model. A possible alternative would exist if the investment equation(s) were to contain an exogenous variable occurring nowhere else in the model. In that case, we could use the impact multipliers for this exogenous variable, multiplying them by its coefficient in the investment equation. But no such exogenous variables exist in either model.

with an exogenous disturbance in spending work themselves out in a single quarter; the impact multipliers computed from these models therefore catch only something like the first round of expenditure adjustments entailed by the disturbance. Dynamic multipliers show the desired cumulative change in a given endogenous variable in response to a unit change in an exogenous variable after n time periods, but only if the model properly captures the structure of lagged relations in the economy. Neither model at hand can make strong claims on this score. Furthermore, the only remotely convenient way to calculate such dynamic multipliers is to employ the linearized form of the model used to extract the impact multipliers. Both the Officer and Rhomberg models are in fact nonlinear and were linearized by the same process as that employed on the original Klein-Goldberger model.[16] Possible errors due to this linearization increase as responses of the endogenous variables through successive time periods take them farther and farther from their mean values at which the linearization was made. How large these errors are in practice depends on the particular model, but one experiment has shown that the differences in the incremental changes of the endogenous variables in time periods after the first, when calculated from the linearized and nonlinear versions of a model, are great.[17]

The existence of these problems does not render the multipliers drawn from econometric models unusable, but it certainly reduces their standing against relations estimated by

16. Arthur S. Goldberger, *Impact Multipliers and Dynamic Properties of the Klein-Goldberger Model*, Contributions to Economic Analysis, no. 19 (Amsterdam: North-Holland Publishing Company, 1959), pp. 18–21.

17. Sydney May, "Dynamic Multipliers and Their Use for Fiscal Decision-Making," *Conference on Stabilization Policies Convened by the Economic Council of Canada at the University of Western Ontario, London, Aug. 30 to Sept. 1, 1965* (Ottawa: Queen's Printer, 1966), pp. 175–177. Inspection of the second-period increments to the endogenous variables in this (annual) model shows the changes in the linearized version exceeding those calculated from the nonlinear version by amounts ranging from about 15 to 50 percent.

simpler procedures. Keeping these drawbacks in mind, let us consider the evidence. Table 7.2 presents a small set of com-

TABLE 7.2. Selected impact and dynamic multipliers, Rhomberg and Officer econometric models (effect of $100-million change in government purchases of goods and services)

Dependent variable	Units	Time period (quarter)					
		1	2	3	4	6	8
Rhomberg model							
Real GNP	$ million	148	240	275	331	358	325
Money GNP[a]	$ million	588	891	997	1,218	1,316	1,165
Investment[b]	$ million	−41	68	113	177	215	189
Current-account balance	$ million	−35	−130	−168	−223	−257	−236
Capital-account balance[e]	$ million	33	57	74	99	127	139
Exchange rate[d]	U.S. cents	.7	.9	1.1	1.2	1.3	1.5
Officer model							
Real GNP	$ million	105	105	111	125	168	210
Money GNP	$ million	129	135	151	168	212	265
Investment[b]	$ million	−30	−26	−22	−9	36	82
Current-account balance	$ million	−26	−30	−26	−32	−65	−91
Capital-account balance[e]	$ million	2.0	2.0	1.5	2.0	1.5	−2.1
Exchange rate[d]	U.S. cents	−.001	−.002	−.003	−.004	−.007	−.011

Source: Rudolf R. Rhomberg, "A Model of the Canadian Economy under Fixed and Fluctuating Exchange Rates," *Journal of Political Economy*, LXXII (February, 1964), table 7; calculated (see app. B for details) from Lawrence H. Officer, *An Econometric Model of Canada under the Fluctuating Exchange Rate* (Cambridge, Mass.: Harvard University Press, 1968), table 7.

[a] Rhomberg's model contains an equation explaining the change in the GNP deflator; the multiplier for money income was derived by assuming that initial income took its mean value for the period of Rhomberg's observations.

[b] Business plant and equipment, residential construction, change in nonfarm business inventories.

[e] Long-term capital, including trade in outstanding securities.

[d] Price of the Canadian dollar, in U.S. cents.

parable impact and dynamic multipliers from the Rhomberg and Officer models, taking an increase in government expenditures on goods and services as the exogenous disturbance. The two models yield very different multipliers. In Rhomberg's model the induced increases in income and imports are large due to a strong accelerator and the high marginal import content of investment. Officer's model also contains an accelerator term; but his formulation causes it to take a number of quarters to get started, hence the low income multiplier and the reduction in investment for the first few periods. Rhomberg's model shows a large response in prices; Officer's a smaller one that dies away quickly. In neither model is improvement in the long-term capital-account balance sufficient to offset deterioration in the current account; for Officer there is a minute depreciation of the exchange rate, for Rhomberg a rather puzzling appreciation.[18] Clearly, these models reach little useful consensus.

A different approach to the problem of relating income and imports to changes in domestic expenditure has been taken by Robinson in an unpublished doctoral dissertation.[19] His effort, employing a simple model and least-squares estimation, is less elaborate than the Officer and Rhomberg models but contains some attractive features in view of our own aims. Investment is treated as including both endogenous and exogenous components, the former governed by the long-term interest rate. A thorough analysis of Canada's demand for imports is undertaken, showing its dependence on the exchange rate and on the composition of Canadian gross national expenditure.

To secure an estimate of the response of total income to exogenous changes in various categories of expenditure, Robinson combines simple estimates of leakages into taxation and

18. For further discussion of the dynamic properties of the Officer model, see Appendix C.
19. Robinson, "Foreign Trade and Economic Stability," chaps. iii–v.

corporate and personal saving with his own relatively elaborate estimates of import leakages. The latter, in his most suitable set of estimates, are built up for consumption and investment spending separately from average import propensities for separate commodity groups[20] taken from input-output data and weighted according to cyclical importance of the different commodity groups in consumption and investment spending. Marginal propensities to import from investment spending enter the multiplier expression because Robinson employs a series of alternative estimates of the "marginal propensity to invest" in lieu of a conventional accelerator. Table 7.3 presents

TABLE 7.3. Estimated cumulative income multipliers, allowing for various responses of investment to changes in income

Investment response to income change	Number of rounds of expenditure change				
	1	2	3	4	∞
None	1.373	1.512	1.564	1.583	1.595
Response to current change	1.400	1.560	1.624	1.649	1.666
Full distributed-lag response	1.540	1.832	1.989	2.074	2.174

Source: Calculated from T. Russell Robinson, *Foreign Trade and Economic Stability: the Canadian Case*, unpub. diss. (Yale University, 1966), chap. v.

multiplier values that illustrate the range of his results, covering: the case in which the effect of income on investment is

20. He fails to find significant differences between the average and marginal propensities to import for individual commodity groups — i.e., the share of imports in the domestic market for each major group tends to remain constant, although the importance of the groups in total expenditure (and therefore the *total* import share) does not.

ignored; a case in which its influence is taken into account through a distributed-lag function, with the lag assumed brief relative to the income-expenditure lag; an intermediate case in which only the current influence of income on investment is considered.[21] Note that the figures for successive rounds of expenditure do not correspond to actual time periods, since Robinson does not employ an explicit dynamic formulation for all of his relations. A valuable contribution of Robinson's work is his estimation of the fraction of a dollar of increased spending of various types that would leak into imports on the first round. Given a one-dollar change in *total* expenditure, the following injections to *domestic* expenditure would occur: government expenditure, $.867; transfer payments or tax reduction, $.724; exports, $.838; total investment, $.643; construction, $.897; consumer durables, $.725; consumer nondurables, $.795; consumer services, $.850.[22] Applying one of these fractions to any multiplier in Table 7.3 provides an estimate of the effect of that type of expenditure change.

INDUCED ADJUSTMENTS IN THE BALANCE OF PAYMENTS

It is necessary at this point to return briefly to the theoretical models which motivated this assembly of data. Can a nation's balance of payments adjust to a disturbance in capital flows, the models inquire, through income changes alone? Do price changes — the exchange rate, or relative commodity and factor prices — play an essential part in the process, and are the directions of these changes predictable? So far, we have con-

21. That is, the income-expenditure lag is assumed short relative to the investment-income lag.
22. Robinson, "Foreign Trade and Economic Stability," table 5.4.

sidered the total impact of capital-flow disturbances on the domestic economy only. These measurements, of course, hold interest in themselves because of policy significance attached to full employment, income stability, and growth as influenced by the share of national income devoted to investment. We have now to ask about the size of the change in imports associated with the changes computed above in gross national product in response to capital-flow disturbances.

Income-induced changes in imports are the foremost, but not the only, response of the balance of payments to the impact of capital-flow changes on the domestic economy. When increased capital inflows raise the level of domestic output, exports may be discouraged if domestic money prices and factor-costs are adversely affected. If increased domestic activity levels tend to push up domestic interest rates, then there will be induced secondary damping of capital inflows to set against the initial exogenous disturbances.

Finally, the whole of the argument to this point has assumed that, flexible exchange rate or no, variations in the exchange rate due to the capital-flow disturbances themselves do not significantly affect the adjustments taking place in domestic income circuits and capital markets. As pointed out in Chapter 1, this simplification is valid even if it does violence to the facts if the operative relations are all linear, or if the time lag with which the exchange rate affects the current account is no shorter than the lag with which expenditure changes affect the account through domestic income circuits. Chapter 3 noted the extent to which stabilizing expectations concerning the exchange rate induce changes in capital flows that make the rate behave like one fixed by public authorities. The consequences of exchange-rate responses come clear below when we consider whether or not capital inflows are inflationary.

Two approaches can be employed to answer the questions

raised at the beginning of this section. The hypothetical approach lies directly parallel to the "transfer problem" in economic theory in asking whether income adjustments would suffice to change the current account by enough to offset an assumed disturbance in the capital account. The historical approach explores the actual relation between these disturbances and adjustments in Canada, to determine whether capital-flow disturbances contributed to the variability of the exchange rate or to pressures leading aggregate demand away from an optimal level.

Do Income Effects "Requite" Exogenous Transfers?

Table 7.4 adapts materials discussed in the preceding section to provide estimates of response of the current account to disturbances in the major types of international capital flows. We pose the question in the form made familiar by simple multiplier sequences in modern income analysis: if capital flows shift by an arbitrary amount in quarter t and remain at the new level, how soon (if ever) will income-induced changes in the current account attain the same change? This mode of investigation departs from the dictates of neoclassical theory only in emphasizing the amount of adjustment attained in the current account at various points in time rather than hypothetical final equilibrium positions. It is our choice for two reasons. First, deficiencies of the available econometric models render their predictions for small dynamic disturbances suspect and their predicted equilibrium values doubly so. Second, the question of how soon income adjustments can be expected to offset the effects of a capital disturbance seems more relevant to public policy than the question of whether they would do so after an unlimited period of time.

To construct Table 7.4, we depended primarily on Officer's

TABLE 7.4. Estimates of cumulative response of current account of Canadian balance of payments to exogenous disturbances in capital inflows (dollars)

Type of disturbance	Period (quarter)						
	1	2	3	4	5	6	7
1. Increase direct investment by $100							
a. Full employment conditions	25.6	51.2	83.6	105.7	145.0	192.9	236.6
b. Less than full employment	6.9	13.8	22.6	28.5	39.2	52.1	63.9
2. Increase portfolio capital inflow by $100							
a. Due to U.S. interest rate fall	6.2	10.0	15.4	16.9	20.8	25.4	29.2
b. Best guess[a]	2.1	3.3	5.1	5.6	6.9	8.5	9.7
c. Minimum effect[b]	0.6	0.9	1.4	1.6	1.9	2.4	2.7
3. Increase short-term capital inflow by $100							
a. No forward rate change[e]	4.6	4.6	5.8	8.6	11.6	14.4	16.4
b. Best guess[d]	2.9	2.9	3.7	5.7	7.3	9.1	10.3
c. Full forward rate change[e]	2.2	2.2	2.8	4.0	5.5	6.8	7.8
4. Reduce U.S. corporate liquidity by $100							
a. Average U.S. conditions	0	0	0.5	0.6	0.7	0.7	0.7
b. U.S. moderate unemployment	0	0	0.9	1.1	1.3	1.2	1.3

Source: Calculated from Tables 7.1 and 7.2, plus other sources indicated in text.

[a] Two-stage least-squares estimate of effect of autonomous disturbance in net new issues of securities.

[b] Ordinary least-squares estimate of effect of autonomous disturbance in net new issues of securities; statistical biases known to yield minimum estimate of effect.

[e] Forward exchange rate assumed respectively to be unaffected by exogenous changes in short-term capital inflows and to adjust completely to eliminate profitable covered interest arbitrage.

[d] Estimated typical behavior of forward exchange rate.

multipliers relating the current account to autonomous changes in domestic expenditure, applying them to the expenditure changes listed in Table 7.1 as the normal consequences of disturbances in capital flows. We made one major adjustment in these multipliers, however, collapsing the second and third quarter values (Table 7.2) and moving everything up one quarter. This seemingly cavalier maneuver is motivated by a great deal of evidence — drawn from otherwise less satisfactory models — that Canadian income responses get off the ground faster than Officer's multipliers suggest. It can be justified on close inspection of his model, which contains little dynamic structure except for that generated by his accelerator function.

If this procedure is unedifying, the alternatives either inspire no more confidence or make little difference empirically. Rhomberg's dynamic multipliers imply marginal propensities to import of about two-thirds and thus fly in the face of all historical evidence on the economy's behavior. We experimented with adjusting Officer's multipliers to take into account the greater first-round leakage to imports from investment expenditure than from government purchases of goods, the exogenous variable which generates the multipliers used in Table 7.4. This correction shifts the import leakage of a given disturbance forward in time, increasing the initial leakage but reducing subsequent ones (because the net domestic disturbance after the initial leakage is smaller). The net impact on the estimates of Table 7.4 is too small to change the broad qualitative conclusions.

Although this study concentrates on adjustments within Canada, Table 7.4 includes a quick estimate of the impact on Canada's current-account balance of foreign long-term investment emanating from the United States. Briefly: we suppose that an increase of U.S. lending, either direct or long-term portfolio, might affect U.S. domestic investment in the same way as a reduction in corporate liquidity (depreciation plus retained earnings). The results of Meyer and Glauber suggest that a reduction of $100 million in corporate liquidity might typically cut investment spending (after one quarter) by $25 million, or as much as $45 million in periods of slow domestic expansion.[23] The Brookings model supplies the obvious source of dynamic income multipliers, and we have used an average of the multipliers for constant-dollar GNP following changes in government purchases of durable goods and government construction activity.[24] The estimates of Ball and Marwah allow a satisfactory estimate of overall United States propensity to import goods and services (out of real GNP).[25] Finally, the net impact of overall change in the U.S. current-account balance must be converted to a net effect on Canada. A recent paper by Piekarz and Stekler provides a basis for estimating both the direct change in U.S. purchases of Canadian goods and services and the indirect change in third-country purchases from Canada caused by reduced third-country sales of exports

23. John R. Meyer and Robert Glauber, *Investment Decisions, Economic Forecasting and Public Policy* (Boston: Division of Research, Graduate School of Business Administration, Harvard University, 1964), chap. vii. Most specifications of the Meyer and Glauber equations for the whole period 1949–1958 give coefficients between .25 and .30; some are outside these limits. They argue that liquidity is a more important determinant of investment in recession than in prosperity. Bifurcated equations for recession periods give coefficients of about .40 and .50; our .45 is a midpoint.

24. Gary Fromm and Paul Taubman, *Policy Simulations with an Econometric Model* (Washington, D.C.: Brookings Institution, 1968), p. 48. The Brookings investment equations contain no exogenous corporate-liquidity terms suitable for developing such multipliers directly.

25. They present demand equations for six categories of U.S. imports of goods and services, using as an income variable either personal disposable income or GNP less government wage and salary payments. We have adjusted their coefficients to a full GNP basis, assuming that these GNP components hold the same average share of total GNP as during the period of their calculations. Aggregating the adjusted income coefficients gives a marginal propensity to import from GNP of 0.0459 (lagged one quarter). See R. J. Ball and K. Marwah, "The U.S. Demand for Imports, 1948–1958," *Review of Economics and Statistics,* XLIV (November, 1962), 395–401.

to the United States.[26] Line 4 of Table 7.4 results from assembling these various estimates; it testifies once more to the small import propensities characteristic of the U.S. economy.

Table 7.4 shows clearly enough that an increase in direct investment, under conditions of Canadian full employment, rather quickly generates current-account changes large enough to offset the initiating inflow disturbance and thus tends to be inflationary and also to depreciate the exchange rate. In "average" circumstances, direct investment disturbances are at least requited. For direct investment in times of Canadian unemployment and for other capital flows under all circumstances, the income-induced change in the current account is not sufficient (within a reasonable time period) to effect the transfer, causing an appreciation of the price of the currency or other adjustment to the residual payments surplus. Income adjustments in the United States, as the predominant lending country, are too small to change the picture much, although proportionally they make a significant addition to the estimated minimum income effects of portfolio and short-term inflows taking place within Canada.

Are Capital-Inflow Disturbances Inflationary?

Underlying Table 7.4 are estimates of the direct effect of a sustained upward shift in each capital-flow category on Canadian GNP. These are partial effects, in that they neglect an

26. R. Piekarz and L. E. Stekler, "Induced Changes in Trade and Payments," *Review of Economics and Statistics*, LXIX (November, 1967), 517–526. Piekarz and Stekler do not calculate U.S. marginal import shares from the various members of their *n*-region model (because the U.S. reflection ratio is estimated to be zero); so we supplied these, using similar estimation methods. The Canadian current-account balance worsens by 26.5 percent of a reduction in total U.S. imports of goods and services; direct reductions in U.S. purchases from Canada account for 20.8 percent, third-country effects for 5.7 percent.

important factor which we have put aside. With a flexible exchange rate, an increased capital inflow that remains underrequited will maintain upward pressure on the exchange rate. This appreciation of the currency itself deteriorates the current-account balance, and this exchange-rate-induced deterioration serves as another exogenous influence on domestic income. Whether a capital-inflow disturbance under the flexible exchange rate is inflationary thus depends on the outcome of upward pull of the direct expenditure effect and downward pull of the exchange-rate-induced change in the trade balance. An inflow that is promptly over-requited must be inflationary; one that is under-requited may or may not be, depending on these pulls.

In Table 7.5, we present an estimate of the net income im-

TABLE 7.5. Estimates of net effect on Canadian GNP of selected disturbances in capital inflows, allowing for current-account response to exchange-rate adjustment (dollars)

Type of disturbance	Period (quarter)					
	1	2	3	4	5	6
1b.[a] Increase direct investment by $100, less than full employment	28.4	13.2	8.0	17.1	30.7	46.7
2a. Increase portfolio capital inflow by $100 due to U.S. interest-rate fall	13.8	7.3	23.9	72.6	111.1	145.8
2b. Increase portfolio capital inflow by $100, most likely Canadian GNP response	4.6	−32.6	−64.1	−54.1	−52.3	−55.1
3a. Increase short-term capital inflow by $100, no forward rate change	17.9	−31.2	−80.6	−83.3	−91.5	−104.5

Source: Table 7.4 and calculations described in text.
[a] Numbers correspond to lines in Table 7.4.

pact of capital inflows in four sets of circumstances. (Line numbers in Table 7.5 correspond to those in Table 7.4.) By subtracting the income-induced changes in the current-account balance (calculated in Table 7.4) from the initiating disturbances, we estimate the extent to which the capital flow is under-requited in each quarter and thus the associated net excess demand in the exchange market. The question is: how much change should it be assumed this excess demand causes in the exchange rate and current account? A theorist would probably reply that the current-account change must equal the excess demand because only then is the upward pressure on the exchange rate eliminated. Our numbers in fact support this position but with one important qualification.

An under-requited capital inflow putting upward pressure on the Canadian dollar brings about two consequences. (1) The exchange-rate sensitivity of portfolio and short-term capital flows helps mitigate the upward pressure. (2) To the extent that upward pressure is not mitigated, the current account deteriorates by an amount governed by price elasticities of exports and imports. Regarding the first consequence, we found (Chapter 2) very high sensitivities of capital flows to the exchange rate. Equations 2.15–2.20 consistently show a large response of (total) short-term capital in one quarter to the exchange-rate change of the preceding quarter. Portfolio capital (equation 2.10) responds with less strength and is delayed one quarter. The outflow of short-term capital due to a one-cent increase in the exchange rate is about as large as the portfolio flow necessary (equation 2.10) to cause the one-cent increase.[27] So much for "this period" and "the preceding period" — what about the multiple-period analysis developed around

27. Following the analysis of equation 2.11, we interpret the coefficient of *RS* in equation 2.10 as measuring the effect of *PC* on *RS*, rather than vice versa. These coefficients of *PC* and *STK* on *RS* may well reflect unlagged negative relations between *PC* and *STK* operating through other channels.

Table 7.4? Does this offsetting of capital-flow disturbances to the exchange rate continue, quarter after quarter, if the disturbance is sustained? Our equations in Chapter 2 do not really answer this question,[28] but evidence in Chapter 6 (Table 6.5) argues strongly that the effect on the exchange rate of a capital-flow disturbance is postponed a quarter or two but then makes itself felt. Therefore, we shall interpret this exchange-rate damping as a one-shot phenomenon that wipes out the effect of a capital-flow disturbance in the first quarter and cuts it in half in the second, but then allows its full influence to be felt. This is fully consistent with the regression results in Chapter 2.

To test exchange rate influence on the current account, we ran simple regressions relating total constant-dollar imports of goods and services (quarterly) to Canadian GNP, an estimate of potential minus actual GNP,[29] and the exchange rate lagged up to three quarters.[30] Similarly, total Canadian exports of goods and services were related to United States GNP, potential minus actual U.S. GNP, and the exchange rate lagged up to three quarters.[31] Except for substantial sensitivity to the time

28. Because of pessimism about simple distributed-lag formulations, we avoided trying to measure the time shape of influences beyond the hypotheses described in the text.

29. This quarterly series is estimated by T. Russell Robinson on the basis of Drabble's annual figures for the Economic Council of Canada; use of the variable was suggested by Robinson's work. See B. J. Drabble, *Potential Output 1946 to 1970*, Economic Council of Canada, Staff Study no. 2 (Ottawa: Queen's Printer, 1964).

30. Careful study of demand elasticities governing Canada's trade is a formidable undertaking, and the calculations described represent a casual effort designed to serve limited purposes. We used only the exchange rate, rather than price indexes adjusted by the exchange rate; in view of our evidence on price formation in Canada (Chapter 5), however, this apparent simplification may make considerable sense. Compare Murray C. Kemp, *The Demand for Canadian Imports, 1926–1955*, Canadian Studies in Economics, no. 15 (Toronto: University of Toronto Press, 1962).

31. With no constant-dollar series available for quarterly exports of goods and services to the U.S. we chose to work with total exports. The GNP gap series was supplied by Otto Eckstein.

period chosen, the results are quite good, with all coefficients highly significant and import exchange-rate elasticities of at least unity and export elasticities of at least 0.35.[32] Furthermore, the total coefficient for the response of the current account to the exchange rate (including the U.S. income change) is high enough to suggest that any capital-flow disturbances of the arbitrary size assumed for purposes of Table 7.4 would be offset within one quarter by trade responses to the induced exchange-rate change.

This statistical interpretation led us to assume that, when a capital flow disturbance remains under-requited, the current-account balance changes each quarter by enough to offset the excess demand for foreign exchange; but exchange-rate sensitivity of capital flows themselves modifies the excess demand as specified above. Using Officer's income multipliers and these assumptions, Table 7.5 can be calculated. Only a few strategic cases are presented. Even when Canadian unemployment renders the expenditure effects of direct investment weakest, we still find it inflationary by a small margin. A portfolio capital disturbance is also inflationary when due to a fall in the general level of North American long-term interest rates but deflationary under other circumstances. Finally, short-term disturbances (because of their weak measured effects on Canadian expenditure) are deflationary even in the most favorable case.

32. Running the trade flow on the income variables and, in separate equations, RS, RS_{-1}, RS_{-2}, and RS_{-3}, we obtained about the same coefficient and degree of significance for the exchange rate in each equation. This odd pattern held equally for imports and exports. It might be given two quite different interpretations. The first, implied in the text, holds that the result stems from autocorrelation in the exchange rate, especially since most variation in the trade flow is explained by the income variable; therefore the elasticity (at the mean) is given by any one of the slope coefficients, and the lag is somewhere between zero and three quarters. The second interpretation is that Canadian trade flows are influenced by the exchange rate with a rectangular lag pattern stretching over four quarters; in this case the elasticities would be approximately four times those quoted in the text — the basis for our cautionary "at least."

These results are not particularly sensitive to the use of alternative sets of income multipliers, since the induced consequences of the domestic expenditure and current-account balance changes work against each other.

Did Income Adjustments Stabilize the Canadian Economy?

These hypothetical sequences of adjustment tell something about the direction of disturbance to be expected in Canadian employment and the exchange rate (or balance of payments, under the fixed rate), and the stability properties of the economy as an equilibrium system. They fail, however, to indicate whether or not exogenous disturbances in the capital accounts and the adjustments they entailed contributed to the stability of the Canadian economy over the 1951–1962 period. These stabilizing properties depend on the historical pattern of disturbances, as well as upon the size and timing of the adjustments they brought about.

In the first section of this chapter we isolated the portion of variation in historic capital flows that could be called "exogenous" to movements in Canadian variables that lie within the control of Canadian authorities. These calculations provide an estimate of the exogenous disturbance in each quarter of the period. The materials presented in the preceding tables can be used to estimate the effect on the current account in each quarter of capital disturbances occurring in that and the previous quarters. The income mechanism obviously tends to stabilize *this* quarter's disturbance so far as the current-account effects are felt immediately: an exogenous improvement in the capital account raises domestic income and deteriorates the current account. But the income adjustments responding to capital disturbances in the preceding quarters need not be stabilizing in the current one. Indeed, if the disturbances in all recently preceding quarters were of opposite sign to that in the current

293

quarter, they would be destabilizing. Whether the adjustment mechanism is typically stabilizing or destabilizing thus depends both on the historical pattern of capital-account disturbances and on the timing and strength of the adjustment mechanism. Given the historic disturbance pattern, it is not obvious that an income mechanism requiting capital disturbances rather quickly would contribute more to stability than one requiting them rather slowly. It is simply an empirical question.

To explore whether or not capital disturbances and income-induced responses in the current account have tended to stabilize the Canadian exchange rate, we developed series of quarterly estimates of capital-account disturbances and current-account responses for each individual type of capital flow and for the aggregate. In the aggregate, income adjustments proved to be slightly stabilizing. We reached this conclusion by examining the mean absolute values of our estimates of capital disturbances, of trade responses, and of the algebraic sum of each quarter's disturbance and response. If the response were typically destabilizing, then a negative (in its effect on the balance of payments) disturbance would be associated with a negative response and the sum of the two would be greater than the initial disturbance. Conversely, a stabilizing response would be of opposite sign and the sum would have a smaller absolute value. The average absolute value of the sum was less than the value of the disturbance by a modest 6.4 percent.

Direct investment, portfolio investment, and short-term flows were studied individually in the same way, assuming full employment for the first and employing our best-guess estimates for the second and third. The responses to short-term flows were also marginally stabilizing, reducing the average absolute quarterly value of the disturbance by 3.1 percent. But the responses to both direct and portfolio investment were destabilizing, increasing the average quarterly disturbances by 21.7 and 2.0 percent respectively. How could the aggregate response of the current account be more stabilizing than the response imputed to any of its components separately? The capital flows tend themselves to be mutually stabilizing, with a positive disturbance in the long-term flows typically associated with a negative disturbance in the short-term flows; thus the aggregate income response tends to come out right. Note that this accommodation of exogenous disturbances in long and short flows did not operate through Canadian interest rates, for interest rates were among the policy variables whose influences were removed in deriving these estimates of exogenous disturbances. The important stabilizing interaction of long and short flows operates through other channels as well. The probable explanation is simply the Canadian practice of borrowing abroad and holding the proceeds initially in foreign currency, repatriating them only at a rate geared to desired rates of expenditure.

This analysis of the effect of exogenous capital inflows and their consequences on economic stability can be pushed one step farther by comparing these net pressures on the foreign exchange market under the fluctuating exchange rate with actual movements of that rate. We ran a simple correlation between the two quarterly series. The correlation of $+0.074$ was not significantly different from zero. It appears that the net disturbances impinging on the foreign exchange market were too small and unsystematic to contribute significantly to explaining movements of the flexible exchange rate. To put it another way, they were not a substantial source of instability in the exchange rate.[33]

If the exchange rate had shown a substantial correlation with the net pressure of capital disturbances on the foreign

33. One might wonder about the stabilization properties of total capital inflows and their induced adjustments, not just the exogenous components of the flows. It seemed to us that domestically-caused capital disturbances are likely to be linked to current-account changes by other relations than those considered here, rendering the results hopelessly ambiguous.

balance, we would have searched further for evidence of the working of the price mechanism of adjustment. An enormous volume of theoretical work on the balance of payments generates predictions — not always of unambiguous sign — about relations among the exchange rate, terms of trade, and the prices of traded and nontraded goods. But the failure of our quest for effects on the exchange rate, plus the statistical weaknesses of the available price indexes, led us to restrict our efforts.[34] Even so, the results were miserable. The annual index of Canada's overall terms of trade proved unrelated to our measure of net pressure on the balance of payments, the latter leading by six months. The same was true of an index of domestic relative to export prices. A significant relation emerged with the ratio of domestic to import prices, but its sign was perverse! We were compelled to let the price mechanism of adjustment slumber on in darkness.[35]

Capital-account disturbances failed to contribute significantly to instability in the exchange rate. What about the level of Canadian employment during the period? Using the type of calculations underlying Table 7.5, one might conceivably compute the same sort of quarterly series of imputed effects of capital disturbances on GNP. The framework of assumptions

34. Some appropriate price indexes are available only on an annual basis. In any case, the rather long and variable lags built into price responses suggest the folly of trying to work with quarterly rather than annual data. Furthermore, of course, the unit-value basis for constructing trade-price indexes sharply limits the precision with which we can expect them to reflect market behavior.

35. These results do not, of course, imply that the price mechanism was not operating during the period; rather, it was energized by a set of disturbances in which the net impact of exogenous changes in capital flows played an insignificant role. A case in point is that appreciation of the Canadian dollar in the late 1950's is clearly associated with the bulge of long-term capital inflow at that time: however, we discovered at the beginning of this chapter that the bulge was mostly endogenous and should be viewed as a result of the (mis?)management of Canadian monetary policy.

needed for this, however — especially concerning the exchange-rate stabilizing behavior of capital flows — becomes complex enough to render the results arbitrary, and so no full-scale experiment was undertaken. But the relation was computed between the *direct* expenditure changes induced by capital flows and the level of employment,[36] taking no account of income disturbances caused by capital flows through the exchange rate. The correlation was −0.646, a significant relation indicating that the direct effect of exogenous variations in capital inflows, 1951–1962, tended to move Canadian GNP toward the full employment level. This was on the basis of Officer's multipliers; using Rhomberg's, the negative correlation was smaller but still significant.

The "classic" transfer problem concerns the adequacy of income adjustments in the lending and borrowing countries to alter current transactions between them by enough to "requite" an autonomous change in capital movements. Coupling our own estimates of the effect of capital flows on expenditure with other investigators' findings concerning the effect of expenditure variation on the current account, we found that income changes associated with direct investment will more than requite the capital flow within a year in times of full employment, but fall short when unemployment is significant in Canada. They are insufficient at all times for portfolio and short-term capital inflows, to a degree depending on the source of disturbance and on the special factor affecting covered interest arbitrage. Income effects of capital flows in the United States, as the predominant lender, help render the Canadian current-account adjustment more adequate, but not to a large degree. Increases in direct investment are normally inflationary, as are

36. Actually the series of actual minus potential GNP described in n. 29, expressed as a percentage of potential.

portfolio capital inflows due to reductions in United States long-term interest rates. Other portfolio and all short-term capital disturbances tend to be deflationary.

Whether or not capital-flow disturbances have historically tended to stabilize the Canadian balance of payments and employment level is a different question. It depends both on the size of income adjustments and the historical pattern of exogenous disturbances in the capital account, defined in this chapter as capital-flow variations not associated with shifts in Canadian policy instruments. On this historical basis we found aggregate exogenous capital disturbances to the balance of payments (or exchange rate) slightly stabilized by income responses. In any case, the residual disturbance was uncorrelated with movements of the rate over the period 1951–1962. Furthermore, the income changes induced directly by exogenous capital-flow variations over the same period made a contribution to the stability of income around the full employment level. It is regretful that these cheerful conclusions must be doused with historical relativism: there is no guarantee that the same stabilizing behavior would prevail in a different time period with a different pattern of disturbances in the capital account and the domestic income stream.

8 Endogenous Capital Flows and Responses to Domestic Policy

Attention focused in Chapter 7 on the response of Canadian investment and economic activity to exogenous flows of foreign capital. In this chapter we look at induced capital flows, concentrating on the response of foreign capital flows to changes in economic policy and the implications of the responsiveness of foreign capital flows for the effectiveness of the major instruments of stabilization policy — fiscal policy, monetary policy, and debt-management policy.

The theoretical relationships to be considered in this connection, and our empirical evidence on them, have been outlined in earlier chapters. Here we marshal that evidence along with evidence provided in other studies, in order to ascertain the constraints and opportunities created by highly mobile capital flows for Canadian economic policy.

RESPONSES OF GNP TO EXPENDITURE AND TAX CHANGES

Fiscal, monetary, and debt management policies affect the level of GNP and employment by altering the level of domestic expenditure. These expenditure changes may emanate from changes in private investment, changes in direct government outlays, changes in the current-account balance, and changes in consumption induced by the effect of altered tax rates on personal disposable income.[1] Although the multiplier effects on GNP emanating from the first three of these categories may not be the same, they are likely to be similar; for purposes of this chapter we have assumed that they are identical.[2] The multiplier effects of tax changes, on the other hand, are significantly different from a dollar-equivalent change in government spending because of additional leakage through saving; this necessitates working with different estimates of expenditure multipliers and tax multipliers. Within the government sector, we have given no attention to complications that arise from changing the composition of government spending or the tax structure. We assume that the structure of public expenditure is given and address ourselves to the question of how GNP responds to changes in the level of public spending. On the tax side, we concentrate on the effect of a change in personal income taxes.

Empirical estimates of the multipliers associated with changes in government expenditure — which, we assume, apply to private expenditure as well — and taxes are available from both the Officer and Rhomberg models referred to previously and from a model developed by Sydney May.[3] Less

1. Here and elsewhere in this study we ignore changes in expenditure resulting from policy-induced changes in wealth.
2. The estimates made by T. Russell Robinson of the import leakages associated with different types of expenditure indicate that the multipliers associated with various types of expenditure changes do in fact differ somewhat; T. Russell Robinson, "Foreign Trade and Economic Stability: The Canadian Case," unpub. diss. (Yale University, 1966), table 4.2, and "Canada's Imports and Economic Stability," *Canadian Journal of Economics,* I (May, 1968), table 10. The same conclusion is supported by unpublished econometric research done at the Bank of Canada.
3. This model and its predecessors were developed primarily by T. M. Brown and S. May while each was employed with the Economics Branch

sophisticated estimates, not derived from a full econometric model, are provided in the *Report of the Royal Commission on Taxation,* commonly referred to as the Carter Report.[4] Analysis in the sections that follow is based on Officer's estimates of income and current-account multipliers during the period in question. The accuracy of the estimated responses to changes in policy depends to an important degree on the validity of these multiplier estimates. In order to gain some impression of what biases, if any, may arise from relying on Officer's estimates, it is helpful to begin by briefly comparing his estimates with those available from other sources.

Table 8.1 presents a summary of the estimated multipliers derived from the four sources cited above. As indicated, three sets of estimates are based on quarterly data, and the estimates derived from May's model are based on annual data. Because of this the estimates are not strictly comparable: an injection of x dollars of new spending for one quarter is not the same as an injection of x dollars over a full year. We have made an adjustment to Officer's quarterly estimates that makes it feasible to compare them very roughly with May's estimates.[5]

---

of the Canadian Department of Trade and Commerce. The model, together with applications to fiscal policy questions, is in Sydney May, "Dynamic Multipliers and Their Use for Fiscal Decision-Making," *Conference on Stabilization Policies Convened by the Economic Council of Canada at the University of Western Ontario, London, Aug. 30 to Sept. 1, 1965* (Ottawa: Queen's Printer, 1966), pp. 155–187. An earlier model of this species is given in T. M. Brown, "A Forecast Determination of National Product, Employment, and Price Level in Canada from an Econometric Model," in National Bureau of Economic Research, *Models of Income Determination,* Studies in Income and Wealth, vol. XXVIII (Princeton, N.J.: Princeton University Press, 1964), pp. 59–86. The *Conference on Stabilization Policies* volume just cited also includes an annual model by Rhomberg, that complements his quarterly model; Rudolf R. Rhomberg, "Effects of Exchange Depreciation in Canada, 1960–64" (pp. 109–119).

4. *Report of the Royal Commission on Taxation* (Ottawa: Queen's Printer, 1966), vol. II: *The Use of the Tax System to Achieve Economic and Social Objectives,* App. D, pp. 305–323.

5. It is assumed that the *average* annual increase in income over the first full year resulting from an injection of x dollars per quarter is approximated

TABLE 8.1. Effect on income realized at the end of the specified period following an exogenous change in government expenditure or personal income tax (millions of dollars)

	Time base	Quarters								Years		Equilibrium effect
		1	2	3	4	5	6	7	8	1	2	
Government expenditure change in income:		100	0	0	0	0	0	0	0	100	0	–
Cumulative change in income:												
Officer[a]	quarterly	105	111[e]	124	144	168	191	210	221	111[f]	191[f]	438[g]
Rhomberg[b]	quarterly	148	240	275	331	360	358	349	325			73
Carter[c]	quarterly	136[h]								129	163	191
May[d]	annual											232
Personal income tax change in income:		–100	0	0	0	0	0	0	0	–100	0	–
Cumulative change in income:												
Officer[a]	quarterly	55	56[e]	63	72	83	93	102	107	56[f]	93[f]	207[g]
Carter[c]	quarterly	74[h]								65		159
May[d]	annual										113	205

[a] Government expenditure on goods (1957 = 100) and net direct taxes on wage income (1957 = 100) related to GNP (1957 = 100); Lawrence H. Officer, *An Econometric Model of Canada under the Fluctuating Exchange Rate* (Cambridge, Mass.: Harvard University Press, 1968).

[b] Government expenditure on goods and services (1957 = 100) related to GNP excluding change in farm inventories (1949 = 100); Rudolf R. Rhomberg, "A Model of the Canadian Economy under Fixed and Fluctuating Exchange Rates," *Journal of Political Economy,* LXXII (February 1964), 1–31.

[c] Federal government expenditure on goods and services (1957 = 100) and personal income tax (1957 = 100) related to GNP (1957 = 100); *Report of the Royal Commission on Taxation* (Ottawa: Queen's Printer, 1966), vol. II: *The Use of the Tax System to Achieve Economic and Social Objectives,* app. D, pp. 305–323.

[d] Government expenditure on goods and services (1957 = 100) and personal income tax (1957 = 100) related to nonfarm output (1957 = 100), based on Sydney May's linearized model ("Dynamic Multipliers and Their Use for Fiscal Decision-Making," *Conference on Stabilization Policies Convened by the Economic Council of Canada at the University of Western Ontario, London, Aug. 30 to Sept. 1, 1965* [Ottawa: Queen's Printer, 1966], p. 176).

[e] The second and third periods have been collapsed to provide an estimate of the second quarter; other periods then follow in turn.

[f] The multiplier for the second quarter is related to the first year and that for the sixth to the second year.

[g] This is not, strictly speaking, the equilibrium multiplier, but the value of the multiplier when the system is truncated at the end of 24 periods. The model converges slowly and the equilibrium multiplier is in fact considerably larger.

[h] Based on the first "round" of expenditure; the Carter estimates do not allow for lags, and "rounds" do not correspond to quarters,

Differences among the various estimates also arise out of differences in the definitions used for government expenditure, taxes, and the dependent national income variable. In addition, differences in the specification of the models from which these estimates have been derived are also reflected in the figures.[6]

Both impact and equilibrium multipliers are shown in Table 8.1. Except for the Carter Report multipliers, the impact multipliers are defined to show the effect of an exogenous change in spending or taxes in period t on GNP in period t. The equilibrium multipliers are defined to indicate the ultimate effect of an exogenous change in spending or taxes after a new equilibrium has been attained and all lagged effects have been exhausted. The Carter Report multipliers have been calculated on the basis of expenditure rounds rather than quarters.[7]

---

by the increase in income attained during the second quarter of that year. This procedure rests on the assumption that multipliers in an annual model reflect the average response of the system to disturbances distributed in duration throughout the year, with an average duration of about two quarters. The *average* increase in income over the second full year is then approximated by the increase in income during the sixth quarter of the second year.

6. The estimates derived from Officer's and Rhomberg's models are discussed in detail in Chapter 7 and in Appendix C.

7. What the Carter Report labels the first-round effect of increased government expenditure on GNP differs from the concept used here. As stated in the Report, the first-round government expenditure multiplier reported by the Commission is simply $(1 - mix)$ where mix is the direct and indirect import requirement per dollar of final demand for government expenditure. For personal income tax changes, the first-round effect as recorded in the Report is $mpc (1 - mix)$ where mpc is the marginal propensity to consume out of personal disposable income. In the case of government expenditures, this concept of the impact multiplier simply removes foreign leakage from the initial injection of spending and does not indicate what the effect on GNP is after one round of the remaining domestic component of spending has taken place. The latter is regarded as the impact effect in this chapter, since this concept conforms more closely with the concept of impact effect which emerges from the Officer, Rhomberg, and May models. Redefined thus, the impact expenditure multiplier indicated by the Carter estimate is equal to $(1 - mix) + (1 - mix) b$ where $b = [mpc (1 - ml) + mI + mG]$ $- [mic \cdot mpc (1 - ml) + miI \cdot ml + miG \cdot mG]$ and where the notation and values of the variables are as shown in the Carter Report. It is im-

This study is primarily concerned with impact multipliers and subsequent adjustments over a period of a year and a half, rather than with long-run equilibrium multipliers. Nevertheless, long-run equilibrium multipliers are of passing interest, because of both their implications about characteristics of the models from which they were derived and their implications about the proportion of final adjustment realized after the passage of some defined period of time — in other words, because of what these multipliers imply about the speed of adjustment.[8]

The impact expenditure multiplier derived from Officer's model is 1.05, which is significantly less than the corresponding estimates based on Rhomberg's model and the Carter estimate. In addition, when adjusted to an annual basis, the impact multiplier derived from Officer's model is considerably less than the estimate based on May's model. From these estimates, and assuming that Officer's estimate errs on the low side, one might conclude that the impact expenditure multiplier lies in the range of 1.2 to 1.5.

The evidence on equilibrium multipliers also differs somewhat. The estimate derived from Officer's model seems obviously too large. This can be explained by the specification of the accelerator relationship assumed in his model as outlined in Chapter 7. At the same time, the estimate derived from Rhomberg's model seems implausibly small. His model suggests that an extra dollar of expenditure, maintained over time, fails not only to generate additional expenditure, but in fact

---

portant to note that the multipliers presented in the Carter Report do not allow for lags, and that "rounds" as defined above do not correspond to quarters.

8. As noted in Chapter 7, dynamic multipliers for all these models are based on their linearized form. Because the models in fact are not linear, the estimated dynamic multipliers for more remote periods may be highly unreliable.

shrinks to three-quarters of the injection. The May and Carter estimates, suggesting a long-run multiplier ranging from 1.9 to 2.3, seem more plausible than either the Officer or Rhomberg estimates.

Estimates of the tax multipliers diverge much less from each other than do the expenditure multiplier estimates. The estimated impact tax multipliers range from .55 to .74 and the equilibrium multipliers from 1.59 to 2.09. Again, because of the sluggish response built into the Officer model, it is likely that estimates of the initial effects based on this model are on the low side and that the equilibrium multiplier is too high. Discounting these estimates, one might regard the range for the impact tax multiplier as approximating .69 to .70.

To summarize, the evidence available suggests that an exogenous increase in $100 million in expenditure might be expected to increase GNP by between $105 and $150 million almost immediately and by some $230 million after the full effects of the expenditure change have been realized. At the same time, a reduction in personal income taxes of $100 million might be expected to enhance GNP by between $55 and $70 million immediately and by between $160 and $210 million ultimately. Suppose government expenditures are increased $100 million and personal income taxes are raised $100 million to cover the extra expenditure. The evidence implies that the impact effect on GNP will be an increase ranging from $50 to $90 million. In the long term the effect is more uncertain. The evidence suggests that the repressive effect of higher taxes could more than offset the stimulating effect of increased expenditure. At the other limit, the long-term effect might be to increase GNP on the order of $70 million. This evidence on the long-term equilibrium effect is very shaky, however, and is of only limited interest from the standpoint of this study.

In addition to indicating the impact and equilibrium effects of changes in expenditure and taxes, the figures given in Table 8.1 indicate the speed with which GNP responds to these changes. Because the dynamic properties of the May model seem somewhat superior to those of the Officer and Rhomberg models, we attach rather more significance to the timing it indicates. The estimates based on the May model indicate that about 55 percent of the ultimate effect of a change in government expenditure can be expected to be realized within a year and 70 percent within two years. The time pattern suggests a rather faster reaction time than that indicated by the Officer model. The estimates based on Rhomberg's model, on the other hand, suggest a very rapid and large buildup of induced income effects during the first two years after an exogenous change. This buildup reaches a peak at the end of the fifth quarter after the initial change in government expenditure, when the change in income is estimated as 3.6 times greater than the change in government expenditure! These estimates are quite different from those of both Officer and May. For this and other reasons, it seems doubtful whether GNP is as sensitive to changes in government expenditure policies as Rhomberg's estimates suggest.

The response rate for a change in personal income tax as indicated by May's estimates is slower than that for a change in expenditure. Only 32 percent of the ultimate effect appears during the first year, 55 percent at the end of the second year, and about 82 percent at the end of five years. The Officer model, if one collapses the first two periods, suggests that the timing of expenditure and tax effects is quite similar.

These comparisons suggest that, as a result of relying on Officer's multiplier estimates, the estimated short-run expenditure effects of various policy changes presented below may be somewhat understated. In addition, the speed of adjustment in

GNP to policy changes implicitly assumed in deriving the estimates may be somewhat slower than in reality.

RESPONSES TO FISCAL POLICY

A change in fiscal policy initiates both expenditure and monetary effects to which the balance of payments responds. Under a free exchange rate, this response may give rise to further adjustments via the exchange rate. It will facilitate comprehension of this rather complicated process to consider each of these adjustments in turn.

Response of the Balance of Payments to the Expenditure Effects of Fiscal Policy

The studies from which the income multipliers presented above have been taken also include estimates of the effect of fiscal policy changes on imports and exports. These are shown in Table 8.2, together with an indication of the timing with which the effects of fiscal policy changes can be expected to manifest themselves. Comparison of Officer's estimates with Rhomberg's and May's is subject to the qualification that they include exports and imports separately only for trade with the United States; but unlike the other two studies, Officer's allows one to derive an explicit estimate of the net effect of a change in fiscal policy on the current-account balance with all countries.

According to this evidence, an increase in government expenditures of $100 million might be expected to increase Canadian imports immediately by $6 to $24 million. Ultimately, the increase in imports might be between $58 and $83 million (discounting the Rhomberg estimates, which are open

TABLE 8.2. Effect on current account realized at the end of the specified period following exogenous changes in government expenditure and personal income tax (millions of dollars)

	Quarters								Years		Equilibrium effect
	1	2	3	4	5	6	7	8	1	2	
Government expenditure change:	100	0	0	0	0	0	0	0	100	0	–
Cumulative change in:											
Officer[a] Imports (U.S.)	6	7	10	15	21	26	30	33	7	26	83
Exports (U.S.)	0	-2	-2	-2	-3	-4	-5	-6	-2	-4	-15
Net current-account balance, all countries	-26	-26	-32	-47	-64	-80	-91	-95	-26	-80	-197
Rhomberg Imports	24	115	151	205	234	237	232	213	–	–	-17
Exports	-11	-15	-17	-18	-19	-20	-22	-23	–	–	-23
May Imports	–	–	–	–	–	–	–	–	11	29	58
Personal income tax change:	-100	0	0	0	0	0	0	0	-100	0	–
Cumulative change in:											
Officer[a] Imports (U.S.)	7	8	9	11	14	16	18	19	8	16	43
Exports (U.S.)	0	-1	-1	-1	-2	-2	-2	-3	-1	-2	-7
Net current-account balance, all countries	-26	-23	-26	-33	-39	-45	-49	-52	-23	-45	-98
May Imports	–	–	–	–	–	–	–	–	21	37	70

Source: See sources given in Table 8.1.
[a] Second quarter effect equated with effect after three periods; equilibrium effect equated with effect after 24 periods.

to the same doubts raised in connection with his estimates of the change in income). As is evident from Table 8.2, between a fifth and a tenth of this increase might be expected within the first year after the change in government expenditure and between a half and a third within two years. In the May model imports are less responsive to changes in government expenditure than in the Officer model and the effects show up somewhat more slowly.

In the May model, exports are exogenously determined. In the Rhomberg and Officer models, exports are endogenous. In both cases, exports respond negatively to an increase in government expenditures; but this response is small. According to Officer's model, a $100-million increase in spending induces a reduction of $1 million in exports to the United States fairly soon and leads to an ultimate decrease of $15 million. The timing of this induced change coincides fairly well with the timing of the change in imports.

The current-account balance in the May model deteriorates by the amount of the induced change in imports, since exports are assumed to be exogenously determined. From Officer's model one can calculate explicitly the net effect on the current-account balance with all countries as already noted. Such calculations indicate that the impact effect on the current account of a $100-million increase in government expenditure is a negative change in the current-account balance of $26 million. Over the long term, the negative effect on the current account is substantially larger according to Officer's estimates.

The Officer and May models also provide some evidence of the induced effect on foreign trade of a change in personal income tax, as shown in Table 8.2. According to these estimates, a $100-million reduction in taxes can be expected to increase imports by $8 to $21 million within the first year after the reduction and by $43 to $70 million in the long run.

Between 18 and 30 percent of this ultimate increase can be expected within the first year after the tax change and about 40 percent by the end of the second year. As for exports, the Officer estimates suggest that United States exports will be slightly deterred by a reduction in taxes which stimulates domestic demand. This effect on U.S. exports manifests itself with about the same timing as the effect on U.S. imports.

As before, the change in the current account indicated by the May model is shown by the change in imports. Figures calculated from Officer's model indicate that a $100-million reduction in taxes has an immediate negative impact of $26 million on the current account, a negative effect of about the same magnitude by the end of the first year, and a negative effect of some $45 million by the end of the second year.[9]

A final point may be noted in connection with these figures. Officer's estimates suggest that a change in government expenditure has a greater impact on imports than a change in personal taxes; May's estimates suggest the opposite. The evidence provided in Russell Robinson's study, referred to earlier, tends to support May's results. His estimate of the implicit marginal import propensity for consumer expenditure is .205, and for government expenditure it is .133.[10] Thus, there appears to be a considerable difference in the effect on imports in the first round of expenditure. In the light of Robinson's estimates, one might argue that May's estimates seem somewhat more plausible than Officer's.

9. Officer's estimates of the impact effects of fiscal policy are open to some doubt: despite an estimated impact income multiplier that is twice as large for government expenditure changes as for tax changes, the impact of these two policy changes on the current-account balance is estimated to be the same and to remain similar during the first three quarters of the adjustment process.

10. Robinson, "Canada's Imports and Economic Stability," table 10, p. 425.

Response of the Balance of Payments to the Monetary Effects of Fiscal Policy

In addition to the expenditure effects just considered, exogenous changes in fiscal policy affect the balance of payments through monetary channels. If one assumes that the money supply is given, a rise in GNP induced by expansionary fiscal policy can be expected to raise interest rates and vice versa. The change in interest rates will, in turn, induce capital flows which will have further repercussions on interest rates and output.

How much and how fast can interest rates be expected to rise if a change in government expenditure or personal income taxes induces the effects on GNP indicated earlier in this chapter, assuming that the money supply remains constant? The models developed by Officer and May, to which we have been referring, are unsatisfactory for evaluating this question: Officer's dynamic interest rate multipliers have the wrong sign, and May's model ignores interest rates. Rhomberg's model, on the other hand, provides multiplier estimates relating to both short- and long-term rates; it suggests, as shown in Table 8.3, that a $100-million increase in government expenditure might immediately raise short rates by .2 percentage points and long rates by .65 percentage points. Ultimately, short rates would rise .4 percentage points and long rates by .25. These long-run estimates are open to doubt, however, if one does not accept Rhomberg's estimate of the income multiplier. For instance, if, as our earlier discussion suggests, the equilibrium multiplier is on the order of 2.3 rather than .75, as Rhomberg's work suggests, then presumably the ultimate increase in interest rates can also be expected to be greater than Rhomberg's interest-rate estimates suggest.

The Johnson-Winder estimates shown in Table 8.3 are not

311

TABLE 8.3. Estimated changes in interest rates induced by changes in fiscal policy

		$100-million increase in government expenditure		$100-million reduction in personal income tax	
		Impact effect	Equilibrium effect	Impact effect	Equilibrium effect
	Change in interest rates (percentage points)				
Rhomberg:[a]	Short term	.20	.40	–	–
	Long term	.65	.25	–	–
Johnson-Winder:[b]	Short term	.44	.26	.22	.24

[a] Rudolf R. Rhomberg, "A Model of the Canadian Economy under Fixed and Fluctuating Rates," *Journal of Political Economy*, LXXII (February, 1964), 14.

[b] Based on the equations given in Harry G. Johnson and John W. L. Winder, *Lags in the Effects of Monetary Policy in Canada*, working paper prepared for the Royal Commission on Banking and Finance (Ottawa: Queen's Printer, 1962), pp. 165–166. The estimated effect on interest rates is equal to the difference between $\hat{r}_t$ and r'_t. $\hat{r}_t$ is estimated from the equilibrium equation given in *ibid.*, p. 166, assuming mean values for A and M/Y. r'_t is estimated from the fitted equation p. 165, assuming mean values of A, M/Y for $(M/Y)_{t-1}$, and M and the estimated impact and equilibrium changes in income indicated by May's multiplier estimates.

derived from a full-scale model of the economy but are based on a partial analysis of the demand for money.[11] These estimates, relating only to short-term rates, indicate that the impact effect of a change in income induced by government expenditure changes might be on the order of half a percentage point. For a change in income induced by tax changes, the impact effect on interest rates might be on the order of a quarter of a percentage point. The long-run equilibrium effect indi-

11. Harry G. Johnson and John W. L. Winder, *Lags in the Effects of Monetary Policy in Canada,* working paper prepared for the Royal Commission on Banking and Finance (Ottawa: Queen's Printer, 1962), pp. 165–167.

cated in both cases is about one quarter of a percentage point.

Interest-rate changes can be expected to induce a response in foreign capital flows and, in turn, to be dampened by the capital-flow responses. These induced effects are not explicitly allowed for in Rhomberg's model, nor are they reflected in the figures derived from the Johnson-Winder equations on the demand for money. When they are allowed for, our own estimates suggest that the effect on interest rates of changes in fiscal policy is likely to be much less than suggested by the estimates in Table 8.3.

In order to estimate the effect of a fiscal policy change on interest rates when induced capital flows are allowed for, we start from the proposition that if the government embarks on a fiscal policy change in the form of either increasing expenditure or reducing taxes, and if the money supply is held constant, the result will be an increase in its new security issues to the public. The annual increase in new issues will eventually be less than the amount of the new expenditure or the tax reduction because of induced effects on revenue. But these induced revenue effects in the long run will cover only part of the annual deficit that has been generated initially; and in the first instance, because of lags, the induced effects may be very small and most of the deficit may have to be financed through an increase in the public debt.

Therefore, to estimate the monetary consequences of a fiscal change, we need to know how government revenues respond over the first year and a half following a change in fiscal policy. Unpublished econometric research in progress at the Bank of Canada encompassing simulations based on the period from the beginning of 1958 to mid-1959, when the economy was operating at less than full employment, indicates that a $100-million increase in Canadian government expenditure on goods, given the employment and other circumstances of that period, was associated with the following approximate changes in revenue collections and the government deficit:

	Quarters ($ million)					
	1	2	3	4	5	6
Increase in tax revenues	10	15	19	29	37	45
Change in government deficit	90	85	81	71	63	55

Government revenues can be expected eventually to reach a new equilibrium in relation to the new equilibrium level of GNP induced by changes in fiscal policy. Estimates presented in the Carter Report indicate that as a result of a $100-million increase in government expenditures, the federal deficit might be about $52 million greater per quarter after a new equilibrium has been reached.[12] Although we are principally interested in short-run adjustments, this estimate provides a check on the Bank of Canada's estimates, which imply a change in the long-run equilibrium level of the deficit that is similar to the Carter estimate.

The Bank of Canada's estimates do not readily lend themselves to estimating the effect on the government's deficit of a $100-million decrease in personal income taxes that is sustained over time. Carter Report estimates indicate that a $100-million reduction in personal income taxes would lead eventually to an increase in government revenues of $40.3 million per quarter — compared to an estimate of $48.2 million in the case of a $100-million increase in government expenditures. Our estimate of the time pattern of response of the deficit to a change in taxes assumes it is the same as the time pattern of response to a change in expenditure, estimated by econometric work at the Bank of Canada. The quarter-to-quarter changes in government revenues arising from tax changes are

12. *Report of the Royal Commission on Taxation,* vol. II, app. D, pp. 305–323.

assumed to equal 40.3/48.2 of the estimates of changes in revenues arising from expenditure changes.[13]

Given the money supply, government deficits arising from changes in fiscal policy are financed by increases in the public debt which, in turn, influence interest rates as portfolios are readjusted to accommodate additional government bonds. The reduced-form multipliers based on ordinary least-squares shown in Table 3.1 and equations 3.8 and 3.10 indicate that an increase in NNS of $100 million might be expected to increase long-term interest rates by .02 or .03 percentage points when the effect of induced capital inflows is taken into account. The reduced-form multipliers shown in Table 3.2, based on the two-stage least-squares equations, indicate that the increase in long-term interest rates is unlikely to exceed .07 percentage points. As for short-term rates, our estimates suggest that the effect of increasing the public debt by $100 million may be to increase rates from .04 to .12 of a percentage point.[14] Our best point estimates for the induced changes in interest rates are assumed to be .06 for long-term rates and .08 for short-term rates.

The other side of this adjustment is the increased inflow of

13. Implicitly it is assumed that the only difference between the tax and expenditure revenue multipliers is the effect on GNP resulting from extra leakage through saving in the first instance when taxes are reduced, as compared to the alternative of increasing government expenditures.

14. $(\partial CL/\partial NNS)\ (\partial CS/\partial PCMS)\ /\ (\partial CL/\partial PCMS)\ =\ \partial CS/\partial NNS$. $\partial CS/\partial PCMS$ is equal to $-.03893$ from equation 3.20, assuming FP to be determined exogenously, or $-.09106$ from equation 3.20, assuming FP to be determined endogenously by equation 3.25. As indicated in n. 27 below, the estimated value of $\partial CS/\partial PCMS$ falls within this range if it is assumed that FP is endogenously determined and that parity prevails. The values of $\partial CL/\partial PCMS$ are given in Table 3.2. The values of $\partial CL/\partial NNS$ are also given in Table 3.2, except in the case where CL is determined according to equation 3.14.

The values of $\partial CS/\partial NNS$ calculated on this basis range from a low of $-.000402$ to a high of $-.00120$. If FP is assumed to be endogenously determined, and interest parity is also assumed, $\partial CS/\partial NNS$ falls within this range. Our best estimate is $-.000823$, based on equation 2.6, as shown in Table 3.2, and equations 3.20 and 3.24.

315

foreign capital induced by fiscal policy changes. As a consequence of an increase of $100 million, the inflow of long-term capital might be expected to increase by $8 to $46 million, judging from the reduced-form multipliers shown in Tables 3.1 and 3.2;[15] our best estimate is $42 million. Short-term flows would also increase — one of our estimates is in equation 2.15. At a maximum, short-term inflows might reach $80 million; the most likely estimate is $33 million.[16] And when exchange-rate adjustments are allowed for, the inflow of both long- and short-term capital is in fact likely to be less than these figures suggest.[17]

All of the foregoing estimates assume that Canadian interest rates in fact do respond to changes in *NNS* and completely ignore the influence of expectations. If, however, Canadian interest rates are largely governed by expectations based on United States rates — which, evidence introduced earlier indi-

15. $\partial PC/\partial NNS = .0831$ from equation 2.10 and .4612 from equation 2.7, Tables 3.1 and 3.2.

16. From equation 2.15 $\partial STK/\partial DS = 602$, assuming *FP* to be determined exogenously; when *FP* is assumed to be determined endogenously in accordance with equation 3.24, $\partial STK/\partial DS = 404.3$. Throughout this chapter the expressions "best" or "most likely" will serve as a shorthand for calculations that embody the two-stage least-squares estimates from Chapter 3 of the effects of disturbances on the Canadian short- or long-term interest rates when the adjustment of capital inflows is taken into account. As explained there, the alternative estimates embody statistical biases of known direction, assume different economic specifications, or both. These alternative estimates might more appropriately be used to illuminate economic circumstances which match their assumptions. Our "best" estimates thus are put forth as embodying the following virtues: (1) they are as free from bias as the estimation methods we employ seem willing to permit; (2) they embody specifications that deal with reasonably general, if not with necessary economic circumstances.

17. Here and elsewhere in this chapter only short-term and portfolio capital flows are considered and direct investment is ignored. As indicated in Chapter 2, direct investment also seems responsive to interest-rate changes, though much less so than other categories of foreign investment. But there is some question of whether this apparent sensitivity in fact is a sensitivity to interest rates or whether interest rates are serving as a proxy for some other variables, such as the level of business activity. To the extent that direct investment is sensitive to interest rates, our estimates of the responsiveness of capital flows to interest-rate changes are low.

cates, is more important than expectations based on Canadian rates — and the other factors included in equation 3.14, then no change is likely in either long- or short-term rates or in international capital flows as a consequence of changes in fiscal policy. Thus, our minimum estimates of the monetary effects of fiscal policy on interest rates, GNP, the current account, and capital flows are zero.[18]

In Tables 8.4 and 8.5, the various pieces of the statistical puzzle are fitted together to show the combined primary expenditure and monetary effects of a change in government expenditure on GNP and the balance of payments. The minimum estimate in each case assumes that the monetary effects of fiscal policy changes are nil because Canadian rates are tied to United States rates through expectations. The other two estimates reflect the assumption, which Chapters 2 and 3 support, that capital flows adjust to interest-rate changes without a lag. The figures shown in line 10 are an approximation to what the change in Canada's foreign exchange reserves would have been during our sample period, had the country adhered to a fixed exchange rate and implemented the assumed expansionary fiscal policies.[19]

Response of the Exchange Rate to the Effects of Fiscal Policy

In the past it has generally been assumed that an expansionary fiscal policy could be expected to lead to a depreciation in

18. The coefficient of *NNS* is not statistically significant and has the wrong sign when *USL* is included in equation 3.14. If $\partial CL/\partial NNS \approx 0$, then from n. 14 above, $\partial CS/\partial NNS \approx 0$.

19. This assumes that changes in foreign-exchange holdings would have been sterilized, as in fact they have been since Canada adopted a fixed rate in 1962. Foreign exchange is bought and sold by the Exchange Fund Account, and payments made to or from the chartered banks are debited or credited to the government's Canadian dollar balances. Thus, the ownership of deposits changes, but the total amount of deposits and the level of bank reserves remains unchanged; *Report of the Royal Commission on Banking and Finance* (Ottawa: Queen's Printer, 1964), p. 293.

TABLE 8.4. Size and timing of the primary income and monetary effects of an increase in government expenditure on the balance of payments

	Quarters					
	1	2	3	4	5	6
1. Change in government expenditure ($ million):	100	0	0	0	0	0
2. Effect on government deficit ($ million) = NNS:	90	85	81	71	63	55
3. Change in interest rates (percentage points)[a]:						
a. Best estimate:						
CL	.055	.052	.050	.043	.039	.034
CS	.074	.070	.067	.058	.052	.045
b. Maximum estimate: CL	.066	.062	.059	.052	.046	.040
CS	.108	.102	.097	.085	.076	.066
4. Domestic expenditure effects of interest-rate change ($ million)[b]:						
a. Change in consumer durable spending	−2.15	−1.51	−1.45	−1.25	−1.13	−0.99
b. Change in residential construction	−.99	−2.42	−4.60	−5.68	−5.68	−5.12
c. Change in total business fixed investment	−.66	−1.83	−3.27	−4.71	−5.90	−6.68
d. Total: best estimate	−3.80	−5.76	−9.32	−11.64	−12.71	−12.79
maximum estimate	−5.11	−8.06	−12.27	−14.91	−16.07	−16.03
5. Income response to expenditure change, l. 4 ($ million)[e]:						
a. Best estimate	−3.99	−6.28	−10.63	−14.29	−17.28	−19.75
b. Maximum estimate	−5.37	−8.77	−14.02	−18.47	−22.15	−25.21
6. Current-account response to expenditure change, l. 4 ($ million)[e]:						

	.99	1.50	2.61	3.89	5.28	6.86
	1.33	2.10	3.45	5.05	6.87	8.89
a. Best estimate	.99	1.50	2.61	3.89	5.28	6.86
b. Maximum estimate	1.33	2.10	3.45	5.05	6.87	8.89
7. Combined income response, Table 8.1 and 1.5 ($ million):						
a. Best estimate	101	105	113	130	151	171
b. Minimum estimate	105	111	124	144	168	191
c. Maximum estimate	100	102	110	126	146	166
8. Combined current-account response, Table 8.2 and 1.6 ($ million):						
a. Best estimate	−25	−24	−29	−43	−59	−73
b. Minimum estimate	−26	−26	−32	−47	−64	−80
c. Maximum estimate	−25	−24	−29	−42	−57	−71
9. Capital-account response ($ million):						
a. Best estimate: long-term	23.4	22.0	21.0	18.4	16.3	14.3
short-term	29.9	28.3	26.9	23.6	20.9	18.3
b. Maximum estimate: long-term	30.4	28.7	27.3	24.0	21.3	18.6
short-term	65.0	61.4	58.5	51.3	45.5	39.7
10. Net change in balance of payments ($ million):						
a. Best estimate	28.3	26.3	18.9	−1.0	−21.8	−40.4
b. Minimum estimate	−26.0	−26.0	−32.0	−47.0	−64.0	−80.0
c. Maximum estimate	70.4	66.1	56.8	33.3	9.8	−12.7

[a] Best estimates assume: $\partial CL/\partial NNS = .0611$ and $\partial CS/\partial NNS = .0823$ percentage points; $\partial PC/\partial CL = 42.46$ and $\partial STK/\partial CS = 40.43$ millions. Maximum estimates assume: $\partial CL/\partial NNS = .0732$ and $\partial CS/\partial NNS = .120$ percentage points; $\partial PC/\partial CL = 46.12$ and $\partial STK/\partial CS = 60.2$ millions. Interest-rate changes are equal to NNS times the appropriate interest-rate factors.

[b] Based on the response rates given in Table 7.1.

[c] Using Officer multipliers.

[319]

TABLE 8.5. Size and timing of the primary income and monetary effects of a reduction in personal income taxes on the balance of payments[a]

	Quarters					
	1	2	3	4	5	6
1. Personal income tax change ($ million):	−100	0	0	0	0	0
2. Effect on government deficit ($ million) = *NNS*:	92	88	84	76	69	62
3. Change in interest rates (percentage points):						
a. Best estimate: *CL*	.056	.054	.051	.046	.042	.038
CS	.076	.072	.069	.063	.057	.051
b. Maximum estimate: *CL*	.067	.064	.062	.056	.051	.045
CS	.110	.106	.101	.091	.083	.074
4. Domestic expenditure effects of interest-rate change ($ million):						
a. Change in consumer durable spending	−2.20	−2.09	−2.00	−1.83	−1.65	−1.48
b. Change in residential construction	−1.01	−2.49	−4.73	−5.90	−5.96	−5.48
c. Change in total business fixed investment	−.67	−1.89	−3.37	−4.89	−6.15	−7.02
d. Total: best estimate	−3.88	−6.47	−10.10	−12.68	−13.76	−13.98
maximum estimate	−5.22	−8.29	−12.64	−15.52	−16.90	−17.15
5. Income response to expenditure change, l. 4 ($ million):						
a. Best estimate	−4.07	−7.02	−11.50	−15.54	−18.70	−21.56
b. Maximum estimate	−5.48	−9.01	−14.45	−19.18	−23.10	−26.68
6. Current-account response to expenditure change, l. 4 ($ million):						

a. Best estimate	1.01	1.68	2.82	4.20	5.72	7.46
b. Maximum estimate	1.36	2.16	3.55	5.23	7.15	9.33
7. Combined income response, Table 8.1 and 1. 5 ($ million):						
a. Best estimate	51	49	51	56	64	71
b. Minimum estimate	55	56	63	72	83	93
c. Maximum estimate	50	47	49	53	60	66
8. Combined current-account response, Table 8.2 and 1. 6 ($ million):						
a. Best estimate	−25	−21	−23	−29	−33	−38
b. Minimum estimate	−26	−23	−26	−33	−39	−45
c. Maximum estimate	−25	−21	−22	−28	−32	−36
9. Capital-account response ($ million):						
a. Best estimate: long-term	23.86	22.84	21.78	19.70	17.92	16.09
short-term	30.60	29.27	27.93	25.27	22.96	20.62
b. Maximum estimate: long-term	31.04	29.70	28.36	25.64	23.29	20.94
short-term	66.46	63.57	60.68	54.90	49.85	44.79
10. Net change in balance of payments ($ million):						
a. Best estimate	29.5	31.1	26.7	16.0	7.9	−1.3
b. Minimum estimate	−26.0	−23.0	−26.0	−33.0	−39.0	−45.0
c. Maximum estimate	72.5	72.3	67.0	52.5	41.1	29.7

[a] Notes to Table 8.4 apply to Table 8.5.

[321]

the exchange rate if the country was on a flexible exchange rate, and vice versa if a contractionary fiscal policy was adopted. This conclusion was arrived at by concentrating on the current-account effects — especially on the change in imports — resulting from the change in expenditure induced by the change in fiscal policy. The most serious empirical challenge to this conventional view is provided by Rhomberg's work, as noted earlier. His estimates suggest that, ceteris paribus, pressure on the exchange rate arising from the expenditure effects induced by a change in fiscal policy will be more than offset by pressure on the exchange rate arising from induced monetary effects, which, in turn, induce foreign capital movements. A $100-million increase in government expenditure can be expected to increase capital inflows by $33 million immediately and by $63 million ultimately. The exchange rate is estimated to appreciate initially by about two-thirds of a cent and ultimately by one and a half cents.

This result is difficult to reconcile with the evidence referred to earlier suggesting that Rhomberg's estimates of the effects of GNP changes on the current account seem too large in the short run and too small in the long run; this would tend to produce the opposite pattern of exchange-rate movement. From the estimates presented in Tables 8.4 and 8.5, it is evident that, in the short run at least, the monetary effects of a change in fiscal policy via the capital account are likely to outweigh the expenditure effects via the current account if we ignore the possibility that Canadian interest rates are closely linked to United States rates via expectations.[20] Over subsequent periods, how-

20. As explained in Chapter 2, our empirical estimates relate the flow rather than the stock of financial assets to the interest-rate differential. This means that, rather than view the interest rate as the price paid for holding the outstanding stock of securities, we regard it as the price necessary to place in the hands of the public a disturbance in the flow of securities. The short-run income multipliers estimated by Officer and others, as well as our monetary-sector equations, all are calculated by methods that fail to treat the historic average growth rate of real income flows and asset stocks as en-

ever, expenditure effects gradually become larger relative to monetary effects, and by the sixth quarter they are likely to outweigh the monetary effects as rising revenues in response to rising GNP reduce the size of the deficit. In sum, our evidence suggests that in the short run an expansionary fiscal policy is likely to put upward pressure on the exchange rate, as Rhomberg suggests; however, within a year and a half of the change in policy, downward pressure on the rate is likely to develop as suggested by conventional views of the adjustment process. And if interest rates in Canada are closely geared to United States rates via expectations, downward pressure on the exchange rate will be felt in both the short and the long run.[21]

During the period on which our estimates are based, Canada's exchange was in fact free to move in response to market forces, and exchange-rate movements provided another avenue of adjustment through both current and capital accounts. Economic theory predicts that, under a flexible rate system, changes in fiscal policy will induce important feed-back effects due to exchange-rate adjustments whereby the monetary effects of fiscal policy changes pull contrary to the expenditure effects. As a consequence, fiscal policy is less effective as an instrument of stabilization policy under a flexible rate system than under a fixed rate system, except under highly unlikely circumstances. How much the effectiveness of fiscal policy is impaired by exchange rate variations is an empirical question that has remained open to which we now turn.

---

dogenous and thus do not hold these real magnitudes constant. If real growth were halted, excepting that due to capital accumulation, the income multipliers might not necessarily be much different, but the monetary coefficients might alter considerably because the growth trend would be pulled out from under the demand for securities.

21. Officer's estimates indicate that the exchange rate is likely to depreciate in the short run; this implies that, even in the short run, expenditure effects outweigh monetary effects. But his estimate of the monetary effect, and hence of the exchange rate effect, is open to serious doubt because his model gives the wrong sign for the interest-rate multiplier.

If, as our earlier evidence strongly indicates, the elasticity of expectations vis-à-vis exchange-rate movements is less than one, any tendency for the rate to appreciate or depreciate will serve to choke off or stimulate capital flows. From equation 2.15 one can derive minimum and maximum estimates of the effect of a change of one cent in the exchange rate on short-term capital flows, depending on what assumptions are made about the forward premium. These estimates are $35.1 and $57.5 million respectively. Our best point estimate, based on equations 2.15 and 3.24, is assumed to be $51.4 million.[22] According to the evidence presented in Chapter 2, exchange-rate movements also influence long-term portfolio capital flows but do not have a discernible effect on direct investment. Equation 2.10 indicates that a one-cent appreciation in the exchange rate in the current quarter results in an outflow of portfolio capital in the *next* quarter of $23.7 million.

In addition to the repercussions of exchange-rate adjustments on the capital account, such adjustments also affect the current-account balance; this in turn leads to further adjustments in GNP. Appreciation of the exchange rate by one percent, according to estimates described in Chapter 7, can be expected to increase imports of goods and services by at least one percent and to decrease exports by at least .35 percent.[23]

22. From equation 2.15 $\partial STK/\partial RS = -35.1$ when CRS is rewritten as $RS - RS_{-1}$ and FP is assumed to be given exogenously. The other extreme is to assume that FP is endogenous and that interest parity prevails. On these assumptions, $\partial STK/\partial RS = -35.12 - 314.5 \ (CS - USS)/(100 + CS)$. For mean values of CS and USS this expression is equal to $57.5 million. Equation 3.24 provides a direct estimate of the relation between RF and RS; when this is substituted into equation 2.15, $\partial STK/\partial RS = $51.4 million.

23. This implies that an appreciation of one cent results in a deterioration of $94.5 million in the current-account balance, calculated at the mean values of exports, imports and the exchange rate for the period 1952–1961. Here and elsewhere in this chapter it is assumed that the estimated price elasticities reflect the response of exports and imports in the current quarter. Another interpretation of our estimates might be that lagged responses of comparable size follow in each of the next three quarters. On this assump-

What will be the net effect on GNP of the assumed change in fiscal policy when these expenditure-damping effects of exchange-rate adjustment are taken into account along with the rate's effect on capital flows?

Equation 2.11 provides direct estimates on linkages between changes in various payments categories and the exchange rate. As explained earlier, the estimated parameters are biased downward by varying amounts because of strong simultaneous relations between the dependent and independent variables. The bias is likely to be greatest for the coefficients of CA and STK, which, the evidence suggests, both cause and are affected by exchange-rate changes. The coefficient for PC seems likely to be less biased, since apparently most of the response in PC to changes in exchange rates occurs with a mean lag of one quarter. The coefficient for DIC is probably the least biased since there is no evidence that DIC responds to changes in the exchange rate. On the plausible assumption that a net demand for one Canadian dollar on the exchange market has the same effect on the exchange rate whatever the source of the demand, the difference between the coefficients for DIC and for CA, STK, and PC may provide some indication of the degree of bias in the coefficients for these other variables. On this test the coefficient for PC is also biased downward, though less so than the coefficients for CA and STK.[24] In effect, the coefficients

---

tion all our estimates of the secondary effects of policy changes via exchange-rate movements are substantially too low. A third possible interpretation of our estimates is that one quarter of the estimated effect is realized in the current quarter, the remainder showing up in the next three quarters. On this interpretation, the estimated secondary exchange rate effects emanating from the current account would show up much more slowly than has been assumed.

24. Apparently the estimate of $\partial RS/\partial DIC$ in equation 2.11 cannot be regarded as the partial effect of changes in DIC on RS on the assumption that the other exchange-rate-sensitive components in the equation remain constant. The figures given in the text indicate that $\partial Pi/\partial RS = -\$146$ million, where Pi indicates the responsiveness of the balance of payments to exchange-rate changes. If $\partial RS/\partial Pe = \partial RS/\partial DIC = .0182$, then the net effect

for *PC, CA,* and *STK* are reduced-form coefficients rather than estimates of the structural relations between these variables and the exchange rate.

Although it would be preferable to work with the latter, in the absence of structural estimates one may proceed on the assumption that these direct estimates of the reduced-rate coefficients are reasonably accurate approximations of the reduced-form coefficients one would derive from direct estimates of the structural parameters if these were available. This assumption is somewhat heroic, but it does make feasible a rough estimate of the combined external and domestic effects on GNP of the assumed changes in fiscal policy under a flexible rate system.

The estimates presented in Table 8.6 are based on the assumption just described. What is labelled "minimum estimate" has been calculated on the assumption of no link between *NNS* and interest rates as explained in the previous section; consequently, the entire adjustment occurs through the current account. In this situation, effects via exchange-rate adjustments considerably enhance the other effects of expansionary fiscal policy, as is evident from a comparison of lines 5b and 10b of Table 8.6 with lines 7b of Tables 8.4 and 8.5.

The lines labeled "best estimate" and "maximum estimate" indicate that capital flows, responding to changes in the government's budgetary position, substantially reduce the effectiveness of fiscal policy in the short run under a flexible exchange-rate system.[25] This is evident from a comparison of

---

of an exogenous increase in international receipts, *Pe*, of $1 million on *RS* is equal to $\partial RS/\partial Pe + (\partial RS/\partial Pe)(\partial Pi/\partial RS) = .0182 - (.0182)(146) = -2.66$. This implies the implausible conclusion that an increase in international receipts results in depreciation of the exchange rate. The estimated coefficient for *DIC* in equation 2.11 should probably be viewed as the net effect on *RS* after the other components have made the simultaneous adjustment that they typically have made over our period of observation.

25. The terms "best," "minimum," and "maximum" are defined in relation to the responsiveness of capital flows to changes in fiscal policy as shown in Tables 8.4 and 8.5.

lines 5a, 5c, 10a, and 10c of Table 8.6 with lines 7a and 7c of Tables 8.4 and 8.5. Our best estimates show the following response patterns of GNP (millions of dollars) with and without exchange-rate adjustments:

	Quarters					
	1	2	3	4	5	6
$100 million increase in government expenditure:						
Without exchange-rate adjustments	101	105	113	130	151	171
With exchange-rate adjustments	77	81	91	115	144	173
$100 million reduction in personal income taxes:						
Without exchange-rate adjustments	51	49	51	56	64	71
With exchange-rate adjustments	26	22	24	31	39	47

It is also interesting to observe that exchange-rate adjustments have a greater debilitating effect on the effectiveness of fiscal policy when fiscal policy changes are enacted through tax changes than when they are enacted through expenditure changes. As the foregoing figures indicate, by the end of a year and a half the changes in GNP induced by expenditure changes are as large with exchange-rate adjustments as without; the changes in GNP induced by tax reductions, on the other hand, remain substantially less with exchange-rate adjustments. This result reflects the higher cost to the government, in terms of the size of its deficit, of the assumed changes in taxes compared to the assumed change in expenditures — higher cost stemming from the additional leakage through savings on the first round of expenditure associated with a tax cut, compared to an expenditure increase. Because of this differential effect on the deficit, the monetary effects are larger relative to the expenditure effects for a tax change than for a change in government expenditures.

TABLE 8.6. Size and timing of the external effects and the combined domestic and external effects of changes in fiscal policy on GNP, allowing for exchange-rate adjustments (millions of dollars)

	Quarters					
	1	2	3	4	5	6
A. Increase in government expenditure of $100 million						
1. Current- plus capital-account adjustment, Table 8.4:						
a. Best estimate	28.3	26.3	18.9	−1.0	−21.8	−40.4
b. Minimum estimate	−26.0	−26.0	−32.0	−47.0	−64.0	−80.0
c. Maximum estimate	70.4	66.1	56.8	33.3	9.8	−12.7
2. Exchange-rate adjustment (cents)						
a. Best estimate	.2497	.2326	.1882	.0682	−.0545	−.1648
b. Minimum estimate	−.1430	−.1430	−.1760	−.2585	−.3520	−.4400
c. Maximum estimate	.4542	.4269	.3725	.2362	.1011	−.0286
3. Change in the current account induced by exchange-rate adjustments:						
a. Best estimate	−23.0	−21.4	−17.3	−6.3	5.0	15.2
b. Minimum estimate	13.2	13.2	16.2	23.8	32.4	40.5
c. Maximum estimate	−41.8	−39.3	−34.3	−21.8	−9.3	2.6
4. Change in income induced by the change in the current account, 1. 3:[a]						
a. Best estimate	−24.2	−23.9	−22.5	−15.0	−6.9	1.7
b. Minimum estimate	13.8	14.6	19.5	30.3	43.3	56.9
c. Maximum estimate	−43.9	−43.8	−43.8	−38.4	−33.0	−26.1
5. Combined domestic and external effects on GNP:						
a. Best estimate	77	81	91	115	144	173
b. Minimum estimate	119	126	144	174	211	248
c. Maximum estimate	56	58	66	88	113	140

B. *Decrease in personal income taxes of $100 million*

6. Current- plus capital-account adjustment, Table 8.5:						
a. Best estimate	29.5	31.1	26.7	16.0	7.9	-1.3
b. Minimum estimate	-26.0	-23.0	-26.0	-33.0	-39.0	-45.0
c. Maximum estimate	72.5	72.3	67.0	52.5	41.1	29.7
7. Exchange-rate adjustments (cents):						
a. Best estimate	.2576	.2626	.2342	.1667	.1152	.0574
b. Minimum estimate	-.1430	-.1265	-.1430	-.1815	-.2145	-.2475
c. Maximum estimate	.7422	.6939	.6733	.6535	.6296	.6058
8. Change in the current account induced by exchange-rate adjustments:						
a. Best estimate	-23.7	-24.2	-21.6	-15.4	-10.6	-5.3
b. Minimum estimate	13.3	11.8	13.3	16.9	20.0	23.0
c. Maximum estimate	-68.4	-63.9	-62.0	-60.2	-58.0	-55.8
9. Change in income induced by the change in the current account, 1.8:[a]						
a. Best estimate	-24.9	-26.8	-27.2	-25.3	-25.2	-23.5
b. Minimum estimate	14.0	13.2	16.4	22.7	29.1	36.0
c. Maximum estimate	-71.8	-71.2	-77.9	-88.9	-101.1	-112.8
10. Combined domestic and external effects on GNP:						
a. Best estimate	26	22	24	31	39	47
b. Minimum estimate	69	69	79	95	112	129
c. Maximum estimate	-22	-24	-29	-36	-41	-47

[a] Using Officer's multiplier estimates.

These estimates bear directly on a central question in the theory of economic policy: to what extent, given a change in fiscal policy, do changes in GNP attributable to exchange-rate adjustments wipe out changes in GNP attributable to net employment effects not associated with exchange-rate movements? Theoretically, it is conceivable that the first set of effects may wipe out the second. Among other things, this theoretical possibility requires that capital flows be infinitely elastic with respect to interest rates and completely inelastic with respect to the exchange rate. Empirically, this theoretical possibility apparently did not arise in Canada during the flexible rate period. For one thing, capital flows, though highly elastic vis-à-vis interest rates as shown in Table 2.2, were substantially less than infinitely elastic. For another, exchange-rate changes evoked large equilibrating movements in capital flows — also evident from Table 2.2. In addition, the effects on GNP induced by exchange-rate movements failed to outweigh the changes in GNP attributable to the other expenditure and monetary consequences of a change in fiscal policy because of the special circumstances resulting from our assumption of a growing rather than a static state.

Two additional features of these estimates should be noted. First, they do not allow for the lagged response of portfolio capital flows in response to exchange-rate adjustments which our evidence, as described in Chapter 2, indicates is significant. The figures presented in Table 8.6 assume that the coefficients estimated in equation 2.11 allow for the current response of portfolio capital flows to changes in exchange rates. It is further assumed that any effect that lagged portfolio capital flows may have on the exchange rate will be at least offset by compensating short-term capital flows.[26] Secondly, these estimates

26. $\partial PC/\partial RS_{-1} = -2374$ from equation 2.10 is consistently less than $\partial STK/\partial RS$ from the equations summarized in Table 2.2, ignoring equation 2.21 for which the estimated coefficient is insignificant.

do not allow for second-order effects on interest rates as capital flows respond to changes in the exchange rate. The inflow of capital induced by exchange-rate adjustments will further dampen interest rate changes which, in turn, will somewhat reduce the monetary consequences of fiscal policy in relation to the expenditure consequences.

In addition to considering how GNP responds to changes in fiscal policy, the estimates presented in Table 8.6 indicate the extent of the adjustment in the exchange rate associated with the assumed changes in fiscal policy. As noted earlier, Rhomberg's estimates suggest that, as a consequence of a $100-million increase in government expenditures, the exchange rate might be expected to appreciate by $.0067 initially and $.015 eventually. Our evidence suggests that exchange-rate movements are likely to be smaller, and that after a year and a half the rate will begin to depreciate. As capital flows respond to changes in the government's deficit, line 2a of Table 8.6 indicates that, initially, the exchange rate may appreciate about $.0025; at the end of a year it may have appreciated by $.0074; after that it begins to depreciate, and at the end of a year and a half it may be $.0052 higher than initially. If, on the other hand, one assumes that interest rates in Canada were governed by expectations related to United States rates, the exchange rate immediately depreciates by $.0014; at the end of a year it has depreciated by $.0072; at the end of a year and a half by $.0151. As for tax changes, if one assumes that interest rates respond to changes in the deficit, line 7a of Table 8.6 indicates that, initially, the rate might have appreciated by $.0026; at the end of a year it may have appreciated by $.0092; at the end of a year and a half by $.0109. Alternatively, if Canadian interest rates are linked to U.S. rates via expectations, the assumed reduction in taxes is associated with an immediate depreciation of $.0014, one of $.0059 at the end of a year, and one of $.0106 after a year and a half.

331

RESPONSES TO MONETARY POLICY

The first link in the chain of reactions running from changes in monetary policy is the effect of a change in the money supply on interest rates as asset portfolios are readjusted to accommodate this change. The series of experiments undertaken to analyze the interdependent relations between the money supply, interest rates, and foreign capital flows have been described and analyzed in considerable detail in Chapter 3; consideration of this question here can be brief. As already indicated, our best estimate of the determinants of the long-term interest rate, *CL*, in Canada appears in equation 3.1. Equation 3.1 indicates that, given the influence of other factors affecting interest rates, an increase in the rate of growth in the money supply (*PCMS*) of one percent is likely to result in a decrease in *CL* of .0613 percentage points in the same quarter. In the corresponding equation in which *MWL* (McLeod Weir 40-bond average long-term interest rate) was used as the dependent variable in place of *CL*, the estimated coefficient of *PCMS* is —.0552. In the two-stage least-squares equation (3.17) explaining *CL* the coefficient of *PCMS* is —.103.

When allowance is made for induced capital flows, as in the reduced-form multipliers in Tables 3.1 and 3.2, the effect on *CL* of a one-percent increase in *PCMS* is reduced somewhat. If, alternatively, it is assumed that long-term interest rates are based on expectations about future interest rates that are closely geared to the level of United States rates, as assumed in equation 3.14, the effect on *CL* of a one-percent increase in *PCMS* is reduced to —.010 of a percentage point. As far as short-term interest rates are concerned, equation 3.20 indicates that a one-percent increase in *PCMS* might be expected to reduce *CS* by between .039 to .092 of a percentage point, depending on what assumptions are made about the forward premium.[27] For working purposes, we assume that our best estimates of the effect of a one-percent change in *PCMS* are a reduction in *CL* of .059 and a reduction in *CS* of .080 of a percentage point.

Estimates of the induced change in capital flows serving to constrain the reduction in long-term interest rates range from $23.8 to $44.6 million, according to Tables 3.1 and 3.2. If, however, one again assumes that expectations about the future of *CL* are based on United States rates and severely limit the impact of changes in *PCMS* on *CL*, then the induced changes in capital flows will be substantially less — on the order of $4 to $8 million, according to the estimates presented in Table 2.2.[28] The induced short-term capital outflow generated by the interest-rate reduction is given by equation 2.15.[29] Depending on the assumptions made about the forward premium, the estimates range from $23.4 to $34.2 million. The capital flow estimates corresponding to the assumed best estimates of the change in interest rates given above are an outflow of $41.1 million in long-term portfolio capital and one of $32.2 million in short-term capital.

Effects of a Change in Monetary Policy

The building blocks assembled thus far allow us to construct estimates of the size and timing of effects of a change in

27. If equation 3.24 is substituted for FP in equation 3.20, $\partial CS/\partial PCMS = -.07966$. If equation 3.25 is substituted for FP, $\partial CS/\partial PCMS = -.09209$. Assuming that FP is determined endogenously and that interest parity prevails, one can approximate $\partial CS/\partial PCMS$ by assuming further that $FP = RF - RS$ and substituting the mean values for RS and CS into the expression $-RS (CS - USS)/(100 + CS)$. On this basis $\partial CS/\partial PCMS = -.08141$. If FP is assumed to be determined exogenously, $\partial CS/\partial PCMS = -.03893$ from equation 3.20.

28. From equation 3.14 $\partial CL/\partial PCMS = -.01018$ and estimates of $\beta = \partial PC/\partial CL$ for equation listed in Table 2.2 range from 424 to 806.

29. Since equation 2.15 is in reduced form, the estimated interest-rate changes may be applied directly to obtain estimates of the induced capital flow.

333

monetary policy similar to those presented earlier for changes in fiscal policy. These building blocks include evidence developed in Chapters 2 and 3 and summarized above on relations between interest rates and money supply changes and between interest rates and capital flows. Also included is the evidence assembled in Chapter 7 on the relation between interest-rate changes and domestic expenditure. The other set of building blocks consists of measures of the income and current-account responses to changes in domestic expenditure reviewed at the beginning of this chapter, along with our evidence on the interaction between exchange rates, the capital account, and the current account.

Table 8.7 presents a summary of our estimates of size and timing for the primary effects of a change in monetary policy that takes the form of increasing the rate of growth of the money supply by one percent. Line 2 indicates the induced change in interest rates that our evidence suggests is likely to follow from the increase in the money supply, as summarized earlier. The associated changes in capital flows are shown in line 6. In developing the estimates presented in Chapters 2 and 3, extensive tests were made to discover lagged relationships between interest-rate changes and capital flows; no evidence was found to suggest that lags are important. Accordingly here, as elsewhere in this chapter, it is assumed that changes in capital flows manifest themselves in the same quarter as changes in interest rates.

The other channel of response is via domestic expenditure changes, GNP changes, and current-account changes. Table 7.1 (Chapter 7) shows evidence we have derived from several sources on the response of various expenditure items to a change of .1 percentage point in interest rates. When our estimates of the change in interest rate are applied to these factors, we arrive at the estimates shown in line 3 of Table 8.7. If Officer's income and current-account multipliers are

TABLE 8.7. Size and timing of the primary effects of a change in monetary policy on the balance of payments

	Time period (quarter)					
	1	2	3	4	5	6
1. Increase in the rate of growth in money stock (%):	1.0	—	—	—	—	—
2. Induced change in interest rates, present study (percentage points):						
a. Short-term rate (CS) (−.039 to −.092)[a]	−.080[b]	—	—	—	—	—
b. Long-term rate (CL) (−.010 to −.071)[a]	−.059[b]	—	—	—	—	—
3. Direct domestic expenditure effects, present study ($ million):						
a. Change in consumer durable spending	2.32	0	0	0	0	0
b. Change in residential construction	1.06	1.59	2.48	1.48	.47	0
c. Change in total business fixed investment	.71	1.30	1.65	1.77	1.65	1.36
d. Total: best estimate	4.09	2.89	4.13	3.25	2.12	1.36
minimum estimate	1.43	.49	.70	.55	.36	.23
maximum estimate	4.80	3.48	4.97	3.91	2.56	1.63
4. Income response, present study ($ million):[c]						
a. Best estimate	4.30	3.28	5.04	4.86	4.48	4.44
b. Minimum estimate	1.50	.59	.95	.97	.93	.91
c. Maximum estimate	5.04	3.94	6.05	5.82	5.37	5.26
5. Current-account response, present study ($ million):[c]						
a. Best estimate	−1.06	−.75	−1.27	−1.60	−1.89	−2.23
b. Minimum estimate	−.37	−.13	−.25	−.37	−.44	−.49
c. Maximum estimate	−1.25	−.90	−1.53	−1.91	−2.26	−2.68
6. Capital-account response ($ million):						
a. Short-term (−23 to −34)[a]	−32[b]	—	—	—	—	—
b. Long-term (−4 to −45)[a]	−41[b]	—	—	—	—	—

[a] Range of estimates.
[b] Best estimate.
[c] Using Officer multipliers.

now applied to these investment expenditure changes, the figures shown in lines 4 and 5 of the table are obtained. If the multipliers from either May's or Rhomberg's models had been used instead, the estimates would differ in detail but would not materially alter the findings of this study.

At this point, the picture that emerges from Table 8.7 can be briefly summarized. The primary effect on the balance of payments of increasing the rate of growth in the money stock by one percent is to increase international net payments immediately by something like $74 million, of which some $73 million reflects an induced outflow of capital and about $1 million an increase in current-account payments. The outflow of capital is induced by a decrease in short-term rates of about .08 percentage points and in long-term rates of .06 percentage points. This conforms roughly to what one might expect under a fixed exchange-rate system. Apparently, an increase in the rate of growth in money supply of one percent under a fixed rate system might be expected to lead to a foreign-exchange drain of some 70 million, followed by much smaller drains in subsequent periods as current-account effects work themselves out.

The foregoing picture needs modification in at least two respects so that light will be shed on the adjustment process under a flexible rate system. First, no attempt is made in Table 8.7 to allow for any reactions on interest rate of the changes in GNP and the exchange rate induced by the initiating change in monetary policy. Second, it is evident that pressure on the exchange rate emanating from the effects of monetary policy on current and capital accounts will result in exchange-rate adjustments with further effects on GNP and interest rates.

The first of these reactions is likely to be small and has been ignored in the estimates that follow. For one thing, the initial change in GNP, as shown in Table 8.7, is small. According to equation 3.20 an increase in GNP of $4 million can be expected to increase short-term interest rates by .0006 percentage points. Moreover, the increase in GNP will generate additional government revenue which, other things equal, will reduce government borrowing, thereby exerting some downward pressure on interest rates.

Much more important is the chain of reactions running from induced changes in the balance of payments and the exchange rate to changes in GNP and employment. The estimates shown in Table 8.8 have been calculated on the same assumptions made to calculate the effects of fiscal policy in Table 8.6. Our best estimates indicate the following response patterns of GNP (millions of dollars) with and without exchange-rate adjustments:

	Quarters					
	1	2	3	4	5	6
Without exchange rate adjustments	4	3	5	5	5	4
With exchange rate adjustments	64	7	13	17	19	19

It is evident that exchange-rate adjustments greatly enhance the effectiveness of monetary policy — particularly in the short run, but also in the longer term.

Line 2 of Table 8.8 shows the size of the estimated exchange-rate adjustments associated with the assumed change in monetary policy. According to the best estimate, the exchange rate can be expected to depreciate $.0062 cents immediately following the change in monetary policy. A year after the change in policy, exchange rates would have depreciated $.0064, a year and a half later by $.0066.

RESPONSES TO DEBT MANAGEMENT POLICY

By debt management we mean policies that change the average term to maturity of the public debt. The first ques-

TABLE 8.8. Size and timing of the external effects and combined domestic and external effects of changes in monetary policy on GNP, allowing for exchange-rate adjustments (millions of dollars)

	Quarters					
	1	2	3	4	5	6
1. Current- plus capital-account adjustment, Table 8.7:						
a. Best estimate	-74.1	-0.8	-1.2	-1.6	-1.9	-2.2
b. Minimum estimate	-27.4	-0.1	-0.3	-0.4	-0.4	-0.5
c. Maximum estimate	-80.3	-0.9	-1.5	-1.9	-2.3	-2.7
2. Exchange-rate adjustment (cents):						
a. Best estimate	-0.6151	-0.0044	-0.0072	-0.0088	-0.0105	-0.0121
b. Minimum estimate	-0.1290	-0.0007	-0.0014	-0.0020	-0.0024	-0.0027
c. Maximum estimate	-0.6715	-0.0050	-0.0084	-0.0105	-0.0124	-0.0147
3. Change in the current account induced by exchange-rate adjustments:						
a. Best estimate	56.66	0.40	0.67	0.81	0.97	1.11
b. Minimum estimate	11.88	0.07	0.13	0.18	0.22	0.25
c. Maximum estimate	61.86	0.46	0.77	0.97	1.15	1.36
4. Change in income induced by the change in the current account, 1. 3:[a]						
a. Best estimate	59.49	3.82	8.09	12.27	14.27	14.58
b. Minimum estimate	12.47	0.78	1.68	2.59	3.00	3.07
c. Maximum estimate	64.95	4.19	8.88	13.49	15.68	16.12
5. Combined domestic and external effects on GNP:						
a. Best estimate	63.79	7.10	13.13	17.13	18.75	19.02
b. Minimum estimate	13.97	1.37	2.63	3.56	3.93	3.98
c. Maximum estimate	69.99	8.13	14.93	19.31	21.05	21.38

[a] Using Officer multipliers.

tion to be considered in assessing the effects of such policies is how short- and long-run rates of interest respond to a change in the average term to maturity of the public debt. From this we can proceed to estimate what effect induced changes in the term structure of interest rates are likely to have on GNP, capital flows, the current account, and the exchange rate.

It will be recalled that equation 3.1 explicitly includes the average term to maturity (ATM) as a determinant of the long-term interest rate (CL). The same variable is highly significant statistically when included as a determinant of MWL. The reduced-form multipliers shown in Tables 3.1 and 3.2 indicate that a reduction in ATM by one month can, everything else given, be expected to reduce long-term interest rates by .0022 to .0049 percentage points. These estimates allow for the influence of induced capital inflows responding to the decrease in interest rates. When the possibility is allowed for that long-term interest rates in Canada are determined by expectations based on long-term rates in the United States and the other factors included in equation 3.14, evidence suggests that changes in ATM have no significant influence on CL. Our best estimate of the effect on CL of decreasing ATM by one month is assumed to be a reduction of .0024.

Equation 3.20, explaining short-term interest rates, does not include ATM as an explanatory variable. Our best estimate including ATM follows:

$$CS = -.709 - .53FP - .0771PCMS + .0026ATM$$
$$(5.48) \quad (5.05) \quad (4.87) \quad (1.88)$$
$$+ .0001GNP$$
$$(7.34)$$

$$RSQC = .83$$
$$DW = .84. \quad (8.1)$$

339

Although ATM in this equation is not significantly different from zero at the 95-percent confidence level if one uses a two-tailed test, it is significantly different from zero on a one-tailed test. This equation is inferior to equation 3.20 in two other respects as well: the portion of the variance explained is somewhat lower and the value of the Durbin-Watson statistic is very low, indicating serious autocorrelation in the residuals; in addition, when USS is added to the equation, the coefficient for ATM becomes quite insignificant. These qualifications notwithstanding, equation 8.1 provides the best estimate we could develop of the influence of ATM on CS. According to equation 8.1, a reduction in ATM of one month can be expected to lower short-term interest rates from .0026 to .0057 percentage points depending on what assumptions are made about the forward premium. The best estimate is assumed to be .0039.[30] As before, these estimates of short-term interest-rate effects allow for the influence of induced capital flows responding to changes in interest rates.

It is not possible to say with any assurance what effect changes in ATM will have on the term structure of interest rates on the basis of our calculations. A comparison of the assumed best estimates suggests that a reduction in ATM by one month will reduce short-term rates relative to long-term rates ($-.0039$ compared to $-.0024$ percentage points). This picture is generally consistent with evidence presented earlier on the effect of a change in the money supply. Increasing the money supply may be viewed as reducing the average length of the debt by issuing noninterest-bearing, fully liquid government liabilities. As shown in Table 8.7, the effect of increasing the rate of growth in the money supply apparently

30. If FP is assumed to be determined exogenously, $\partial CS/\partial ATM = .0026$; if FP is assumed to be determined endogenously according to equation 3.24, $\partial CS/\partial ATM = .0039$; if FP is assumed to be determined endogenously and interest parity is also assumed to prevail, $\partial CS/\partial ATM = .0057$.

is to reduce short-term relative to long-term rates ($-.080$ compared to $-.059$ percentage points for long-term rates).

The reduced-form multipliers given in Tables 3.1 and 3.2 also show the effect of a change in *ATM* on long-term capital flows. This evidence indicates that an increase of one month in *ATM* can be expected to induce an outflow of long-term capital ranging from $1.2 to $3.7 million; our best estimate is $1.6 million. If one assumes that *CL* is not significantly influenced by changes in *ATM*, as suggested by equation 3.14, then a minimum estimate of the effect of changes in *ATM* on long-term capital flows is zero.

Our estimates do not directly indicate what effect a change of one month in *ATM* is likely to have on short-term capital flows. However, this relationship may be inferred indirectly from equations 3.20 and 8.1. Depending on assumptions about the forward premium, the estimates range from $1.57 to $1.61 million; our best estimate is assumed to be $1.58 million.

Effects of a Change in Debt Management

Table 8.9 corresponds to Table 8.7. It provides estimates of the effect of a decrease in *ATM* on GNP and on the current and capital accounts. Because changes in *ATM* imply changes in the level of rates, as well as in the term structure of rates, it was more interesting to trace through the response to a change in debt management policy that in some sense is comparable to the change in monetary policy considered earlier. As indicated in Chapter 3, an increase in the rate of growth in the money supply in Canada during our sample period evidently had about the same effect on long-term interest rates as a decrease in the average term to maturity of the public debt (11.39 months). For ease of calculation, a decrease in *ATM* of ten months has been assumed in the dis-

TABLE 8.9. Size and timing of the primary effects of a change in debt management policy on the balance of payments

	Time period (quarter)					
	1	2	3	4	5	6
1. Decrease in *ATM* (months):	10.0	0	0	0	0	0
2. Induced change in interest rates, present study (percentage points):						
a. Short term (CS):	−.039[b] (−.026 to −.057)[a]	–	–	–	–	–
b. Long term (CL):	−.024[b] (0 to −.049)[a]	–	–	–	–	–
3. Direct domestic expenditure effects, present study ($ million):						
a. Change in consumer durable spending	.11	.06	.10	.06	.02	0
b. Change in residential construction	.04	.05	.07	.07	.07	0
c. Change in business fixed investment	.03	.11	.17	.13	.09	.07
d. Total: best estimate	.18	.13	.21	.20	.09	.07
minimum estimate	.15	.11	.15	.13	.08	.05
maximum estimate	.32	.24	.35	.27	.18	.11
4. Income response, present study ($ million):[c]						
a. Best estimate	.19	.13	.21	.20	.18	.20
b. Minimum estimate	.16	.13	.19	.19	.16	.17
c. Maximum estimate	.34	.27	.42	.39	.38	.37
5. Current-account response, present study ($ million):[c]						
a. Best estimate	−.06	−.03	−.05	−.06	−.08	−.10
b. Minimum estimate	−.04	−.03	−.05	−.06	−.07	−.07
c. Maximum estimate	−.08	−.06	−.10	−.12	−.16	−.17
6. Capital-account response ($ million):						
a. Short term	−15.8[b] (−15.7 to −16.1)[a]					
b. Long term	−16.4[b] (0 to −36.9)[a]					

[a] Range of estimates.
[b] Best estimate.
[c] Using Officer multipliers.

cussion that follows. This amounts to assuming a very sub-stantial change in debt management policy. If one excludes the 1958 Conversion Loan episode, during which the average term to maturity of government securities changed from six years four months to ten years six months, quarter-to-quarter changes in the average term to maturity have consistently been substantially less than ten months. The mean value of *ATM* used in our regressions is 101 months and its standard deviation 21.8 months including the Conversion Loan. For the period 1952-I to 1956-IV the mean value is 88.5 months and the standard deviation 5.9 months.

Line 2 of Table 8.9 shows the changes in long- and short-term interest rates to be expected as a result of the assumed change in *ATM*; these estimates are based on discussion in the preceding section. Line 3 shows the changes in investment expenditure which can be expected to result from the induced interest-rate changes; these figures are based on the estimates presented in Table 7.1. Lines 4 and 5 indicate the income and current-account changes that are likely to ensue follow-ing the change in investment expenditure, based on Officer's multiplier estimates. Line 6 indicates the reduction in capital inflows due to the lower interest rates. Adding up the effects of the interest-rate change on the current account through income changes and its direct effects on the capital account, it can be said that the primary effects of decreasing *ATM* by ten months are likely to increase external payments by about $27 million, virtually all due to a capital outflow.

Under a fixed exchange-rate system, a loss of reserves of approximately this amount could be expected. Under a flexible rate system, on the other hand, the pressure these additional payments exert on the rate results in a depreciation. Proceed-ing on the assumptions made earlier in connection with fiscal and monetary policy changes, estimates have been made of the effects on GNP via exchange-rate adjustments arising from the assumed change in debt management policy. The series of best estimates derived on this basis is shown in Table 8.10.

Apparently, flexible exchange rates enhance the effectiveness of debt management policy even more than the effectiveness of monetary policy. With exchange-rate adjustments the initial bite of changes in debt management policy on GNP is something like 13.0 times greater than without exchange-rate adjustments, and it remains on the order of ten to 20 times greater after the first quarter. Virtually all adjustment in the exchange rate occurs in the same quarter as the change in policy. For a decrease in *ATM* of ten months, the implied depreciation of the exchange rate is $.0025, according to Table 8.10.

Before attempting to draw together some of the more important implications of this analysis, it is important to mention three characteristics of our evidence. First, given the variety of sources and the series of partial equilibrium estimates upon which we have drawn, the foregoing evidence necessarily is imprecise and the estimates can only be viewed as approximations. Consequently, not much can or should be made of small differences in the estimates of the same parameter, or of small differences between the estimates presented here and those provided by other investigators. This said, it is also true that the authors are quite confident in the reliability of the broad picture of the relationships examined.

Second, and perhaps more important, it should be recognized that the estimates presented have been based on the structure of the Canadian economy and the state of expectations prevalent during the decade ending in 1961. It is reasonable to believe that the performance of the economy during these years is relevant to an assessment of Canadian policy beyond this period, as well as to policy assessment in other countries. Nevertheless, the estimates are based upon a particular set of circumstances, including time and place, and should not be projected uncritically beyond. Expectations per-

TABLE 8.10. Size and timing of the external effects and the combined domestic and external effects of changes in debt management policy on GNP, allowing for exchange-rate adjustments[a] (millions of dollars)

	Quarters					
	1	2	3	4	5	6
1. Current- plus capital-account adjustment, Table 8.9	−32.3[b]	−.03	−.05	−.06	−.08	−.10
2. Exchange-rate adjustment (cents)	−.2538	–	–	–	–	–
3. Change in the current account induced by exchange-rate adjustments	23.38	–	–	–	–	–
4. Change in income induced by the change in the current account, 1. 3[c]	24.55	1.40	3.04	4.68	5.38	5.38
5. Combined domestic and external effects on GNP of a 10-month increase in the average term to maturity of the public debt	24.74	1.53	3.25	4.88	5.56	5.50

[a] All calculations based on our best estimate of the change in capital flows plus the change in the current-account balance shown in Table 8.9.
[b] Range: $−7.3 to $−52.6 million.
[c] Using Officer multipliers.

haps warrant special mention in this context. Our estimates are based on responses to policy changes under relatively "normal" circumstances, implying marginal adjustments made in fairly conventional ways. It seems likely that a different policy strategy that introduced major shocks and discontinuities would change at least some of the parameters on which our conclusions are based.

Third, although the adjustment process has been traced through the major channels of response, it is evident that a number of tributaries have been bypassed en route on the assumption that their quantitative significance is relatively minor. Nor have the interconnections between the major channels of response been circumnavigated repeatedly to insure that all interdependent effects have been entirely taken into account. First- and second-order effects having been evaluated, we have assumed that tertiary and higher order effects are of marginal quantitative significance and may safely be ignored. This neglect, inherent in the methodology of this study, occurs both in the choice of estimation methods that neglect some simultaneity in the underlying economic relations and in the use of assembly or simulation procedures that take only limited account of interdependent relations.

These caveats aside, what conclusions does the foregoing analysis suggest about the constraints and opportunities afforded Canadian economic policy by highly mobile international capital flows? Table 8.11 presents a summary of the evidence developed in earlier sections of this chapter on the response in GNP to changes in fiscal, monetary, and debt management policies with and without exchange-rate adjustments. For each type of policy change a distinction is made between the response in GNP with foreign capital flows and without. A comparison of these figures indicates roughly the extent to which capital flows strengthened or weakened these instruments of Canadian economic policy during the decade ending in 1961, and what effect capital flows would have had on the leverage of these policy instruments had Canada been operating under fixed exchange rates rather than flexible rates.

Before considering the figures, something should be said

TABLE 8.11. Summary of estimated effects on GNP of changes in fiscal, monetary, and debt management policies with and without foreign capital flows and with and without exchange-rate adjustments (millions of dollars)

	Without exchange-rate adjustments						With exchange-rate adjustments					
	1	2	3	4	5	6	1	2	3	4	5	6
Increase in government expenditure of $100 million:												
Without foreign capital flows	97	98	103	117	136	154	110	111	120	143	173	202
With foreign capital flows	101	105	113	130	151	171	77	81	91	115	144	173
Percentage[a]	104	107	110	111	111	111	70	73	76	80	83	86
Decrease in personal income tax of $100 million:												
Without foreign capital flows	47	43	42	44	49	54	60	54	55	62	71	80
With foreign capital flows	51	49	51	56	64	71	26	22	24	31	39	47
Percentage[a]	109	114	121	127	131	131	43	41	44	50	55	59
Increase in rate of growth in money supply of 1 percent:												
Without foreign capital flows	8.6	5.6	8.7	8.5	7.9	7.8	9.7	6.4	10.1	10.4	10.3	10.8
With foreign capital flows	4.3	3.3	5.0	4.9	4.5	4.4	63.8	7.1	13.1	17.1	18.8	19.0
Percentage[a]	50	59	57	58	57	56	658	111	130	164	183	176
Decrease in average term of the public debt by 10 months:												
Without foreign capital flows	3.9	2.3	3.6	3.5	3.3	3.3	4.5	2.7	4.2	4.4	4.4	4.6
With foreign capital flows	.2	.1	.2	.2	.2	.2	24.7	1.5	3.3	4.9	5.6	5.5
Percentage[a]	5	4	6	6	6	6	549	56	79	111	127	120

a "With foreign capital flows" as a percentage of "without foreign capital flows."

about the sources of these estimates. The lines showing the adjustment with foreign capital flows have been taken directly from the estimates presented earlier and no further comment is required. The basis of the estimates showing the change in GNP without capital flows is necessarily rather tentative, since the situation that is assumed might well imply far-reaching effects not allowed for therein. The estimates are therefore largely hypothetical, and their principal purpose is to illustrate how, in general, capital flows affect the adjustment process.

From the structural estimates of the determinants of long-term interest rates, it is a straightforward matter to determine the effect of a change in fiscal, monetary, and debt management on long-term interest rates. Unfortunately, we do not have comparable structural estimates for the determinants of short-term interest rates. Equations 3.20 and 8.1 are reduced-form estimates, as noted earlier. This means that the estimated parameters are biased downward, reflecting the dampening effects of capital flows on interest-rate changes initiated by changes in monetary, debt management, and fiscal policies. However, the figures summarized in Table 3.3 indicate the extent to which exogenous changes in short-term Canadian interest rates are dampened by capital flows. If the forward premium is assumed as determined endogenously, and if some deviation from interest parity is also assumed, the figures relating to equations 2.15 and 2.16 indicate that about 55 percent of any exogenous change in short-term rates is wiped out by capital flows. Accordingly, it has been assumed that the estimated responses when capital flows are allowed for, as reported earlier in this chapter, are equal to 45 percent of the response that would have occurred in the absence of capital flows.[31]

Several features of the figures shown in Table 8.11 may

31. On this assumption the estimated responses of short-term interest rates without capital flows are as follows: $\partial CS/\partial NNSC = .182$; $\partial CS/\partial PCMS = -.178$; and $\partial CS/\partial ATM = .087$.

be especially noted:

1. Under the flexible exchange-rate system adhered to during the 1950's, the effectiveness of Canadian fiscal policy as an instrument to regulate GNP and employment apparently was substantially impaired by mobile capital movements. The degree of impairment was considerably greater for changes in tax policy than for changes in expenditure policy. Under fixed rates exactly the opposite would have been true. Capital inflows induced by the interest-rate effects of expansionary fiscal policy would have dampened the increase in interest rates, and the expansion in GNP would have been greater. Capital flows would especially have increased the efficiency of tax policy changes. Under flexible rates the initial efficiency of expenditure policies was reduced by about 30 percent by capital flows; after a year and a half the degree of impairment was reduced to about 14 percent. The initial efficiency of tax policy was reduced by about 57 percent by capital flows, and this was reduced to about 40 percent within a year and a half. Had Canada adhered to fixed rates, capital flows would have increased the effectiveness of expenditure policy by about 4 percent initially and by some 11 percent after a year and a half. The initial increase in effectiveness in tax policy would have been about 9 percent, and after a year and a half this would have increased to 31 percent.

2. In the case of monetary policy, capital flows evidently enhanced the effectiveness of Canadian policy substantially while the free rate prevailed. Had Canada adhered to fixed-rates their effect would have been the opposite. With the exchange rate flexible, the immediate impact of a change in monetary policy was tremendously increased by capital flows. In subsequent periods a sharp reduction occurs in the gain obtained from capital flows at first, but then greater gains in the effectiveness of monetary policy because of capital flows are again evident. According to the third panel of Table 8.11, had Canada been on fixed exchange rates during this period,

the efficiency of monetary policy would have been reduced by about 50 percent because of international capital flows.

3. The pattern for debt management policy is naturally somewhat similar to that for monetary policy. Given a flexible exchange rate for Canada, the initial impact of a change in debt management policy on GNP was tremendously increased by the mobility of capital flows. This was followed for two quarters by an impairment of the effects of changes in debt management policy. In the subsequent three quarters, the efficiency of debt management policies was again substantially enhanced by capital flows. Under fixed rates, by contrast, the efficiency of debt management policies would have been virtually wiped out by capital mobility.

4. Given mobile capital movements, the estimates indicate that flexible exchange rates greatly enhanced the efficiency of monetary and debt management policies. Flexible rates, on the other hand, seriously impaired the efficiency of fiscal policy, particularly tax policy. The effectiveness of expenditure policy was significantly reduced by exchange-rate adjustments in the short run; after a lag of a year and a half, the impact of expenditure policy changes on GNP was about the same under flexible rates as it would have been under fixed-rates.

The magnitudes of the changes in policy assumed in this chapter are arbitrary and, with the exception noted earlier, are not intended to be dimensionally equivalent in any sense. Hence, the figures shown in Table 8.11 are not by themselves of much help in comparing the efficiency of the various instruments of policy in regulating GNP. They indicate only the output, defined as the effect on GNP, of various policy changes, but tell nothing about the costs of implementing these changes. Only after such costs have been adequately specified can we go on to compare the relative efficiency of various policy instruments in terms of output gains per unit of cost. The notion of the "cost" of using an instrument of economic policy means different things to different people. For some it appears to be based only on the trouble or subjective disutility associated with revising established attitudes and analytical habits, as well as conventional practices. In the modern theory of economic policy, however, "cost" is employed in the specific sense of policy opportunity cost: the incidental displacement of the economy's performance with respect to other policy objectives that may occur when policy instruments are manipulated to improve the economy's performance on one particular target that conflicts to some degree with these other objectives. Given interdependencies among policy objectives, among policy instruments, and among objectives and instruments, an optimum policy is sought in terms of developing a procedure for simultaneously adjusting a series of policy instruments so that the marginal gain of moving closer to one target is matched by the marginal opportunity cost of falling somewhat further short of other targets in conflict with the one which has been more fully attained.

The discussion of the so-called "assignment problem" that has commanded considerable attention in recent years hangs critically on specification of the opportunity cost, as defined above, associated with the use of each instrument of policy. If each implies the same cost, then the underlying rationale for assigning instruments to targets breaks down. Much of the literature on the assignment problem concentrates on development of a procedure for simultaneously setting a series of n policy instruments, so that when all side effects on other targets are allowed for, n targets that have been prespecified are squarely hit.[32] And, in a more pessimistic view, these

32. This is the approach followed in Appendix A. It differs from the more general approach developed, for example, by H. Theil in *Economic Forecasts and Policy*, Contributions to Economic Analysis, no. 15 (Amsterdam: North-Holland Publishing Co., 1958).

351

policy-opportunity cost data are used to assign responsibility for particular targets to the wielders of policy instruments in the hope of minimizing the mischief that ensues when the side effects on other policy instruments are neglected.

The principal purpose of this study has been to present estimates of the effectiveness of the major instruments of stabilization policy under different institutional circumstances with respect to capital flows and exchange rates. The purpose has not been to try to close the circle by specifying and estimating the opportunity costs associated with the use of various policy instruments; nevertheless, in the course of deriving our estimates, some information has been developed which is relevant to this question and may be briefly considered.

First: as noted earlier, the assumed changes in monetary and debt management policy are approximately equivalent in terms of the effect of assumed changes in policy on long-term interest rates. On this criterion, monetary policy is substantially more efficient than debt management policy in regulating GNP, as is evident from Table 8.11.

Second, another base of comparison might be provided by considering how much additional GNP is generated by the use of each policy instrument in relation to the level or stability of foreign-exchange reserves, assuming fixed rates, or to the level or stability of exchange rates, assuming flexible rates. This criterion would be relevant to assessing the efficiency of the various instruments of policy, to the extent that the level or stability of reserves or exchange rates is included in the objective function of policy-makers. In addition, one would wish to consider the efficiency of the various instruments of policy in relation to the level or stability of interest rates, if the interest-rate level or stability were included in the objective function of the authorities. And, finally, one might wish to distinguish between the efficiency of the various instruments of policy in the short and in the long run, on the ground that relative efficiency over time is another factor that could be included in the objective function of the authorities.

Table 8.12 summarizes estimates relating to both the short- and longer-term efficiency of the major instruments of stabilization policy. Both the immediate and longer term changes in GNP induced by assumed policy changes are shown, together with the interest-rate changes and exchange-reserve or exchange-rate changes associated with these policy maneuvers. In all cases the figures distinguish between situations where capital is mobile and where it is not. Table 8.13 shows the amount of GNP created per unit change in interest rates and per unit change in either exchange reserves or exchange rates.

No attempt will be made to comment in detail on the figures shown in Tables 8.12 and 8.13; but the following points suggested by these tables may be briefly noted:

1. Irrespective of the exchange-rate system, under conditions of high capital mobility, changes in fiscal policy that gave rise to increases in GNP also gave rise to improvement in the international payments position, both in the short and longer terms. Improvement in the payments position per unit of newly created GNP was substantially greater for expenditure changes than for tax changes. By contrast, changes in monetary and debt management policies giving rise to an increase in GNP were associated with a deterioration of the payments position, defined either in terms of exchange depreciation or reserve losses. It is, accordingly, not feasible to compare the efficiency of fiscal policy and monetary and debt management policies on this basis, since the direction of their effects on the payments position is opposite: some amount of either fiscal or monetary-debt management policy will always be preferable, initially, to any use of the other, but the choice of which to use depends on the nature of the policy problem.

2. Had capital not been mobile, the picture would have been different. In this case it is possible to compare the efficiency

TABLE 8.12. Comparison of changes in GNP and changes in interest rates, and foreign-exchange rates as a consequence of changes in fiscal, monetary, and debt management policies, with and without foreign capital flows

| | Impact effects | | | | | | Cumulative effect after six quarter | | | | | |
| | Without exchange-rate adjustments | | | With exchange-rate adjustments | | | Without exchange-rate adjustments | | | With exchange-rate adjustments | | |
	GNP ($ million)	Long-term interest rate (%)	Foreign-exchange reserves ($ million)	GNP ($ million)	Long-term interest rate[a] (%)	Foreign-exchange rate (cents)	GNP ($ million)	Long-term interest rate (%)	Foreign-exchange reserves ($ million)	GNP ($ million)	Long-term interest rate[a] (%)	Foreign-exchange rate (cents)
Increase in government expenditure of $100 million:												
Without foreign capital flows	97	.106	−24.0	110	+	−.1320	154	.106	−235	202	+	−1.2925
With foreign capital flows	101	.055	28.3	77	+	.2497	171	.273	10.4	173	+	.5194
Decrease in personal income tax of $100 million:												
Without foreign capital flows	47	.106	−24.0	60	+	−.1320	54	.106	−149	80	+	−.8195
With foreign capital flows	51	.056	29.5	26	+	.2576	71	.287	110	47	+	1.0937
Increase in the rate of growth in the money supply of one percent:												
Without foreign capital flows	8.6	−.103	−2.1	9.7	−	−.0117	7.8	−.103	−16.0	10.8	−	−.0878
With foreign capital flows	4.3	−.080	−74.1	63.8	−	−.6151	4.4	−.080	−81.8	19.0	−	−.6581
Increase in average term of the public debt by 10 months:												
Without foreign capital flows	3.9	−.041	−1.0	4.5	−	−.0054	3.3	−.041	−6.8	4.6	−	−.0376
With foreign capital flows	.2	−.024	−32.3	24.7	−	−.2538	.2	−.024	−32.6	5.5	−	−.2538

[a] The direction of the change in interest rates is apparent, but the magnitude of the change is not.

[354]

TABLE 8.13. GNP per unit cost in terms of changes in interest rates and in foreign-exchange reserves or exchange rates associated with changes in fiscal, monetary, and debt management policies, with and without capital flows[a]

	Impact effects				Cumulative effects after 6 quarters			
	Without exchange-rate adjustments		With exchange-rate adjustments		Without exchange-rate adjustments		With exchange-rate adjustments	
	GNP created per unit change in:		GNP created per unit change in:		GNP created per unit change in:		GNP created per unit change in:	
	l-t i.r.[b]	f.x.r.[c]	l-t i.r.[b]	f.e.r.[d]	l-t i.r.[b]	f.x.r.[c]	l-t i.r.[b]	f.e.r.[d]
Increase in government expenditures:								
Without foreign capital flows	+92	−4	+	−83	+145	−.7	+	−16
With foreign capital flows	+184	+4	+	+31	+63	+2	+	+34
Decrease in personal income taxes:								
Without foreign capital flows	+44	−2	+	−48	+51	−.4	+	−1
With foreign capital flows	+91	+2	+	+10	+25	+.7	+	+5
Increase in the rate of growth in the money supply:								
Without foreign capital flows	−8	−4	−	−83	−8	−.5	−	−12
With foreign capital flows	−5	−.06	−	−10	−6	−.05	−	−3
Increase in the average term of the public debt:								
Without foreign capital flows	−10	−4	−	−83	−8	−.5	−	−12
With foreign capital flows	−8	−.006	−	−10	−8	−.006	−	−2

[a] Unit changes in interest rates are defined as .1 percentage points, unit changes in exchange reserves as $1 million, and unit changes in exchange rates as .1 cent. Plus signs indicate an increase in GNP associated with an increase in interest rates, an accumulation of reserves, or an appreciation in the exchange rate; minus signs indicate the opposite.

[b] Long-term interest rates.

[c] Foreign-exchange reserves.

[d] Foreign-exchange rates.

of various instruments in terms of the change in GNP per unit change in foreign exchange reserves or rates. In the short run, whether under a fixed- or flexible-rate system, the efficiency of monetary, debt management, and expenditure policies would have been about the same, and tax policies would have been less efficient. Much the same holds true for the longer term.

3. An alternative approach to evaluating the efficiency of policy instruments under flexible exchange rates might be to consider the degree of change in either direction in the exchange rate associated with policy changes.[33] On this criterion, capital flows impair the efficiency of all the policy instruments under review in the short run and the efficiency of monetary and debt management policies in the longer term as well. The efficiency of fiscal policy is, however, increased by capital mobility in the longer term by this criterion.

4. If the effectiveness of policy instruments is looked at in terms of their influence on interest rates and GNP, it is evident that in both the short and the long run, irrespective of capital mobility and the exchange-rate system, changes in fiscal policy have the opposite effect on interest rates from changes in monetary and debt management policy when all are regulated to change GNP in the same direction. Hence, as before, the efficiency of fiscal policy cannot be compared with monetary and debt management policy on this criterion. Within the realm of fiscal policy, however, one can argue that under a fixed-rate system in both the short and the longer term: (a) expenditure policy is more efficient than tax policy, whether capital is mobile or not, and (b) capital mobility more than doubles the efficiency of both expenditure and tax policy. As far as monetary and debt management policies are concerned,

33. This criterion might be based, for example, on such considerations as the alleged deleterious effects of exchange-rate movements on the value of trade.

their efficiency is about the same if capital immobility is assumed and debt management is somewhat more efficient if high capital mobility is assumed.

5. If one wishes to evaluate the various policy instruments in terms of changes in GNP per unit change in interest rates, irrespective of whether interest rates rise or fall, it is evident that fiscal policy is much more efficient than either monetary or debt management policies in both the short and the long run and regardless of whether capital flows are mobile or not.[34]

All of these comments are based on the assumption of a relatively simple world in which there are only a few well-defined objectives matched by an equal number of policy instruments that can be freely manipulated without constraints. As soon as greater realism is introduced into this picture by allowing for more objectives, disparity between the number of objectives and instruments, constraints on the use of instruments and a wider range of interdependencies among objectives and instruments, we find ourselves in a much more complicated world — a world that we leave as a challenge for the reader to explore.

34. This criterion might presumably be included in the objective function of the authorities because of the effect of changes in interest rates upon asset values.

Appendixes   Bibliography   Index

Appendix A The Effectiveness of Monetary and Fiscal Policies under Pegged and Floating Exchange-Rate Systems

Primary interest here is in presenting a reasonably rigorous comparison of the relative effectiveness of monetary and fiscal policies under pegged and floating exchange-rate systems. A simple model of income determination is developed in order to illustrate some of the more interesting relations that exist between endogenous movements of international capital and domestic income-generating policies.[1]

Income is determined under the usual Keynesian conditions; the analysis is short-run in nature. Thus, the effect of net investment upon capacity is ignored, and the debt-servicing obligations generated by net inflows of capital are excluded from consideration. Employment is not explained explicitly but is assumed to vary directly

1. The model developed below is general enough to reproduce the major conclusions of the more important contributions to the theoretical literature, such as J. Marcus Fleming, "Domestic Financial Polices under Fixed and Floating Exchange Rates," *IMF Staff Papers* (November, 1962), 369–379; Robert Mundell, "Capital Mobility and Stabilization Policy under Fixed and Flexible Exchange Rates," *Canadian Journal of Economics and Political Science,* XXIX (November, 1963), 475–485; and Anne O. Krueger, "The Impact of Alternative Government Policies under Varying Exchange Systems," *Quarterly Journal of Economics,* LXXIX (May, 1965), 195–209. The model builds upon one by Harry G. Johnson, "Some Aspects of the Theory of Economic Policy in a World of Capital Mobility," *Essays in Honor of Marco Fanno* (Padua: Cedam, 1966), II, 345–359.

with income. Prices are also assumed to be stable enough so that distinction between real and money income is not necessary. Finally, we assume that the rest of the world, which in the Canadian context refers mainly to the United States, is unaffected by Canadian developments. If Canadians purchase more imports, the effect of this upon foreign income and hence Canadian exports is ignored. A rise in the Canadian interest rate is assumed as equivalent to a rise in the Canadian-foreign interest-rate differential by the same amount. In short, the focus is entirely upon adjustments within the Canadian economy and influences upon Canadian economic policy. Although similar adjustment processes are presumably set in motion within the lending countries as well — particularly the United States — there seems to be little hope in detecting the income linkages in their case. Variations in capital flows to Canada constitute such a small portion of the disturbances affecting the United States economy that the chances of isolating their effects empirically are very slight.

The model contains eight basic equations, five of which are behavioral and three of which are identities.

(1) Income is defined as the sum of private, public, and net foreign expenditures on domestic goods and services:

$$Y = X + G + C$$

where X is private expenditure on consumption and investment, G is government expenditure — a predetermined policy variable — and C is the net balance of payments on current account, defined as exports of goods and services minus imports of goods and services.

(2) Private expenditures on consumption and investment are determined by disposable income and rate of interest:

$$X = X(D, R)$$

where D is disposable income and R is the rate of interest. Private expenditures are assumed to vary positively with disposable income and negatively with the rate of interest. Thus

$$\partial X / \partial D > 0 \quad \text{and} \quad \partial X / \partial R < 0.$$

Henceforth, partial derivatives like these will be written as X_d and X_r respectively.

(3) Disposable income is defined as national income minus personal and corporate income taxes:

$$D = Y - T.$$

(4) Personal and corporate income taxes are determined by income:

$$T = T(Y)$$

where $T_y > 0$.

(5) The rate of interest is determined by the money supply and the level of income:

$$R = R(M, Y)$$

where M is the stock of money — a predetermined policy variable — and R is, ideally, the expected net effective yield obtained on all securities held for any defined period of time, regardless of their term to maturity. It is assumed that $R_m < 0$ and $R_y > 0$.

(6) The net balance on current account is determined by expenditure or absorption and the exchange rate:

$$C = C(E, F)$$

where F is the price of the domestic currency in terms of the foreign currency. If the usual conditions for exchange-market stability are met, $C_f < 0$ is expected. Absorption, E, is a sort of corrected national income — national income gross of foreign lending. If the domestic economy increases its imports of goods and services by borrowing abroad, expenditure increases because more can be consumed or invested than in the absence of foreign lending. Income or production remains unchanged, however. Since an increase in expenditures will be devoted partly to imports and partly to exportables, the net balance on current account will deteriorate with a rise in expenditures, and $C_e < 0$.

(7) Absorption is defined as total domestic expenditures:

$$E = X + G.$$

(8) The net balance of payments on capital account is determined by the rate of interest, the level of income, and the exchange rate:

$$K = K(R, Y, F)$$

where $K_r > 0$, $K_y > 0$, and $K_f < 0$.

THE PEGGED EXCHANGE-RATE CASE

If the exchange rate is pegged by official sales and purchases of foreign exchange (and zero margins are assumed) our system can be closed by adding the equation $dF = 0$.

The expenditure multipliers. The change in the equilibrium level of income resulting from changes in our predetermined policy variables is obtained by totally differentiating $Y = X(D, R) + G + C(E, F)$. Thus,

$$dY = \frac{(1 + C_e)[dG + X_r R_m dM]}{1 - (1 + C_e)X_d(1 - T_y) - (1 + C_e)X_r R_y}, \quad (A.1)$$

and the multipliers resulting from changes in government expenditures and the money stock are, respectively,

$$\frac{dY}{dG} = \frac{(1 + C_e)}{1 - (1 + C_e)X_d(1 - T_y) - (1 + C_e)X_r R_y} \quad (A.2)$$

and

$$\frac{dY}{dM} = \frac{(1 + C_e)X_rR_m}{1 - (1 + C_e)X_d(1 - T_y) - (1 + C_e)X_rR_y}. \quad (A.3)$$

The multipliers are positive if the denominator is positive, or

$$(1 + C_e)X_d(1 - T_y) + (1 + C_e)X_rR_y < 1.$$

The first term in this expression is the marginal propensity to spend on domestic goods and services. Since the marginal propensity to spend out of total income, $X_d(1 - T_y)$, is less than unity and the proposition of marginal expenditures devoted to domestic goods and services, $1 + C_e$, lies between zero and unity, the product of these two numbers is also less than unity. The second term is negative because it measures the reduction in expenditures on domestic goods and services resulting from the income-induced rise in the interest rate.

If we define a constant monetary policy in terms of an unchanged interest rate instead of an unchanged money stock, the government expenditure multiplier increases to

$$\frac{dY}{dG} = \frac{(1 + C_e)}{1 - (1 + C_e)X_d(1 - T_y)} \quad (A.4)$$

because the increase in the demand for money as income rises is met through increases in the stock of money rather than increases in the velocity of circulation. This may be seen most clearly by noting that $dR = 0$ when $dY > 0$ if

$$dM = -(R_y/R_m)dY > 0.$$

In other words, the money stock must be increased in proportion to the increase in income with the factor of proportionality being the incremental demand for money. This violates our assumption of a pure fiscal policy because the monetary authorities are effectively financing the increase in the government's budget deficit — monetary policy is automatically coordinated with fiscal policy.

If we return to the assumption that government expenditures are deficit-financed — that is, that $dM = 0$ when $dG > 0$ — expressions A.2 and A.3 indicate that, dollar for dollar, monetary policy has a larger impact on income than fiscal policy if $X_r R_m > 1$: a one-dollar increase in the money stock will, through its effect on the interest rate, induce an increase in the flow of private expenditures by more than one dollar.

Balance of payments implications. The net change in foreign-exchange reserves resulting from changes in the money stock and the flow of government expenditures is measured by

$$dC + dK = K_r R_m dM + \left[\frac{C_e}{1 + C_e} + K_r R_y + K_y \right]$$

$$\left[\frac{(1 + C_e)(dG + X_r R_m dM)}{1 - (1 + C_e)X_d(1 - T_y) - (1 + C_e)X_r R_y} \right]. \quad (A.5)$$

Thus an expansionary fiscal policy will improve the balance of payments while raising income if

$$\left[\frac{C_e}{1 + C_e} + K_r R_y + K_y \right] dG > 0$$

or

$$K_r R_y + K_y > -\frac{C_e}{1 + C_e}. \quad (A.6)$$

In other words, the responsiveness of the capital account to both the income-induced change in interest rates and the change in income itself must exceed the responsiveness of the current account to change in income (note that $-C_e/(1 + C_e) = -C_y$).

An expansionary monetary policy will improve the balance of payments while raising income if

$$K_y > -\left[\frac{C_e}{1 + C_e} \right] - \frac{K_r}{X_r} \left[\frac{1 - (1 + C_e)X_d(1 - T_y)}{1 + C_e} \right] \quad (A.7)$$

or, in words, if the improvement on capital account due to income-mobile flows exceeds the deterioration on current account induced by rising income plus the deterioration in capital account accompanying a unit increase in income brought about by lower interest rates. This latter effect varies directly with the interest sensitivity of capital flows and inversely with the interest sensitivity of private consumption and investment expenditures.

Clearly, monetary policy is more likely than fiscal policy to deteriorate the balance of payments while raising income. In the absence of endogenous capital flows, of course, both policies will deteriorate the balance of payments. Equation A.1 shows that income will increase if

$$dG + X_r R_m dM > 0,$$

while equation A.5 shows that the balance of payments will improve if

$$\left(\frac{C_c}{1 + C_e}\right)(dG + X_r R_m dM) > 0.$$

Thus, any policy or policy combination which raises the level of income must deteriorate the balance of payments via the income-induced deterioration in current account.

If capital movements do respond to changes in interest rates and the level of income, however, it is possible to discover policy combinations that will simultaneously raise the level of income and improve the balance of payments. Thus, equation A.5 indicates that the balance of payments will improve if

$$[dG + X_r R_m dM]\left[\frac{C_e}{1 + C_e} + K_r R_y + K_y\right]$$
$$+ K_r R_m dM\left[\frac{1 - (1 + C_e)X_d(1 - T_y) - (1 + C_e)X_r R_y}{1 + C_e}\right] > 0.$$
$$(A.8)$$

The first term in expression A.8 is positive if

$$K_r R_y + K_y > -\frac{C_e}{1 + C_e}.$$

The second expression will be positive if the policy combination used to increase income involves contractionary monetary policy ($dM < 0$). On the other hand, if capital flows are very sensitive to changes in interest rates and/or income, it is conceivable that a combination where monetary and fiscal policies are both expansionary will improve the balance of payments and simultaneously raise the level of income. We can go much further than this, however. With certain exceptions, endogenous capital flows permit the combination of monetary and fiscal policies to simultaneously attain any income target and any balance of payments goal.

Internal and external balance. In order to investigate more precisely the problem of discovering the correct policy combinations required to simultaneously achieve internal and external balance, it is useful to construct "iso-income" lines (the loci of all combinations of monetary and fiscal policies that will generate any given change in the level of income) and "iso-payments" lines (the loci of all policy combinations producing given changes in the balance of payments). The iso-income equation is derived by solving equation A.1 for dG in terms of dM and dY. This gives

$$dG = dY\Delta - X_r R_m dM \tag{A.9}$$

where Δ is the reciprocal of the autonomous expenditure multiplier. A family of iso-income lines is depicted in Figure A.1.

The iso-payments equation is similarly derived from equation A.5 by solving for dG in terms of dM and $(dC + dK)$. Thus

$$dG = (dC + dK)\left(\frac{\Delta}{\dfrac{C_e}{1 + C_e} + K_r R_y + K_y}\right)$$
$$- \left[X_r R_m + K_r R_m \left(\frac{\Delta}{\dfrac{C_e}{1 + C_e} + K_r R_y + K_y}\right)\right]. \tag{A.10}$$

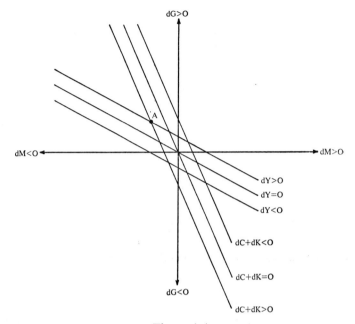

Figure A.1

Here we must distinguish among three cases. If interest-sensitive and income-sensitive capital flows are insufficient to finance the current-account deficit arising from a policy-induced expansion in income, that is, if

$$K_r R_y + K_y < -\frac{C_e}{1 + C_e},$$

the iso-payments line will have a negative intercept on the ordinate for positive changes in the balance of payments, and its slope will be negative and algebraically smaller than that of the iso-income line. A family of iso-payments lines for this case is superimposed upon Figure A.1, illustrating the typical textbook generalization that interest-sensitive capital flows permit us to obtain any desired increase in income and any desired improvement in the balance of

369

payments by using a policy combination involving easy fiscal policy and tight monetary policy (see point A in Figure A.1).

The textbook generalization is upset if

$$K_r R_y + K_y > -\frac{C_e}{1 + C_e}.$$

In this case, the slope of the iso-payments line may be positive or negative depending upon whether

$$-\left[X_r R_m + K_r R_m \left(\frac{\Delta}{\dfrac{C_e}{1 + C_e} + K_r R_y + K_y} \right) \right]$$

is greater than or less than zero. If this expression is positive, it can be rewritten as

$$K_r R_y + K_y < \frac{C_e}{1 + C_e} - \frac{K_r}{X_r} \Delta, \qquad (\text{A.11})$$

which, in words, states that fiscal policy improves the balance of payments while raising income, whereas monetary policy deteriorates the balance of payments while raising income. A family of iso-payments lines is depicted for this case in Figure A.2. It is clear that the simultaneous achievement of any given increase in income and any given improvement in the balance of payments may require a combination of easy fiscal and tight monetary policies or a combination where both policies are expansionary (see points A and B, respectively, in Figure A.2).

If inequality A.11 is reversed, then both fiscal and monetary policies will improve the balance of payments while raising income, and the slope of the iso-payments line will again be negative but algebraically larger than that of the iso-income line. Solution of the internal-external balance problem may now require a third type of policy combination — contractionary fiscal policy and expansionary monetary policy (see points A, B, and C in Figure A.3).

This analysis demonstrates that, although our two policy instruments can generally be combined so as to simultaneously secure any income and payments target, mere knowledge that capital movements are interest-elastic is insufficient to permit the a priori specification of the correct policy combination. There are, of course, limiting cases where it is impossible to solve the internal-external balance problem (even at our level of abstraction). Thus, if $K_r = 0$, the iso-income and iso-payments equations are linearly dependent and the iso-payments line coincides with the iso-income line. If K_y is also zero, or, at least, less than $-C_e/(1 + C_e)$, then any increase in the level of income is at the expense of the balance of payments and vice versa. If $K_r = 0$ and K_y exceeds $-C_e/(1 + C_e)$, then a combination of easy fiscal and tight monetary policies will raise income and improve the balance of payments; but we cannot achieve *any* two targets. We can have any desired increase in income and some payments improvement (which may be more or less than desired), or we can have any desired improvement in the balance of payments and some increase in income; but that is as far as we can go. These conclusions also hold if capital flows are interest-elastic, but a liquidity trap exists. Interest-elastic capital flows are irrelevant because the interest rate is pegged by expectations and fiscal policy is the only operative policy tool. In the case of a liquidity trap, the iso-income and iso-payments lines coincide and are parallel to the monetary policy axis.

Nonsterilization of foreign-exchange reserves. The expenditure multipliers derived above measure the potential effects of changes in the money supply and the flow of government expenditures upon the equilibrium level of income when the monetary base is insulated from changes in the stock of foreign exchange reserves by offsetting open market operations. If changes in foreign-exchange reserves are permitted to feed into the monetary base, the money supply will increase when the balance of payments improves and vice versa. In this case we can write

$$dM = dM^* + dC + dK$$

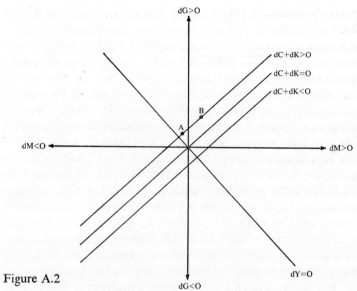

Figure A.2

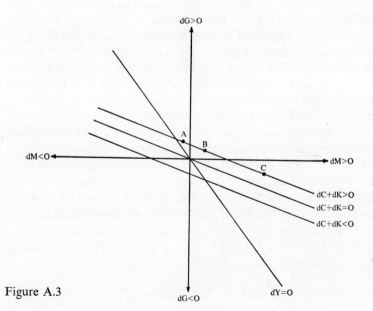

Figure A.3

where dM^* represents the initial open market operation and dM is the actual change in the money stock that materializes in the final equilibrium. It might be noted that the institutional fact of fractional reserve banking is irrelevant for our purposes. It has long been recognized that the mechanism of adjustment under the gold standard and other fixed exchange-rate systems did not require or even imply the necessity of a multiple change in the monetary circulation resulting from a net gold movement. The only essential part of the mechanism is that transfer of purchasing power which is equivalent in amount to the international payment that gives rise to it.

The substitution of $dM^* + dC + dK$ for dM in the totally differentiated income equation gives the following multiplier expressions:

$$\frac{dY}{dG} = \frac{1}{\dfrac{\dfrac{1}{1 + C_e} - X_d(1 - T_y) - X_r R_y - X_r R_m \left(\dfrac{C_e}{1 + C_e} + K_y\right)}{1 - K_r R_m}}$$

(A.12)

$$\frac{dY}{dM^*} = \frac{\dfrac{X_r R_m}{1 - K_r R_m}}{\dfrac{\dfrac{1}{1 + C_e} - X_d(1 - T_y) - X_r R_y - X_r R_m \left(\dfrac{C_e}{1 + C_e} + K_y\right)}{1 - K_r R_m}}$$

(A.13)

These expressions are easy to interpret. Looking first at the government expenditure multiplier, three interesting cases can be distinguished:

(1) If capital flows are completely unresponsive to changes in interest rates the multiplier becomes

$$\frac{dY}{dG} = \frac{1}{\dfrac{1}{1 + C_e} - X_d(1 - T_y) - X_r R_y - X_r R_m \left(\dfrac{C_e}{1 + C_e} + K_y\right)}$$

(where we are now dividing numerator and denominator by $1 + C_e$ to reduce clutter). If the income sensitivity of the capital account is equal to the income sensitivity of the current account, the fiscal multiplier has the same magnitude as the "sterilized" multiplier. On the other hand, if

$$K_y > \frac{-C_e}{1 + C_e},$$

fiscal policy improves the balance of payments while raising income, and the resulting monetary expansion curtails the income-induced rise in interest rates and hence the dampening effect upon private expenditures. The expenditure multiplier is therefore larger than in the case where the domestic money stock is completely insulated from changes in the reserve position.

(2) If capital flows are perfectly interest-mobile, the multiplier on government expenditures becomes

$$\frac{dY}{dG} = \frac{(1 + C_e)}{1 - (1 + C_e)X_d(1 - T_y)},$$

and this is clearly larger than the "sterilized" multiplier because the depressing effects of the income-induced rise in interest rates upon private expenditures are completely eliminated by the inflow of perfectly interest-mobile capital. In this case the demand for money as income rises is satisfied entirely by the creation of new money balances rather than an interest-rate-induced increase in the velocity of existing money balances. The multiplier is therefore identical to the sterilized multiplier which arises when a constant monetary policy is defined in terms of an unchanged rate of interest (see equation A.4).

(3) In the empirically relevant case where capital movements are somewhat interest-elastic, it is clear from a comparison of equations A.2 and A.12 that fiscal policy will be more effective when changes in foreign-exchange reserves are permitted to affect the money supply if

$$K_r R_y + K_y > \frac{-C_e}{1 + C_e}.$$

If this inequality holds, expansionary fiscal policy will be associated with a net improvement in the balance of payments, and the resulting monetary expansion will temper the interest-rate-induced reduction in the flow of private expenditures.

Looking now at the multiplier on monetary policy, three interesting cases can again be distinguished:

(1) If capital flows have zero interest elasticity, the sterilized and nonsterilized multipliers will have the same magnitude only if income-mobile capital flows exactly offset the income-induced deterioration on current account.

(2) In the limiting case of perfectly interest-elastic capital movements, the multiplier becomes

$$\frac{dY}{dM^*} = \frac{0}{1 - (1 + C_e)X_d(1 - T_y)} = 0$$

because the capital outflow prevents any net change in the rate of interest, and hence the flow of private expenditures and income, from taking place. Since the equilibrium rate of interest and level of income remain unchanged, we can infer that the money supply is also unchanged in the final equilibrium. In effect, the newly created money balances disappear through the capital account in exchange for foreign securities — a situation which can be sustained only so long as foreign exchange reserves hold out. In the absence of sterilization, each dollar of newly created money is destroyed as it is used to purchase an equivalent amount of foreign exchange to finance acquisitions of foreign securities.

Mundell argues that sterilization operations fail to work in the case of perfectly interest-elastic capital flows. Suppose that deficit-financed government expenditures increase. As income rises, the increased demand for money bids the interest rate upward as the private sector attempts to unload securities for money balances. The movement of the interest-rate differential in favor of Canada in-

375

duces foreigners to provide a market for the excess supply of Canadian securities, and the resulting capital inflow increases the stock of foreign exchange. If the monetary authorities sterilize the reserve buildup by selling securities on the open market at the same rate at which they are buying reserves, the increase in sales to residents places continued pressure on the interest rate and the capital inflow continues. The problem here is that product-market equilibrium requires an increase in income which, in turn, requires a larger money supply or a rise in the rate of interest. Sterilization prevents the money stock from increasing and the capital inflow pegs the interest rate. Something has to give. If foreign-exchange reserves are purchased at a rate sufficient to prevent currency appreciation, the money supply rises. If securities are sold at a rate sufficient to prevent a rise in the money supply, the capital inflow appreciates the currency. Reasoning along similar lines, the attempt to increase the money supply will be frustrated by a continuing capital outflow as the monetary authorities attempt to sterilize the foreign exchange loss through open market purchases of securities. Eventually, the stock of reserves is depleted and the initial increment in the money stock disappears.[2]

(3) In the case where interest sensitivity is positive, but less than infinite, a comparison of equations A.3 and A.13 shows that monetary policy will be more effective when changes in reserves are not sterilized if

$$K_y > -\left(\frac{C_e}{1 + C_e}\right) - \frac{K_r}{X_r}\left[\frac{1 - (1 + C_e)X_d(1 - T_y)}{1 + C_e}\right].$$

If this inequality holds, monetary policy will improve the balance of payments while raising income, and the actual increase in the money supply, dM, will exceed the initial policy increase of dM^*.

In summary, interest-elastic capital flows must reduce the relative effectiveness of monetary policy when changes in foreign-exchange reserves are not sterilized or are incompletely sterilized because of

2. Mundell, "Capital Mobility," p. 481.

the opposite interest-rate effects of expansionary monetary and deficit-financed fiscal policies. Dollar for dollar, monetary policy will have a larger impact on income than fiscal policy will have if

$$\frac{X_r R_m}{1 - K_r R_m} > 1, \tag{A.14}$$

but it is clear that this measure of relative effectiveness diminishes as K_r increases.

We now have two sets of multipliers, each of which may be compared with the floating exchange-rate multipliers to be developed in the next section. Since the monetary authorities are probably successful in partially isolating the money supply from changes in the foreign exchange position, the sterilized and nonsterilized multipliers can be used to provide minimum and maximum estimates of the relative effectiveness of monetary and fiscal policies under the two types of exchange-rate systems.

THE FLOATING EXCHANGE-RATE CASE

Under a floating exchange-rate system, the foreign currency price of the Canadian dollar will adjust to preserve overall balance of payments equilibrium. Since changes in reserves of gold and foreign exchange are not required to preserve external balance, the equation

$$dC + dK = 0$$

replaces the equation

$$dF = 0$$

used to close the model in the case of officially pegged exchange rates.

The expenditure multipliers. The change in the equilibrium level of income that results from changes in the policy variables, G and M, is again discovered by totally differentiating $Y = X(D, R) + G + C(E, F)$. Thus dY is equal to

$$\frac{(1 + SC_e)dG + [(1 + SC_e)X_r - (1 - S)K_r]R_m dM}{1 - (1 + SC_e)[X_d(1 - T_y) + X_r R_y] + (1 - S)(K_r R_y + K_y)}$$

(A.15)

where $S = \dfrac{K_f}{C_f + K_f}$. This term measures the effect of speculative or exchange-rate-sensitive capital flows upon domestic policy leverages, and it assumes a zero value if such behavior is absent.

In order to comprehend expression A.15 more fully, the multipliers prevailing in the absence of endogenous capital flows will first be examined. We will then assume that capital flows respond to changes in the interest rate, then to changes in income, and finally to changes in the exchange rate.

Case 1: $K_r = K_y = K_f = 0$

Monetary and fiscal policies will both have a larger impact on income when the exchange rate floats than when it is pegged, because as income rises, the income-induced deterioration on current account is offset by currency depreciation, export expansion, and import contraction. The expenditure multipliers operate without any foreign leakage and thereby attain a higher value than they would under an officially pegged exchange rate — indeed, the multipliers attain the same values they would have in a completely closed economy. Thus, in this special case where $K_r = K_y = K_f = 0$, expression A.15 collapses to

$$dY = \frac{dG + X_r R_m dM}{1 - X_d(1 - T_y) - X_r R_y}.$$

(A.16)

If this expression is compared with A.1, it is clear that the multipliers, dY/dG and dY/dM, are larger when the exchange rate floats as long as the marginal propensity to import is positive.[3] This conclusion is reinforced if, under pegged exchange rates, the money supply is reduced by the drainage of foreign-exchange reserves through the income-induced deterioration on current account. It is equally clear that floating exchange rates per se confer no special leverage on the effectiveness of one policy relative to the other; the effectiveness of each increases in the same proportion when the exchange rate floats. Finally, we might note that, as in the pegged rate case, monetary policy has a larger impact on income than fiscal policy has if $X_r R_m > 1$.

Case 2: $K_r > 0$, $K_y = K_f = 0$

Interest-sensitive capital flows reduce the effectiveness of fiscal policy under a floating exchange-rate regime. In the absence of credit creation, deficit-financed government expenditures imply net new issues of securities with a consequent rise in bond yields and fall in bond prices. The resulting inflow of interest-sensitive capital tends to stem the depreciation of the currency induced by rising imports. This permits the development of a net foreign leakage which offsets some of the effects of higher domestic expenditures on the level of income. The fiscal multiplier implied by equation A.15 when $K_r > 0$ is

$$\frac{dY}{dG} = \frac{1}{1 - X_d(1 - T_y) - X_r R_y + K_r R_y}. \qquad (A.17)$$

When this is compared with the multiplier prevailing under officially pegged rates (equation A.2), it is clear that fiscal policy remains more effective under a floating exchange-rate regime as long as

3. The expression $\dfrac{C_e}{1 + C_e} = -C_y$ is the marginal propensity to import if exports are unrelated to expenditure.

$$K_r R_y < -\frac{C_e}{1 + C_e};$$

or, the capital inflow induced by the rise in interest rates as income increases must be smaller than the deterioration on current account induced by the rise in expenditures. If this condition is met, a net depreciation in value of the domestic currency must take place in order to preserve equilibrium in the balance of payments. The net foreign leakage is therefore smaller than it would be under officially pegged rates where some reduction in foreign-exchange reserves would take place to finance that part of the current-account deficit not covered by capital inflows. Since the condition for fiscal policy to be more effective under a floating rate is the converse of the condition for its improving the balance of payments under pegged rates, it is clear that the relative effectiveness of fiscal policy is enhanced if changes in the stock of reserves are not or cannot be sterilized.

It is interesting to note that a nominally floating exchange rate may be effectively pegged by offsetting movements in the current and capital accounts. In this case, fiscal policy will have the same impact on income under a floating rate as it would have under an officially pegged rate. The sterilization issue is irrelevant here, of course. Further increases in the interest sensitivity of the capital account render fiscal policy less effective under floating than under pegged rates because preservation of payments equilibrium then necessitates a net appreciation of the currency. The resulting expenditure leakage through the current account will exceed that which would take place under a system of officially pegged rates because, in the latter case, the leakage will be restricted to the income effect — price effects are absent. If the increase in reserves that would result under pegged rates is permitted to expand the money supply, fiscal policy will be even more effective under that system because the negative effect of the income-induced rise in interest rates upon the flow of private expenditures will be mitigated by monetary expansion. It should be pointed out that, in the case of incomplete sterilization under officially pegged rates, we are no longer comparing the effectiveness of identical policies, but rather the effectiveness of a deficit-financed policy with one that is, in effect, partly financed by credit creation.

In the limiting case of perfectly interest-sensitive capital movements, fiscal policy will be totally ineffective under a floating exchange-rate regime. An increase in income requires either an increase in the money supply or a rise in the interest rate to induce more economic utilization of the existing stock of money. The perfectly interest-mobile capital flow prevents the rate of interest from rising, while the attempts of capital importers to exchange the foreign currency proceeds of their security sales abroad for domestic balances merely appreciates the currency until the deficit on current account completely offsets the budgetary deficit. In equilibrium, the interest rate, the money stock, and the level of income are all unchanged — the public sector has simply enlarged itself at the expense of the private sector.

Interest-sensitive capital flows increase the effectiveness of monetary policy under a floating exchange-rate system. An expansionary monetary policy creates an excess demand for income-earning assets and the rate of interest falls. The reduction in the capital inflow complements the expenditure-induced currency depreciation operating through the current account, thus providing an additional source of expenditures on domestically produced goods and services. Monetary policy therefore affects the level of income through two channels: (1) directly, by changing the price and quantity of money, and hence the volume of domestic expenditures, and (2) indirectly, by changing the supply of foreign capital, the exchange rate, and hence the volume of foreign expenditures flowing through the current account. Since the indirect channel is closed under officially pegged exchange rates, monetary policy will always be more powerful when the exchange rate floats. To prove this rigorously, note that the money stock multiplier implied by equation A.15 when $K_r > 0$,

$$\frac{dY}{dM} = \frac{X_r R_m - K_r R_m}{1 - X_d(1 - T_y) - X_r R_y + K_r R_y}, \quad (A.18)$$

is larger than the multiplier prevailing under pegged rates (equation A.3) if

$$\frac{K_r}{X_r}\left[\frac{1 - (1 + C_e)X_d(1 - T_y)}{(1 + C_e)}\right] + \frac{C_e}{1 + C_e} < 0.$$

Because both terms in this expression are negative, it can be concluded that monetary policy will always be more effective when the exchange rate floats because it will require a net depreciation in the value of the currency to preserve equilibrium in the balance of payments. A comparison of the inequality above with A.7 again demonstrates that if a policy is more effective under a floating exchange rate, it will lead to a loss of exchange reserves when the rate is officially pegged. Alternatively, if a policy depreciates a floating exchange rate net, it will lead to reserve losses under an officially pegged rate. This conclusion rests upon the assumption that adoption of a floating exchange rate will not significantly alter the values of the parameters of the model.

The proportion of the total effect of monetary policy flowing through the indirect channel varies directly with the interest sensitivity of the capital account. In the limiting case where capital flows are perfectly interest-mobile, foreign purchasers stand willing to buy all Canadian securities offered at the prevailing price and yield differentials disappear. In this case the total effect of monetary policy is indirect. An expansionary policy will induce capital outflows at a rate sufficient to prevent any net fall in the rate of interest from taking place. The flow of private expenditures is not directly stimulated. The outflow of interest-arbitrage capital will, however, depreciate the currency and improve the balance of payments on current account. The first round of the multiplier will then operate on the increase in expenditures on import-competitive goods and Canadian exports. Since the interest rate remains unchanged in equilibrium, it is clear that the level of income will rise in proportion to the increase in the money supply, with the factor of proportionality being the incremental velocity of circulation. Thus

$$\lim_{K_r \to \infty} \frac{dY}{dM} = \lim_{K_r \to \infty} \left[\frac{X_r R_m - K_r R_m}{1 - X_d(1 - T_y) - X_r R_y + K_r R_y} \right]$$

$$= -\frac{K_r R_m}{K_r R_y} = -\frac{R_m}{R_y} = \frac{dY}{dM}$$

where $dR = 0$. The predictions of the classical quantity theory are realized in a world of floating exchange rates and perfectly interest-mobile capital flows.

We have demonstrated that interest-sensitive capital flows always increase the relative effectiveness of monetary policy under a floating exchange rate. On the other hand, the relative effectiveness of fiscal policy under a floating rate decreases with the interest sensitivity of the capital account. Although fiscal policy may remain more effective under a floating exchange rate, it is clear that the effectiveness of monetary relative to fiscal policy will be greater under a floating than under a pegged rate system as long as international capital flows are somewhat responsive to interest-rate differentials. This statement is proved if the relative effectiveness of monetary policy under a floating exchange rate, $X_r R_m$, exceeds the relative effectiveness of monetary policy under an officially pegged system, $X_r R_m$. Clearly, $X_r R_m - K_r R_m > X_r R_m$ if $K_r > 0$. An empirical measure of the relative advantage of monetary policy is provided by the ratio $-K_r/X_r$. If $K_r = 0$, for example, the ratio is equal to zero, and this means that the impact of monetary relative to fiscal policy is no greater under a floating exchange-rate than under an officially pegged rate system. The absolute effectiveness of both policies will, of course, be greater under the floating rate system. On the other hand, if the responsiveness of the capital account to changes in the interest rate is numerically equal to the interest sensitivity of private expenditures, the ratio would be equal to unity — monetary policy would be 100 percent more effective, relative to fiscal policy, when the rate floats than when it is pegged. The economic interpretation of this is that the increase in the flow of expenditures induced by an increase in the money stock will be twice as large when the rate floats, because the increase in the flow of domestic expenditures induced by the fall in interest rates is matched by an equal increase in the flow of foreign expenditures through the current account (equal to the interest-rate-induced reduction in the net capital inflow). Under pegged rates, the second source of new spending is absent because price effects are eliminated by official maintenance of the exchange rate. These conclusions are reinforced if changes in reserves are not or cannot be fully sterilized when the exchange rate is pegged. Indeed, all of our measures of relative effectiveness are conservative estimates because they are based upon comparisons of the floating rate multipliers with the ones that would prevail under pegged rates in the case where the money supply is completely insulated from changes in foreign-exchange reserves by offsetting open market operations.

Case 3: $K_r > 0, K_y > 0, K_f = 0$

If components of the capital account are responsive to changes in the level of income,[4] this response will reduce the effectiveness of both monetary and fiscal policies under a floating exchange rate

4. A positive response of capital flows to changes in Canadian income can be expected on several grounds. In our empirical work, we discovered that direct capital inflows were significantly related to income movements and argued that income probably served as a proxy for profit expectations. A positive response is also consistent with Malach's relative cycle hypothesis, which argues that the current account deteriorates and the capital account improves when domestic expansion exceeds foreign expansion. The capital exporter's cycle hypothesis, on the other hand, argues that a rapid expansion in the United States will be associated with an expanding supply of capital and hence with a capital export. If Canadian investment expenditures rise pari passu with capital imports, the current account deteriorates because of the high import content of these expenditures; see Paul Wonnacott, *The Canadian Dollar: 1948–1962* (Toronto: University of Toronto Press, 1965), pp. 127–150. Although independent movements in Canadian income are unlikely to have much effect on U.S. income, movements in U.S. income will affect Canadian income. A positive sign for K_y is therefore clearly inadequate to disentangle the theories, but the ultimate results will be the same — the current account deteriorates because of the rise in income; the income-induced capital flow appreciates the currency, leading to further deterioration of the current account.

by curtailing the currency depreciation induced by the tendency of the current account to deteriorate as income rises. The multiplier on government expenditures implied by equation A.15 when $K_y > 0$ is

$$\frac{dY}{dG} = \frac{1}{1 - X_d(1 - T_y) - X_r R_y + K_r R_y + K_y}, \quad (A.19)$$

and, following the procedure of the previous section, it is clear that fiscal policy will remain more effective under a floating exchange rate as long as

$$K_r R_y + K_y < -\frac{C_e}{1 + C_e}. \quad (A.20)$$

If this condition is not met, the tendency for the capital account to improve will exceed the tendency for the current account to deteriorate, and a net appreciation in the value of the currency will take place to preserve equilibrium in the balance of payments. Net foreign leakage will therefore be greater under a floating than under an officially pegged rate and the multiplier will be correspondingly reduced.

Similarly, as monetary policy stimulates expenditure and income under a floating exchange rate, income-sensitive capital flows will counter the currency depreciation induced by capital outflows on interest-arbitrage account and the income-induced deterioration on current account. The money-stock multiplier implied by equation A.15,

$$\frac{dY}{dM} = \frac{X_r R_m - K_r R_m}{1 - X_d(1 - T_y) - X_r R_y + K_r R_y + K_y}, \quad (A.21)$$

remains larger than the multiplier that would prevail under an officially pegged rate as long as

$$K_y < \frac{-C_e}{1 + C_e} - \frac{K_r}{X_r}\left[\frac{1 - (1 + C_e)X_d(1 - T_y)}{1 + C_e}\right]. \quad \text{(A.22)}$$

If this condition is not met, the income-induced capital inflow will exceed the interest-rate-induced capital inflow plus the income-induced deterioration on current account and the currency will on balance appreciate. Income-mobile capital flows therefore open the possibility that monetary policy may induce a larger net foreign leakage under a floating than under an officially pegged exchange rate. Our previous conclusion that monetary policy is *always* more effective when the exchange rate floats is destroyed.

In the limiting case of perfect income mobility, the slightest tendency for income to rise in response to either an increase in the money stock or an increase in the flow of public expenditures will evoke a capital inflow large enough to completely offset the increased flow of private or public expenditures by appreciating the currency and producing an equivalent adverse shift in the net balance on current account. There can be no permanent rise in the level of income. If there were, the result in capital inflow would lead to continuous currency appreciation and current-account deterioration until income returned to its initial level. This solution is proved by noting that K_y appears in the denominators, but not the numerators, of the expenditure multipliers. Thus, referring to equations A.19 and A.21,

$$\lim_{K_y \to \infty} \frac{dY}{dG} = \lim_{K_y \to \infty} \frac{dY}{dM} = 0.$$

Although the presence of income-sensitive capital movements implies that we can expect less from monetary and fiscal policies when the exchange rate floats than would be the case if this type of capital-account response were absent, income-mobile flows do not affect the relative leverage of one policy with respect to another. Referring again to equations A.19 and A.21, it is clear that monetary policy will continue to have a larger impact on income than fiscal policy has if

$$X_r R_m - K_r R_m > 1.$$

It also remains true that the effectiveness of monetary policy relative to fiscal policy is greater when the exchange rate floats than when it is pegged, provided that capital flows are interest-elastic.

Case 4: $K_r > 0, K_y > 0, K_f < 0$

Exchange-rate movements leave the capital account unchanged only in the special case where expectations about future exchange-rate movements are unit-elastic. In this case, actual and expected future rates change in the same proportion — a current movement in the rate is expected to be a once-and-for-all or permanent alteration in the price of the currency, and capital flows should remain completely unaffected because expected exchange profit or loss is nil. If exchange-rate expectations are elastic, a current appreciation in the value of the Canadian dollar will increase the relative value of future proceeds expected by lenders and decrease the cost of debt servicing expected by borrowers. Speculative capital inflows therefore increase to take advantage of the expected exchange profit; in so doing they accentuate movements in the rate, making the expectations more or less self-fulfilling. If exchange-rate expectations are inelastic, on the other hand, a current appreciation in currency value will decrease the relative value of proceeds expected by lenders, and speculative capital inflows will decrease in order to avoid the expected exchange loss when Canadian dollar investments are repatriated. Expectations are again self-fulfilling because the reduction in capital inflow on speculative account speeds the return of the currency toward its previous value. In summary, a change in the exchange rate will affect the net capital inflow (1) negatively when exchange-rate expectations are inelastic, (2) positively when exchange-rate expectations are elastic, and (3) not at all when expectations are unit-elastic.

The empirical evidence presented in Chapter 2 supports the hypothesis that speculative capital movements were stabilizing — net capital inflows were negatively related to changes in price of the Canadian dollar during the floating exchange-rate period. This type of behavior reduces the leverage of monetary relative to fiscal policy when the exchange rate floats. Thus, an expansionary monetary policy will induce a capital outflow on interest-arbitrage account which depreciates the currency and improves the balance of payments on current account. The greater the interest-elasticity of capital flows, the greater the fall in the value of the currency and improvement in the current account. In the case where interest elasticity is infinite, the total effect of monetary policy is indirect and the money-stock multiplier attains its maximum value because none of the newly created money balances are absorbed into private asset holdings. With inelastic exchange-rate expectations, however, speculators will believe that the currency is "undervalued" and that a return toward its previous value is imminent. They will speed the return of the dollar toward its previous value by moving into Canadian dollar assets in order to take advantage of the exchange profit when the expected appreciation takes place. Thus the currency depreciation induced by the downward pressure of lower interest rates on capital inflows itself tends to stay the reduction of the inflows. By stabilizing the exchange rate, inelastic expectations block the indirect route through which monetary policy gains its greater effectiveness under floating rates. Indeed, in the limiting case of perfectly inelastic exchange-rate expectations, the exchange rate will be pegged by stabilizing capital flows on speculative account and the total effect of monetary policy will be direct. The money stock multiplier will be no larger under the nominally floating exchange rate than it would be under an officially pegged rate system because the foreign leakage induced by the rise in income will not be eliminated by currency depreciation. These conclusions are proved by noting that the money stock multiplier implied by equation A.15 when $K_f < 0$, dY/dM is equal to

$$\frac{(1 + SC_e)X_rR_m - (1 - S)K_rR_m}{1 - (1 + SC_e)[X_d(1 - T_y) + X_rR_y] + (1 - S)(K_rR_y + K_y)}$$

$$(A.23)$$

is larger than the multiplier prevailing under an officially pegged rate if $K_f > -\infty$. In the limiting case of perfectly stabilizing capital movements,

$$\lim_{K_f \to -\infty} S = \lim_{K_f \to -\infty} \frac{K_f}{C_f + K_f} = 1$$

and the money stock multiplier becomes

$$\frac{dY}{dM} = \frac{(1 + C_e)X_r R_m}{1 - (1 + C_e)[X_d(1 - T_y) + X_r R_y]},$$

which is identical to the multiplier prevailing under pegged rates.

The effect of stabilizing capital flows on the leverage of fiscal policy under a floating exchange rate cannot be ascertained on a priori grounds alone. If it is discovered empirically that

$$K_r R_y + K_y < \frac{C_e}{1 + C_e},$$

then fiscal policy will be more powerful under a floating rate because currency depreciation will eliminate some of the foreign leakage induced by income expansion. But the tendency for the currency to depreciate net will be countered by inward capital movements on speculative account, and the leverage of fiscal policy will be correspondingly reduced. On the other hand, if capital inflows on interest-arbitrage and income accounts are sufficiently large to more than offset the tendency for currency to depreciate as income rises, the resulting expenditure leakage through the current account renders the policy less effective than it would be under officially maintained rates. By bucking the tendency for the exchange rate to appreciate, capital outflows on speculative account will in this case increase the leverage of fiscal policy. In the limiting case of perfectly stabilizing capital flows, the multiplier implied by equation A.15,

$$\frac{dY}{dG} = \frac{(1 + SC_e)}{1 - (1 + SC_e)[X_d(1 - T_y) + X_r R_y] + (1 - S)(K_r R_y + K_y)}$$

(A.24)

rises to the value it would have under a system of officially pegged exchange rates,

$$\frac{dY}{dG} = \frac{(1 + C_e)}{1 - (1 + C_e)[X_d(1 - T_y) + X_r R_y]}.$$

To conclude, the leverage of any income-increasing policy or combination of policies that would be larger under a floating exchange rate in the absence of exchange-rate-stabilizing capital flows will be reduced when these flows are in fact present. We can further conclude that the leverage of monetary policy will fall relative to that of fiscal policy when speculative capital flows are stabilizing. The increased effectiveness given by a floating rate to monetary relative to fiscal policy when capital flows are interest-mobile is due to the stronger influence exercised by monetary policy upon the exchange rate. Even if a net depreciation of the currency is required to balance the external accounts when fiscal policy is used to expand income, the key point is that an expansionary monetary policy will require a deeper depreciation to equilibrate the balance of payments because the current and capital accounts both move in the same direction — both tend to deteriorate. By limiting or eliminating the fluctuations in exchange rate upon which the greater relative effectiveness of monetary policy depends, exchange-rate-stabilizing capital movements reduce the effectiveness of monetary policy relative to fiscal policy. To prove this we note from equations A.23 and A.24 that the effectiveness of monetary relative to fiscal policy is given by

$$X_r R_m - \left[\frac{1 - S}{1 + SC_e}\right] K_r R_m.$$

Although we can say nothing about the size of this ratio a priori, it is clear that interest-sensitive capital flows increase it while exchange-rate-sensitive capital flows decrease it. The latter point can be seen more clearly if S is expressed in terms of C_f and K_f. Because

$$S = \frac{K_f}{C_f + K_f}$$

we can re-express the measure of relative effectiveness of monetary policy as

$$X_r R_m - \left[\frac{C_f}{C_f + K_f(1 + C_e)} \right] K_r R_m. \qquad \text{(A.25)}$$

Since the three parameters, C_f, K_f and C_e, are all theoretically negative, the ratio

$$\frac{C_f}{C_f + K_f(1 + C_e)}$$

will be a positive number which can assume values between zero and unity. If speculative flows are absent, $K_f = 0$ and the relative effectiveness of monetary policy is measured as $X_r R_m - K_r R_m$. In the limiting case of perfectly stabilizing capital flows, the relative effectiveness of monetary policy falls to $X_r R_m$, which is identical to the estimate obtained for the pegged rate case. Of course, monetary policy remains relatively more effective under a floating than under a pegged rate when changes in foreign-exchange reserves under the latter system are allowed to affect the size of the monetary base. The reason for this is that the interest rate effects of expansionary monetary and fiscal policies run in opposite directions so that fiscal policy will always be accompanied by a greater increase (or smaller decrease) in reserves than will monetary policy. The relative effectiveness of monetary policy under a floating rate that is pegged by stabilizing capital flows is measured by the ratio

$$\frac{X_r R_m}{\dfrac{X_r R_m}{1 - K_r R_m}} = 1 - K_r R_m,$$

which exceeds unity if capital flows are somewhat interest-elastic. The increase in relative effectiveness of monetary policy under a floating rate arises in this case solely from the different monetary effects that the two policies have under an officially pegged rate.

The main conclusions reached above can be recapitulated as follows.

1. When capital flows are not responsive to changes in domestic variables, both monetary and fiscal policies are more effective when the exchange rate floats because the currency will depreciate until foreign leakage is eliminated.

2. Interest-sensitive capital flows lead to a deeper currency depreciation under floating rates and a greater reserve drain under officially pegged rates when monetary policy is used to raise income than when fiscal policy is employed. The increase in the flow of foreign expenditures through the current account raises the relative effectiveness of monetary policy from $X_r R_m$ under officially pegged rates to $X_r R_m - K_r R_m$ when the rate floats. If the relatively larger reserve drain induced by an expansionary monetary policy is permitted to feed back into the monetary base, the effectiveness of monetary relative to fiscal policy is further reduced under an officially pegged exchange rate regime to

$$\frac{X_r R_m}{1 - K_r R_m}.$$

Although interest-sensitive capital flows increase the effectiveness of monetary policy under a floating rate because of greater improvement in the current account and reduce it under an officially pegged rate if changes in reserves are not sterilized, it cannot be concluded that monetary policy will be absolutely more effective than fiscal policy when the rate floats or absolutely less effective when the rate is pegged. This is an empirical rather than a theoretical question.

3. Fiscal policy will be most effective under a floating exchange-rate system if the net inflow of capital induced by the rise in interest rates accompanying a unit increase in income is less than the deterioration on current account induced by a unit increase in income, because the currency must then depreciate net to eliminate that part of the foreign leakage not covered by the capital inflow. Under a pegged rate, foreign-exchange reserves would be expanded to finance the portion of the current-account deficit not covered by capital inflows, and the larger foreign leakage would remain to reduce the multiplier. On the other hand, if

$$K_r R_y > \frac{C_e}{1 + C_e},$$

the currency will appreciate net and the multiplier will operate with a larger foreign leakage than under an officially pegged rate.

4. The counterpart of a policy-induced appreciation in the value of currency under a floating exchange rate is an influx of foreign-exchange reserves when the rate is officially pegged. If induced changes in foreign-exchange reserves are not sterilized by offsetting open market operations, then expansionary monetary and fiscal policies will have secondary monetary effects which alter the degree but not the direction of our conclusions. In the limiting case of perfect interest mobility, four polar cases can be distinguished. Fiscal policy will be totally ineffective under a floating exchange rate because the currency will appreciate to the point where the resulting deficit on current account just offsets the increased flow of government expenditures. The net addition to the expenditure stream therefore disappears and income reverts to its initial level. This conclusion is reversed for monetary policy which attains maximum effectiveness because, at an unchanged rate of interest, the total increment in money balances is utilized to transact increased expenditures on goods and services — none of the increment is absorbed into idle cash holdings. These conclusions are exactly

393

reversed when the exchange rate is officially pegged. Fiscal policy now attains maximum effectiveness because the rise in income is financed by monetary expansion rather than by an interest-rate induced increase in the circulation velocity of the existing money supply — private expenditures are therefore not reduced by rising interest rates. Monetary policy now becomes totally ineffective because initial injections of new money are destroyed as capital exporters purchase foreign exchange to finance purchases of foreign securities. Continuous credit creation is required to produce a given increment in the money stock, and the policy is sustainable only so long as foreign exchange reserves hold out; ultimately, the stock of reserves is eliminated, the increase in the money stock disappears, and income reverts to its initial level.

5. Income-sensitive capital flows reduce the effectiveness of both policies when the exchange rate floats by curtailing the tendency for the currency to depreciate as imports increase and outflows of capital on interest-arbitrage account take place. Monetary and fiscal policies remain more effective under a floating rate if

$$K_y < -\frac{K_r}{X_r}\left[\frac{1 - (1 + C_e)X_d(1 - T_y)}{1 + C_e}\right] - \frac{C_e}{1 + C_e}$$

and

$$K_r R_y + K_y < \frac{-C_e}{1 + C_e},$$

respectively. When these conditions are not met, expansionary monetary and fiscal policies will be accompanied by net appreciation in currency value, and the resulting foreign leakage will exceed that which is induced by income effects alone under officially pegged rates. Income-sensitive capital flows complement the effects of interest-sensitive flows in reducing the leverage of fiscal policy; in the limiting case of perfect income mobility, fiscal policy will be rendered totally ineffective for the reasons outlined above. Monetary policy, too, becomes totally ineffective when capital flows are perfectly income-mobile, because as long as income is above its initial level, the currency will appreciate and the current account will deteriorate until the net foreign leakage offsets the net increase in the flow of private expenditures induced by the interest-rate reduction. Income therefore reverts to its initial level, and the increase in the money supply disappears into idle cash holdings — the velocity of circulation declines by the same proportion that the money stock is increased.

6. The condition for an income-raising policy or policy combination to be more effective under a floating exchange rate is that it leads to a net depreciation in the value of the currency, and hence to a smaller foreign leakage than would result under an officially pegged rate. By curtailing the tendency for the currency to depreciate, exchange-rate-stabilizing capital flows will permit the development of a larger foreign leakage than otherwise, and the multipliers will be correspondingly reduced. In the limiting case of perfectly stabilizing capital flows, the multipliers will fall to the values that would prevail under officially pegged rates. Conversely, if monetary and/or fiscal policies are less effective under floating rates because of relatively high interest and income sensitivities in the capital account, exchange-rate-sensitive capital flows will raise the effectiveness of the policies, at most, to levels that would prevail under a rate pegged by official sales and purchases of foreign exchange.

The relative effectiveness of monetary to fiscal policy is greater under floating than under officially pegged rates because a relatively deeper currency depreciation is required to balance the external accounts when monetary policy is used to raise income. By limiting exchange-rate fluctuations, speculative capital flows curtail the relative advantage that interest-sensitive capital flows give monetary policy. We can therefore conclude that, regardless of whether speculative capital flows increase or decrease the absolute leverages of monetary and fiscal policies under a floating exchange rate, they will always reduce the leverage of monetary policy relative to fiscal policy, measured by

$$X_r R_m - \left[\frac{C_f}{C_f + K_f(1 + C_e)} \right] K_r R_m.$$

If the exchange rate is pegged by perfectly stabilizing capital flows, the relative effectiveness of monetary to fiscal policy is no greater under floating than under officially pegged rates — namely, $X_r R_m$.

Again, the qualification must be added that secondary monetary effects are absent under floating exchange rates when movements in the exchange rate alone are relied upon to balance the external accounts, whereas secondary monetary effects will be present when the exchange rate is officially pegged and changes in reserves are not sterilized. In the latter case, monetary policy will remain relatively more effective under a floating rate pegged by speculative capital flows than under a rate pegged by official sales and purchases of foreign exchange because it will induce a larger decrease (or smaller increase) in reserves than will fiscal policy. Thus

$$\frac{\left[\dfrac{dY}{dM} \Big/ \dfrac{dY}{dG}\right] dF \neq 0}{\left[\dfrac{dY}{dM} \Big/ \dfrac{dY}{dG}\right] dF = 0} = \frac{X_r R_m - \left[\dfrac{C_f}{C_f + K_f(1 + C_e)}\right] K_r R_m}{\dfrac{X_r R_m}{1 - K_r R_m}}$$

exceeds unity in the limiting case of perfectly exchange-rate-sensitive capital flows ($K_f = -\infty$) provided that some components of the capital account are interest-sensitive.

Appendix B   Methods Employed to Investigate Lag Patterns

The simple correlation procedure employed to derive the estimates presented in Chapter 6 is subject to a number of well-known statistical limitations that need not be listed here. Moreover, the procedure implies discrete rather than distributed lags, and no allowance can be made for seasonality.

In trying to circumvent some of these limitations, extensive experiments were made employing distributed lag formulations. Seasonality was allowed for by including quarterly dummy variables, Q_i, in the relationships. In these experiments linear equations of the following form were fitted by ordinary least-squares to data from the last quarter of 1951 to the end of the first quarter 1962.

1. $y_0 = f_1(x_{-7}, x_{-6} \ldots x_{+6}, x_{+7}, Q_i)$

This form is a modified version of the distributed lag formulation used by M. Friedman and D. Meiselman in their study for the United States Commission on Money and Credit.[1] These equations were fitted using a step-wise regression program which included variables in the equation in order of their degree of statistical significance. In applying this procedure, the hope was that the order

1. "The Relative Stability of Monetary Velocity and the Investment Multiplier in the United States, 1887–1957," *Stabilization Policies: A Series of Research Papers Prepared for the Commission on Money and Credit* (Englewood Cliffs, N.J.: Prentice-Hall, 1963), pp. 209–213.

397

in which the independent variables entered the equation would indicate the nature of the lag structure. High multicollinearity between successive values of the independent variables seriously impairs the reliability of this approach.

2. $y_0 = f_2(x_0, y_{-1}, y_{-2}, y_{-3}, Q_i)$

This equation follows the formulation developed by L. M. Koyck and extended by R. M. Solow.[2] Koyck's formulation, which includes only one lagged value of the dependent variable, avoids the problem of multicollinearity but gives rise to the problem of autocorrelated error terms which result in biased estimates of the parameters and make the normal tests of randomness in the residuals inconclusive. In addition, Koyck's formulation imposes a geometric sequence of weights on the lag structure being estimated. Also, the formulation assumes that the initial impact of x on y occurs in the current period. Solow's formulation avoids assuming the form of the lag structure by including additional lagged values of the dependent variable. One cost of doing this is the reintroduction of multicollinearity. Although Solow's formulation was used in our tests, the estimates derived indicate that if one eliminates those lagged variables with regression coefficients less than twice their standard errors, one almost always ends up with a Koyck-type distributed lag.

3. $y_0 = f_3(x_i, y_{-1}, y_{-2}, y_{-3}, Q_i)$,

where x_i is preselected on the basis of the highest $r(x_i, y_0)$.

This form relaxes the assumption that the current value of x should be related to the current value of y by allowing lagged values of x to be related to current values of y.

4. $y_0 = f_4(x_0, x_{-1}, x_{-2}, x_{-3}, Q_i)$.

2. L. M. Koyck, *Distributed Lags and Investment Analysis,* Contributions to Economic Analysis, no. 4 (Amsterdam: North Holland Publishing Co., 1954); Robert M. Solow, "On a Family of Lag Distributions," *Econometrica,* XXVIII (April, 1960), 393–406.

As with the first approach outlined above, this procedure runs into a serious problem of multicollinearity between successive values of the independent variable.

5. $y_0 = f_5(\hat{y}_{-1}, x_0, Q_i)$,

where $\hat{y}_0$, the estimated value of y, is derived from $y_0 = f_0(x_0, x_{-1}, x_{-2}, x_{-3})$.

This procedure has been suggested as a way of overcoming the problem of autocorrelated error terms that impair estimates based on a Koyck-type distributed lag.[3]

6. A number of equations were estimated using two-stage least-squares to try to circumvent the problem of simultaneous relations between current- and capital-account variables. Koyck-type lag structures were included in these two-stage least-squares estimates. In addition, in some experiments lagged values of the explanatory variables were included in place of lagged values of the dependent variables.

As mentioned in Chapter 6, the evidence on lag structures obtained by applying the foregoing methods, while generally consistent with the evidence presented there and supplementing this evidence in a number of respects, did not add materially to the information about lag structures obtained by applying the simple correlation procedure outlined in Chapter 6.

3. N. Liviatan, "Consistent Estimation of Distributed Lags," *International Economic Review*, IV (January, 1963), 44–52.

Appendix C Dynamic Multipliers
Derived from Officer's Quarterly Model
of the Canadian Economy*

To provide a basis for estimating the dynamic response of the Canadian economy to disturbances associated with international capital flows, we computed the dynamic multipliers for the Canadian economy implied by Lawrence H. Officer's econometric model, the most complete one available when this project was begun. The estimation procedure and subsequent analysis is similar to that presented by A. S. Goldberger in *Impact Multipliers and Dynamic Properties of the Klein-Goldberger Model.*[1] The process used was an iterative one: impact multipliers were applied to initial (arbitrary) changes assumed in a selected group of exogenous variables (for example, a change in government purchases of goods and services of one million dollars). Successive application of the reduced form (impact multipliers) of the model gives the changes in all endogenous variables for the desired number of subsequent periods.

The changes in all endogenous variables of the system can easily be calculated for the first period from the reduced form given by

* This appendix was prepared by Mr. Peter K. Clark, Harvard University.
1. Contributions to Economic Analysis, no. 19 (Amsterdam: North-Holland Publishing Co., 1959).

400

Officer.[2] Rather than explore the dynamic variation of all endogenous variables in the model, we confined our attention to such interesting ones as real GNP, money GNP, and 14 others, plus all those that appear lagged in the predetermined set. Transformation of them becomes the "exogenous" disturbance for the second period,[3] and the change in the endogenous set for the second period is then determined. We continued this process through a total of 24 periods; since a quarterly model was used, this corresponds to predicting the dynamic behavior of the system over a period of six years.

As an illustration of this calculation, suppose that π is the reduced form of the econometric model. Then, by changing a policy variable (such as government expenditure), we determine the changes in those endogenous variables that interest us directly or that appear lagged. Call this vector of changes y_1^i.[4] We now form the matrix A from π by striking out all the rows corresponding to endogenous variables that are of no interest, and all the columns corresponding to predetermined variables that are truly exogenous and contain no lagged endogenous variables. All the changes in these variables are assumed to equal zero; therefore, any column of $\pi.0 = 0$, and these columns do not contribute to the analysis. Now suppose that other predetermined variables include lagged endogenous variables and can be written as linear transformations of these and other exogenous variables. Changes in them will be linear combinations of changes in the lagged endogenous variables only.[5] If we call this transformation T, then $y_2^i = AT y_1^i$ where A is nxm, and T is mxn. In general,

2. Lawrence H. Officer, *An Econometric Model of Canada under the Fluctuating Exchange Rate* (Cambridge, Mass.: Harvard University Press, 1968), chap. iv.

3. Note that only variables with one-period lags appear in the predetermined set for the second period; those with two-period lags appear initially only in the third round.

4. *i* means "due to unit change in policy variable *i*."

5. This is for the case of single lags only. In the case of multiple lags, the formula for y_k^i is much more complicated but still linear in the same sense.

401

$$y_k{}^i = (AT)^{k-1}y_1{}^i,$$

and it is easily shown that $y_n{}^i$ is linear in the sense that multiplying the change in policy variable i by a constant multiplies $y_n{}^i$ by the same constant; if

$$y_n{}^i = (AT)^{n-1}y_1{}^i \quad \text{and} \quad y_n{}^j = (AT)^{n-1}y_1{}^j,$$

then changing both policy variables i and j at the same time results in changes $y_n{}^i + y_n{}^j$.

The procedure used to obtain dynamic multipliers from Officer's econometric model is identical with the above, except that two-period lags are sometimes used and the transformation (T) is not linear. $y_n{}^i$ is now not linear in either of the ways defined above; a change of government expenditure of \$10 million will not have ten times the effect of a \$1-million change. Also note that the changes are not independent of the values of the truly exogenous variables; if A is lagged endogenous and B is exogenous, and $TA = \left(\dfrac{B}{A}\right) - 1$, then

$$TA = \frac{-\overline{B}_{-1}\Delta A_{-1}}{A_{-1}{}^2}.^6$$

In cases such as these, all terms of the form $\overline{B}$ are taken as the average values during the period covered by the Officer model. This dependence would obtain even if the transformation (T) were linear, since the impact multipliers were estimated for a particular span of years. This appearance of the exogenous variables is clearly the largest source of error in the computation; if they were truly exogenous, inserting them at mean value would do no harm, but they obviously are not. There are 100 input ("predetermined") variables, and only 17 have lagged endogenous terms. This 1:6 proportion is much too small. If any of the exogenous variables

6. Subscript $_{-1}$ means "lagged once"; the bar $(-)$ notation signifies average value.

are really endogenous, the insertion of mean values is invalidated, and transformations of the form

$$\Delta T(A, B) = \Delta(A + B - C - D)_{-1}$$
$$= \Delta A_{-1} + \Delta B_{-1}$$

where A and B are endogenous and C and D are falsely exogenous lead to large errors.

Other sources of error include: insertion of price indexes at one when their average over the period 1951–1962 could not be determined from Officer's work; the fact that even the average is slightly incorrect when variables have changed; and, of course, all of the vagaries inherent in simultaneous equation estimation.

The most noticeable dynamic characteristic of the model is the accelerator variable that appears among the predetermined set; this is the regression coefficient of $\log(YG)_{-2}, \ldots, \log(YG)_{-7}$ on $t = (1, \ldots, 6)$, which has very large coefficients in the reduced-form matrix.[7] It is this accelerator which drives the system after three or four periods. Table C.1 shows this qualitatively by comparing the change in real national income over a six-year period (computed in regular fashion) to the change computed with the accelerator (artificially) set at zero.[8] Table C.2 illustrates the changes induced in a few other key endogenous variables by disturbances in government purchases of goods and services. They behave in about the manner one would expect after considering the GNP multiplier.

After some meaningless results for the very early periods,[9] money income rises faster than real income and prices rise gen-

7. Where YG is output of goods constituting final sales, in terms of constant dollars.
8. Not that this procedure invalidates all the impact multipliers because they were computed with the accelerator left in; the comparison is presented only to give the reader a feeling for what is happening in the model.
9. The erratic coefficients in periods two and three are clearly due to the discrete lag structure of the model and its reaction to a discontinuous change in exogenous variables after eight periods of (assumed) constancy of all variables. The Officer model was estimated from a continuously changing economy with no long stagnant periods and cannot be expected to perform well until all the variables are changing (i.e., period four).

403

TABLE C.1. Comparison of dynamic multipliers for real GNP in response to change in government purchases of goods and services, computed with and without accelerator term

	Change in real GNP ($ million)[a]	
Period	With accelerator	Without accelerator
1	1.05	1.05
2	.00093	.00093
3	.062	.062
4	.13	.0041
5	.20	.0053
6	.23	.0012
7	.23	.0018
8	.19	.0013
9	.11	.00095
10	.16	.00061
11	.18	.00039
12	.18	.00022
13	.16	.00010
14	.15	.00003
15	.14	−.00002
16	.14	−.00004
17	.15	−.00005
18	.14	−.00005
19	.14	−.00005
20	.13	−.00004
21	.13	−.00003
22	.13	−.00002
23	.13	−.00001
24	.12	−.00001

[a] If government purchases are assumed to increase by $1 million in the first period and remain at the new higher level, then each entry represents the resulting change in GNP from the preceding period.

erally, with the prices of investment goods rising faster than those in other sectors. The percentage of the labor force employed grows slowly, which conforms closely to theoretical expectations for expansionary fiscal policy in times such as 1951–1962, when large amounts of excess capacity and unemployment did not exist. Also, some of the variables included in the calculations, but not in Table C.2, move as expected; for instance, inventories fall, while residential construction, nonresidential construction, and machinery production increase. The results for the Canadian interest rates and the exchange rate are not so good; during the six-year period shown above, the interest rates on short- and long-term government bonds fall slowly as the Canadian dollar appreciates in terms of United States dollars. These results seem both self-contradictory and inconsistent with the other changes occurring in the economy; the inconsistencies could be due to changes in exogenous variables that occurred during the period for which the reduced form was estimated (1951–1962) or to original mis-specification of the model. Note that if the interest rate rose instead of falling, the appreciation of the Canadian dollar might be realistic, due to a capital inflow that would more than offset the trade deficit. Thus, only the interest-rate movement may be incorrect. Also, as interest rates have fallen in contractionary periods, the Canadian government has engaged in countercyclical fiscal policy, leading to a negative correlation between government expenditure and interest rates. Note that if United States interest rates were rising collinearly with Canadian rates in 1951–1962, and if U.S. rates were taken as exogenous to the system, then the model would be inadequate to predict changes in Canadian interest rates when U.S. rates were assumed constant. The induced changes in interest and exchange rates are quite small,[10] however; so the other results may be trusted to a certain extent.

Changes in monetary policy were examined, as well as those in fiscal policy. Changing the excess reserve ratio by +1 percent (using whatever monetary policy variables necessary) brought

10. The changes in interest rates are less than $.13 \times 10^{-4}$ in every period and most of them are much smaller. The exchange-rate changes are even smaller: less than $.25 \times 10^{-4}$ in every period.

TABLE C.2. Changes in selected endogenous variables in response to change in government purchases of goods and services

Period	Money GNP ($ million)	Exports to U.S. ($ million)	Merchandise imports from U.S. ($ million)
1	1.29	0	.057
2	−.061	−.017	.0035
3	.17	−.0037	.011
4	.16	−.0006	.030
5	.20	−.0034	.049
6	.24	−.0064	.056
7	.27	−.0080	.054
8	.26	−.0087	.044
9	.21	−.0082	.025
10	.27	−.0063	.036
11	.26	−.0065	.042
12	.26	−.0071	.042
13	.24	−.0072	.038
14	.23	−.0068	.034
15	.23	−.0063	.033
16	.22	−.0059	.033
17	.22	−.0060	.035
18	.21	−.0058	.033
19	.21	−.0057	.032
20	.20	−.0055	.030
21	.20	−.0053	.030
22	.19	−.0051	.030
23	.19	−.0050	.029
24	.18	−.0049	.028

TABLE C.2 — *Continued*

Period	Consumer goods price index 1957 = 1 ($\times 10^{-5}$)	Investment goods price index 1957 = 1 ($\times 10^{-5}$)	Proportion of labor force employed ($\times 10^{-5}$)
1	−.96	−.16	5.38
2	−.12	−.33	.0048
3	.32	1.02	.32
4	−.07	.78	.67
5	−.30	.87	1.04
6	−.28	1.13	1.19
7	−.15	1.38	1.17
8	.045	1.49	.98
9	.28	1.41	.58
10	.24	1.65	.82
11	.096	1.52	.93
12	.086	1.48	.92
13	.13	1.46	.83
14	.17	1.43	.77
15	.17	1.39	.73
16	.14	1.34	.74
17	.11	1.31	.76
18	.10	1.26	.74
19	.11	1.23	.70
20	.12	1.19	.67
21	.11	1.16	.66
22	.10	1.13	.65
23	.093	1.10	.64
24	.092	1.07	.62

TABLE C.3. Changes in selected endogenous variables in response to change in excess reserve ratio (+1 percent)

Period	Real GNP ($ million)	Money GNP ($ million)	Exports to U.S. ($ million)	Merchandise imports from U.S. ($ million)
1	.79[a]	−35.6	0	−.70
2	−2.54	10.4	0.70	−.35
3	−5.35	5.96	−.40	−1.49
4	.92	8.54	−.067	.049
5	.20	4.24	−.083	.016
6	−.51	2.50	−.064	−.14
7	−1.01	1.07	−.0075	−.26
8	−1.21	−.089	.037	−.29
9	−1.20	−.88	.059	−.27
10	−.82	−1.08	.067	−.17
11	−.46	−1.13	.061	−.086
12	−.81	−1.62	.048	−.17
13	−.95	−1.61	.048	−.21
14	−.92	−1.56	.049	−.21
15	−.81	−1.46	.046	−.18
16	−.73	−1.36	.040	−.16
17	−.70	−1.28	.035	−.16
18	−.73	−1.23	.032	−.17
19	−.76	−1.19	.030	−.18
20	−.72	−1.11	.030	−.17
21	−.67	−1.04	.029	−.16
22	−.65	−1.01	.027	−.15
23	−.64	−.98	.026	−.15
24	−.64	−.95	.025	−.15

[a] It is hard to see why this impact multiplier is positive.

TABLE C.3 — *Continued*

Period	Consumer goods price index 1957 = 1 ($\times 10^{-4}$)	Investment goods price index 1957 = 1 ($\times 10^{-4}$)	Proportion of labor force employed ($\times 10^{-4}$)
1	−12.9	−26.5	.41
2	6.31	13.0	−1.30
3	5.97	8.36	−2.73
4	3.12	6.92	.47
5	1.75	3.75	.10
6	1.35	2.40	−.26
7	.99	−1.25	−.51
8	.59	.28	−.62
9	.24	−.42	−.61
10	−.073	−.77	−.42
11	−.29	−.94	−.24
12	−.26	−1.14	−.42
13	−.18	−1.06	−.49
14	−.17	−1.02	−.47
15	−.18	−.96	−.42
16	−.18	−.90	−.37
17	−.16	−.83	−.36
18	−.12	−.77	−.37
19	−.080	−.71	−.39
20	−.068	−.66	−.37
21	−.068	−.63	−.35
22	−.064	−.60	−.33
23	−.055	−.58	−.33
24	−.047	−.57	−.33

about the results summarized in Table C.3. As might be expected, the relative weakness of the financial sector of the model makes these results much less reliable than those for fiscal policy. The initial change in prices is violently downward, but real income rises in the first period.[11] Reactions to this change cause all other variables to oscillate before attaining the steady trend normally expected. After the ninth period,[12] most of the variables have signs matching a priori expectations. Considering the fluctuations in periods one through nine, however, the estimates of size of these changes are much less trustworthy than those in Table C.2. This time the interest rate moves upward, its usual course in periods of monetary restraint; but the Canadian dollar depreciates in terms of American dollars, which is contradictory to concurrent deflation. Again, multicollinearity of Canadian and U.S. variables seems the only explanation for this obviously incorrect result.

As a direct comparison with previous work, the effect of a $100-million increase in government expenditure in period one was calculated. This is exactly the initial change used by Rudolf Rhomberg in deriving his dynamic multipliers.[13] As can be seen from the results in Table C.4, the income multiplier is smaller than Rhomberg's in the short run but larger in the long run. This is to be expected, due to the oscillatory nature of the Rhomberg model and the damped behavior of the dynamic multipliers from the Officer model.

In terms of traditional "rounds" of expenditure due to autonomous investment, the Officer model implies a marginal propensity to consume of .85 and an average length of time for each round of about 15 months. This is clearly too slow, but the sluggishness might have been expected of a model in which so few variables contribute to the dynamic structure.

11. This might be due to a lag in output decisions during the 1951–1962 period or some other aberration. It is hard to believe that falling prices would cause output to *rise*, especially since exports have a two-period lag.
12. Notably, this is when the initial violent disturbance of period one finally gets out of the accelerator relation.
13. Rudolf R. Rhomberg, "A Model of the Canadian Economy under Fixed and Fluctuating Exchange Rates," *Journal of Political Economy*, LXXII (February, 1964), 1–31.

TABLE C.4. Cumulative change in endogenous variables due to $100-million increase in government expenditure in period 1 (millions of dollars)[a]

A. Calculated from Officer model

Period	Real GNP	Money GNP	Exports to U.S.	Merchandise imports from U.S.
1	105	129	0	5.68
2	105	123	−1.72	6.04
3	111	139	−2.10	7.09
4	124	155	−2.15	10.1
5	145	176	−2.50	14.9
6	168	200	−3.13	20.4
7	190	226	−3.94	25.8
8	209	252	−4.79	30.1
9	220	272	−5.61	32.6
10	236	298	−6.22	36.1

B. Calculated by Rhomberg for case of fluctuating exchange rate (1949 prices)

Period	GNP − Δ farm inventories	Exports of goods and services	Imports of goods and services
1	148	−11	24
2	240	−15	115
3	275	−17	151
4	331	−18	205
5	360	−19	234
6	358	−20	237
7	349	−22	232
8	325	−23	213
9	286	−25	180
10	240	−26	141

Source: Calculations described in text, and Rudolf R. Rhomberg, "A Model of the Canadian Economy under Fixed and Fluctuating Exchange Rates," *Journal of Political Economy*, LXXII (February, 1964), 26.

[a] Officer's results for Canadian trade with the United States can be compared with Rhomberg's for total trade by remembering that exports to and imports from the U.S. constituted about 60 and 70 percent of total trade respectively during the period on which these models are based.

Comparison of a $100-million change in government expenditure with a $1-million change reveals that the model is very nearly linear in the sense mentioned above. A $100-million change has effects almost exactly 100 times as large as a $1-million change, which indicates that a very good approximation to the response of the economy to changes in more than one policy variable may be calculated by adding the responses to each single variable. Of course, if the results are not particularly good for one of the policy variables, the response to a multiple policy including this variable would be just as unreliable.

In general, then, the dynamic structure of the Officer model can be described as not oscillatory and is damped after an initial accelerating response to changes in policy variables. This damping is clearly the dominant reaction after nine quarters, and it belies the fact that only then do none of the (assumed) constant observations affect the accelerator relation. Some type of distributed lag in the accelerator would have given smoother results. The second- and third-period changes must be ignored as spurious; they also contribute to slowness of the reactions in the first year. A better approximation to the truth might be obtained by merely discarding them and moving the other changes forward two periods, since Officer does not justify the introduction of this lag in specifying his model.

Regularity of the response to fiscal policy as the changes in variables accelerate to a peak about two years hence and then decline exponentially into the future should elicit at least some confidence in the numbers.

Bibliography

BOOKS, GOVERNMENT DOCUMENTS, AND
UNPUBLISHED DISSERTATIONS

Anderson, W. H. Locke. *Corporate Finance and Fixed Investment.*
Boston: Division of Research, Graduate School of Business Administration, Harvard University, 1964.

Baguley, Robert W. "International Capital Flows and Canadian Monetary and Fiscal Policies, 1951–1962," unpub. diss. Harvard University, 1969.

Barber, Clarence L. *The Canadian Economy in Trouble: A Brief to the Royal Commission on Banking and Finance.* Privately printed, 1962.

Boarman, Patrick M. *Germany's Economic Dilemma: Inflation and the Balance of Payments.* New Haven, Connecticut: Yale University Press, 1964.

Bodkin, Ronald G., Elizabeth P. Bond, Grant L. Reuber, and T. Russell Robinson. *Price Stability and High Employment: The Options for Canadian Economic Policy.* Economic Council of Canada, Special Study no. 5. Ottawa: Queen's Printer, 1966.

Brecher, Irving. *Capital Flows Between Canada and the United States.* Washington and Montreal: Canadian-American Committee, 1965.

Breton, Albert J. "The Demand for Money in Canada, 1900–1959," unpub. diss. Columbia University, 1963.

Brown, T. M. *Canadian Economic Growth.* A Study Prepared for the Royal Commission on Health Services. Ottawa: Queen's Printer, 1965.

Canada. Bank of Canada. *Statistical Summary.* Various issues.

——— *Statistical Summary: Supplement.* Various issues.

Canada. Department of Labour. *Labour Organizations in Canada.* Ottawa: Queen's Printer (annual).

Canada. Department of National Revenue. *Taxation Statistics.* Various issues.

Canada. Department of Trade and Commerce. *Public and Private Investment.* Various issues.

Canada. Dominion Bureau of Statistics (D.B.S.). *The Canadian Balance of International Payments: A Compendium of Statistics from 1946 to 1965.* Ottawa: Queen's Printer, 1967.

—————— *The Canadian Balance of International Payments and International Investment Position.* Ottawa: Queen's Printer. Various issues.

—————— *Index of Industrial Production.* Various issues.

—————— *Indexes of Real Domestic Product by Industry of Origin, 1935–61.* Ottawa: Queen's Printer, 1963.

—————— *Industry Selling Price Indexes, 1956–59.* Ottawa: Queen's Printer, 1961.

—————— *Man-Hours and Hourly Earnings.* Various issues.

—————— *National Accounts, Income and Expenditure by Quarters.* Various issues.

—————— *Prices and Price Indexes.* Various issues.

—————— *Quarterly Corporate Profits.* Various issues.

—————— *Review of Man-Hours and Hourly Earnings.* Various issues.

—————— *Revised Index of Industrial Production, 1935–1957.* Ottawa: Queen's Printer, 1959.

—————— *Trade of Canada.* Various issues.

Canada. *Report of the Royal Commission on Banking and Finance.* Ottawa: Queen's Printer, 1964.

Canada. *Report of the Royal Commission on Taxation.* Ottawa: Queen's Printer, 1966.

Canada. Task Force on the Structure of Canadian Industry. *Foreign Ownership and the Structure of Canadian Industry.* Prepared for The Privy Council Office. Ottawa: Queen's Printer, 1968.

Crispo, J. H. G. *The Role of International Unionism in Canada.* Washington and Montreal: Canadian-American Committee, 1967.

Curtis, John M. "Direct Linkages Between Canadian and United States Prices and Wages: A Disaggregated Study, 1957–1966," unpub. diss. Harvard University, 1969.

Drabble, B. J. *Potential Output 1946 to 1970.* Economic Council to Canada, Staff Study no. 2. Ottawa: Queen's Printer, 1964.

Drummond, Ian M. *The Canadian Economy: Organization and Development.* Homewood, Ill.: Richard D. Irwin, 1966.

Duesenberry, James S. *Business Cycles and Economic Growth.* New York: McGraw-Hill, 1958.

Freund, John E. *Mathematical Statistics.* Englewood Cliffs, N.J.: Prentice-Hall, 1965.

Fromm, Gary, and Paul Taubman. *Policy Simulations with an Econometric Model.* Washington, D.C.: Brookings Institution, 1968.

Goldberger, Arthur S. *Impact Multipliers and Dynamic Properties of the Klein-Goldberger Model.* Amsterdam: North-Holland Publishing Company, 1959.

Grubel, Herbert G. *Forward Exchange, Speculation, and the International Flow of Capital.* Stanford: Stanford University Press, 1966.

Hansen, Bent. *Foreign Trade Credits and Exchange Reserves.* Amsterdam: North-Holland Publishing Company, 1961.

Helliwell, John F. *Public Policies and Private Investment.* Oxford: Clarendon Press, 1968.

Holmes, James M. *An Econometric Test of Some Modern International Trade Theories: Canada, 1870–1960.* Institute for Research in the Behavioral, Economic, and Management Sciences, Institute Paper no. 170. Lafayette, Ind.: Herman C. Krannert Graduate School of Industrial Administration, Purdue University, 1967.

Iversen, Carl. *Some Aspects of the Theory of International Capital Movements.* Copenhagen: Levin & Munksgaard, 1936.

Johnson, A. W., and J. W. Andrews. *Provincial and Municipal Governments and the Capital Markets.* Working paper prepared for the Royal Commission on Banking and Finance. Ottawa: Queen's Printer, 1962.

Johnson, Harry G. *The Canadian Quandary.* Toronto: Macmillan, 1963.

———— *International Trade and Economic Growth.* Cambridge, Mass.: Harvard University Press, 1958.

Johnson, Harry G., and John W. L. Winder. *Lags in the Effects of Monetary Policy in Canada.* Working paper prepared for the Royal Commission on Banking and Finance. Ottawa: Queen's Printer, 1962.

Johnston, J. *Econometric Methods.* New York: McGraw-Hill, 1963.

Kemp, Murray C. *The Demand for Canadian Imports, 1926–1955.* Toronto: University of Toronto Press, 1962.

Kent, Frederick C., and Maude E. Kent. *Compound Interest and Annuity Tables.* New York: McGraw-Hill, 1963.

Kindleberger, Charles P. *International Short-Term Capital Movements.* New York: Columbia University Press, 1937.

Koyck, L. M. *Distributed Lags and Investment Analysis.* Amsterdam: North-Holland Publishing Company, 1954.

Lubitz, Raymond. "United States Direct Investment in Canada and Canadian Capital Formation, 1950–1962," unpub. diss. Harvard University, 1966.

415

Meiselman, David. *The Term Structure of Interest Rates.* Englewood Cliffs, N.J.: Prentice-Hall, 1962.

Mellish, G. Hartley, and Robert G. Hawkins. *The Stability of Flexible Exchange Rates — The Canadian Experience.* Bulletin no. 50–51. New York: Institute of Finance, Graduate School of Business Administration, New York University, 1968.

Meyer, John R., and Robert Glauber. *Investment Decisions, Economic Forecasting and Public Policy.* Boston: Division of Research, Graduate School of Business Administration, Harvard University, 1964.

Meyer, John R., and Edwin Kuh. *The Investment Decision.* Cambridge, Mass.: Harvard University Press, 1957.

Officer, Lawrence H. *An Econometric Model of Canada under the Fluctuating Exchange Rate.* Cambridge, Mass.: Harvard University Press, 1968.

——— "An Econometric Model of the Canadian Economy under the Fluctuating Exchange Rate," unpub. diss. Harvard University, 1964. Abbreviated in notes as Officer, unpub. diss.

Pitchford, J. D. *A Study of Cost and Demand Inflation.* Amsterdam: North-Holland Publishing Company, 1963.

Reuber, Grant L. *The Objectives of Monetary Policy.* Working paper prepared for the Royal Commission on Banking and Finance. Ottawa: Queen's Printer, 1962.

Reuber, Grant L., and Frank Roseman. *The Takeover of Canadian Firms, 1945–61: An Empirical Analysis.* Economic Council of Canada, Special Study no. 10. Ottawa: Queen's Printer, 1969.

Reuber, Grant L., and Ronald J. Wonnacott. *The Cost of Capital in Canada.* Washington: Resources for the Future, 1961.

Robinson, T. Russell. "Foreign Trade and Economic Stability: The Canadian Case," unpub. diss. Yale University, 1966.

Rosenbluth, G. *Concentration in Canadian Manufacturing Industries.* Princeton, N.J.: Princeton University Press, 1957.

Safarian, A. E. *Foreign Ownership of Canadian Industry.* Toronto: McGraw-Hill, 1966.

Shapiro, Harold T. "The Canadian Monetary Sector: An Econometric Analysis," unpub. diss. Princeton University, 1965.

Shearer, Ronald A. *Monetary Policy and the Current Account of the Balance of International Payments.* Working paper prepared for the Royal Commission on Banking and Finance. Ottawa: Queen's Printer, 1962.

Slater, David W. *Canada's Balance of International Payments — When Is a Deficit a Problem?* Montreal: Canadian Trade Committee, 1964.

Smith, Lawrence Berk. "The Postwar Canadian Residential Mortgage

Market and the Role of Government," unpub. diss. Harvard University, 1966. To be published by University of Toronto Press.

Sohmen, Egon. *Flexible Exchange Rates: Theory and Controversy.* Chicago: University of Chicago Press, 1961.

—— *International Monetary Problems and the Foreign Exchanges.* Special Papers in International Economics, no. 4. Princeton, N.J.: International Finance Section, Princeton University, 1963.

Stewart, Ian A. "A Quarterly Econometric Model of the Canadian Economy, 1951–1962," unpub. diss. Cornell University, 1966.

Stovel, John A. *Canada in the World Economy.* Cambridge, Mass.: Harvard University Press, 1959.

Theil, Henri. *Economic Forecasts and Policy.* Amsterdam: North-Holland Publishing Company, 1958.

United States. Department of Commerce, Office of Business Economics. *Balance of Payments: Statistical Supplement,* rev. ed. Washington: Government Printing Office, 1962.

—— *Survey of Current Business.* Various issues.

United States. Department of Labor, Bureau of Labor Statistics. *Employment and Earnings Statistics for the United States, 1909–66.* Washington: Government Printing Office, 1966.

—— *Wholesale Prices and Price Indexes.* Washington: Government Printing Office, 1967.

Viner, Jacob. *Canada's Balance of International Indebtedness, 1900–1913.* Cambridge, Mass.: Harvard University Press, 1924.

—— *Studies in the Theory of International Trade.* New York: Harper, 1937.

Williams, John H. *Argentine International Trade under Inconvertible Paper Money, 1880–1900.* Cambridge, Mass.: Harvard University Press, 1920.

Wilson, Thomas A. *Capital Investment and the Cost of Capital: A Dynamic Analysis.* Studies of the Royal Commission on Taxation, no. 30. Ottawa: Queen's Printer, 1967.

Wonnacott, Paul. *The Canadian Dollar, 1948–1962.* Toronto: University of Toronto Press, 1965.

Wonnacott, Ronald J. *Canadian-American Dependence: An Interindustry Analysis of Production and Prices.* Amsterdam: North-Holland Publishing Company, 1961.

Wonnacott, Ronald J., and Paul Wonnacott. *Free Trade Between the United States and Canada: The Potential Economic Effects.* Cambridge, Mass.: Harvard University Press, 1967.

BIBLIOGRAPHY

ARTICLES

Almon, Shirley. "The Distributed Lag Between Capital Appropriations and Expenditures," *Econometrica,* XXXIII (January, 1965), 178–196.

Altman, Oscar L. "Canadian Markets for U.S. Dollars," *Factors Affecting the United States Balance of Payments, Compilation of Studies,* U.S. Congress, Joint Economic Committee. 87th Cong., 2nd sess. Washington: Government Printing Office, 1962. Pages 525–540.

Arndt, Sven W. "International Short-Term Capital Movements: A Distributed Lag Model of Speculation in Foreign Exchange," *Econometrica,* XXXVI (January, 1968), 59–70.

Ball, R. J. "Capital Imports and Economic Development: Paradoxy or Orthodoxy?" *Kyklos,* XV, no. 3 (1962), 610–623.

Ball, R. J., and K. Marwah. "The U.S. Demand for Imports, 1948–1958," *Review of Economics and Statistics,* XLIV (November, 1962), 395–401.

Barber, Clarence L. "On Surplus Budgeting," *Canadian Tax Journal,* XIII (July–August, 1965), 319–322.

Bell, P. W. "Private Capital Movements and the U.S. Balance of Payments," *Factors Affecting the United States Balance of Payments.* United States Congress, Joint Economic Committee, 87th Cong., 2nd sess. Washington: Government Printing Office, 1962. Pages 399–481.

Black, Stanley W. "Theory and Policy Analysis of Short-Term Movements in the Balance of Payments," *Yale Economic Essays,* VIII (Spring, 1968), 5–78.

Bloomfield, Arthur I. "The Significance of Outstanding Securities in the International Movement of Capital," *Canadian Journal of Economics and Political Science,* VI (November, 1940), 495–524.

Borts, George H. "A Theory of Long-Run International Capital Movements," *Journal of Political Economy,* LXXII (August, 1964), 341–359.

Brown, T. M. "A Forecast Determination of National Product, Employment, and Price Level in Canada from an Econometric Model," in National Bureau of Economic Research, *Models of Income Determination,* Studies in Income and Wealth, vol. XXVIII. Princeton, N.J.: Princeton University Press, 1964. Pages 59–86.

Cavalieri, D. "Stabilisation des prix et ré-équilibre de la balance des paiements en periode d'inflation," *Economie Appliquée,* XX, no. 3 (1967), 347–388.

418

Courchene, Thomas J. "An Analysis of the Price-Inventory Nexus with Empirical Application to the Canadian Manufacturing Sector," *International Economic Review,* X (October, 1969), 315–336.

———— "Inventory Behavior and the Stock-Order Distinction: An Analysis by Industry and by Stage of Fabrication with Empirical Applications to the Canadian Manufacturing Sector," *Canadian Journal of Economics and Political Science,* XXXIII (August, 1967), 325–357.

Davis, Thomas E. "A Model of the Canadian Current Account," *Canadian Journal of Economics and Political Science,* XXXII (November, 1966), 468–488.

de Leeuw, Frank. "The Demand for Capital Goods by Manufacturers: A Study of Quarterly Times Series," *Econometrica,* XXX (July, 1962), 407–423.

Diamond, Marcus. "Trends in the Flow of International Private Capital, 1957–65," *International Monetary Fund Staff Papers,* XIV (March, 1967), 1–39.

Eckstein, Otto, and Thomas A. Wilson. "The Determination of Money Wages in American Industry," *Quarterly Journal of Economics,* LXXVI (August, 1962), 379–414.

Fleming, J. Marcus. "Domestic Financial Policies under Fixed and under Floating Exchange Rates," *International Monetary Fund Staff Papers* (November, 1962), 369–379.

Ford, A. G. "Flexible Exchange Rates and Argentina, 1885–1900," *Oxford Economic Papers,* X (October, 1958), 316–338.

Friedman, Milton, and David Meiselman. "The Relative Stability of Monetary Velocity and the Investment Multiplier in the United States, 1887–1957," *Stabilization Policies: A Series of Research Papers Prepared for the Commission on Money and Credit,* Englewood Cliffs, N.J.: Prentice-Hall, 1963, pp. 165–268.

Gray, H. Peter. "The Demand for International Travel by the United States and Canada," *International Economic Review,* VII (January, 1966), 83–92.

———— "International Short-Term Capital Movements: Comments," *American Economic Review,* LVII (June, 1967), 548–551.

Griliches, Zvi. "Distributed Lags: A Survey," *Econometrica,* XXXI (January, 1967), 16–49.

Grubel, Herbert G. "Internationally Diversified Portfolios: Welfare Gains and Capital Flows," *American Economic Review,* LVIII (December, 1968), 1299–1314.

Hanson, J. A., and Philip A. Neher. "The Neoclassical Theorem Once Again: Closed and Open Economies," *American Economic Review,* LVII (September, 1967), 869–878.

Häuser, Karl. "Das Inflationselement in den deutschen Exportüberschussen," *Weltwirtschaftliches Archiv*, LXXXIII (1959), 166–187.

Helleiner, Gerald K. "Connections Between United States and Canadian Capital Markets, 1952–1960," *Yale Economic Essays*, II, no. 2 (1962), 351–400.

Helliwell, John. "A Structural Model of the Foreign Exchange Market," *Canadian Journal of Economics*, II (February, 1969).

Hendershott, Patric H. "International Short-Term Capital Movements: Comments," *American Economic Review*, LVII (June, 1967), 560–563.

Jamieson, Stuart M. "Trade Unions and Inflation: United States and Canada," *Canadian Issues: Essays in Honour of Henry F. Angus*, ed. R. M. Clark. Toronto: University of Toronto Press, 1961. Pages 309–324.

Johnson, Harry G. "Some Aspects of the Theory of Economic Policy in a World of Capital Mobility," *Essays in Honor of Marco Fanno*, ed. Tullio Bagiotti. Padua: Cedam, 1966. Volume II, pp. 345–359.

Jones, Ronald W. "Monetary and Fiscal Policy for an Economy with Fixed Exchange Rates," *Journal of Political Economy*, LXXVI, pt. 2 (July–August, 1968), 921–943.

Jorgenson, Dale W. "Anticipations and Investment Behavior," *Brookings Quarterly Econometric Model of the United States*, ed. J. S. Duesenberry et al. Chicago: Rand McNally, 1965.

Kareken, John, and Robert Solow. "Lags in Monetary Policy: A Summary," *Stabilization Policies: A Series of Research Papers Prepared for the Commission on Money and Credit*. Englewood Cliffs, N.J.: Prentice-Hall, 1963. Pages 3–7.

Kenen, Peter B. "Short-Term Capital Movements and the U.S. Balance of Payments," *United States Balance of Payments*. United States Congress, Joint Economic Committee, Hearings, 88th Cong., 1st sess. Washington: Government Printing Office, 1963. Pages 153–191.

Krueger, Anne O. "The Impact of Alternative Government Policies under Varying Exchange Systems," *Quarterly Journal of Economics*, LXXIX (May, 1965), 195–209.

Kuh, Edwin, and John R. Meyer. "Investment, Liquidity and Monetary Policy," *Impacts of Monetary Policy: A Series of Research Papers Prepared for the Commission on Money and Credit*. Englewood Cliffs, N.J.: Prentice-Hall, 1963. Pages 339–474.

Lee, C. H. "A Stock-Adjustment Analysis of Capital Movements: The United States-Canadian Case," *Journal of Political Economy*, LXXVII, pt. 1 (July–August, 1969), 512–523.

Lintner, John. "Distribution of Incomes of Corporations Among Dividends, Retained Earnings and Taxes," *American Economic Review,* XLVI (May, 1956), 97–113.

Liviatan, N. "Consistent Estimation of Distributed Lags," *International Economic Review,* IV (January, 1963), 44–52.

MacDougall, I. "Non-traded Goods and the Transfer Problem," *Review of Economic Studies,* XXXII (January, 1965), 67–84.

Massell, B. F. "Exports, Capital Imports, and Economic Growth," *Kyklos,* XVII, fasc. 4 (1964), 627–634.

May, Sydney. "Dynamic Multipliers and Their Use for Fiscal Decision-Making," *Conference on Stabilization Policies Convened by the Economic Council of Canada at the University of Western Ontario, London, Aug. 30 to Sept. 1, 1965.* Ottawa: Queen's Printer, 1966. Pages 155–187.

Meier, G. M. "Economic Development and the Transfer Mechanism: Canada, 1895–1913," *Canadian Journal of Economic and Political Science,* XIX (February, 1953), 1–19.

Melvin, James R. "Capital Flows and Employment under Flexible Exchange Rates," *Canadian Journal of Economics,* I (May, 1968), 318–333.

Mundell, Robert A. "The Appropriate Use of Monetary and Fiscal Policy for Internal and External Balance," *International Monetary Fund Staff Papers,* IX (March, 1962), 70–77.

———— "Capital Mobility and Stabilization Policy under Fixed and Flexible Exchange Rates," *Canadian Journal of Economics and Political Science,* XXIX (November, 1963), 475–485.

———— "Problems of Monetary and Exchange Rate Management in Canada," *National Banking Review,* II (September, 1964), 77–86.

Neher, Philip A. "Natural Rates of Economic Growth and International Interest Rates," *Kyklos,* XXI, no. 2 (1968), 326–335.

Penner, Rudolph G. "The Inflow of Long-term Capital and the Canadian Business Cycle, 1950–1960," *Canadian Journal of Economics and Political Science,* XXVIII (November, 1962), 527–542.

Phillips, A. "An Appraisal of Measures of Capacity," *American Economic Review,* LIII (May, 1963), 275–292.

Piekarz, R., and L. E. Stekler. "Induced Changes in Trade and Payments," *Review of Economics and Statistics,* LXIX (November, 1967), 517–526.

Poole, William. "The Stability of the Canadian Flexible Exchange Rate, 1950–62." *Canadian Journal of Economics and Political Science,* XXXIII (May, 1967), 205–217.

Powrie, T. L. "Short-term Capital Movements and the Flexible Exchange Rate," *Canadian Journal of Economics and Political Science,* XXX (February, 1964), 76–94.

Radford, R. A. "Canada's Capital Inflow, 1946–53," *International Monetary Fund Staff Papers,* IV (February, 1955), 217–257.

Reuber, Grant L. "The Objectives of Canadian Monetary Policy, 1949–61: Empirical 'Trade-Offs' and the Reaction Function of the Authorities," *Journal of Political Economy,* LXXII (April, 1964), 109–132.

——— "Wage Adjustments in Canadian Industry, 1953–66," *Review of Economic Studies* XXXVII (October, 1970). Forthcoming.

Rhomberg, Rudolf R. "Effects of Exchange Depreciation in Canada, 1960–64," *Conference on Stabilization Policies Convened by the Economic Council of Canada at the University of Western Ontario, London, Aug. 30 to Sept. 1, 1965.* Ottawa: Queen's Printer, 1966. Pages 99–125.

——— "A Model of the Canadian Economy under Fixed and Fluctuating Exchange Rates," *Journal of Political Economy,* LXXII (February, 1964), 1–31.

Robinson, T. Russell. "Canada's Imports and Economic Stability," *Canadian Journal of Economics,* I (May, 1968), 401–428.

Robinson, T. R., and T. J. Courchene, "Fiscal Federalism and Economic Stability: An Examination of Multi-Level Public Finance, 1952–1965," *Canadian Journal of Economics,* II (May, 1969), 697–715.

Romanis, Anne. "Cost Inflation and Incomes Policy in Industrial Countries," *International Monetary Fund Staff Papers,* XIV (March, 1967), 169–206.

Samuelson, Paul A. "The Transfer Problem and Transport Costs," *Economic Journal,* LXII (June, 1952), 278–304; LXIV (June, 1954), 264–289.

Schultze, Charles L. "Recent Inflation in the United States," *Materials Prepared in Connection with the Study of Employment, Growth and Price Levels.* United States Congress, Joint Economic Committee, Study Paper no. 1. Washington: Government Printing Office, 1959.

Schwartzman, David. "The Effect of Monopoly on Price," *Journal of Political Economy,* LXVII (August, 1959), 352–362.

——— "Monopoly and Wages," *Canadian Journal of Economics and Political Science,* XXVI (August, 1960), 428–438.

Scitovsky, Tibor. "Two Concepts of External Economies," *Journal of Political Economy,* LIII (April, 1954), 143–151.

Scott, Ira O., Jr., and Wilson E. Schmidt. "Imported Inflation and Monetary Policy," *Banca Nazionale del Lavoro Quarterly Review,* no. 71 (December, 1964), 390–403.

Slater, David W. "International Factors in Canadian Credit Conditions," *The Canadian Banker,* LXXV (Spring, 1968), 5–14.

Smith, Lawrence B. "A Model of the Canadian Housing and Mortgage Markets," *Journal of Political Economy,* LXXVII (September–October, 1969), 795–816.

Solow, Robert M. "On a Family of Lag Distributions," *Econometrica,* XXVIII (April, 1960), 393–406.

Stein, Jerome L. "International Short-Term Capital Movements," *American Economic Review,* LV (March, 1965), 40–66.

Stein, Jerome L., and Edward Tower. "The Short-run Stability of the Foreign Exchange Market," *Review of Economics and Statistics,* XLIX (May, 1967), 173–185.

Stevens, Guy V. G. "Fixed Investment Expenditures of Foreign Manufacturing Affiliates of U.S. Firms: Theoretical Models and Empirical Evidence," *Yale Economic Essays,* IX (Spring, 1969), 137–200.

Stoll, Hans. "An Empirical Study of the Forward Exchange Market under Fixed and Flexible Exchange Rate Systems," *Canadian Journal of Economics,* I (February, 1968), 55–78.

Tobin, James. "Liquidity Preference as Behavior Towards Risk," *Review of Economic Studies,* XXV (February, 1958), 65–86.

Triffin, Robert, and Herbert Grubel. "The Adjustment Mechanism to Differential Rates of Monetary Expansion among the Countries of the European Economic Community," *Review of Economics and Statistics,* XLIV (November, 1962), 486–491.

Vanderkamp, John. "Wage and Price Level Determination: An Empirical Model for Canada," *Economica,* XXXIII (May, 1966), 194–218.

Waterman, A. M. C. "Some Footnotes to the 'Swan Diagram' — or How Dependent is a Dependent Economy?" *Economic Record,* XLII (September, 1966), 447–464.

Wilson, John S. G. "The Canadian Money Market Experiment," *Banca Nazionale del Lavoro Quarterly Review,* XI (March, 1958), 19–55.

——— "The Internationalisation of Capital Markets," *Three Banks Review,* no. 62 (June, 1964), 3–24.

Young, John H., and John F. Helliwell. "The Effects of Monetary Policy on Corporations," in Royal Commission on Banking and Finance, *Appendix Volume.* Ottawa: Queen's Printer, 1964. Pages 303–435.

423

Index

ences during recession, 175–178; determinants, by industry, 186–189; endogenous in econometric models, 277, 287; marginal propensity to invest, 281

Carter Report, 301–304, 314

Commercial paper, 74, 135n

Common stocks, 58

Consumer durables industry: wage linkages, 222; short-term capital flows, 273

Conversion Loan, 343

Courchene, T. J., 225, 274n

Credit rationing, 17, 37

Current account: effect on exchange rate, 64; historic changes, 92–93; capital-account changes, 236–237, 240; autocorrelation, 240; direct investment changes, 241, 243; effect of fiscal policy, 307–310; effect of monetary policy, 333–336; effect of debt-management policy, 343–345. *See also* Exports; Imports; Invisibles trade; Trade balance

Debt-management policy: effect on long-term interest rate, 107, 112–113, 114, 339; effect on short-term interest rate, 339–340; effect on term structure, 340–341; effect on capital flows, 341; effect on current account, 343–345; effect on GNP, 343–345; effect on exchange rate, 344; effect of capital mobility, 345–348, 350; exchange-rate flexibility, 345–350; relative efficiency, 353–357

Degrees of freedom, 49, 53

de Leeuw, F., 270

Deliveries of securities: lag contract date, 35–36, 249–250

Depreciation: effect on portfolio capital flows, 39–40, 47; effect on capital formation, 153

Differentiated products, 207, 215

Direct investment: Canadian share, 2; transfer theory, 12; price linkages, 26–27, 214–215, 216, 217,

230; wage linkages, 26–27, 223; portfolio investment, 47; effect on exchange rate, 64, 325; short-term flows, 85; effect of interest rate, 87–89, 245, 316n; effect on domestic investment, 146–147, 157, 179–180; effect on business capital formation, 156–157, 168–171, 175–178, 265–267; measurement, 161–163, 166, 180–182, 185n; in recession, 176–178; by industry, 186–189; takeovers, 192–194; leads current-account changes, 241, 243; induced component, 245–246, 262–263, 264; requiting of transfer, 285, 288; inflationary effects, 289, 292–293; payments stability, 294–295

Distributed lags: term structure, 42; speculative supply forward exchange, 131–132; autocorrelated series, 131–132, 151, 270; multiple predetermined variables, 151–152, 166; portfolio capital flows, 241

Dividends: effect on portfolio capital, 58–59; relation to residual funds, 149

Domar, E. D., 23

Duesenberry, J. S., 149

Dummy variables, 49

Dumping, 213

Eckstein, O., 224

Equity capital, 58–59

Errors and omissions, 71

Estimation, choice of methods, 65, 104–105, 158–159. *See also* Indirect least squares; Two-stage least squares

Exchange control, 2

Exchange Fund Account, 91, 317n

Exchange market stability: theory, 8, 11, 20; effect of exogenous capital flows, 293–295; disturbances by policy instruments, 353–357. *See also* Exchange rate

Exchange rate, Canada: unemployment, 2–3; flexible rate introduced,

300–307, 327; effect on current account, 307–310; effect of capital mobility, 349; effect of exchange-rate flexibility, 350; relative efficiency, 353–357. *See also* Fiscal policy

Taxes, corporate profits: effect on short-term capital flows, 74; effect on residual funds, 153, 161

Terms of trade: capital transfer theory, 6, 8; evidence, 296

Term structure, interest rates: effect on portfolio capital flows, 41–46, 58; effect on short-term capital flows, 81-82; transmission of U.S. influences, 247–248; effect of debt-management policy, 340–341

Textile and clothing industries, 222

Tinbergen, J., 6

Trade balance: effect on short-term capital flows, 73; effect on forward exchange rate, 130–131, 134–135; leading capital flows, 237, 241, 243. *See also* Current account; Exports; Imports

Trade credit: short-term capital flow, 73, 134n; relation to forward market, 75n, 77

Trade participation: transmitting price changes, 213–214, 216, 217, 228, 230; measurement, 213n

Trade unions: transmitting wage changes, 26–27, 219, 222–223, 225, 228; wage-setting practices, 198

Transfer problem: theory of, 6–16; Rhomberg, Officer estimates, 280; evidence, 284–288

Transport costs, 9–10

Treasury bills, 71, 72, 73–74, 83

Two-stage least squares, 65–66, 105, 119–125, 140–144

Unemployment: variations in, 2, 3, 174–175; relation to price level, 24, 196–197, 229; effect on portfolio capital, 246–247; expected securities yields, 261; effect on

direct investment, 266; effect on exports, 283; requiting of transfers, 288

United Kingdom: international lender, 1, 71; effect of short-term interest rate, 83, 138–139

United States: balance-of-payments problem, 2, 4

— predominance: direct investment, 2, 162; other capital flows, 2, 32, 35; size of capital market, 57; lag structure, Canadian balance of payments, 241–243

— international corporations: transmitting price changes, 26, 214–217, 230; finance and liquidity, 74, 162–163, 170–172; risks, 147; export markets, 157; data on direct investment, 161–162, 166, 180–182; transmitting wage changes, 223, 225

— long-term interest rate: measurement, 34–35; effect on portfolio capital flows, 54–55; effect on direct investment, 87–89, 245; effect on Canadian long-term interest rate, 108–109, 113–119, 125

— trade balance: effect on short-term capital flows, 73, 78–86 *passim;* effect on forward exchange rate, 130–131

— short-term interest rate: effect on Canadian short-term interest rate, 127, 139–140

— price level: inflation mechanism, 198; effect on Canadian prices, 201, 212–213

— wages: transmission to Canada, 219, 221–222. *See also* Trade unions

— GNP: effect on U.S. current account, 286–288; effect on Canadian exports, 291–292

United States-pay securities, 60, 250

Unit labor costs, 225, 227

Utilities investment, 186–188, 191–192

Vanderkamp, J., 202n